MAKING SHORT FILMS

The complete guide from script to screen

THIRD EDITION

Max Thurlow and
Clifford Thurlow

BLOOMSBURY
NEW YORK • LONDON • NEW DELHI • SYDNEY

Bloomsbury Academic
An imprint of Bloomsbury Publishing Plc

50 Bedford Square
London
WC1B 3DP
UK

1385 Broadway
New York
NY 10018
USA

www.bloomsbury.com

British Library Cataloguing-in-Publication Data
A catalogue record for this book is available from the British Library.

ISBN: HB: 978-0-8578-5386-8
PB: 978-0-8578-5387-5
ePDF: 978-0-8578-5432-2
ePub: 978-0-8578-5433-9

Library of Congress Cataloging-in-Publication Data
Thurlow , Max.
Making short films : the complete guide from script to screen / Max Thurlow & Clifford Thurlow. -- 3rd edition.
pages cm
Includes bibliographical references and index.
ISBN 978-0-85785-386-8 (Hardcover : alk. paper) -- ISBN 978-0-85785-387-5 (Paperback : alk. paper) 1. Short films--Production and direction. 2. Short films--Authorship. I. Thurlow, Clifford. II. Title.
PN1995.9.P7T49 2013
791.43'6--dc23

2012049671

Typeset by Fakenham Prepress Solutions, Fakenham, Norfolk NR21 8NN
Printed and bound in Great Britain

CONTENTS

1 Lights, Camera, Action

INTRODUCTION TO MAKING SHORT FILMS, 3rd Edition

In the long, hot summer of 1929, Luis Buñuel set out for Cadaqués, an isolated fishing village clinging to the last rocky outcrops of the Pyrenees and inaccessible except by sea. Under his arm, Buñuel carried the first draft of a short film and was making the journey from Aragon to the Spanish coast to see Salvador Dalí, his collaborator.

They had already made *Un Chien Andalou* and *L'Âge d'Or*, the latter "a uniquely savage blend of visual poetry and social criticism," according to writer Paul Hammond,[1] this surreal masterpiece being banned from public viewing thanks to Dalí's "subversive eroticism" and the film's "furious dissection of civilized values." Vicomte Charles de Noailles and his wife Marie-Laurie, a descendant of the Marquis de Sade, had promised funds for the new film and Buñuel was anxious to have his writing partner on board.

But Dalí that summer had other manias in mind. He needed a muse and was pursuing the Russian beauty Gala, wife of poet Paul Éluard, and a significant, if controversial figure in the Surrealist Movement. It was said that if one of the artists—Max Ernst, Yves Tanguy, Man Ray et al—did a particularly fine piece of work, the others would nod judiciously and whisper: "Ah, but of course, he was having an affair with Gala at the time."

Buñuel, with all the determination that was to characterize his career, followed Dalí from the shingle beach where fishermen repaired their nets, to the dining table where the local wine was said to have the bitter taste of tears, to the modest hut where his old student chum from Madrid's Residencia de Estudiantes had set up a studio. All to no avail.

In desperation, Buñuel tried to throttle Gala, to the consternation of the rest of the party: René Magritte, his dull wife Georgette, art dealer Camille Goemans, and his svelte girlfriend Yvonne Bernard. Cadaqués, despite its lack of a road, had been discovered by the Paris avant-garde and the appearance of this exotic group would be covered in the columns of the fortnightly *Sol Ixent*. Finally, his fingers prised from Gala's white throat, Buñuel packed his bag, shoved the script under his arm and sailed back around the coast, the still surface of the Mediterranean doing little to calm his fury. Salvador Dalí had worked on the scripts for two short films and Buñuel was now on his own.

He did not see Dalí again until 1937. Civil War had broken out in Spain. Fascist thugs had murdered their fellow student, the poet Federico García Lorca, and fearing that he was next on the list, Buñuel fled to New York, where Dalí, always one jump ahead, was safely ensconced with Madame Éluard. He was making a handsome living painting portraits of society ladies and collaborating on movie sets with Alfred Hitchcock.

Buñuel asked him for a $50 loan. But, just as Dalí had spurned working on short film number 3, he refused his request and ended their long and fruitful friendship with a letter of such eccentric misanthropy that Buñuel's son, filmmaker Juan Luis Buñuel (*Calanda; La Femme aux Bottes Rouges*), carries the offensive missive folded in his wallet to remind him of the joys of generosity.

Filmmaking is tough. Buñuel's flight from Spain at the outbreak of Civil War, the banning of *L'Âge d'Or* and the long years of exile in Mexico were not wasted years, however, but the very experiences that infused the wit and imagination that would make him one of the greatest filmmakers of the twentieth century, as indeed, Salvador Dalí, who suffered his own array of paranoias and phobias, would become one of its great painters.

Buñuel's early films were random, scattered, indeed surreal, but he came to understand that the key to a great film is the script. If anything, the script for a short film is more important and perhaps more difficult to write than a feature, simply because the brush strokes by necessity must be fine and detailed, each moment perfect. He was learning his craft by trial and error and would have been the first to admit that he still had a long way to go. *Un Chien Andalou* and *L'Âge d'Or* always head the Buñuel filmography, but he had already made with cameraman Albert Duverger back in 1929 the forgotten, five-minute short *Menjant garotes* (*Eating Sea Urchins*) on 35mm. Illustrating, perhaps, the incestuous nature of filmmaking, it was Salvador Dalí's young sister Ana María who had kept *Menjant garotes* stored in a biscuit tin where it remained until her death more than half a century later.

Shot for the most part in harsh sunlight, the film follows Dalí's plump father and stepmother as they stroll through the terraces of Cadaqués before sitting down to a plate of sea urchins. Buñuel had planned his setups with care, the light filtering through the window as Dalí senior slices into his *garotes* revealing the first glimpse of a visual style that he would come to develop. But, a vital lesson to Buñuel, and all first-time filmmakers, that for all the extravagance of camera angles and lighting effects, in spite of the Hannibal Lecter grin of Señor Dalí as he slurps down the first sea urchin, the film is so slender on story it is at best rather ordinary and, at worst, plain boring.

Buñuel needed Dalí's inspired if contradictory logic and had taken the train from Aragon in the hottest month of the year to try and get it. A phrase, a gesture, a jump-cut between unrelated events, a moment's silence or the introduction of music can make all the difference between success and failure, a story that grabs you and one that's as flat as the bay of Cadaqués in summer.

Filmmaking is a team process. Often, contacts made and films shared in the early days will last through a filmmaker's career. Each film is a voyage of discovery and adventurers who have made the journey together before know they are with people they can rely on. Buñuel mastered his craft making short films and that is how most filmmakers start. From Charlie Chaplin and Buster Keaton with their first silent movies to the current young auteurs Lynne Ramsey (*Ratcatcher; Morvern Callar*), Phillip Noyce (*American Pastoral, Dead Calm*), Robert Rodriguez (*Sin City, El Mariachi*), and Christopher Nolan (*Memento*, *Insomnia, The Prestige*), before tackling a feature, they cut their teeth on the silver ring of shorts.

It was Luis Buñuel's passion to make films that made him a filmmaker, but there is another lesson to be learned from his flurry of activity that summer in 1929. *Menjant garotes* had been financed by his family, but getting it in the can, even if it was to remain hidden for decades, gave Buñuel the experience and, in turn, the confidence to go out and source funds for future projects.

For anyone on the same path today, the journey has never been easier. Cameras are smaller, lighter, less expensive and easier to use. A laptop with a few basic programs is sufficient to edit, compose music and add sound effects to a film. Since the publication of the second edition of *Making Short Films* in 2008, innovative changes in distribution are making it easier than ever to get films shown. It is an exciting time to be a filmmaker.

Anyone can do it, but how do you stand out in the crowd? How do you bring your movie gems in front of those who can make a difference to a new filmmaker's career?

The aim of *Making Short Films* is to answer those questions and to inspire filmmakers through the stages of writing, producing, financing, casting, directing, editing and distributing short films. The book includes an analysis of the scripts of six very different shorts: a 2012 Oscar-nominated comedy, a modern surrealist film, a country-house haunting, a high-tech horror, a mockumentary with Nick Moran as a fighter pilot, and a *noir* thriller adapted from a short story. There are introductions to essential industry software, advice on what camera to buy, basic sound and lighting tips and an extra 20 interviews with filmmakers in all areas of the industry.

In Buñuel's era, revolutionary politics or a flash of thigh was enough to make a film controversial. In an age when almost nothing is controversial, films will need other qualities. *L'Âge d'Or* would remain banned for many years, but has since been shown on television, it can be viewed at the surrealist galleries at the Tate Modern, and of course on YouTube. When it was first screened in Britain, in Cambridge, in 1950, the sole complaint was from the Royal Society for the Protection of Animals. Bare breasts and a nun being thrown from a window caused no offence, but one of the characters is seen booting a small dog up the backside. Social mores had changed, but not the English.

TITLE

The holy trinity

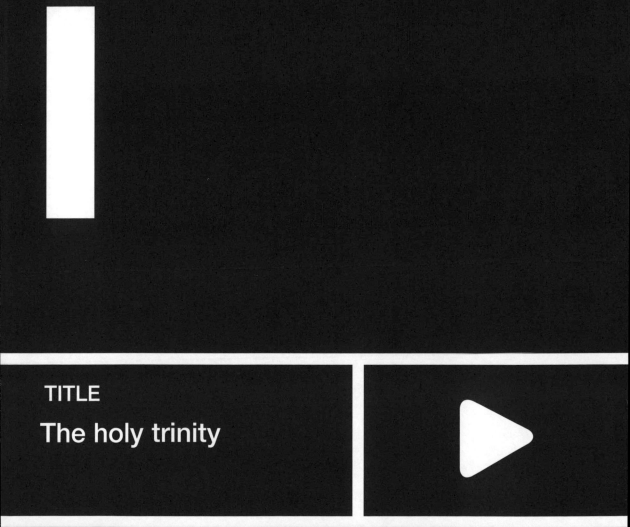

START

CHAPTER 1

The Writer

How do you write a short film?

There is a certain irony in the question in as much as the secret of writing a short film is the same as writing anything: first, it ain't easy, and second, the secret is there is no secret. It's plain hard work. Scriptwriting is re-writing. Whatever goes down on paper, however well it looks, and with the abundance of scriptwriting programs and story-creating paradigms, it's probably going to look super, that first gush of words is unlikely to produce anything of great value.

What that gush will do is give you something to work with. It is the cloth from which the tailor fashions a suit, the fittings are the re-writes, the new drafts.

It is often said that you should write about what you know about. I would amend that to say, better still, write about what moves you, your passions, dreams and desires. You have to get into the midst of the story before even you, the writer, knows what it is you are trying to say. Character drives plot, but the underlying theme, the message, is what holds the narrative together.

CHARACTERS

Once you give birth to your characters, they are responsible for their own actions, and the effects caused by those actions. Put a volatile character in a compromising situation and he will swing out with both fists; neither he nor you will be able to prevent it.

Put temptation in the way of a thief and just watch his eyes light up as he sees the main chance. Are we, the reader or viewer, interested in these people? Do we want to follow their story? Do the characters start at point A and shift subtly, cleverly, gradually and convincingly through dilemma, reversals and crisis to point B? Will the brute learn self-control; the thief not to take what isn't given? Do they have obstacles to overcome? Most important: is there conflict? All stories progress through conflict: action and reaction.

Boy asks Girl: Will you go to the movies with me? Girl says: Yes. No conflict, no story. Boy asks Girl: Will you go to the movies with me? Girl says: No. I can't stand men with beards.

Now we have a story. Will he shave off his beard for her? Will he shave it off in order to get her to see the movie with him, then grow it again once they're an item? And if he does regrow his beard, will she break off the relationship?

THEME

Now, we have conflict, the grist of every TV soap, but what underpins the story is the theme: the writer's viewpoint, the attitudes and issues the writer wants to explore. A theme can normally be expressed by a well-known saying, in this case: You can't tell a book by looking at the cover. In *The Wizard of Oz*, Dorothy discovers there's no place like home. *Rocky* learns if at first you don't succeed, you try, try, try again.

The Boy With The Beard is about superficiality, the comical aspects integral to the plot adding light relief, and underpinning the theme. When the Boy sees that the Girl is merely frivolous, he will stop pursuing her. The Girl, oblivious to her own nature, rather than looking introspectively, will look outside herself and seek ways of punishing the Boy. The initial point of conflict is the beard. The first turning point is when the Boy shaves off his beard to get a date. The plot requires another turning point, the second hook, to swing the story into a new direction.

In this case, we will add the Rival, the key element to most love stories and the third spar in the eternal triangle. Our Rival is a clean-shaven shallow character with an equal fondness for taking girls to the movies. When the Girl goes out with the Rival, she finds him self-centered, conceited, his conversation dull. She still hates beards, but she will now look inside herself and realize that she has been superficial worrying over such trivialities. She has started to look inside the book, not just at the cover, and, as if she is looking in the mirror, she will glimpse in the reflection the danger of losing the man she really loves.

It is the emotional journey that holds readers and grabs an audience. To begin with, the Boy was pursuing the Girl. Now, the turnaround is complete. She will start pursuing him, extending the theme and highlighting this aspect of human nature: the tendency to reject what we have and miss it the moment it's gone.

With the story dynamic in flux and the characters now familiar, the scenes should turn with greater urgency, racing us to a conclusion that should achieve two goals:

1. to be both what the audience expects
2. yet not exactly in the way they expect it.

The audience wants to be surprised, not disappointed by the obvious.

CONSTRUCTION

Each scene should have its own beginning, middle, and end, a minor conflict leading to resolution and on to the next scene, the characters growing from each development. The effect is like placing tiles on a mosaic path, each contributing to the story's journey and driving us forward to a satisfying conclusion.

If the story has been well told, the characters would have gone through changes. We will have observed their small imperfections, foibles and flaws, the acts of kindness and humanity that add up to the sum total of what they are, a representation of ourselves.

The metaphor of the sculptor releasing the figure from the block of marble is familiar and can be extended to the part played by the writer, the unique mannerisms, word patterns, strengths and weaknesses of his characters[1] laid bare as each new challenge chips away the outer layers to reveal the individual beneath. Our own dreams and deepest desires often remain a mystery to us; we are a collage of inconsistencies. But the writer must know his characters and their motivations; they must remain consistent *even as they change* in order for them to become interesting to the audience.

The Girl of our story will have fallen in love with the Boy for what he is, not how he appears, and will accept his facial hair. The Boy, conscious of her love and aware of the compromises she has made, will stop being so obstinate about his beard, perhaps shave it off for their wedding day, when the priest—this now being a Greek Orthodox story—has the longest beard known to mankind. The Rival, too, will have changed. He lost the girl, but has learned that you can't tell a book by looking at the cover. He'll probably grow a beard as well.

The Boy With The Beard is a morality play that evolved *while I was writing it*. It began as a romantic comedy, but the weighty undertones could with careful writing and re-writing draw us into new depths: perhaps the Boy is a recent immigrant and wears the beard for religious reasons? Perhaps the Girl was once assaulted by a bearded man carrying a knife and the memory still haunts her?

If we take the cross-cultural theme, I would now name my characters: let's give the Boy the heroic-sounding name Alexander, the Girl Wendy, something fresh and easy on the tongue. The Rival we'll call Dirk, for reasons that will become clear. Writers keep books with titles like "Naming Your Baby" on their shelves and pay as much attention christening their characters as parents give to naming their new-born infants. In Spain, people remember Don Quixote more than Cervantes, his creator. Great names of fiction live forever in our minds, Scarlett O'Hara, Sam Spade, Luke Skywalker, Lolita, Robin Hood, Nurse Ratched, Scrooge, Bond—James Bond. In *Pat Garrett & Billy the Kid* the chameleon-like Bob Dylan is named Alias.

The film *In The Heat of the Night* turns on the scene when gum-chewing police chief Rod Steiger asks Sidney Poitier his name.

1.1 *In the Heat of the Night* (1967)

▶▶ P.17

"So, boy, what do they call you up there in the north?"
"They call me Mr Tibbs."

The response earns Poitier respect and he states his name with such power the producers used the line to title the sequel. Good line, bad script. In the original, Poitier is picked up on a murder rap for no other reason than he's black. His knowledge, detective skills and humanity move the plot along and secure his release, but as a gritty look at Southern racism, the film is not about Poitier, but Steiger, as he comes to terms with his bigotry, his lack of humanity and, for good measure, his personal loneliness.

They Call Me Mr Tibbs is about *what it's about*, without subplots or theme; it lacks authenticity, the quality the writer should be striving for. If a scene doesn't work, only by looking for the veracity of the scene, for the authenticity of the characters' needs, desires and actions, will we unearth its weaknesses.

When a scene is stuck in as a device to move the plot along—*'Hi, John, fancy seeing you here. Are you going to Anne's party at the country club Saturday?'*—the filmgoer knows he's being made a fool of, it's a subtle thing like an instrument out of tune in an orchestra, but you can sense it in the auditorium when, instead of watching the screen, people are glancing around or—the ultimate nightmare: talking. You still see the above "Hi, John" scene, or the girlfriend opening a drawer by "chance" and finding a gun hidden among the handkerchiefs, but this is lazy writing and it's growing harder to get away with it.

In this chapter and throughout the text, examples have been taken from features, not short films, simply because there are so few universally recognized short films to quote from. The structure of short films, and all stories, is essentially the same, and writers of short films are presented with special difficulties, the challenge of space and time, or the lack of it. Once they overcome those challenges, they will be ready to write a feature.

Going back to Wendy, if we want to run with the idea that she was assaulted, we could remap the story as Gothic horror, a now clean-shaven Alexander becoming an avenging hero who pursues the bearded attacker to a haunted house on a windy cliff top where the rivals fight to the death. And who is the bearded attacker: Dirk, of course, in another guise, so named for the knife he carries.

When I was looking for a story to make the above example, a number of films rushed into my mind. But I needed something less complex, a fable, more than a feature. I was sitting with my morning coffee flicking through the local paper, avoiding the computer hum in the office next door. Writing is hard; it's always hard, any diversion to avoid it will do. I turned finally to the newspaper's back page and there was an attractive woman and a young man with a full beard pictured at their wedding; in their optimistic expressions was *The Boy With The Beard*, waiting to be found.

PAUSE

HOLLYWOOD REPORTER'S TOP 10 SCRIPTS:

1. **Casablanca (Epstein-Epstein-Koch)**
2. **The Godfather (Puzo-Coppola)**
3. **Chinatown (Towne)**
4. **Citizen Kane (Mankiewicz-Welles)**
5. **All About Eve (Mankiewicz)**

6. Annie Hall (Allen-Brickman))
7. Sunset Boulevard (Brackett-Wilder-Marshman)
8. Network (Chayefsky)
9. Some Like It Hot (Wilder-Diamond)
10. The Godfather II (Coppola-Puzo)

Most scripts can be found on the Internet Movie Script Database: www.imsdb.com.

STORYTELLING

According to American writer and scholar Joseph Campbell, the stories are already there, inside us, bursting to come out.

Whether we listen with aloof amusement to the dreamlike mumbo jumbo of some red-eyed witch doctor of the Congo, or read with cultivated rapture thin translations from the sonnets of the mystic Lao-tsu; now and again crack the hard nutshell of an argument of Aquinas, or catch suddenly the shining meaning of a bizarre Eskimo fairy tale: it will be always the one, shape-shifting yet marvelously constant story that we find, together with a challengingly persistent suggestion of more remaining to be experienced than will ever be known or told.[2]

The above paragraph comes from *The Hero With A Thousand Faces*, Campbell's analysis of world folk tales that shows how common threads and themes in storytelling bridge the frontiers of culture, religion, and time. It was Campbell's study that inspired Christopher Vogler's *The Writer's Journey*, an insider's look at how writers can utilize mythic structures to create powerful narratives that are dramatic, entertaining and psychologically authentic. Since its first publication in 1998, *The Writer's Journey* has become the Hollywood "bible" on the screenwriting craft.

The stories are there aplenty, in the depths of our own subconscious, and I quote Campbell to counter the post-modern belief that everything under the sun has already been seen and every story has already been told. In writing classes and spats among movie addicts someone will invariably remark that there is only a handful of different stories—the exact number always varies—and writers throughout time just keep retelling them: *The Boy With The Beard* is *Romeo and Juliet*; the man with the fatal flaw—*Achilles*; the precious gift taken away—*Orpheus*; virtue finally recognized—*Cinderella*; a deal with the devil—*Faust*; the spider trapping the fly—*Circe;* change or transformation—*Metamorphosis*; the quest—*Don Quixote*.

To the list we can add the coming-of-age plot (*Gregory's Girl, On the Waterfront*); rivals (*Chicago, Amadeus* and Nolan's *The Prestige,* mentioned above); escape (*The Great Escape, The Shawshank Redemption*); revenge (*Hamlet, Gladiator*); the con (*House of Games, The Sting*); manipulation (*Svengali*). These stories have been reshaped over and over again, but it is the reshaping and combination of plots that makes them fresh and original. Cross *Romeo and Juliet* with *Cinderella* and what do we end up with: the Richard Gere/Julie Roberts film *Pretty Woman*; change *Cinderella* for *Orpheus* and we have Nabokov's *Lolita*. The genius of George Lucas is that he borrowed from them all to create *Star Wars*, a mythical adventure in the tradition of *Gilgamesh*, the pre-Biblical epic still on the bookshelves today.

The themes running through Clint Eastwood's Oscar-winning *Million Dollar Baby* are little different from Stallone's *Rocky*. Rocky transforms to the girl fighter Maggie Fitzgerald (Hillary Swank), but the story in this incarnation is more about Frankie Dunn (Eastwood), her trainer. The most important lesson Dunn teaches his fighters is "always protect yourself." But we discover that Dunn, on bad terms with his daughter, is himself emotionally vulnerable. Maggie Fitzgerald is a poor waitress already past 30 trying to make something of her life through boxing. At first reluctant to allow a female boxer in his gym, old Frankie finally takes on the girl, teaches her everything he knows, and puts the emotional heart back in his own life. Maggie realizes her dream, she becomes a great boxer, and the conclusion does just what it's supposed to do: it takes us to the big fight and pummels the wind out of us with a knock-out punch of a surprise ending not to be given away here.

Million Dollar Baby is an old story made fresh in its modification. In the time of the Greeks they were saying there's nothing new under the sun. The fact is in art, each new creation is a reworking of the old, and it is that reworking that gives a story new life. We are still discovering species of bird, insect and fish unknown to mankind. Every generation has its own hopes and fears, its own tales to tell: melting ice caps, vanishing rain forests, GM crops, terrorism. What makes our story special, what draws in the reader or viewer, then, is not the underlying mechanics of plot, but the characters. Great characters move the audience and, as plot unfolds through conflict, great villains make great stories.

Once born, before a word of narrative goes down on paper, writers should sketch out complete biographies of their characters, their ages, idiosyncrasies, disappointments, hopes and dreams, not caricatures or stereotypes, but flesh-and-blood originals with all the qualities, doubts and nervous tics that make us all one-offs. Characters need a past, a network of relationships. They will show the audience just a fraction of this in the drama, the tip of the iceberg, and then usually at a time of crisis. But from this study, you should be able to extract the essence of your characters and summarize them in a few sentences.

1.2 *Thelma and Louise* (1991)

▶▶ P.17

Callie Khouri does it marvelously in her screenplay *Thelma and Louise*, describing Thelma's husband (the perfectly-named carpet salesman Darryl) in three swift brushstrokes:

Darryl comes trotting down the stairs. Polyester was made for this man and he's dripping in men's jewelry. He manages a Carpeteria.

Darryl is checking himself out in the hall mirror and it's obvious he likes what he sees.

He exudes overconfidence for reasons that never become apparent. He likes to think of himself as a real lady killer. He is making imperceptible adjustments to his over moussed hair. Thelma watches approvingly.[3]

What Callie Khouri did was take the traditional buddy movie and put two girls in the lead roles. In the story, while Louise is fighting the demons from the past, Thelma is finding herself, both in their own way "coming-of age." When they have fully matured into new beings, they know they can never go back to what they were; they are ready for the ultimate metamorphosis: the drive over the cliff edge into the Grand Canyon.

Each story will have running through it what's called the Active Question: will they get married? Will she stop using drugs and run in the Olympics? Will he get revenge? Will they escape—the robbers with the bank haul, Thelma and Louise from the tyranny of men?

If the characters we create have a tale worth telling, they will *want* something: to get the girl, revenge, justice, to steal the Goose that laid the Golden Egg, a sign of self-worth, find the road to El Dorado. A story becomes interesting when the writer sets up obstacles that prevent their heroes getting what they want (Thelma and Louise first lose their money, essential for their flight). The story hooks us as they overcome those obstacles and/or villains and thereby grow and change in the process.

In order to grip the audience, the characters must be seen to go through a range of emotions: fear, self-doubt, sorrow, elation. The screen-writer achieves this through conflict *(you will never marry that man; I will never go out with a boy with a beard; you'll never be good enough to run in the Olympics).*

As the conflict unwinds, the audience will be seeing themselves in the hero or heroine and will be sharing those emotions. Conflict is to drama what sound is to music. It is the heart of drama, the soul of drama, the secret of suspense, the key to emotional engagement, that thing that keeps filmgoers on the edge of their seats. If you laugh out loud while reading a book or feel a tear jerk into your eye while you are watching a movie, the writer has done his job.

Thelma and Louise is often quoted on film courses and Callie Khouri's script should be on the reading list of every writer who wants to turn their pen to film, shorts or a feature, not only for its pace and dialogue, but for the symbolism neatly woven into the plot. *Thelma and Louise* is about male dominance. Darryl's comic machismo, the attempted rape and the truck driver's lecherous behavior subliminally underpin that theme. Male domination is an abstract concept, but Callie Khouri has written scenes as symbols of that concept to make the abstract real and more easy to understand.

On the list of memorable names above is Nurse Ratched (Louise Fletcher) from *One Flew Over the Cuckoo's Nest*. The perfect use of symbolism is explored in this movie through the use of the water fountain McMurphy (Jack Nicholson) has failed to budge on the various occasions when he tries to lift it. McMurphy is a free spirit gradually crushed by the institution. In the final scene, Big Chief (William Sampson) seizes the fountain and crashes it through the bars—to escape from the despotic asylum.

As a sub-plot, Big Chief's strand of the story tells us more about McMurphy, Nurse Ratched and oppression, underlining the theme. Sub-plots contribute color, comedy and nuance; they serve to confirm the main plot, reveal the contradictions of the principal characters and place obstacles in the hero's path. Characters who serve this function need as much fleshing out and, ideally, will go through changes during the course of events from one state to another, in the case of Big Chief, from tyranny to freedom.

One Flew Over the Cuckoo's Nest holds our attention because of the power of the characters drawn in Ken Kesey's novel. We as people are interested in the joys and sufferings, the ups and downs of our neighbors and friends; as Marcel Proust once said, at heart everyone is a gossip. Disney cartoons and science fiction monsters are anthropomorphic, and it will take rare skill for a writer to keep us involved in a plot where the hero goes into battle against some anonymous adversary like nature, disease, the tobacco companies or big business. The enemy needs a human face—Christopher Eccleston in Danny Boyle's virus nightmare *28 Days Later*; Michael Douglas as Gordon Gekko in *Wall Street*. In *El Laberinto del Fauno* (*Pan's Labyrinth* in English), writer/director Guillermo del Toro combines the harsh reality of Franco's Spain with the imaginary, fairy tale world seen through the mind of a young girl played by Ivana Baquero. But it is the human face of fascism brutally revealed by Sergi López that allows us to comprehend the human cost of the dictatorship.

In life, the whistle blower usually loses his battle against the corporate giants. It is the role of the writer to put the world back in balance and show us the little guy fighting back; except in downbeat *noir* and ironic tales, people come away from films more satisfied with positive endings. As Oscar Wilde reminds us: The good ended happily, the bad unhappily—that is fiction. Whether it's James Bond entering Ernst Blofeld's fortress, Rocky Balboa in the boxing ring, or Charlie Sheen challenging Michael Douglas in *Wall Street's* final reel, the hero and the antagonist must have this conclusive, face-to-face confrontation to send the audiences home contented. The little guy rising to the challenge and overcoming evil appeals to our deepest humanity. We are the little guy.

THE WRITER'S CRAFT

One thing that first-time writers and filmmakers need to prevail over is that everyone has grown up on the same diet of countless movies and endless hours of television. We know how it's done because we've seen it done, over and over again. It looks easy. Film courses and text books, including this one, light the road before us. The struggle then, as Luis Buñuel understood, is to break the mold of our education and environment, think in fresh ways and use new technology to find our own originality.

Writing has laws of perspective, of light and shade, just as painting does, or music. If you are born knowing them, fine. If not, learn them. Then rearrange the rules to suit yourself.

What Truman Capote[4] is saying in the above is that storytelling has rules, but like the moon and stars to the navigator at sea, we must still pilot our own course through the darkness.

Imagine a journey by land from London to Athens. We may take the ferry to Bilbao in Spain, cross the Pyrenees and hug the Mediterranean coast. Alternatively, we can take the tunnel to France, slip through Germany and Austria, then follow the Adriatic. The two journeys will be touched by different languages, foods, customs and landscapes; different people with different skills and knowledge will cross our paths along the way. But the destination is the same and the journey will be the hero's own personal and unique experience, the material face of the more profound internal journey.

While the script for a short film will require conflict, emotional engagement and resolution, as discussed above, there is the added difficulty of wrapping it all up, preferably, in under ten minutes. Surreal or experimental short films may be useful for filmmakers to show a new narrative or visual style. In drama, the best short films have a simple plotline and, in my experience, can generally be noted for containing these three elements:

One main character
One story or conflict
One result or resolution

1.3 Ashvin Kumar directing (2004)

▶▶ P.17

On the list of "Ten Short Films You Must See" (see *Part VIII: A Brief History of Short Films*), is Ashvin Kumar's 2004 Oscar-nominated short *Little Terrorist*. This perfectly illustrates the point made above: one main character, one story, one result.

Ten-year-old Jamal is playing cricket with his friends on the Muslim side of the Indian/Pakistan border. When the ball is hit into the minefield dividing the two countries, Jamal slips under the barbed wire and picks his way among the mines to rescue the ball (a cricket ball in this poor community would have greater value than in our consumer driven society).

Jamal is seen by guards and escapes their gunfire by fleeing into India. Hunted by the police, he is taken in by a Hindu Brahmin who disguises Jamal by shaving his head and leaving a single curl of hair at the crown, a Hindu custom. The audience sees that life in the Hindu village is the same as life in the Muslim village beyond the barbed wire and that "common human decency" is the same the world over.

The Brahmin knows his way across the minefield and returns the boy that night. They stop at a tree with cricket stumps painted on the trunk: as a boy, before India—Pakistan partition, the old Brahmin played cricket in this very place. Jamal runs safely home to his village, only to be given a good spanking by his mother for cutting off his hair. Result: boys will be boys, mothers will be mothers, and Jamal has seen a glimpse of life beyond the minefield. The plot of *Little Terrorist* is simple, but Kumar's non-partisan exploration of universal themes and his eye for detail makes the story compelling to watch and satisfying in resolution.

www.little-terrorist.com

1.4 Oscar nominee Ashvin Kumar

▶▶ P.18

TIPS

All stories, long or short, for film or the written word, benefit from structure. In *The Writer's Journey*, cited above, Christopher Vogler outlines the 12-stage journey the hero normally takes in those stories we find ultimately satisfying. A short film will lack time for all the intricate stages and archetypes, but a sense of structure is still crucial.

1.5 *Babel* (2006)

▶▶ P.18

The 8-Point Guide below remains true to Vogler's principle, but is more practicable for a short film. We have applied the framework to both the short story and short film script in *Part VI, Greta May—The Adaptation*, and a careful reading reveals the 8 steps that hold the story in place. The 8-Point Guide is not a formula, but a road map, and the best stories will take the framework and bend it into a new shape. Note also, that the 8 points do not have to be in sequence; with flashbacks and flashforwards, they may appear in any order (except, perhaps, the resolution), for example *Pulp Fiction* and Alejandro González Iñárritu's dazzling multi-linear, multi-lingual and multi-faceted *Babel*, a film every new writer and director should watch many times.

PAUSE

8-POINT GUIDE TO MAKING SHORT FILMS

1. Introduce main character(s); set the scene.
2. Give the character a problem, obstacle, obsession or addiction.
3. Let the character work out a plan to overcome the problem.
4. Before setting out to solve the problem, there may be a moment of doubt that will require the hero to seek advice from a mentor: teacher, best friend. This is an opportunity to let the audience know more about the problem and weigh it up in their own minds. What would they do?
5. With new resolve (and often a ***magical*** gift from the mentor: the watches Q gives James Bond; Dorothy's ruby slippers), the hero sets out to overcome the problem, obstacle, obsession or addiction.
6. Overcoming the problem or challenge (getting the girl; escaping tyranny; saving the world) will be met by extreme opposition from the rival, who will usually have greater but different strengths and will in some ways bear similarities to the hero: the nemesis is the hero's dark side.
7. The hero will appear to fail in his quest. He will give up or glimpse defeat, even death, and will require superhuman effort to overcome this daunting final task.
8. The hero wins the final battle, with an opponent, or enemy, or with himself, and returns to his natural state wiser, or stronger, or cured, but not necessarily happier. The journey has made him a different person. He has glimpsed death and can never go back to the simplicity of what he once was.

To the 8-point guide above, I would add the following recommendations when tackling a script.

10 TIPS

- Don't trust in inspiration, unless you want to be a poet. The first idea you get is often borrowed from every movie you've seen and book you've read.
- If you do work on that inspired project: re-write, re-write; re-write. That is the most important three things you will ever learn about scriptwriting, and I repeat: ***re-write, re-write, re-write.***

- See your writing from the other side of the screen, from the audience point of view; if there is no audience, there is no message.
- Do not adjust your writing to the market by attempting to stay abreast, or even ahead of changing trends; such work is a form of cultural static lacking veracity and, often, even relevance.
- Be true to your own vision. Write about what you know about? Absolutely. But then write what you believe in.
- Four steps to writing a short film scenario: find the ending; then the beginning; then the first turning point – the event that gets the story going; then the second turning point, the scene that swings the story around and sets up the ending.
- Enter your story a short time before the crisis that ignites the drama.
- Scenes are like parties: arrive late and leave early.
- Persevere.
- Listen to criticism. But don't always take it.

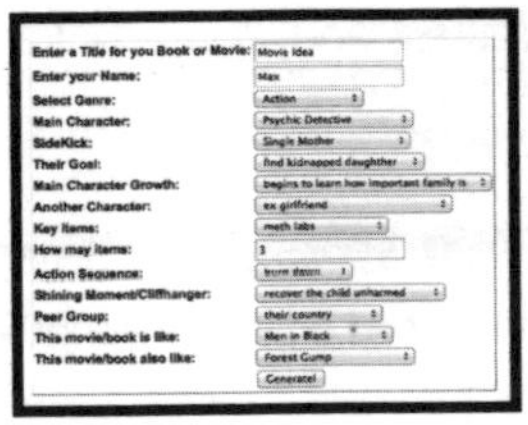

1.6 Myers

▶▶ P.18

If you are really stuck for ideas, Bill Myers has created a free piece of online software on his website www.bmyers.com.

The program is easy to use. Just complete the blanks, click Generate, and your movie treatment is created instantly for you.

From the above, I created an action film, where a psychic detective and single mother join forces to find her kidnapped daughter. A single click on "Generate" gave me the following movie idea:

Movie Idea
An original screenplay concept by
Max

Action: A Psychic Detective teams up with a Single Mother to find kidnapped daughter. As the story unfolds, the Psychic Detective begins to learn how important family is with a ex-girlfriend.
By the finale, they manage to burn down 3 meth labs, recover the child unharmed and win the respect of their country.
Think Men in Black meets Forest Gump.

SOFTWARE FOCUS – SCREENWRITING

There are literally dozens of programs that help you, as the writer, to format and present a screenplay properly. These range from specialized applications to word processor add-ons to web-based resources.

The two industry leading applications are Final Draft and Movie Magic Screenwriter, both available on Mac and Windows. Both programs will remember and automatically fill in information like character names, scene headings and transitions. They will also automatically paginate and format your script to industry standards. Script elements such as Action, Character, Dialogue and Shots will be formatted as you type. A personal favorite is the option to keep track of ideas via Script Notes. Information can be added, but hidden, so it doesn't disrupt the flow of the text and can be returned to at a later time. Scenes can also be viewed in different ways to get a better view of the script as a whole. Chapter 27 is a detailed guide to using Final Draft.

For writing a short script, both of the above could well be over budget, but the good news is there is a lot of excellent freeware that provide the same features. Screenpro is a good formatting template for Microsoft Word with a range of functions, and is available at a very low price. Page 2 Stage for Windows, and Montage for Mac, are both reliable—and free.

One of the many free web-based scriptwriting programs is Five Sprockets—www.fivesprockets.com—which describes itself as an "online production studio," and has many of the expected features in its script-writing section. It also helps you network with other writers and producers.

However good your script is, if it doesn't meet industry standards or is filled with typos, it is likely to be in the producer's bin before he's even finished reading the first page (see the AMPAS'S fourteen points below[5]). But remember the point of this chapter: that writing a good screenplay takes time, hard work, and rewriting. While time can be saved with good software, it doesn't help you to be more imaginative or do the writing for you.

Once the screenplay has been polished, redrafted and is ready for Hollywood, be sure to format it in the right way.

PAUSE

Fourteen foibles that might invoke a poor first impression (based only on a script's title page and page one):

- **Typo/misspelling on the title page.**
- **Typo/misspelling in the first scene header.**
- **Typos/misspellings in the first sentence or paragraph or page.**
- **Triple/double spacing of every/many line(s) on first page.**
- **Lack of spacing between scene header and description and/or between description and dialogue and/or between dialogue and dialogue.**
- **Use of font other than Courier 12-point, ten-pitch, non-proportional.**
- **Extensive use of bold print.**
- **Dialogue that stretches from the left margin to the right margin.**
- **Extra space between character name and dialogue.**
- **Description and/or dialogue typed ALL CAPS.**
- **Extremely narrow or extremely wide outside margins.**
- **Long, long, long descriptive passages.**
- **Handwritten or hand-printed script.**
- **Other glaring, non-standard format usage.**

THE WRITER'S GUILD OF AMERICA (WWW.WGA.ORG)

If you are serious about writing and are based in the states, it's worth joining the Writers Guild of America, a labor union composed of the thousands of writers who write the content for television shows, movies, news programs, documentaries, animation, and Internet and mobile phones (new media).

Their primary duty is to represent their members in negotiations with film and television producers to ensure the rights of screen, television, and new media writers. Once a contract is in place, they enforce it. Due to the WGA's efforts, writers can receive pension and health coverage, and their financial and creative rights are protected.

The WGA is also responsible for determining writing credits for feature films, television, and new media programs and also monitors, collects, and distributes residuals (payments for the reuse of movies, television, and new media programs) for writers each year.

Register Your Screenplay

The WGA is also the world's leading screenplay registration service, registering more than 65,000 pieces of literary material every year. Submitting your work to be archived by the WGA Registry will document your authorship and establish the completion date of an original work.

Though the Registry does not claim it can prevent plagiarism, it can produce the registered material to any legal proceeding or arbitration regardless of location or membership as a neutral third party.

Registering can be done online, by mail or in person and costs $20 for non-members per screenplay. Almost any type of creative work can be registered, and material is kept on file for five years.

PAUSE

TOP 5 HIGHEST PAID SPEC SCRIPTWRITERS[6]

As with all aspects of filmmaking, scriptwriting is a tough area to get into. But some people make more than a decent living out of it. Spec scripts are sold on the open market, not written at the behest of a studio.

1. Déjà Vu (2006)
Screenwriters: Terry Rossio and Bill Marsilii
Fee: $7 million ($2 million guarantee and $5 million production bonus)
2. The Long Kiss Goodnight (1996)
Screenwriter: Shane Black
Fee: $4 million
3. Panic Room (2002)
Screenwriter: David Koepp
Fee: $4 million ($2 million guarantee, $1 million production bonus and $1 million for serving as a producer)
4. Talladega Nights: The Ballad of Ricky Bobby (2006)
Screenwriter(s): Will Ferrell and Adam McKay
Fee: $4 million
5. Basic Instinct (1992)
Screenwriter: Joe Eszterhas
Fee: $3 million

To repeat the first line of this chapter: How do you write a good short film? It requires the same intense work as writing a feature or novel, it's just shorter. Finally, a quote from Jean Cocteau:

Listen carefully to first criticisms of your work. Note just what it is about your work the critics don't like – then cultivate it. That's the part of your work that's individual and worth keeping.

Poet, dramatist, novelist, film director, the kind of guy you could really grow to hate, Cocteau began his career with *The Life of a Poet*, a short film.[7]

STOP

1.1 Sidney Poitier and Rod Steiger reaching boiling point in the racially charged *In the Heat of the Night*. (1967)

1.2 Ready for the long ride; Geena Davis and Susan Sarandon in *Thelma and Louise*. Photo Roland Neveu. (1991)

1.3 Ashvin Kumar directing *The Little Terrorist*. (2004)

1.4 Oscar nominee Ashvin Kumar

1.5 *Babel* film poster. (2006)

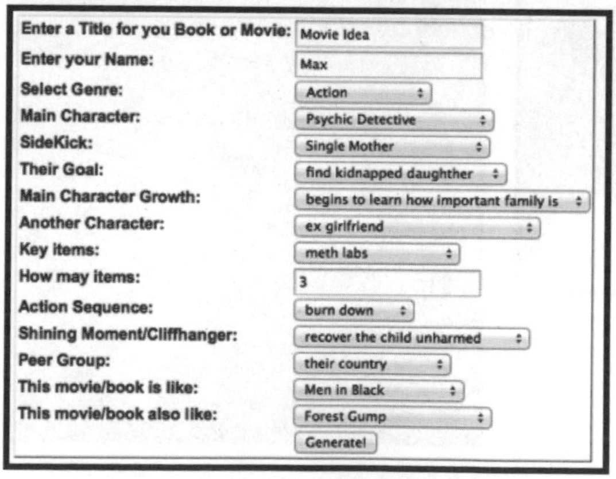

1.6 Screenshot of www.bymers.com.

START

CHAPTER 2

The Producer

When a novelist completes his manuscript, apart from the re-writes and brawls with the editor, the job is done. With a screenplay, the journey is about to begin.

With short films, the writer, director and producer will often be one and the same. Filmmakers, though, will mostly find that life is too short to keep so many balls in the air all at once and, when they find what they are best at, they stick to it.

The foundation of every film, as the previous chapter makes clear, is the script, but it is the producer who will nurture the writer through the new drafts, fork out for the cappuccinos, then present the final version to the director, casting agent, actors, and funders. He will draw up contracts, speak to lawyers, settle feuds and stroke the highly-strung sensitivities of his family of creatives.

In the 2002 *Simone*, Winona Ryder is furious with Al Pacino because her trailer, while the biggest on the lot, isn't actually the highest. At first Pacino tries to let the air out of the tires on the offending vehicle, but when his patience runs out, he does the only self-respecting thing left to him and fires her.

In this parody on the movie business, Miss Ryder, in a refreshing self-parody, is replaced with a computer-generated star character. Such technology isn't yet with us, but the scene illustrates perfectly the relationship between the producer and his team, his role as best friend, adviser, marriage-counselor, guru, psychiatrist and, ultimately, the boss. From the moment a film goes into production, whether it's a Hollywood feature or a first short, the meter is running and the producer has to keep his eyes on the clock.

FINANCE

It is often assumed outside the industry that the producer has a fat wallet from which he pulls fists full of dollars like Michael Lerner as the odious Jack Lipnick in *Barton Fink*. Not in real life.

Tim Bevan and Eric Fellner at Working Title are responsible for more than 60 films with hits including *Four Weddings and a Funeral*, *Notting*

Hill, Bridget Jones's Diary, Atonement, and *Anna Karenina*, a fresh new vision of Leo Tolstoy's epic love story adapted by Oscar-winning writer Tom Stoppard and starring Keira Knightley.

It's a great track record, but Working Title is backed by American studios. The producer uses other people's money, and only when he hands that money back with a slice of the profits will he raise funds for the next project.

There is another common misconception to bear in mind: even a no-budget film is going to cost somebody something somewhere along the line: the camera and equipment, postage, labels, pre-production planning, post-production film developing or transfer, and that's apart from the bus fares and bacon sandwiches during production. The producer with his pared-down micro-budget short may not have investors to worry about, but will need to show flare with his début in order to attract some cash next time around.

It's not essential for the producer to have a sister working in Barclays in Soho or a college buddy at the Chase Manhattan. What he does need is a nose for a story and the passion to convince backers and funders (more on that later) to finance his project over the many competing and perhaps equally good packages that flood across their desks. You will notice that in the mind of the producer, the script has become the product and the product, with its added elements, becomes a package.

DIFFERENT HATS

The producer, then, is a salesman, a PR shapeshifter. He can sell plans for a bridge when there isn't a river; he is a UN peacekeeper between warring factions—the writer, director, leading lady—a shepherd who should guide his creatives and as such is a creative himself. You don't have to be able to score music to appreciate Mozart or Ry Cooder's seductive blues. Likewise you don't need to know what the *f* stops do on a camera, or how an editor adds fades on Final Cut. What the producer understands is human nature. He knows how to get the best out of his people and gives the best in return.

Producers are characterized as tough guys, the cigar-chomping tight wad, and while this might be true of a Hollywood Jack Lipnick, the parody is the exception and, in my own encounters with industry heavyweights, I have experienced only kindness and that species of vibrant, boundless energy it takes to be interested in everything and everyone they come across, the energy it requires to make movies.

PAUSE

6 QUESTIONS TO ASK WHEN YOU READ A SCRIPT

1. **Who is the hero?**
2. **What is the active question: will he, will she, will they ...?**
3. **Who or what opposes the hero?**
4. **From whose point of view is the story being told?**
5. **Theme: What's it about?**
6. **What is the visual style of the film?**

One time, when I was writing a book about Salvador Dalí, I met Hal Landers, the man behind such classics as *What Ever Happened To Baby Jane?* I mentioned that I was a writer—writers can't help themselves—and Hal asked to read the manuscript. It was something I would not normally have done, showing someone unfinished work, but I was swept along by Hal's enthusiasm.

The following morning, he insisted on calling a publisher he knew. That same day, the publisher was calling me and, by the end of the week, I was reading a contract. There was nothing in this for Hal Landers—except the dedication in the book—but he had used his contacts to pull the deal together, extended his own network and made life seem truly magical.

Hal Landers once bumped into Queen Juliana of Holland in a store in Paris. "Hey," he said, "aren't you the Queen of Holland? I'm from New Jersey, I've never met a Queen before. Why don't you let me buy you a cup of coffee?" The Queen was so overwhelmed by the approach she agreed, and they remained friends from that day on.

What these anecdotes illustrate is that the qualities Hal Landers brought to his daily life are the very qualities required by a producer: enthusiasm, energy, generosity, a good eye for product (the Dalí book is now in its fifth edition), an agile mind, the verve to think laterally and the personality to do the unusual. Like invite Queens for coffee.

ALEXANDER SALKIND

One time when I was in Paris, I was invited to the première of *The Rainbow Thief*, a whimsical fantasy written by Berta Dominguez D, directed by Alexandro Jodorowsky and pairing Peter O'Toole with Omar Sharif for the first time since *Lawrence of Arabia*. I met the producer, Alexander Salkind, and at his prompting I told him that I was trying to interest broadcasters in a documentary project. He didn't make any phone calls on my behalf, but led me to the bar and told me how he got started in the film business.

He had arrived penniless in France from Russia and was taking a train from Paris to Lyon where he thought he might have more luck finding work. In the carriage, he met a man who owned three shoe shops. Alex told him a story he wanted to turn into a short film. By the time they arrived at their destination, the shoe shop owner was so intrigued, he decided to sell one of his shops and fund the movie.

Financially, it was a disaster. Salkind was depressed, but it was his first film and his collaborator, the shoe shop guy, considered the experience so valuable, he sold a second shop to finance the next film. That, too, was a flop, but he had started out on a course from which he saw no way back: he sold the last of his shops to fund one more film and lost everything.

Alex Salkind had to go elsewhere for finance, but he now had a showreel and was on his way. As for the shoe shop proprietor, he'd left the footwear business behind him forever. He'd caught the film bug, worked as Salkind's assistant and had a long career as a cinematographer. Salkind had learned the three essential lessons:

1. How to inspire potential finance.
2. How to manage a budget.
3. How to tell a good story.

With these skills he went on to make an enormous variety of movies, from Kafka's impenetrable *The Trial* (1962) to *The Three Musketeers* (1973) to the *Superman* movies where, due to deft negotiations and deceptive scheduling, his name is lent to what lawyers call the Salkind Clause: that an actor must be told *how many movies he's making*. When he filmed Christopher Reeve in the first *Superman* in 1977, the out-takes contained much of the footage used in *Superman II*.

Salkind by then was a powerful figure, "a Russian producer who moves somewhat mysteriously in international circles," according to writer John Walker,[1] but he had learned when he was penniless the value of a penny and never took his eye off the ticking meter.

The producer will always be pushing the production manager and first assistant director (1st AD) to keep to schedule, that's his job. But the enthusiasm and passion he brings to the project must animate them to give their best. He will develop the bi-lingual skill of telling his director two things at once: The rushes are great. Get on with it. He will know when his leading lady needs stroking or firing. Producing is a multi-skilled pursuit and communication skills form the basis of all the others.

The bigger the budget, the more of other people's money he's spending and the good producer will always be aware of that responsibility. He makes a modest living from the fee written into the budget. He makes the big money for those fat cigars from the points, the percentage of profits negotiated with finance or the studios. The success of a film will leverage up those points for future projects. Failure will make it that much more difficult to finance the next one and sobering statistics show that the majority of first-time filmmakers never make a second feature.

To turn the written word into film needs everyone from the stars whose names go up in lights to the runner on a work experience intern scheme. The process of mixing and shaping the many disparate elements is like taking base metal and turning it into gold. The producer is the alchemist. Behind the scenes he will be working harder than anyone. It's his reputation that's on the line.

WRITERS

A variety of hyphenates shore up the title producer: Assistant, Associate, Executive, Line and the modest Co, but what we are dealing with here is *the* producer, the man or woman who finds the raw material: the book, play, short story, original script, a script adapted from another medium, an idea on the back of a pack of *Marlboro*, or inspired by a photograph on somebody's shelf—and what he sees is the film flash before his eyes.

This talent is more acquired than innate and for the producer to get started, the short film provides the same demands of story-telling and filmmaking found in a feature or TV drama. The constraints of budget and the need to answer to backers or broadcasters will encourage the producer to seek out a story that works for a wide audience, and that's not a bad thing.

However, if you do have the urge to make something culturally or socially valid, a personal crusade, a showcase for your six-year-old twins, or something zany and completely off-the-wall like Martin Pickles' *G.M.*, a short homage to Georges Méliès (discussed later), the short film has all the challenges of a feature without the risks, critically as well as financially.

The first job is to find the script or find the story and put a writer to work on it.

Where do you find a writer?

Throw a stone out of the window and you'll probably hit one. Finding a good writer—finding a great writer, that takes time, practice, patience—and luck.

If you announce that you're looking for material, proposals will start dropping through the mail box with whining letters that diligently explain the story, always the kiss of death; if a script needs explaining, it isn't ready. Andrea Calderwood once remarked that when she left BBC Scotland for Pathé, the same scripts followed her down the M6 to the capital. She took on two assistants, they read 700 scripts between them, and rejected the lot. That isn't to say, of course, that the 701st isn't going to be *the one!*

It's an odd contradiction, but even with all those rookie writers out there, producers from the narrow streets of Soho to the gleaming glass offices looming over Santa Monica Boulevard are pulling out their hair weeping over the scarcity of good scripts. There was a time when every man leaning on every bar imagined he had a book in him. Now it's a screenplay. In fact, mention the movie business, and he'll whip it out of his shoulder bag, dog-eared and coffee-ringed, and ask strangers casually met if they would like to take a look. If you meet Andrea Calderwood in the bar she'll probably tell you she's a dentist.

While there are thousands of people writing scripts, producers continue to complain that there isn't anything worth filming, and with the complaint being ubiquitous, there must be something to it. Producers are therefore rejecting the scripts sliding electronically and physically over the transom and are making calls to publishing houses in search of the neglected novel, the remaindered gem, the book out of copyright, the self-published crime novel released digitally through Amazon. Others are venturing out of the West End to see fringe plays, and into the wind-blown canyons off-Broadway to hole-in-the-wall experimental theaters. If it's worth publishing or staging, it must be worth taking a look at.

But here lies the dilemma. The novel is about ideas, about the internal life of the characters. Proust in *Remembrances of Things Past* wanders off for a dozen pages to describe the smell of *madeleines.* Try getting your writer to put that in his screenplay. Or try getting him to take it out if he's attempted to slip it in. The stage play is about words, plays on words, the taste of words. There is a mass of material that can be adapted, but as anyone who has ever done any adapting soon learns, you have to read the original, take out the kernel and sling the rest to the pigeons. An adaptation is just as hard to write as an original screenplay, perhaps harder.

SMILEY FACES

A friend of mine recently quit making corporate videos to adapt a biography, the hardest of genres. Within days he was phoning to chat about migraine and insomnia; his attraction to cliff tops and razor blades. Suddenly he was fighting with his girlfriend—her fault—arrived late for appointments; he was drinking too much or, alternatively, claiming he no longer drank at all (first sign of the alcoholic). Finally, he turned up at a meeting wearing odd shoes. He talked about the "verbal" power of silent movies then handed me a Post-it with this on it:

The true way leads along a tight-rope, which is not stretched aloft but just above the ground. It seems designed more to trip than to be walked along.

He'd found Franz Kafka,[2] or Franz Kafka had found him, and this is where the producer becomes the psychiatrist, the healer, the script editor. My writer friend was filled with self-doubt, not that he had done a bad job with the screenplay, he just needed someone to tell him he'd done a good job, a great job ... just a few tweaks here and there, get the first turning point forward a few pages, put some action into that soggy middle ... maybe cut out that section on page 73 where the cop explains the whys and wherefores to his sergeant.

Producer Maureen Murray (www.foxtrotfilms.com) puts smiley faces beside the bits she likes in a script and her writers are more able to cope with the cold straight lines that slice like razors through the bits she doesn't. She makes suggestions, but expects the writer to find solutions: the two skills are different and must complement each other like *yin* and *yang* in a perfect if reversed fit.

A producer is not a writer who has too much in the in-tray to write, but must be able to distinguish good writing when it's on the page and bad writing that needs erasing. Re-writes are a form of torture, "the main condition of the artistic experience,"[3] according to Samuel Beckett, but no screenplay surfaces through the slush piles without them. A film may not live up to the script's potential, but there has never been a great film made from a bad script.

Producers are not always looking for the best script they can find. They may be looking for a script that appeals to them for their own reasons. J. Arthur Rank[4] was a Methodist lay preacher who showed films to children at Sunday school. In 1932, when he discovered more people went to the cinema than to church, the wealthy young mill owner entered the movie business with the intention of making and distributing films that had a positive social content. In the competitive movie market, the Rank Organization had to make films with one eye on the audience, but Rank in looking at scripts and dealing with producers never lost sight of his original aims.

Rank was concerned with the moral and ethical state of society in his time, as an examination of this theme can provide useful and entertaining material at any time. No one who saw *Syriana* and *Good Night, and Good Luck*, two films in 2005, would have missed the filmmakers' allusions to and reflections on the Iraq War. The actor/producer George Clooney was the prime mover behind them both and his political stance got him in a whole lot of trouble with the American right wing press: If you're not with us you're against us. But Clooney was big enough to swim against that particular tide and come fall 2006, Americans were swimming the same way, voting the Republicans out of power in both Houses of Congress. Clooney's films did that? No, of course not. But they were a valuable part of the drip, drip, drip of opposition that finally encouraged the American people to take a fresh look at the entire Iraq crisis.

2.1 *Goodnight and Good Luck* (2005)

▸▸ P.31

From the early days of Chaplin's Little Tramp movies, film has evolved as a primary source of social and philosophical debate. Film, with greater facility and to a larger audience than literature, can convey complex ideas through the intentions, actions, and relationships of the characters; those actions, and the results of those actions, involve the audience on an emotive level.

Day in and day out on the news we hear stories of rape, robbery, muggings, violence at school, on public transport. We watch a movie about Joe Wright, a man doing two jobs in order to help his sister Maria pay for an operation to right a crooked leg. We meet Bill Black, his neighbor. Black's a small-time dope dealer in trouble with the mob. When he robs Joe Wright at the very moment when enough money has been saved for the operation our heart goes out to Joe and Maria. We are glued to our seats until Bill Black gets his comeuppance, and we'd kind of like to see Maria walk straight again. Audiences will be moved far more deeply watching the soap story of Joe and Maria Wright than listening to the priest in church telling the parable of the Good Samaritan, as J. Arthur Rank realized when he first showed films at Sunday school.

TELLING A STORY WELL

Some writers are good at dialogue, others structure, others still can see the big picture and take on adaptations. There are writers like Paul Schrader—*Taxi Driver, Cat People*—who go alone into the desert for a week, work 20 hours a day and return with a finished scenario.

2.2 *Taxi Driver* (1976)

▸▸ P.31

Maybe it needs fixing, but there's another kind of writer unique to the film industry, the script doctor, and that's what he does, not original work but, like a picture restorer, he fills in the fine details. The role of the producer is to match the writer with the story; in Hollywood, of course, they'll use a combination of expertise and leave the Writer's Guild to resolve the credits.

There is yet another kind of writer the producer must watch out for and he's the one who does a single draft and is reluctant to do more because he knows the script will be overhauled when a director comes on board. He's right, of course, it will be. But a director won't come on board if the script isn't fully developed in the first place. These writers, normally very competent, make a reasonable living writing first drafts and can't understand why it's rare for their scripts to turn into films. They are often wonderful raconteurs and can slip marquee names with their business cards into every conversation. This is the writer to avoid. Their stories are verbal, not on the page, and it is easy to be fooled by a colorful personality unless the producer has knowledge of script mechanics and the insight to enjoy their company and leave it at that.

If the producer has learned the art of managing money, he should max out his credit cards and spend some time on a desert island finding out how stories work. Read Æschylus, the lives of the great Olympians, Oedipus and on to Shakespeare and Chaucer. Dip into the wise worlds of Lao-tsu and Confucius; some Jacobean drama, and don't forget the exquisitely constructed short stories of Hemingway and James Joyce. See Sam Beckett's absurdist plays (demand them on your island) and study the greats: Dickens, Thomas Hardy, E. M. Forster, Daphne du Maurier, F. Scott Fitzgerald, Flaubert, William Golding ... and on to Tolkein, Nick Hornby, J. K. Rowling ... Gore Vidal, José Saramago and Michel Houellebecq. You may not want to produce vampire movies or erotica, but you should certainly be aware of the phenomenon that is *The Twilight Saga* by Stephenie Meyer and *The Fifty Shades Trilogy* by E. L. James.

2.3 *Belle de Jour* (1967)

You can learn a lot about making films by watching films, but you learn story-telling from the written word. Buñuel hitched his wagon on to Dalí's genius to get started, but he was a voracious reader and became a masterly writer with the breathtaking *Belle de Jour* and Academy Award winning *The Discreet Charm of the Bourgeoisie*, to name just two of his many films. To get there, like Buñuel, it makes sense to start with shorts. Once you get those right, you'll have a showreel for Andrea Calderwood to brighten her quest for the perfect script.

SHORT FILM DISCIPLINE

Unlike the United States and in Europe, many short films made in the UK have a sameness about them, no doubt because the majority are produced by young filmmakers eager to enter the industry and whose background and education is similar. They have the mixed good fortune not to have lived through the hard times of Alexander Salkind, who fled Russia, or Hal Landers, who grew up in the mean streets of New Jersey during the Depression, though, naturally, it is those experiences that shaped them and gave them an edge, the nerve it takes to approach strangers on a train and royals out shopping.

According to Dawn Sharpless, creative director at Dazzle Films, one of the UK's top outfits for sales, distribution and the exhibition of short films, shorts in the UK are falling behind because insufficient time is spent on their development. Short films are often seen as merely a stepping stone to features and filmmakers are in such a hurry to take that step they are not putting the time into creating powerful short scripts. The short film discipline is a genre in its own right, and only when that is fully recognized and appreciated will short films improve.

"Occasionally something makes you sit back in your seat and you realize that here's a filmmaker with a story to tell," Dawn adds.[5] "But the sad thing is that for every fifty shorts I see, you sit back only once with real excitement."

What's the problem?

"Inadequate planning. I think the whole secret is in pre-production," she says. "New filmmakers need to be more daring. Stories should take us to places we have never been to before—and that takes courage."

Her observation is substantiated by Elliot Grove, who heads the Raindance Film Festival. Some 2,000 shorts are submitted to him each year from 40 or so countries and 200 make it into the annual festival, the largest showcase of shorts in the UK. He has noticed that every year there is a flood of good shorts from a different country. Last year it was Poland; a few years ago, South Africa. “It’s always somewhere new, but it has been a few years since I have seen anything in the UK that really knocks your socks off.”

Elliot Grove has noticed that most British short films are dialogue driven, while those in the United States and Europe tend to be more visual. “It’s an odd dichotomy, because those British films that are visual usually go around the world winning prizes.”

In the US and Canada, young filmmakers have grown up on a diet of MTV, while in the UK, a lot of scripts and films Grove sees have been inspired by TV soaps with their incessant banter and lack of action.

With shorts, filmmakers should be exploring ideas and learning their craft, says Grove. They should study as many short films as they can, especially at festivals, where they will come in contact with other filmmakers meeting the same challenges and where they can ask each other how they got this effect or that shot. Film is a collaborative process, and Elliot Grove has been constantly and pleasantly surprised at how willing filmmakers are when it comes to sharing information.

Grove compares the difference between writing a short film and a feature as creating a haiku poem and a sonnet. “It requires different techniques, different skills, a different sensibility. With a good short film you have a calling card. And every time we have shown a filmmaker with great story-telling skills, they have moved on to making successful features.”

Raindance first showed Shane Meadows before he made *TwentyFourSeven* and screened Christopher Nolan’s shorts before he made *Following*, *Memento* and that latest incarnation of *Batman*.

USING SHORT STORIES

If in the search for a feature, producers look at novels and plays, for a short film, one surprisingly untapped source of material is the short story, sadly neglected by mainstream publishers and mainly found in the hermetic world of the literary small-press and online magazine.

There are thousands of small-press journals and websites with a constant flow of new stories, usually by writers experimenting with style and who view publication as an end in itself. Few journals can afford to pay contributors, but the competition to get into print is still fierce and the quality of writing often very high.

Short-story writers know every word counts and, as a form, the short story has similarities to the short film that do not apply to the novel and play. Both make use of suggestion, atmosphere, nuance, the subtly implied gesture. Both are a riddle, every word having to carry its own weight, justify its existence. The short story weaves fine lines more than broad strokes. Explanation is death. A published story would have been honed and refined, every gesture and action thought through to such a degree that if the woman in the story runs her tongue over her lips, there is such a good reason for it, you'd better make sure your script contains the same instruction and your director heeds it.

If you do hit on a writer with a fine short story, he will already be well versed in re-writing and prepared for it when you option a short script. And who knows, perhaps he has a feature script lurking in the bowels of his laptop?

Short stories are subtle, often enigmatic, with carefully drawn characters, and when filmmakers alight on them they tend to think in terms of features not shorts. There are many examples of successful adaptations, among the best known coming from three Philip K. Dick stories: Ridley Scott's *Bladerunner*, from the imaginatively titled *Do Androids Dream of Electric Sheep?* Steven Spielberg's *Minority Report*, and John Woo's 2003 adaptation of *Paycheck*, a story about a machine that can read the future and just as relevant in film terms half a century after it was first published in 1953. Dawn Sharpless was unable to come up with any examples of short stories that have been turned into memorable short films, but yearns for the day when that hole in the genre is filled.

As mentioned above, many short-story writers see publication as their main goal. There are many short-story sites. I have found FanStory, ABCtales and the Short Story Library (at Americanliterature.com) particularly good.

www.FanStory.com
www.abctales.com
www.americanliterature.com

SMALL FISH

Instead of doing their research and finding material, producers in frustration will often turn to directors and accept their scripts, not because they're better, often it's the contrary, but at least they know the director is committed and they haven't got to go through the birth pains of yet another draft. The result, though, as Dawn Sharpless has observed, are too many forgettable films—shorts and features—written by non-writers and backed by producers too uncertain of themselves to find a writer and put in the hours bonding and working together.

Writers tend to be introvert. Directors are charming, outgoing, more fun to work with. But producers should be wary and heed William Goldman's haunting counsel: there are three essentials that come before you sign up a director. The Script. The Script. And the Script.

When Goldman's *Butch Cassidy and the Sundance Kid* came out, New York's three leading papers devoted many pages to their reviews. Two of the critics were in raptures over the Redford/Newman coupling and forgot to mention the writer. The third hated the picture and blamed the script. Goldman had spent five years sitting in his New York apartment writing it.

Critics are not going to go easy on writers. The producer must. He should cultivate the wisdom of ancient China where the Emperor once sent an emissary to Lao-tsu asking for advice on how to rule the kingdom. You should rule the kingdom, replied the sage, as you would cook a small fish.

Producers are emperors. Writers are small fish. Don't grill him, don't batter, bone and leave him gutted. Writers are delicate: fine porcelain; thin ice on winter morning ponds; a love affair.

Imagine the plumber coming three days late to repair the loo. He shoves a new tube into the ballcock, fingerprints the tiles with lubricating oil and you feel a wave of gratitude when he accepts $300 cash and agrees to screw the government out of the taxes. Your writer drops in with three typos and an oxymoron fleshing out a secondary character and you want to kill him. Those stains on the bathroom walls have to be douched away and where better to spray some ammonia than at the self-doubting wordsmith. Writers cry easily. Don't use words like: pretentious, slow, lacking, boring, depressing, or another day, as in: "We'll talk about it another day."

He'll worry himself sick waiting for that day. Let slip the word pretentious and you're leaving yourself open to the pretensions of defining the term. Tell a writer his script is slow and he'll shuffle down to *Starbucks* for a double espresso with whipped everything, including the skin on his back. Tell him his work's depressing and he'll get depressed, swallow a fistful of codeine and consider Hemingway's last dance with a shotgun.

The major production companies work with established writers and, more than ever, are sourcing material from novels, biographies, plays, and, a disturbing trend, old movies—*The Wicker Man*, *The Four Feathers*, *Psycho*, *Vanilla Sky* from Alejandro Amenábar's *Abre los Ojos*, all, in my opinion, inferior to the original. The new producer is more likely to be working with an inexperienced writer who, like the producer, is learning his craft. The writer will work for weeks and months before presenting what he believes is a masterpiece and it will require tact and patience for him to see that what he has typed is probably little more than a glorified treatment.

PAUSE

There's a great saying: When nine Russians tell you you're drunk, lie down. I always think of that. If people say, "That's a ghastly idea"—and I'm certainly capable of ghastly ideas—then it might be worth listening. You have to listen, and it's desperately important to find people whose opinions you can respect and value—Anthony Minghella[6]

CUTTING DIAMONDS

When Lee Hall's script for *Billy Elliot* first went to the BBC it was about the miners' strike in Thatcher's Britain. Billy's desire to dance was a subplot. Hall's standpoint was socialist more than aspirational. Three years of development changed a story about class solidarity to class betrayal, from Old Labour to New Labour, and created a film for our times.

Hall's first draft, like all first drafts, was not a film but a road map leading to a film, a guide, not the place it became. When you read first drafts you are looking for a spark, originality, an individual voice, not gold dust but the iron ore that can be mined and shaped into a bridge to span the gulf from development to production. A producer should identify all that is good in a script. If only 10% is good, salvage it, compliment it. Get rid of the 90% and start again.

Billy Elliot spent three years in development. *Good Will Hunting* needed seven. Richard Attenborough was white haired and 20 years older before *Gandhi* was ready to go. Scripts are hard to write, as difficult or more difficult than novels. They need many drafts and time, lots of time. Producers must face that. They choose a companion as much as a project. Their writer becomes their brother, their sister, their child. According to Cyril Connolly, writers are just that, infants crying in their cots for attention. A writer needs faith, patience and passion. A producer needs all of that and a box of Kleenex to wipe away the tears.

When a producer finds his writer he sticks with him. *The Claim* (2000) was produced by Andrew Eaton with Frank Cottrell Boyce writing and, by the time Michael Winterbottom began directing in Canada, they were already working on *24 Hour Party People*, the next project.

At a Script Factory screening of *The Claim* in London, Cottrell Boyce spoke about the long process he'd gone through to take the themes from Thomas Hardy's *The Mayor of Casterbridge* and transpose them to the 1849 gold rush in the American West. He told the audience the first drafts (that's plural) of his script were done *just to see what the themes were.* The next drafts have to be a good read so that the *Suits* with their check books can see the story in their minds. The script that goes out to actors is slightly different again. *But every draft is different to the shooting script*. Those earlier drafts contain an explanation of themselves that you don't need when you're ready to shoot. It's a leaner and fitter thing. "I love this stage. It's really great when you feel something coming to life. It's like cutting diamonds."

Frank Cottrell Boyce did not choose to write *The Claim*. Andrew Eaton chose it and stuck Hardy's novel on his desk. Of course, writers want to write their own stories. But it is the job of producers to know what they can market. With a short film, the producer has an added burden: telling a good story in ten minutes is hard and finding slots for films that are longer is harder still, as we shall discuss later when it comes to distribution.

Once the producer has survived the writing process and has a script in his hand, he moves to the next square on the board where he must find a director and build his team.

STOP

2.1 George Clooney and fellow travellers take on commie hunter Senator Joseph McCarthy in *Good Night and Good Luck* (2005)

2.2 *"Are you looking at me?"* Robert de Niro in *Taxi Driver* (1976)

START

CHAPTER 3

The Director

The writer has labored over his ten, descriptive, lively but tightly-written pages, and the producer hands this precious object to the director. It is hardly surprising that writers want to direct their own work but this impulse is, in a historic sense, a relatively new trend and many subscribe to Hitchcock's faith in what he called The Trinity: Writer. Director. Producer. By keeping the roles of writer and director separate, the producer has greater control.

In the case of Hitchcock, while he was directing one film, every morning he would have breakfast with the writer he'd set to work on a new project. He didn't read the pages or interfere with the ongoing narrative, but like the operator of a Punch and Judy Show, his hand was manipulating the twists and turns from behind the scenes.

The director, whatever his modus operandi, will invariably work on the script and his name often finds its way onto the writing credits, something Hitchcock grandly renounced. The director also gets the debatable designate *A Film By* ... just above or just below the title, depending on his status, and the power of his agent when it comes to negotiating the contracts. The deifying of the director in this way occurs because he is the creator of the finished work, the artist who takes the raw material of the script and combines the elements of mise-en-scène, a phrase borrowed from the theater and meaning "to put on stage."

In film terms, John Gibbs in his excellent study *Mise-en-Scène* suggests a useful definition might be the contents of the frame and the way those contents are organized, both halves of the formulation being significant:

What are the contents of the frame? They include lighting, costume, décor, properties, and the actors themselves. The organization of the contents of the frame encompasses the relationship of the actors to the camera, and thus the audience's view. So in talking about mise-en-scène, one is also talking about framing, camera movement, the particular lens employed and other photographic decisions. Mise-en-scène therefore encompasses both what the audience can see, and the way in which they are invited to see it. It refers to many of the major elements of communication in the cinema, and the combinations through which they operate expressively.[1]

In the novel, the word alone must convey mood and meaning. In film, every frame is packed with information, a shadow, a ticking clock, the breeze fingering the curtains: every detail is significant. Stephen Fry while directing *Bright Young Things* (2003) from the Evelyn Waugh novel *Vile Bodies* was shown by the props department several cigarette cases from the thirties for him to choose from. That cigarette case may only be seen for a fraction of a second—it may be edited out of the final cut—but it is the attention to detail that creates audience identification with character and involvement in their lives.

The director must have an eye for every small detail. He decides who does what, when and why, this multiplicity of detail described by actor Gary Oldman after the first time on the floor as "death by a thousand questions."[2]

The fusion of these disparate parts is the puzzle the director (with the editor's help) assembles and it is his vision that we see on screen. Of all the jobs in film, the director requires the least training and the least experience with technology. That isn't to say that directors do not know their way around an editing suite, or which filters to use on the camera. Most do. The best learn. What the director needs most, however, is the insight to understand immediately what the story is about, what passions drive the characters, and what each actor needs in order for them to make those passions real.

When we think back on any situation, in the pub with friends, a bitter row, a day on the beach, a night of love, we see it from our own point of view. As we piece the memory together, the mind selects the most salient and piquant details with camera angles, distances, juxtapositions, close ups and long shots in a richly woven tapestry.

This selection of fragments is the same as taking frames of film and, in our heads, cutting movies from our recollections. According to anthropologists, once monkeys learn to use tools, to prise open sea shells, for example, future generations are genetically blessed with that knowledge. Likewise, a century after the Lumière Brothers first shot moving pictures, it seems an innate human predisposition to be able to piece together the puzzle of a film story and, perhaps more important, to actively take part in its telling by incorporating our own experience and imagination.

Actors develop and refine this art; the director like a hypnotist will draw out the appropriate memories to bring a scene to life. You don't have to be an out-of-work father with hungry mouths to feed to play the role, as Clint Eastwood showed in *Unforgiven*, the story of a retired gunslinger who crawls back into his old skin in order to put food on the table. Similarly, it's unlikely in Beverly Hills that Sigourney Weaver would have come face to face with an *Alien* bent on genocide (though anything's possible in Beverly Hills). Both performances were convincing because these proficient actors are able to dredge up emotions that inform their characters.

The director must know the character he is creating as well or *even* better than the actor; the evolution of their story will be part of the pattern painted inside his mind. Shooting schedules by necessity divide scripts into convenient but disconnected chunks that are stuck together when filming is completed. Cinema actors are trained to give realistic performances with minimal preparation; it is considered by many that too much preparation can blunt their edge, the reverse of work in theater, where rehearsals are lengthy and stories are told chronologically.

A woman, for example, who stabs her husband and is taken away by *gendarmes* in a rainy Paris exterior, may not get to show what led up to the fatal event until weeks later when the crew moves to do the villa interiors in sun-drenched St Tropez. If the director dresses the woman in the Paris scene in a clinging gown that becomes diaphanous in the spring rain, it's going to look a whole lot different than if she's wearing an anorak and climbing boots. Are her shoulders sagging, or does she hold her head high? Is mascara running in black streams over her cheeks or are her scarlet lips puckered in a defiant smile? Was her husband a brute and we were with her, feeling her pain and relief as she plunged the knife in his back? Or is she a scheming gold digger who deserves the guillotine? How the audience reacts depends on the scene staged by the director and the performance drawn from the actress.

To return to *Unforgiven*, Clint Eastwood would not have approached the role by trying to *act* the feeling of a man suffering the torments of failure. Rather, he would have allowed the appropriate consciousness to take possession of him. That state would generate the emotionally applicable movements, responses, behavior and body language, a glimpse into the inner soul where all sensation occurs on a deeper level. It is the art of restraint and suggestion that Eastwood has mastered, a particular achievement as he normally directs himself.

More than the writer who has shaped his theme, plotted his turning points and set up his surprises, the director would have combed the material for the emotionally charged moments and, through his cast, reveals the heart of character. An actor well directed will make his feelings so clear that lines in the dialogue mentioning love, despair, jealousy, hatred and so on can be edited out of the final cut, the telling having been supplanted by showing, the point made by Frank Cottrell Boyce in the previous chapter, his diamond-cutting analogy for the shooting script being that moment when the last traces of dust are blown away and the sparkling gemstone is revealed.

POV—POINT OF VIEW

A film goes through three stages to reach completion: pre-production, production and post-production. All carry equal weight and, as the producer will remind his director, it is in pre-production where they can save time and money on production and post. The ticking clock is the perfect symbol for the process: for the producer the ticking clock is a meter ringing up the bills; for the director, the ticking clock is more like a metronome guiding rhythm and pace; for the audience the ticking clock is a ticking bomb that holds us breathless waiting for the explosion. The director will keep us waiting, building the sense of urgency, the tension.

Typically, the writer would indicate in a script:

The Firefighter dashes like a 100 meter sprinter into the blazing building to save the baby.

But the Mother's reaction, the Fire Chief's reaction, the play of water arcing from the hoses, the size of the flames leaping from the building, to what degree the staircase inside is turning to ash; when exactly the Mother's reaction and the Fire Chief's reaction are inserted, and how many times they're inserted; the swelling crowd, the swirling police lights and the look on the Firefighter's blackened face as he scoops the infant into his arms: all this—along with set design, costume, the music score—are created by the director from the screenplay's brief scene description.

If the blaze is the first scene in a movie (and it's a powerful opening), how the Firefighter plays it, and how the director guides him, depends on how future events unfold. It certainly looks like this guy is our hero, the character we want to identify with, but it requires the whole story for us to understand his action, his motivations, whether he's a coward overcoming cowardice, an egomaniac playing to the crowd, a man whose wife has just died *in a fire* and has nothing to live for. Perhaps the Fire Chief is his older brother, or *younger* brother. The fact that we don't know is what makes the scene interesting. Conversely, the director may give the audience superior position, whereby we in the darkened auditorium know something the Firefighter doesn't—*perhaps it is his baby in the cot?*—and we watch with vicarious angst as this is revealed.

Don Roos's 1998 *The Opposite of Sex* opens with Christina Ricci contemptuously flicking a cigarette butt on a coffin as it is lowered into the ground. We don't know who lies in that coffin, but we're already hooked.

3.1 *The Opposite of Sex* (1998)

▶▶ P.46

Each scene is described on the page when the producer hands the script to the director, but the director doesn't just turn the material into film. He interprets it, shapes it, gives it pace and inner life. Actors when they're given a script tend to read their parts and count the lines. The director dives in and immerses himself in a script; he'll take it home, turn off the cell phone and read it through in one take without making notes. He will want to get a sense of the story. He will then go back and read it through again, many times, looking for nuance, depth, reversals, surprises. He will need to engage emotionally with the work in order to create an emotional response in the audience. If the story doesn't move him, he should pass on it, because it will remain flat when it reaches the screen.

If the story does grab him, he will undoubtedly percieve elements differently from the writer. That's when the fireworks begin. Perhaps the female screenwriter is telling the above Firefighter's story from the POV of the Mother whose infant is trapped in the building. The director may see the story from the Firefighter's POV, and the entire script will have to be restructured for him to tell the story that way. Imagine *Cinderella* told from the point of view of one of the Ugly Sisters. How does she feel when this pretty, self-effacing waif moves into the family home? It is not necessarily a better story. But if that's the way the director sees it, that's the way it will be done.

Burt Lancaster, after 30 years as a Hollywood leading man, got to direct for the first time and relished being the early bird on set each morning; he enjoyed dealing with "temperamental actors" and their "little problems." At the end of the day he was anxious to pick up the rushes and he'd spend half the night studying them. "When you are a director you are God, and that's the best job in town."[3]

COLLABORATION

Scripts for short films are often burdened with excess characters. The director may see immediately that the cleverly constructed lines given to the Barman in one scene and the Desk Clerk in another can be combined: it saves money and time on an extra actor, gives one actor a better role—a chance to develop that role—and those key lines are still there, the same story is being told.

This is collaboration. The writer has to accept that this is going to happen, and the director has to learn how to oil the squeaky wheel and make the running easy. Re-writes, especially after all the re-writes, are painful and a system has to be established right from the beginning. As Maureen Murray (see Chapter Two: The Producer) with her smiley faces and steely cold lines picks out the best and worst in a script, it is better for the writer, and better for the process, if the director tackles each aspect of the screenplay separately: first structure and plotting, to get the overall *feel* of the piece, before moving on to the finer aspects of dialogue and visual interpretation.

PAUSE

PROBING QUESTIONS

When the director breaks down a script, he will ask himself a number of questions:

1. What's the story actually about?
2. Who is it about?
3. Do we empathize with the main character/s?
4. Are they likeable?
5. What exactly do these people want?
6. Who is stopping them getting it?
7. Why?
8. Are there surprises, thrills, revelations: is the audience led one way before the opposite is revealed?
9. Is the audience lifted and let down and then lifted again, the peaks and troughs going higher and plunging lower as the story builds?
10. Do the main turning points and climaxes appear for maximum impact and interest?
11. Do we have the elements you'd expect for the genre?
12. Have the principal characters gone through major, irreversible changes?
13. Are those changes credible?
14. Will those changes move and affect the audience?
15. Is the underlying theme clearly revealed?
16. Is there a satisfactory ending which gives the audience what they expect, but not exactly how they expected it?

These questions should be applied to the script as a whole before the director moves on to the finer details:

PAUSE

THE FINER POINTS

1. What's this scene about?
2. What does this scene achieve?
3. Is this scene necessary?
4. What does this scene tell us about the main character/s?
5. Do the secondary characters have their own dramatic function?
6. Does this scene have conflict, a beginning, middle, and end?
7. Does this scene contribute to the main character/s' objectives, development, revelations of true nature?
8. Do the characters behave consistently, and where they are inconsistent is that understood and applicable within the narrative?
9. Do the characters have individual voices, word patterns, slang?
10. Can verbal exposition be replaced by the visual?

At the script stage, every detail can be investigated, chewed over, pulled apart and put back together again at little or no cost. It's the time to get things right. There are directors who rush into production (unlike Kurosawa) and try to cover holes in the script once they're on set—but like the writer who's reluctant to write new drafts, this is a director the cautious producer will avoid.

Theme (No. 15 in the first list above) is the essence of the script: the fight against injustice (*The Hurricane*), the search for love (*When Harry Met Sally*), the struggle for freedom (*Gandhi*), the quest for personal validation (*All Or Nothing*), fear of the unknown (*Signs*). The Pulitzer Prize winning playwright Arthur Miller would finish a play before he was fully aware of the theme. Once he got the theme, he would jot it down, stick it on the wall above his desk and write a new draft with the theme informing the characters' decisions and choices. There may be more than one theme; John Malkovich's extraordinary if sometimes muddled *The Dancer Upstairs* (2002) blends love, injustice and the struggle for freedom.

GENRE

An independent film, especially one made by a writer/director, is likely to be an exploration of ideas, an individual voice with a specific viewpoint. Most short films fall into this category: it is the time when new filmmakers will be testing the boundaries of their own creativity, finding their voice. If the short conforms to genre: horror, crime, melodrama, *film noir*, science fiction, comedy, the conventions of that genre need to be observed in order to meet audience expectations.

Film stories, whether they are genre-based or not, are commonly rooted in moral issues and contain lessons on how to behave in a changing world with its myriad anxieties and temptations. The conflict between good and evil is as basic to the modern screenplay as it was to the tribal wise

3.2 *Chinatown* (1974)

P.46

3.3 *Pulp Fiction* (1994)

P.46

3.4 *The Man Who Wasn't There* (2001)

P.46

3.5 *The Girl with the Dragon Tattoo* (2011)

P.47

men, and people are more likely to be pondering the ethical conundrums of capital punishment, immigration and abortion on a Saturday night at the movies than they are in their places of worship in the cold light of day.

Writer Steve Biddulph argues that through television, magazines and other media, children learn values such as "Looks are everything", "Your sexuality is something you trade for being liked", "Money buys happiness", "Friends will come if you have the right stuff."[4] Celebrity, youth and wealth are the idols we have come to revere. In a splintered society shorn of the ethical cornerstones of traditional close-knit communities, movies for many have practically taken the place of religion, giving filmmakers the role of moral arbiters as well as entertainers, an onerous responsibility.

Every decade is marked by its genre: the musicals of the thirties were an escape from the Depression; the forties Westerns saw stories of split families after the uncertainties of the Second World War; the Cold War and the Bomb were reflected in fifties and sixties science fiction; new attitudes to sex, drugs and rock-and-roll marked the seventies; while Schwarzenegger and Stallone were emblematic of the eighties cult of the individual, one man against the world, a drinker, fighter, gambler, veteran, often a loser who, deep down, has the best of human qualities and his heart in the right place.

This, too, can be applied to the protagonists of *film noir*, a style that originated in the 1940s and has continued through the decades, *Chinatown* (1974), *Body Heat* (1981), *Blood Simple* (1985), *Pulp Fiction* (1994), *L.A. Confidential* (1997), *The Man Who Wasn't There* (2001), *The Girl With The Dragon Tattoo* (2011); all exquisite, multifaceted contributions to the genre.

Film noir originated with the writers and directors who adapted the detective novels of such authors as Raymond Chandler, Dashiell Hammett and Cornell Woolrich. The common theme is the dangerous if desirable *femme fatale* who challenges the values of a male-dominated society normally portrayed as decadent and corrupt. Set in a world of small-time hoods and petty, self-seeking officials, the detective central to these stories is an alienated, down-at-heel outsider who maintains a strict moral code while he sets about both solving the crime and dealing with the symbolic temptations of the *femme fatale*. Whether he succumbs or not, his integrity is never in question.

The Blues Brothers (1980) has the catch-phrase "We're on a mission from God." It sounds both silly and unlikely. But is it? John Belushi and Dan Aykroyd are getting their band together for one last gig with Southern rednecks and a scorned woman with a rocket launcher in hot pursuit. They need money, not for a stake in some nefarious venture, but to save their orphanage. We identify with Belushi and Aykroyd, as we identify with the musclemen Schwarzenegger and Stallone, because the characters they play are inherently honorable and uphold the values of our culture.

In Quentin Tarantino's *Pulp Fiction*, Bruce Willis plays Butch, a boxer instructed by gang boss Marsellus Wallace (Ving Rhames) to overcome his pride and throw a fight. Butch, however, backs himself against the odds, kills his opponent in the ring, and picks up a fat pay day. He's about to flee with his girlfriend, but she leaves the watch passed down to him by his father at their apartment, which he knows Marsellus's men will now be watching. But Butch can't go into exile without that watch and, in returning to get it, he has to shoot Vincent Vega (John Travolta) with Vega's own gun to survive.

Fleeing again, he literally runs into Marsellus in a car crash. Both are injured and stumble into a gun shop run by neo-Nazis. Butch escapes, but goes back to save Marsellus from the torture scene unwinding in the basement. Why? It is true to his nature. Butch always does the right thing. In the boxing ring, the death was accidental. In his apartment, he shoots Vega in self-defense. He was told to throw the fight, cheat the punters, swallow his pride. But he remains proud, with the values we admire and to which we all aspire.

During the course of the story, Vincent Vega's partner Jules (Samuel L. Jackson) has seen the hand of God at work in saving him from certain death and decides to give up crime and "wander the earth." Vega not only ridicules this conversion, he has fallen under the spell of Marsellus's wife (Uma Thurman), the *femme fatale*. As a man bereft of ethics, he is the obvious sacrifice to ensure Butch's escape. Vega is not the only character in *Pulp Fiction* to lack morals, but his demise serves to underscore the theme that, while amusing in the world created by Tarantino and Roger Avary, crime still doesn't pay.

The gap between genres has narrowed and blurred—the *Scream* films are slasher comedies; *Chicago* is a crime musical; kick-ass extravaganzas and gross-out comedies will always be crowd pleasers. But while society grows ever more divisive and complex, the cinema becomes the place where serious issues are explored untainted by the hidden agendas of politics and newsprint. It's something of a cliché to say that fact is stranger than fiction. More to the point, it is through fiction that we are best able to articulate fact.

Director Stephen Frears' *Dirty Pretty Things* was enticing people out of the pubs and into cinemas over New Year 2003 with a story set among the illegal immigrants who toil at night in London's mini-cab offices, sweatshops and grubby hotels. With Chiwetel Ejiofor playing a Nigerian who trained as a doctor, and Audrey Tautou as a Turkish asylum seeker who dreams of going to America, Frears captures a cruel, creepy, paranoid city and exposes the human side of immigration as he grapples with the issues of color, race, religion, and the illicit trade in human organs.

To take a horror film example, in Bernard Rose's *Candyman* (1992) the ghost of murdered black slave Daniel Robitaille returns to seek revenge on a complacent white society that has failed to confront racism. Paul Wells in his study *The Horror Genre* describes this as a metaphor on racist culture and the prevailing legacy of slavery.

... the monster—essentially a brutal avenger—is once again morally ambivalent because of the apparent justice that motivates him. Here, the arcane, primitive world perpetrates a seemingly justifiable horror which the contemporary world must confront in order to find understanding and achieve atonement.[5]

ATTITUDES AND MORALS

Cinema is often blamed for creating a moral vacuum with its diet of violence and pornography. But the reverse, not ironically, but typically, is also true. More than contemporary literature, or any other art form, cinema is the place of philosophical and social debate. A serious novel is considered successful if it sells 10,000 copies. A film can reach millions.

That's not to say that the director's job is to come up with quick fixes for our anxieties and problems, to provide morals and meanings. Film's role is not to lead, to teach, but to stimulate debate. A film doesn't need to say: this is wrong and this is how to put it right; it is sufficient to show the audience what is wrong and leave people to make up their own minds. Like the novelist, the director's brief is to set out ideas in new (preferably entertaining) ways and allow the audience to fill in the gaps; as often as not, that there are no simple answers to the big problems, but that is life, and film is a reflection of life. Early talkies found scripts in novels and stage plays. Writers are wedded to the written word, and it was directors like Georges Méliès and William Kennedy-Laurie Dickson who first understood that film is a visual art. "Seeing comes before words. The child looks and recognizes before it can speak."[6]

Film, as no other artifact or memento from the past, painting, written text, even photograph, reveals how the world was when the scenes were shot: the architecture, transport, clothes, the expressions on people's faces. In this respect images, particularly moving images, are more precise and richer than literature. More than the invention of the camera, the movie camera changed the way we as people—our grandfathers and great-grandfathers—viewed and understood the world. People in a Kinetoscope Parlor in Chicago circa 1910 watching one minute of Highland dancing were seeing something those people almost certainly would never have seen before. Now, now they had understanding and empathy with this alien world of bagpipes and men in tartan kilts.

As a director develops his skills, he will not only be able to reveal the world in what we see, but in what we do not see. Often, what is most interesting is what happens in the gaps between images, in the moments between moments. This may come from the action the writer has put in his script (be warned scriptwriters: an excess of directions drives directors crazy!) but more likely it is the director's interpretation of the script inspired by the needs and demands of the characters.

Jenny Borgars, former head of the Film Council Development Fund, told Nic Wistreich on the online film magazine *Film Netribution Network* that new filmmakers need to study the work of people who have excelled in the profession. Training is only one route to knowledge, and an enormous amount can be learned by giving someone ten great American scripts that have been made into movies. The new director can study the pages, study the shots, and see exactly how the transfer to screen is realized.

According to Jenny Borgars, in the United States, scriptwriters have learned to allow the reader enough space to fall into the story, rather than trying to give the reader all the information possible. "A writer/director needs to know what to put down on the page in order to get their film sold into the market—before they actually *make* the film," she continues. "That sounds like a crude distinction but it is quite difficult convincing people of it."

While script development is an on-going process throughout pre-production, the director will also be liaising with the casting director, cameraman, storyboard artist, set director, the props and wardrobe departments, make-up, each element adding shades and layers to the dramatic

3.6 *La Doice Vita* (1960)

▶▶ P.47

3.7 *La Doice Vita*

▶▶ P.47

effect the director wants to achieve, the story he wants to cast before the public.

The infamy of Buñuel's short films reflected his times: the left/right divide, new attitudes to sex and the church. Each generation must tell its own stories and as such the director is the thermometer taking society's temperature. He must see everything, be interested in everything and always seek truth. The Italian director Federico Fellini once said that at school he learned almost nothing except how to observe the silence of passing time, to recognize far-off sounds, rather like an imprisoned person who can tell the sound of the bell of the Duomo from that of San Augustino. "I have a pleasant memory of entire mornings and afternoons spent doing absolutely nothing."[7]

While he was apparently doing nothing, Fellini was meditating on his times, which he captured in *La Dolce Vita*, a film so overpowering when it was released in 1960 that critic Andrew Sarris argued that in terms of social impact "it is the most important film ever made."[8] It was the height of the Cold War; Algeria was fighting the French for independence; thousands perished in the Agadir earthquake, and Fellini, his eyes always half hidden under a black hat, had chronicled the spoiled, confused, aimless lives of those who frequented Rome's Via Veneto: spent writers and bored aristocrats, calculating adventurers, social climbers and the *paparazzi*, from where the generic term originated.

When the film was first released, in the cinema lobby a woman in furs waved her fist at Fellini and screamed: "You are putting Italy into the hands of the Bolsheviks." And a man in a dinner jacket spat in his face, the modern equivalent of challenging Fellini to a duel. As the film moved out across Italy, a civil war erupted in the media, church pulpits, in public debates and in open fights outside movie houses where the police were often called to quell a riot. *L'Osservatore Romano* described the film as disgusting, obscene, indecent, and sacrilegious; *Il Quotidiano* suggested the film's title *The Sweet Life* should be changed to *The Disgusting Life.*

Looking at *La Dolce Vita* today, it is difficult to understand what all the fuss was about. But, as biographer Hollis Alpert explains in *Fellini, A Life*, at the time, while Italians had achieved a post-war miracle, economically and socially, here was a film that implied that the miracle had been reduced to "the shoddy pursuit of materialistic goals and pleasures."[9] This view was not shared when the film was released internationally because Fellini had held up a mirror to *his* world, on Rome. In the reflection the Italian public saw truth and it is truth alone that leads us to greater understanding or to clench our fist in outrage.

La Dolce Vita is set among what at the time was becoming known as the jet-set, but as a portrayal of contemporary society, with its naturalistic acting style and scenes shot on location, it conformed to the tenets of neorealism, a trend that moved across Europe like a breath of fresh air and evolved with a liberal/socialist emphasis on ordinary people living tough, often deprived lives.

When Ken Loach's *Cathy Come Home* was screened on the BBC in 1966, it resulted in angry exchanges about homelessness and social services in the Houses of Parliament and led to the formation of Shelter with actress Carol White its first figurehead. The BBC drama was re-aired

3.8 *Cathy Come Home* (1966)

▶▶ P.47

3.9 *Made in Dangenham* (2010)

▶▶ P.47

in 2006, stimulating public discussion and revealing, sadly, that although some of the worst problems from 40 years ago have been alleviated, there is still homelessness and there are still problems in social services.

The appetite for films that make us laugh, cry, and finally to think about who we are and the world we live in has not diminished and accounts for some of the most successful UK movies in recent years, *The Full Monty, Brassed Off, Billy Elliot, Bend it Like Beckham, Made in Dagenham.* Likewise, in the United States the box office has been ringing out tickets for feature-length documentaries such as former Vice-President Al Gore's 2007 Oscar-winner *An Inconvenient Truth*; Nick Bicanic and Jason Bourque's *Shadow Company*, "a thorough and balanced look at the use of private security forces in Iraq (which) raises serious policy questions," according to the now deceased Senator Ted Kennedy; and Michael Moore's thoughtful polemics *Fahrenheit 9/11*, *Bowling for Columbine* and *Sicko*.

HAVING SOMETHING TO SAY

The need for stories that shed light on the fears and values of the age is as vital, perhaps more vital, now as it ever was and applies, not only to features, but to short films as well. We got the clear impression talking to short-film directors that the ideals held dear by the likes of Loach and Fellini are undimmed and, if anything, are shining ever more brightly. Directing, says Cedric Behrel, is first about *having something to say* and learning your craft in order to be able to say it loud and clear.

You must know how to use the cinematic palette to get across an idea, a vision, a character, and do so with an original, unique interpretation of subject matter. We can't expect a director to be an established writer, essayist or philosopher—he is only a vector of such thoughts, he can only be judged on his capacity to express his material with his tools, the cinematic palette of narration, drama and style. For that, he must make sure he gets the best material possible.[10]

Following the signposts of social realism, Behrel's films include the 20-minute *Lush*, the story of a young woman repressed by her ultra-modern, lifeless environment who sets out on a journey of self-discovery; the 10-minute documentary *Who's Afraid of Vanessa SB?* with artist Tracey Emin; and *St Elucias's Island*, the story of 13-year-old Leah, caught between her abusive mother and the menace of a vicious, small-time businessman, she must succumb to a terrible fate or find the strength to break free.

Behrel finds a common difficulty for shorts directors is that they become *too* involved in aspects of the film that have little to do with directing: writing draft after draft, dealing with production issues, locations and so on. "The focus necessary to direct film—and most of all, direct actors—requires such concentration and energy there isn't enough left in you for anything else," he explains, and remembers driving the lighting van on a film school short because the Director of Photography didn't have a license.

This has a lot to do with budget restrictions and the fact that most filmmakers tend to self-finance their first attempts. Cedric Behrel's advice is to find the most competent people you can and make sure they are placed in key positions: writer, producer, director, the same opinion expressed by Alfred Hitchcock.

"In this spirit I would think it is more important for an apprentice director to have a production manager than, let's say, a camera operator."

PAUSE

BEHREL'S GUIDELINES

1. **Cut down on locations and try to get the locations close together.**
2. **Rehearse. Rehearsal time is cheap and it allows you to save time when you shoot.**
3. **Have post-production in mind before you shoot; what can be done in post-production should reflect the shooting style.**
4. **If you use stage actors (the norm in the UK), get them to "play it down."**
5. **Never shoot a script that you are not at least 300% sure about.**
6. **Know what you are doing: don't try and fit a specific format if you are making an experimental film and, if you are making a genre piece, know the rules and history of the genre you're dealing with.**
7. **Don't expect to earn money from a short.**

Behrel believes that on a short film, a director needs to be persistent but flexible, ambitious but realistic. "You must be hardworking and have vast knowledge of every component of filmmaking," he adds. "You need to be able to talk to everyone on set and be open to nuance. You must know the difference between a good take and a bad one and, more important, know what to do about it."

Being "open to nuance" is much the same as being flexible, which was described by Alexis Bicât as "flashes of inspiration."

"After all the care and planning, once you get on set, those flashes are sacred and can come from anywhere, actors or members of the crew, the sun appearing unexpectedly through the clouds. If you are not open to ideas and prepared to reverse your thinking, you will never be a strong director."

Alexis Bicât directed *Noise Control* (discussed in Chapter 22: Noise Control) with *Lock, Stock and Two Smoking Barrels* star Nick Moran playing a fighter pilot. "As far as I'm concerned, he's Britain's top indie actor and I have to admit I was nervous going on set the first day," he explains. "But the thing with stars is that they get where they are because they are good actors. They are actually more easy to work with because they are more technically proficient."

How do you get a major performer like Nick Moran in your short? "Just ask, they can only say no. And they may say yes," suggests *Noise Control* writer Terence Doyle.

While the director assumes complete creative control and bears responsibility for any problems or errors that occur, Bicât stresses that it is essential to have a close bond with the DP. He is normally more technically trained and will ensure basic things like the film is exposed properly. "The film is preconceived, with each shot and sequence cut in your head, but the DP will know whether what you want to do can be done and how to do it."

Noise Control DP Simon Dinsel had never filmed from a plane before and had to familiarize himself with the specially hired kit, an Aaton Minima camera and the Kenlab stabilizer that operates on a series of gyroscopes. Film can run through this small, versatile camera at 48 frames a second, which makes the action appear smoother when it's slowed down to the standard 24.

"About 95% of people who go up in a training jet throw up and Simon did also," says Bicât. "But he kept going and got all the shots. That's what you need when you're making a short on a tight budget: technicians who are prepared to do anything. Like good actors, they are easy to work with."

Though written as a short in its own right, *Noise Control* was planned as a taster for the feature being developed by the same team and, as such, is rich in feature production values. The film was shot on 35mm with digital composite effects (CGI); video to film transfers; Dolby digital sound mix, the 29 tracks of audio mixed down to 6.

"It was one of the biggest jobs on a short film ever undertaken, which resulted in us being in post-production longer than *Star Wars* waiting for downtime in CGI houses, audio suites and so on," adds Bicât. "It also doubled the production cost."

Downtime means free time, usually in the middle of the night, something short-filmmakers have to consider when they're doing a budget. Was it worth it? After being cut to 8 minutes (a TV 10 minutes), *Noise Control* was sold to BskyB and secured cinema release across Wales. "They do say a short is just a calling card for the director," says Bicât, "but as far as I know, all the creatives involved in *Noise Control* have added the film to their CV."
www.parent.co.uk/noisecontrol

PAUSE

STOP

ARE YOU MAKING THE SAME FILM?

"Lots of problems in film occur when the people are not making the same film; where there are actors in one film and other actors in a different film, or when the production design is not supporting the costume design, or where the camera's not supporting the production design. The task is how you cohere a group of people without inhibiting their own voice, because, chorally, their voices are more interesting than yours is as a solo voice. As a director you must always remember that everybody doing a job on the film is better at that job than you are."
—Anthony Minghella[11]

3.1 Christina Ricci, ready for anything in *The Opposite of Sex* (1998)

3.2 Jack Nicholson and Faye Dunaway in Roman Polanski's noir thriller *Chinatown* (1974)

3.3 John Travolta and Samuel L. Jackson shooting up LA in *Pulp Fiction* (1994)

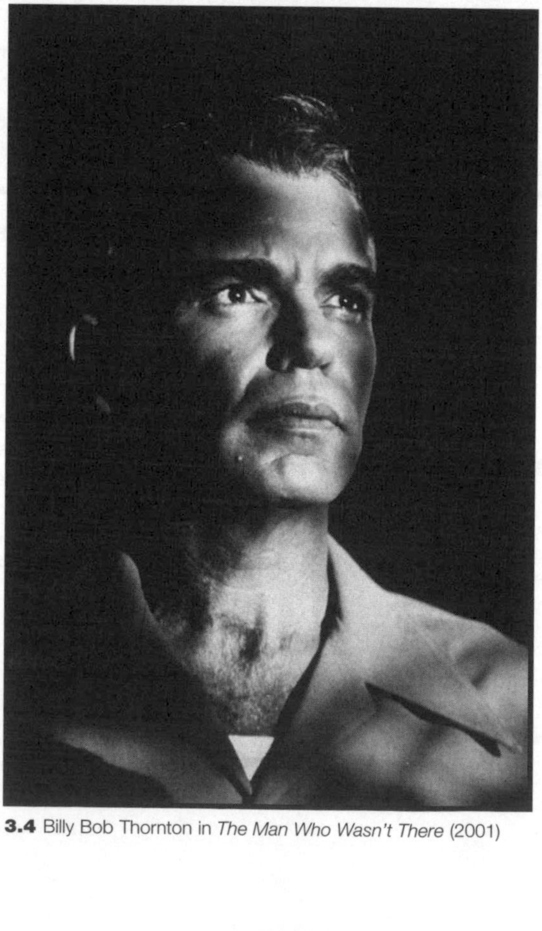

3.4 Billy Bob Thornton in *The Man Who Wasn't There* (2001)

3.5 Rooney Mara in *The Girl with the Dragon Tattoo* (2011)

3.6 *La Dolce Vita* – Marcello Mastroianni and Anita Ekberg in a rainy street (1960)

3.7 *La Dolce Vita* – Marcello Mastroianni and Anouk Aimée in party mood

3.8 Carol White and Ray Brooks in a scene from Ken Loach's moving account of homelessness in *Cathy Come Home* (1966)

3.9 Protesters in Nigel Cole's *Made in Dagenham* (2010)

PART

II

TITLE

Pre-production

START

CHAPTER 4

Scheduling and Budgeting

The script is now polished like a cut diamond. With our passionate producer and director on board, the next step is to plan every aspect of pre-production. This chapter outlines how to schedule and budget, storyboard, insure the film and see how the trade unions work with the film industry.

The first step is to break down the script into a shooting schedule to work out how much each scene is going to cost. In an ideal world, you could create a schedule, then tally up the amount of finance you need. It rarely works that way and, realistically, you will have to make the schedule fit the budget.

In Chapter 28: Movie Magic Budgeting and Scheduling, Laurence Sargent describes how to use the software employed by professionals. This is a useful tool, but if it is out of your price range, more than likely on a short, budgeting and scheduling can be achieved with paper and a pencil. Whether you plan to shoot over four consecutive weekends or in five straight days, the process is the same.

How to pitch is outlined in Chapter 15: Festivals and Distributors, and if your "package" gets that far, you're in with a good chance to get funding or a grant, but to get there you need to work out exactly how much money you need.

1. Breaking Down The Script

Also known as "lining" the script, this is highlighting the different elements of the script in terms of what each department needs in order to shoot each scene, which in turn affects the schedule and budget. Typically, a different color is used for every cost—cast, crew, props, locations, vehicles, effects, wardrobe, set dressing, camera equipment, extras etc. Make sure you make a key on the first page of what each color means. Each shot can also be marked, which will aid storyboarding. Final Draft has the built-in capability to do this, as explained in the Software Focus section.

2. Breakdown Sheets

Every "element" that costs something (or at least needs to be begged, borrowed or stolen, to misquote German director Werner Herzog), must then be transferred into individual breakdown sheets—one for every scene.

We have included a blank example in the appendix. Not all breakdown sheets will look identical, but will include the same information, such as the location, scene number, and script page.

3. Production Boards

Breakdown sheets are in turn transferred to production boards, also known as production strip boards. These boards contain all relevant information on a single scene. Film scenes are rarely filmed in order—instead, group together all of the scenes that happen in the same locations and shoot them together. Finding the best possible shooting schedule is a talent, and needs some time and thought. It generally happens at this stage, by rearranging the production boards—whether by hand if they are on paper, or within software, such as the Stripboard in Movie Magic Budgeting.

THE BUDGET

The budget shows exactly how much the film is going to cost, or, put another way, how much needs to be raised. A well-prepared budget will help secure funding and will make potential investors feel confident that all elements have been thought of and accounted for.

No two budgets will ever be the same as they depend entirely on the script, how it is scheduled, as well as a number of other components, including:

- What filming format is being used. The costs of buying, using, and editing HD, 16mm and 35mm vary immensely. See Chapter 9: Camera for a run-through.
- The number of cast and crew involved will dictate wages and the catering budget.
- The number of locations involved must be factored—not just the cost of each one, but also the cost of transport between them.
- How the film is edited, by whom and whether special effects are needed.
- The costs of submitting to festivals, attending them and other marketing and promotional costs.
- A contingency amount, usually around 10%, for the unexpected.

Film lingo often splits the budget into four categories:

- **Above the line**—mainly the costs of writer, producer(s), director, and principal cast, which may be negotiable.
- **Below the line**—non-negotiable wages and production costs, including everything from staff members to film tape to hard drives to renting sound equipment.
- **Post-production**—all editing, and costs that occur after the final take.
- **Other**—including costs of financing and insurance.

TOP SHEET

This information is collated into a Top Sheet that shows you, and potential investors, how much the film will cost and a one-line breakdown of all expenditures. Following the Top Sheet is a more detailed breakdown of each cost, generally divided by department. In Chapter 32 we have included an example Top Sheet, as well as contracts for paid actors, extras and people who are happy to contribute but who will not be paid.

One trick is to budget your dream schedule, probably spending much more than you can realistically afford, and then "work backwards" seeing where money can be saved. Perhaps a credit could convince a local restaurant to give discounted, or even free, food for the cast.

Could a sequence at one location be shot in a single day instead of two? Maybe the ideal location can be achieved with a favor to the owner—such as shooting a short promo—or replaced with a cheaper set.

Breaking down the script, scheduling and budgeting can be a full-time job. As noted, software can greatly aid the process, but however it is accomplished, it is essential, and will take the creation of your film a giant step closer to being a reality.

Many insiders advise spending an absolute minimum on a first film—even first films. Bigger budgets are only advisable when you've already made all the "rookie errors." Having said that, big budgets don't necessarily equal successful films. While *The Last Broadcast* (1998) had an estimated $900 budget, according to the IMDb, and went on to make $4m in the box office. *The Guardian* newspaper reported *Cutthroat Island* (1995) as the biggest box office flop of all time, with a net loss (adjusted for inflation) of $147.2m.

As well as Movie Magic's Budgeting, other useful software includes:

- Microsoft Excel (with budget template)—www.microsoft.com
- Easy Budget—www.easy-budget.com
- Gorilla—www.junglesoftware.com
- Quick Film Budget—www.quickfilmbudget.com

If the number juggling is too much, hiring a line producer may at first seem expensive, but will often pay off when he/she finds ways to save money you would never have thought of. Many elements of budgeting and scheduling come from experience, and having a sound financial plan is both efficient and will inspire confidence from financiers as well as the cast and crew. Check the listings in Chapter 6: Crewing for how to find a professional line producer.

The Budget Company—www.thebudgetcompany.com and Film Budget—www.filmbudget.com are two companies, with impressive credits, that budget and schedule films for a fee.

RAINDANCE FILM FESTIVAL TIP

10 EXPENSES MOST FIRST TIME FILM DIRECTORS FORGET

1. The Development Budget

When a film goes into production, the story rights need to be acquired and paid for. At this point, the producer controlling the script rights totals up all the money spent to date and presents an invoice so the production team can recoup the money they have paid, plus a profit. Expenses include travel, accommodation and entertainment at places like Cannes Film Festival, location scouting, casting agents fees and that wired one: "Office Overhead." Plus of course option fees paid the writer to date, insurance, banking, and legal fees. This can easily get out of hand, and when the final production budget is in the bank minus the development costs, directors can have a nasty surprise. Directors may have no alternative other than cutting pages out of the script. I know two different writer/directors who found that over 10% of their production budget was gobbled up by extras added to the development budget—make sure you keep on top of it.

2. The DP

Choosing the right Director of Photography will really impact on your budget. Some will literally take over the directing for you, blocking out the scenes in the rush to get the shots completed before wrap. This can lead to a war between the DP and the director. Such conflict can ruin the morale on the set and make the shoot next to unbearable. But at least the film will get shot in this scenario. Other DPs are so eager to please they fall over backwards at each of the director's whims without the benefit of courteous but professional criticism. The resulting shoot meanders and can quickly fall day after expensive day behind schedule (see #10 below).

3. Location, Location, Location

Every time you move from one location to the next the cost rockets. Hence the typically low-to-no budget shoots in a single location movie like *Paranormal Activity*. If you desperately need a second location look out for the two-for-one, i.e. the front of a house can pose as one location and the rear garden as a completely different one.

4. Casting Agent

There are two factors here: First, a skilled casting agent can save you a fortune, which is good. Second, too often directors fantasize about cast until it's too late, and then hire a casting agent to get them out of jail to no avail. Money is flushed down the drain.

5. Let's Fix It In Post

Every time I hear a director say, "We'll fix that shot in post," I cringe. I've worked on 68 features and over 700 commercials. Every time the director made that choice on a set, heads would roll a few days into post-production where the budget would start to rocket. A director who thinks some sort of post-production miracle can save sloppy location shooting is lazy and ultimately a very expensive director.

6. Music

Including uncleared music in a movie is probably the single most costly mistake a filmmaker can make. Over the past 20 years I have had so many bad experiences with festival films that had to be pulled last minute because the filmmaker lied about whether the music was cleared or not. We even had one case where sales agents were nosing around a movie because it had an expensive song like *The Girl from Ipanema* in it (uncleared). Needless to say that movie didn't sell.

7. Catering

This is such a no-brainer you probably are wondering why it's even on this list. Problem is, no one ever considers the cost of the chilli and beans Aunt Emma is going to cook, nor the cost of cutlery and plates. Before long you have blown a good chunk of your budget, and have to decide whether or not your entire cast and crew can survive the next three weeks on nothing but white rice, or cut a special shot to save the catering budget. I once spent two and a half weeks on white rice and I can tell you—it was a thoroughly unpleasant experience.

8. Insurance

If I had a buck for every time we get late afternoon panic calls from filmmakers desperate for a magic insurance telephone number I'd retire to the south of France. No one ever thinks about insurance in time to budget for it properly. And you almost always need it at some point in the process.

9. Transport

I am sure your producer has allocated for car and van rental with the necessary fuel charges, taxes and tolls. But what of the petrol or taxi charges added to invoices of cast and crew? I had such a situation last week where I agreed to the fee but when the invoice arrived it included a whopper taxi bill. When queried, I was asked how else the equipment was going to get there.

10. Shooting Ratio

In the good old days of celluloid it was all about the shooting ratio. Because film stock and processing was so expensive, producers, directors and DPs kept an eagle eye on the ratio between consumed footage and the final film. Most indie films were shot on a ration between 5:1 and 10:1. I.e.: 5:1 ratio means that 5 minutes worth of film stock was used to cover each minute of screen time. In the digital age, image capture and storage is so cheap that some directors shoot over and over—as much as 100:1. Can you imagine the challenges of editing 100 hours of footage into a completed one-hour film? High shooting ratios aren't clever, necessarily. But they sure are expensive.

Elliot Grove

STORYBOARDING

A storyboard is a drawing of each shot that makes up a scene and is used to show what shot is coming up next. Storyboards can be simple stick men or works of art, either way, they are an essential guide for the director.

With a storyboard, it is possible to identify potential shooting problems, they save time on set and great storyboards may be useful in acquiring funding. Seeing your short film in individual panels like a cartoon strip will also make the project appear less daunting by breaking it down into bite-size chunks.

Every panel on a storyboard should represent one shot, or continuous piece of footage with no cuts. For every shot, consider the following:

- Where is it?
- Who is in it?
- What props are in it?
- What type of shot is it? Such as close-up, wide-shot, etc.
- Is there any movement in the shot?
- What lighting is needed?
- Are there any special effects?

Some directors opt to storyboard every shot in their film; others concentrate on complex areas such as action sequences, and rely on shot lists for the rest. This is a personal decision.

4.1 *Ran* (1985)

▶▶ P.61

You can create storyboards by drawing boxes, buy readymade storyboard pads or print them from the Internet (try pdfpad.com/storyboards). Remember the format you are shooting on will affect the dimensions of the boxes you require.

Akira Kurosawa, the legendary writer/director of *Seven Samurai*, spent ten years storyboarding every shot of his film *Ran* with intricate paintings. Each panel is a work of art, the end result a master class in storyboarding.

One filmmaker wrote on indietalk.com: "I don't care about hiring someone to create hundreds of little masterpieces. I am looking for glorified stick figures with camera directions and angle notes etc." For that filmmaker there is a lot of new storyboard-making software available (below, we will look at the professional results possible from a company simply called StoryBoard).

However, it should be noted, that while the Japanese filmmaker dedicated years painting shots in full color, he was picturing scenes, imagining and paring down the dialogue. He visualized the whole film and, on the first day of principal photography, he knew exactly where he was going. Every film is a work of art, a battle against the odds. A film masterpiece is rare. Every film by Akira Kurosawa is a masterpiece.

See an example of a hand-drawn storyboard in Chapter 23: G.M. And remember, the shots sketched on a storyboard are not carved in stone. A new shot may strike you in the middle of shooting, and if there is enough time and money, go for it!

PAUSE

STORYBOARD QUICK – WWW.STORYBOARDQUICK.COM

Described as "clip art with a brain," StoryBoard allows each shot to be set up astonishingly easily. Choose the frame size and start placing objects into the frame by either drawing, importing or choosing an image from the software's library. Each object or character is stored in its own layer, so can easily be moved around or changed in size.

A number of characters, available in different positions (walking, sitting, running etc), can be added, turned around and changed in size. Similarly, locations (a photo of a country lane in this example), props (a car), arrows to show movement and captions can all then be added. The order of shots can later easily be changed.

4.2 Screenshot of StoryBoard Quick

P.61

4.3 Screenshot of StoryBoard Quick

P.61

INSURANCE

The moment the producer starts assembling the crew, he will have to insure the production. There are many specialist companies listed in The Knowledge, KFTV and Kays (see Chapter 33: Useful Links). Film insurance is highly specialized, each production carrying different risks. The types of insurance needed and the level of premium will vary from film to film—but it is the law whether you are in Los Angles or Leeds that all productions are insured. At its most basic, your insurance should cover sickness, accident, death (of crew, cast etc.), physical loss and damage to equipment and assets, employers and public liability.

Producers will need to supply contact details of their insurance company should it be required by equipment houses, local authorities or studios. The cost of insurance on a short? It can vary greatly depending on the number of days, the size of the cast and crew, but you will need to think in terms of several hundred dollars/pounds and, just as you need to cut deals with the facilities houses, you can try the same with insurance companies. If you need advice and you have a location manager, talk to him.

Insurance will also cover any equipment you are hiring, so it is important to find out how much it is worth and get it insured accordingly. There are even types of insurance that will cover bad weather, if a day of shooting is lost due to the rain, although this is generally very pricey.

TRADE UNIONS

When short-film and low-budget filmmakers first make an acquaintance with trade unions they may find themselves in a dilemma. Few people attracted to film are going to be against a worker's right to be in a union and be protected by that union. But here's the crux of the dilemma: they often wonder what this could possibly have to do with them. *We're just trying to make a movie, for heaven's sake.*

Unions, however, play a vital role in filmmaking, not only in fixing rates for their members, but in setting hours, conditions and safety. One of the major reasons for a new production company to sign agreements with unions, actors' and writers' guilds is to be able to hire their members for a production. But here's another side of the dilemma: only films with industry backing and the appropriate budget can afford the wages those unions have negotiated.

The unions recognize that short films and low-budget features are ideal training grounds for technicians and actors entering the industry and have responded by creating a variety of agreements to fit the scarce resources of independent filmmakers. Some low-budget films are actually no-budget films and, while it wouldn't be admitted in those union offices, union bosses tend to turn a blind eye when their members are moonlighting on an indie film. It is to everyone's advantage that the film gets made. On the flip side of the coin, if unions get the impression that their agreements are being flaunted, or their members are being exploited, they will seek an injunction and close down the production.

It is not unusual on a short film that those financing the project (usually a combination of writer/director/producer) will want to put the production on a professional level and will raise sufficient funds to pay the cast and crew at least a nominal sum. Ten-minute shorts require an optimum four-day shoot (at 2½ minutes of usable footage in the can a day, that's still a challenge for novice directors and crews); £100 to £200 or up to £300 for the four days is typical, a modest amount, but when everyone on set is paid equally it inspires a team spirit, a sense that everyone is just as valuable and important as everyone else.

New filmmakers should be aware of what the unions do and how they may be able to help rather than hinder a production. Like flour to the baker, research is the filmmaker's first ingredient. A good place to learn more about unions, wages and rights is FilmMaking.net, which has a lively message board with questions like: "How much should I get paid as ..." and both experts and fellow contributors respond with their views and comments.

Pay is an important factor, although at www.filmmaking.net, Benjamin Craig points out, "If you are a high school student considering whether working in the film industry will be a financially rewarding career, then you are looking down the wrong path. If financial security is your primary career driver, you should consider law, accounting, medicine, or another stable industry with a well defined entry path. You don't become a filmmaker for the money."

There are scores of trade unions and guilds for every branch of the profession, writers, editors, cameramen, musicians, etc. Below is a list of key organizations new filmmakers should be aware of:

UNITED KINGDOM

BECTU—www.bectu.org.uk

The Broadcasting Entertainment Cinematograph and Theatre Union represents permanently employed, contract and freelance technicians primarily based in the UK working in broadcasting, film, theater, entertainment, leisure, and interactive media.

The union negotiates pay, conditions, safety and contracts with employers for its 25,000 members, publishes the magazine *Stage, Screen and Radio* eight times a year and provides a script registration service. "Recommended going rates"—or the amount professionals should be paid for a day's work—are also listed for all sectors of the industry, from lighting technicians to hair and make-up.

Equity—www.equity.org.uk
Equity is the only trade union representing artists from across the entire spectrum of arts and entertainment. Formed in 1930 by a group of West End performers, Equity quickly spread to encompass the whole range of professional entertainment with a membership drawn from actors, singers, dancers, choreographers, stage managers, theater directors and designers, variety and circus artists, television and radio presenters, walk-on and supporting artists, stunt performers and directors and theater fight directors. 5,000 student members can also access information and advice, helping to prepare them for work in the industry.

MU—www.musiciansunion.org.uk
The Musicians' Union was founded in 1893, and now represents over 30,000 musicians working in every sector of the music industry. It maintains links for its members to orchestras, music colleges and various musical resources. The union helps track down stolen instruments, protects copyright, offers contractual advice and sets fees. Short-filmmakers who want to put the Babyshambles or Bruce Springsteen on the soundtrack will need to add several thousand pounds to their budget and may want to consider using original music by an up-and-coming composer. The MU is happy to advise.

UNITED STATES

WGA—www.wga.org
The Writers Guild of America protects writers, settles credits' disputes in the film industry and collects millions of dollars in residuals for its members. The WGA is the leading screenplay registration service in the world, taking in 55,000 pieces of literary material each year. The service costs $20 ($10 for members) and provides legal evidence in fraud, theft and plagiarism cases. Unlike most organizations representing writers (*the lowest man on the film totem pole*), the WGA is a powerful body with a bite as fierce as its bark.

IATSE—www.iatse-intl.org
Renamed in 1995 as the International Alliance of Theatrical Stage Employees, Moving Picture Technicians, Artists and Allied Crafts of the United States and Canada, the union set up shop in 1893 as the National Alliance of Theatrical Stage Employees. Projectionists were the first film technicians to join the union ranks and the membership now comes from all the crafts in film and TV production, as well as product demonstration, conventions, casinos, audio visual, and computer graphics.

SAG-AFTRA—www.sagaftra.org
Representing over 160,000 media professionals, in all fields from actors to DJs to news editors to puppeteers, SAG-AFTRA was formed after a 2012 merger of the Screen Actors Guild and the American Federation of Television and Radio Artists. It promises to negotiate wages, working conditions and pension benefits, expand work opportunities for its members, enforce contracts and protect members from their work being used without authorization.

AUSTRALIA

MEAA—www.alliance.org.au
The Media Entertainment and Arts Alliance in Australia represents people working in the media, entertainment, and arts industries. The website provides information on working in these industries and has a list of wage rates and conditions, upcoming events and membership joining information.

STOP

4.1 Grand Hunt in movie *Ran* (1985)

4.2 Screenshot of *StoryBoard Quick*

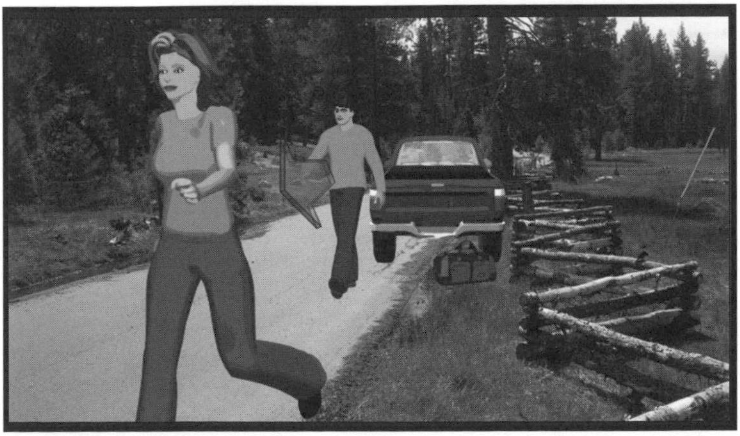

4.3 Screenshot of *StoryBoard Quick*

START

CHAPTER 5

Finance

There is a different stance towards financing short films in the United States and Britain, with Australia and the remainder of the English-speaking world falling somewhere between these contrary positions.

In the US, the attitude is *just do it*.

If making movies is your passion, you beg, borrow or rent the gear, shoot from the hip and see where it leads you. The first film flops, so you go out and do it again. The industry will come calling when what you're making is good enough.

The global film market is worth hundreds of billions of dollars and grows annually. To get a slice of the pie, the UK and Australian governments back their industries to compete with the United States. The result is a double-edged sword: people who may never have got the opportunity to make a film can do so with government grants, while in the US, shorts made without public money or institutional guidance are often more inspired and individual.

5.1 *El Mariachi* (1992)

▶▶ P.**71**

Robert Rodriguez is the archetypal American story: unable to get into film school, he raised $20,000 from family and friends and made his name shooting the acclaimed *El Mariachi*, the film establishing Rodriguez as a hip, indie director with a passport to Hollywood. If you want to know how to take rejection and turn it into a massive career, it's worth reading the inspired and passionate story of the making of *El Mariachi* in his book *Rebel Without a Crew.*

FUNDING

Across the English-speaking world, filmmakers can't help but keep one eye on the vast American market, while in the rest of Europe, short films, features, and television are made principally for the home market and success on the world stage is merely a bonus.

What this all means is that when there's free money available, filmmakers and film funders are locked in an inescapable labyrinth. Applying for funds to make short films is the obvious first step, but the cash available is limited and the number of applications overwhelming. Funders face the unenviable task of sifting through a deluge of paperwork and, to help them select which projects are going to get backing, filmmakers with a track record tend to rise to the top of the pile.

That isn't to say that applying for funds isn't a good idea; it is. The process requires tremendous preparation, an edgy script, a compulsive synopsis, the director's statement, or a mission statement, résumés of key personnel and, of course, a budget. This demanding combination forces the team to focus on every detail, which is exactly what a project needs whether it gets funding or not. Even with such diligence, it is important to realize that it is still a lottery, ironically so, and a good grasp on realism is the best antidote for disappointment.

There are hundreds, if not thousands, of grants available around the world. Outside of government schemes, the majority focus on certain genres, or are designed to support people from certain genders, races, nationalities (or states) and religions. Grants come in many forms, from training to equipment loan. Cash grants can be for all or certain areas of a production, from script development to editing to distribution, the latter two areas being most accessible when low-budget filmmakers have made a little gem with the elements to go big.

This was the case with the 1999 psychological horror *The Blair Witch Project*, written and directed by Daniel Myrick and Eduardo Sánchez. Figures vary, but the film was basically made for about $20,000. It went on to gross almost $250 million at the box office—but only after Artisan Entertainment spent around $1 million on post and marketing.

DOCUMENTARIES

For documentary makers, more grants are available and more slots have opened up at film festivals and in general distribution. In 2011, documentaries had their biggest year to date with big earnings at the box office for *The Interrupters, Senna, Cave of Forgotten Dreams,* and James Marsh's acclaimed *Project Nim*, the story of a chimpanzee taken from its mother at birth.

5.2 *Senna*

▶▶ P.71

According to Carole Lee Dean, at Roy W. Dean film grants, documentary film funding starts with a well-written, organized proposal. It outlines the film's story, background, and what it needs to get made and why it should be made. The proposal also summarizes the approach, structure and style in four to eight pages of "dynamite passion."

She advises applicants to just "write page after page of your vision for the film. Don't worry if you only need a six page proposal and you now have 25 pages, just keep putting down what you see happening in your film." The proposal, she advises, needs to be a visual description of the film. That vision is there, somewhere in those 25 pages, "so read them carefully and find the best visual sections to paste into your proposal."

5.3 *Project Nim* (2011)

▶▶ P.71

Although people applying for grants may have been working on their idea for a year, she adds, it is the first time funders have seen the package and the best way to capture their imagination is by the power contained in the first three paragraphs of the proposal. "It tells us if you are a good writer and it shows us your vision of the film."

All grants are heavily subscribed, so particular attention must be paid to every aspect of an application, and criteria followed to the letter.

In no particular order, here is a small selection of available grants, mainly in the US:

Creative Capital—www.creative-capital.org
A nonprofit organization that provides integrated financial and advisory support for artists.

Panavision's New Filmmaker Program—www.panavision.com
Panavision donates the use of 16mm or 35mm motion picture camera equipment to worthy submissions.

MacArthur Foundation—www.macfound.org
In 2011 alone, this foundation gave $8.5 million in grants for social-issue documentary films on contemporary topics.

Women In Film—Film Finishing Fund Grant—www.wif.org
As the name implies, WIF FFF supports films by, for or about women. Cash grants of up to $15,000 are available for films that are already in the rough cut stage.

Roy W Dean Film Grants—www.fromtheheartproductions.com
A non-profit organization that has given away over £2m since its inception in 1992 for concepts that are "unique and make a contribution to society".

Paul Robeson Fund for Independent Media Film Grant—www.fex.org
Grants that support pre-production and distribution of social issue films.

Cinereach—www.cinereach.org
Grants between $5,000—$50,000 at any stage of a production for feature-films that have "engaging storytelling, visual artistry, and vital subject matter."

Metro Screen (Australia)—www.metroscreen.org.au
Metro Screen offers over AUD$170,000 annually in cash and training with a number of different grants and schemes.

British Film Institute—www.bfi.org.uk
By far the largest source of finance for short films in the UK is managed by the British Film Institute (BFI), a charitable organization that is tasked with managing all aspects of film, television and the moving image. The UK Film Council was formerly responsible for most film grants, but was disbanded in 2011. The BFI has now become the distributor of Lottery money for film funding, and in 2012 announced a five-year plan to inject £273 million into British film, increasing spending on new films by a third, as well as digitizing as many as 15,000 movies, equipping new venues with projectors and promoting training.

As this edition goes to print, it is unclear exactly what funds will be available and how to apply, although the BFI has made it clear that: "We support filmmakers in the UK who are emerging or world class and capable of creating distinctive and entertaining work." Check the website to see how they are realizing this aim, and what grants are available.

As well as the BFI, other places to turn in the UK include local councils and charities. Those that want to attract feature projects to their area will have a film officer in the culture department and some give small grants for short films to local filmmakers, though normally for worthy rather than artistic causes—those that aid the local community or relates to the charity in question in some way.

Screen Australia—www.screenaustralia.gov.au
Screen Australia is the principal agency for funding film and television and operates to ensure that Australians have the opportunity to make and watch their own screen stories. Taking over from predecessor agencies, the Australian Film Commission (AFC), the Film Finance Corporation Australia (FFC) and Film Australia Limited, Screen Australia supports production of a range of content, especially Australian, the growth of screen businesses, and developing scripts.

Canada Council for the Arts—www.canadacouncil.ca
The Canada Council for the Arts gives grants for scriptwriting, production and research twice a year with deadlines on 1 March and 1 October. Canada also has generous tax breaks to attract filmmakers in most provinces.

DUŠAN TOLMAČ

Competition for financing short films from public funds is tough, but filmmakers do come through the process. We spoke to Dušan Tolma[c] about his experience after being awarded £9,000 by the (now defunct) UK Film Council to shoot *Remote Control*, his 6 minute and 40 second digital short about a middle-aged couple fighting over their TV remote.

As part of the award, Dušan attended workshops in script development; he took part in directing sessions with professional actors; there were lectures on the changes in digital technology and conferences with industry experts.

"There doesn't seem to be any secret about getting finance. It doesn't matter how many short films you have made, you can still get turned down. Tastes and views change on an almost daily basis," he says. "I have been working with the same team for three years and it was vital for the award to have the team in place; it means you are taken seriously."

Dušan believes the secret of a good short film is honesty. "You have to be true to yourself and true to your depiction of human situations," he explains. "The beauty of cinema is that the same piece can mean ten different things to ten different people—as long as it is underpinned by an essential truth, it will work for each one of those people on a variety of levels. If you approach the film honestly, the format and length and genre are secondary."

While many people charged with awarding finance are convinced that training is the best medicine for the industry, Dušan Tolma[c] has come to a different conclusion. He has seen what he describes as "genuinely dreadful films" making it to the screen purely based on the persistence or connections of the filmmakers involved. "There are too many films that have nothing to say," he points out, and reiterates the words of director Juan Luis Buñuel: "There are no formats, no short cuts. If films are made from the heart, with sincerity, it shows on the screen and involves the audience."

Dušan made his first short film in 1998 and, after several shorts, pop promos and TV commercials, he is hunting down finance for his first feature. "People say you have to learn your craft. I don't really believe that. I have never read a book on screenwriting, and I never learned to direct. People try to formulize the process, but it's not about formulas, it's about communication. As I've already said, it is your emotional input, your veracity, that will make a film work."

When he shot his first short, he remembers being so involved with getting the crew and locations organized, he walked out of the tube in Notting Hill on the first day and suddenly panicked. "I had no idea what I was going to do, but you go on set and just do it, you let it happen. Of course," he adds wryly. 'It's important that the people you're working with know what they're doing."

TAX BREAKS AND INCENTIVES

Many governments and individual states provide tax incentives to foster their filmmaking industry, or attract foreign productions. One of the most generous incentives in the US is in Michigan, which offers up to 42% of a film's cost in reimbursements. The 2009 film *Whip It* was initially planned to be shot where it is set—in Texas, but the producers put their hands up for Detroit to take advantage of the scheme, according to the website Governing.com.

Another example is Alabama, which offers qualified production companies a 25% rebate of state certified expenditures and 35% of all payroll paid to residents of Alabama for productions costing between $500,000 and $10 million. See www.alabamafilm.org for details. Since the economic downturn, a number of states are reducing their tax breaks for films, so make sure any information you read is up to date.

In the UK a film production company can claim tax relief of up to 25% of 80% of total qualifying UK expenditure, as long as certain criteria are met. Criteria include the film costing less than £20 million, that it is intended for theatrical release and that at least 25% of the production budget was spent within the UK.

COMPANIES AND SELF-FINANCING

Funding schemes and competitions come and go; if those detailed in these pages have since vanished, others will have replaced them. But it doesn't matter how many competitions and grants there are, there will still be thousands of applicants for each film that receives seed money. Being turned down does not necessarily signify that projects are faulty; they may be ahead of their time. Art is subjective. Most artists need to experiment through trial and error before they do their best work, and one must wonder how many great artists there would have been had they only been given the chance.

Self-financing is taking that chance: it is the route chosen by Luis Buñuel, Alexander Salkind, Christopher Nolan and many filmmakers, men and women so driven by their visions to shoot movies they grabbed destiny and a camera in their own hands and went out and did it. Self-financing requires passion and perseverance; kind, trusting friends and parents; the nerve and the ability to inspire others, small businessmen met on trains (as was the case with Salkind) or the local rich guy who fancies seeing himself on the silver screen.

If you are making a short film, a small company—or better an alliance of small companies—may be persuaded to put up some money in order to see their logos on the credits and publicity material, a mention in the local paper, a link on the website. Larger companies only show interest if there is something clear and definite in it for them.

Tiffany Whittome, producer of the 15-minute *Homecoming*, ran a product placement company before forming Piper Films, and in her experience, if you want a name brand to put up the budget for a short film, you have to understand the marketing strategy of that brand. "You need to have a conversation with them before you even start writing the script, you have to work with the brand right from the conception. If they feel that they are in control, they are more likely to agree to the venture."

The ideal situation, she adds, is when you cast a famous actor and the actor is willing to be associated with the brand: beer, alcohol, a clothing line, something that works within the context of the story. "But, again, you have to be in discussions as soon as the actor is attached, and be flexible in changing the script to accommodate the brand,"' she says. "Sometimes the big car companies, like BMW, put up the entire budget for a film if there is a way that they can use the film for their own purposes."

Some companies are more generous with goods than cash; they may supply a vehicle for a specific scene, or bowls of crisps and crates of booze for the wrap party. "Just call the company that does their marketing, or call the brand directly. Tell them the scenario, that you'll credit them on the film, and they will have the pleasure of being associated with supporting the independent films industry," suggests Tiffany. "Perhaps even throw in association at festivals or screenings—especially if it's a drinks brand."

For a funny and eye-opening take on finding sponsors, take a look at Morgan Spurlock's *The Greatest Film Ever Sold*. Morgan's biggest "advertising slot" to sell was above the title, for which he wanted $1m. He managed to sell it to cranberry juice POM, but only if the film grossed $10 million at the box office, sold half-a-million downloads or DVDs, and created 600m impressions in the media.

The qualities needed for raising money have already been covered in Chapter 2: The Producer, and if film funders don't call you in the middle of the night promising to back your opus, then the producer and writer have to sit down with their script and ask themselves some crucial questions:

- How much is the film going to cost?
- How much can we raise?
- Is there a market for this film?
- What is the USP—the unique selling point?
- Would I pay to see this film?
- Or will the making of it be an end in itself?

If the answer to the last question is yes, that the intention is to have some fun and gain experience, the goal when the film is shot has already been accomplished. On the other hand, if the aim is to sail the film into the market-place, it will require sufficient finance to achieve the quality that will ensure distribution. With a feature, it is advisable to have distribution in place at the same time as finance; in fact, a distributor will ordinarily be one of the components that makes up the package. Short films, while less expensive, are more risky because it is the finished product that goes to the distributor.

CROWD FUNDING

5.4 *The Age of Stupid* (2009)

▶▶ P.71

5.5 *The Age of Stupid*

▶▶ P.71

An alternative to seeking one-off grants or central funding is getting a whole load of people to either donate or invest in your film, harnessing the power of friends, social media, and the Internet in general. It's becoming such a big deal, it led Forbes to ask if crowdsourcing is the future of film?

The first major success story of crowd funding was Spanner Films' *Age Of Stupid*, which managed to raise £450,000 between 2004 and 2006 to make the film, another £180,000 in 2009 to launch in the UK and £100,000 for the Global Premiere (over $1m in total). They say they chose the crowd funding route, as opposed to seeking a commission from a broadcaster, so they could own all of the copyright, and in turn control how it is distributed.

They asked donors for a minimum £5,000 investment in exchange for a percentage of profits, if the film made any. One of the creators had already won an Oscar for Best Documentary, so it wasn't such of a long shot it would do ok. There is a detailed guide: "How to crowd fund your film" at their site: www.spannerfilms.net.

Crowd sourcing can also be used for distribution alone, which Kollective Media—www.kollectivemedia.com—describes as the "final stage of true filmmaking independence."

Before you get too excited, *Age Of Stupid* was for a cause many people believe in—trying to make governments reduce carbon emissions. Convincing people to part with their cash is always difficult, but can work if the concept moves people, that they feel like they are making a difference or, at the very least, that they get a tax break for the investment. Forbes concluded that with the Internet giving us the tools to work together in unprecedented ways, maybe crowdsourcing is the future of not just film but music, art, and whatever else you can think of.

STARTING A COMPANY

Starting a production company sounds glamorous. In reality it's time consuming but essential to protect your interests. Failing to start a company leaves you in the category of a sole trader or proprietor, with little protection from lawsuits. If sued, your own assets—and not just those of the company—are liable.

However, an advantage is that it is cheap to run. Types of companies include general partnership, limited partnership, limited liability company

(LLC) and joint ventures. These protect you legally as they are considered separate legal entities from their directors. However, it generally costs to register a company, needs directors and shareholders and is more expensive to run. Choosing the right type of company for you and your film depends on a number of factors, including who owns the company, what taxes need to be paid and who is liable. This needs careful research.

When you've decided what type of company is right for you, the next step is to choose a name. You only get one chance per company, so make sure it's a cracker. Many people choose something edgy that incorporates their ethos. Some just go for their name, such as Laura Ziskin Productions. While others take on parts of their name, such as Tony and Ridley Scott's Scott Free Productions. Some choose confidence: Legendary Pictures, Killer Films or even bigger: DreamWorks, Icon Entertainment. Whatever you choose, make sure no-one else has already bagged it, and ideally that it will be easy to find on Google. With a company and a name, the next step is to set up a business bank account and create a logo, and you're all set to start finding the cast, crew and locations.

PAUSE

PLACES TO CROWDSOURCE

- **Indiegogo—www.indiegogo.com**
The world's funding platform. Go fund yourself.

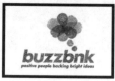

5.6 indiegogo

- **Buzzbnk —www.buzzbnk.org**
Positive people backing bright ideas.

5.7 Buzzbnk

- **Kickstarter – www.kickstarter.com**
A funding platform for creative projects.

5.8 Kickstarter

STOP

5.1 A still from Robert Rodriguez's low budget *El Mariachi* (1992)

5.2 *Senna* (2010) is about the legendary Brazilian Formula One racer

5.3 Nim Chimpsky starring in James Marsh's *Project Nim* (2011)

5.4 Pete Postlethwaite as The Archivist in *The Age of Stupid*. (2009)

5.5 Villagers follow filmmaker Franny.

START

CHAPTER 6

Crewing

It takes an army of people to make a feature film. The art department alone on a big-budget movie can often number in the hundreds. Indeed, the list is so long that auditoriums are often empty before half the crew appears on the end credits.

On short films, on the other hand, a small group of people will generally hold a plethora of job titles. Tight budgets mean limiting the number of crew, so crew members will often do jobs in areas in which they are not necessarily experts. For example, an actress may be in charge of her own wardrobe, and the cinematographer may also be the camera operator. While having several hundred crew for a 10 minute short would be verging on the ridiculous, it is still important to know who does what.

Starting with the Heads of Department, and moving on to the additional crewmembers, this box shows the most relevant crew members. Source: **www.bbc.co.uk/filmnetwork**

PAUSE

CREW

Heads of Department

Line Producer—ensures that the film comes in on time and on budget.

Director of Photography (DP)—in technical charge of how the film is lit and shot.

Production Designer/Art Director—in charge of the production design helps create the style of the set. On low budget films these two roles are often merged.

Gaffer—chief lighting technician.

1st Assistant Director (1st AD)—runs the set according to the needs of the director.

Editor—cuts the film together.

Production Manager—organizes everything and everyone on set.

Sound Recordist—in charge of everything to do with recording sound.

Additional Crew Members

Focus Puller—in charge of focusing the camera.

Clapper Loader—loads the camera, takes care of the stock and records each take.

Location Manager—finds and secures locations

Grip—looks after all the equipment for supporting and moving the camera while shooting (tracking, cranes etc.)

Continuity/Script Supervisor—makes sure everything seen on camera is consistent from shot-to-shot.
2nd Assistant Director (2nd AD)—helps the 1st AD, particularly co-ordinating actors to and from set.
3rd Assistant Director (3rd AD)—is the 1st AD's right-hand person. He/she is always on set and often co-ordinates the runners.
Boom Operator—holds the boom, ensuring that the microphone is as near as possible to the actors without being in shot.
Sparks—lighting technicians.
Costume Designer—designs, purchases, hires, and manages costumes.
Hair/Make-up Designer—designs, and usually executes, hair and make-up.
Production Co-ordinator—works under the production manager to co-ordinate the smooth running of the set.
Storyboard Artist—works with the director to create a shot-by-shot storyboard of the action to be filmed.
Stills Photographer—takes still images of actors and crew for Press Packs and publicity reasons.
Assistants and Runners—needed in every department—the more hands the better.

Only a handful of people can realistically be involved working on most shorts, which means finding the right people is all the more pertinent. Thanks to the profusion of Internet directories, wherever you happen to be in the world, finding crew has become effortless. Knowing who is good at their jobs and who isn't comes from experience, but most technicians will have a showreel and producers can make their choices based on a study of these visual CVs. Anyone without a showreel is either going to be an old hand known by reputation, or a complete novice waiting to get their break as an assistant in one of the crafts.

The Film Centre—www.filmcentre.co.uk—launched a decade ago, maintains a comprehensive database of people working or wanting to work on independent productions on both sides of the camera. The center provides a hire service for cameras, lights, grip, and sound equipment, including owner operators. There are useful tips and the extensive catalog of short films is predominantly British, but with growing representation from the United States and the rest of the world.

Film Centre's founder, Boyd Skinner, says the popularity of the site is down to its easy navigation, and the fact it's free. "There are various sites with crew listings, even IMDb has a directory, but you can be more creative and try the local media colleges," he suggests. "Students are grateful for experience in work placement positions, especially outside the classroom, and if you find a genuinely interested lecturer, he'll probably be keen to give his students a chance at crewing. At the very least, it's a good place to find runners."

Skinner advises producers to find a good all-rounder who knows all the various disciplines. "Most small productions fall down for lack of good organization, or when the *creatives* don't have a strong point of view. So your producer/production manager/AD, often rolled into one, needs to be a good organizer/people mover, but not necessarily with a film/video/media background."

If you can afford to get one key member on the crew, who would it be: sound, lighting, DP?

"I'd still plump for a technical person with some experience, usually the cameraman, provided he doesn't run the show, and it's a plus if he has editing experience. But horses for courses, it goes without saying a proficient sports cameraman isn't necessarily going to be the first choice if you're shooting drama. In fact my ideal person would be an editor with production experience. They would know the shots and coverage you need, and roughly how to achieve it. They are the best judge of whether you actually got the shot, if it will cut, if you need another angle or whether you can move on. These are all the director's decisions, of course, so one would hope then that this is actually the director's background."

There are a number of reasons why experienced crew and well known actors lend their time for little or no wages to new filmmakers making shorts; actors like to act, but more than that, there is a feeling on a film set that you are part of a family and film people openly embrace new members joining that family.

On Terence Doyle's short film (see Chapter 22: Noise Control), Nick Moran joined the cast for two solid reasons: he enjoys making shorts and he got the chance to fly a fighter plane. On Greta May (see Chapter 25: Greta May: The Adaptation), veteran grip Pete Nash joined the crew because he had worked previously with DP Jean-Philippe Gossart; he believed the young cameraman to have a big future and will want to work with him again when he's shooting features. Pete Nash brought an air of professionalism to the team and was quick to remind producer Sacha Van Spall that while he wasn't working for union wages, he did expect hot food "and that doesn't mean pizza." Laying tracks and lifting dollies is hard, demanding work and a film crew functions at its best with decent grub. On *Greta May* we paid the crew a nominal sum, but maintained union standards and the hot food prepared three times a day made a substantial hole in the budget.

Another commonly used system of payment is deferrals: crew and cast may be paid a small sum, or nothing at all, but receive anything from 100% to 200% of the union rate once the film goes into profit. Needless to say, few short films go into profit, but deferrals may be useful for filmmakers making the jump from shorts to a low-budget first feature.

New sites for crewing are constantly appearing. Many US States have their own dedicated sites where local crew can be found, both official and unofficial. An example is the Montana Film Office—www.montanafilm.com. Some established sites dedicated to crewing are listed below.

INTERNATIONAL

IMDbpro—www.imdbpro.com

IMDb—the Internet Movie Database—lists just about every feature ever made and a huge number of shorts. Once people are listed on IMDb, they feel that they've made it. IMDbpro provides professionals in the business a contact listing for crew and cast; films in production and release dates, and the STARmeter to show the popularity of everyone on IMDb. The service costs $15.95 a month, or $124.95 a year and worth every penny according to Fred Baron, executive VP at 20th Century Fox. "An invaluable information resource. I rely on IMDbpro every day."

Mandy—www.mandy.com

The site gets more than six million hits per month and is listed on the first page in a Google search for film production. Mandy describes itself as the "Yellow pages of technicians and facilities". Search for "Sound recordists in Scotland", "Camera rental in South-West USA", or "Producers in Asia Pacific specializing in TV Documentaries"—and you'll find hot bodies looking for work. There are also classifieds for production equipment, casting calls and a "Live Diary," where employers can search for film/TV freelance crew by local town and date-availability.

Shooting People—www.shootingpeople.org

London-based Shooting People is "the voice of independent filmmaking." This Internet information exchange network has over 38,000 members and grows by 200 new members a week. It is a key place for indie and short filmmakers to meet other shooters, find collaborators and follow the triumphs and travails of members as their films enter the market-place. Membership costs £35 (UK); $45 (US). Shooters receive email updates daily. There are regular parties, screenings and Q&As with patrons such as Richard E. Grant and Christine Vachon. The Mobile Cinema travels the highways from New York to LA showing short films made by members. "Shooting People is a necessity for anyone who works, lives and breathes independent film!" Morgan Spurlock *(Supersize Me).*

Crew Connection—www.crewconnection.com

Crew Connection connects people with local video production professionals across the USA and around the globe. With more than 20 years in the business and thousands of shoots to their credit, Crew Connection is one of the most experienced video crew booking service in the world.

Media-Match—www.media-match.com

The Hollywood-based Media-Match is an online directory containing résumés of more than 100,000 film and TV professionals. There is a message board, job vacancy listings and a handy service that allows producers to set their own search criteria, using a combination of job type, program type, specialty, credits, experience, and location. Media-Match serves European as well as US productions and works with all the major studios as well as the BBC, Granada, Hat Trick, the Playboy Channel, and Disney. Freelancers can add photographs to their details and once a week they receive an email with details of which companies have checked out their résumés.

UNITED KINGDOM

Production Base—www.productionbase.co.uk
An online network for people working in film, television, and commercial production, The Production Base website is a multimedia environment which showcases the work, credits, and talent of over 5,000 freelancers working across all grades of pre-production, production and post-production, as well as 13,000 production companies.

Talent Circle—www.talentcircle.org
In true low/no budget indie style, Talent Circle launched without funding in 2003 and has grown into an essential service for the UK film community. Jobs postings, training opportunities and industry news online appear in tandem with offline screenings, networking events, seminars, trade shows, film festivals, and parties. "Our membership consists of directors, producers, actors, writers, crew, editors, music composers and we could go on, but basically if your talent could help get a film or production made at any stage then this site is for you."

Star Now—www.starnow.co.uk
Star Now is one of the leading websites in the UK, Australia, and New Zealand, for casting and crewing, with around 10,000 people joining every week worldwide.

AUSTRALIA

The Film & Television Institute—www.fti.asn.au
Based in Freemantle, the Film & Television Institute is arguably the oldest screen resource organization in Australia. It provides a complete crewing service, widely used by Australians, but also overseas production companies taking advantage of the country's generous allowances to filmmakers and long months of guaranteed sunshine. Supported by Screen Australia, the FTI provides a full production service, hires equipment, and contains at the Adelaide Street offices a 121-seat cinema, video editing suites, an animation center, digital labs, training rooms, studio space, and office accommodation.

VICTORIA POLAND – MAKE-UP DESIGNER

6.1 Victoria Poland

1. What is your job on a film set?
As a make-up artist, my job is to look after the make-up and hair of the actors. You have to use all your technical knowledge and creativity to follow a brief, and create a believable character.

2. What is the difference between a make-up designer and a make-up artist?
A make-up designer breaks down the script and works with the director to make sure you get exactly what the director wants. A make-up artist works under the designer and creates the look the designer has specified.

3. How did you get into the industry?
I trained at *Delamar Academy*, based in Ealing Studios in London. During college I did as many jobs as possible, working for free at weekends. I started by doing a lot of student film shoots, as you all learn together and there is less pressure. Then I moved on to low-budget shoots with professional crews, then bigger-budget shoots. By building up gradually in this way, you learn set etiquette and also what is expected of you in your role. Working on student films first allows you to make mistakes without serious implications. As long as you learn from mistakes they are worth making!

4. How important is training for a make-up artist?
Training is very important as there is a lot of technical skill involved in make-up artistry. You are also taught at college how to behave on set and when working with make-up designers. I would then recommend assisting other make-up artists as much as possible as you will continue to learn from them. This is also a good way of building contacts, as the make-up artist you assist may pass jobs on to you when they are unable to do them.

5. Who do you work most closely with on the set?
You work most closely with the artists and also the costume department (you work together on the look of the character). You also work closely with the director, who will ultimately decide what he wants the character to look like.

6. Are you generally given a strict brief to follow, or can you be as creative as you like?
It depends on how specific the director is on how creative you can be with your characters. Most importantly, you need to decide what is the right look for the character in question. For example, if your character is a dowdy middle-aged housewife who makes very little effort with her appearance, she would not have very glamorous make-up with false eyelashes.

7. How do you prepare for a shoot?
First, you read the script and make a note of each character and also the setting. Does the film require any special effects? Then you speak with the director about his or her ideas for each character. Research is also important, particularly on period films. It is then helpful to do a make-up test with the artists before shooting begins so you can try different make-up and hair looks.

8. Do you generally bring your own kit, or is it supplied for you?
Generally bring your own kit and brushes. You may have a make-up budget to buy specific items such as sfx make-up and consumables, or you may just get expenses to cover the cost of the kit you use.

9. On a short film might you be expected to also run the wardrobe and hair departments?
The role of the make-up artist usually incorporates hair as well as the make-up. There should always be a separate person for the wardrobe department, as this would be too much to take on for one person, and they are two very different areas of expertise.

10. What advice do you have for someone hoping to enter your part of the industry?
Take every opportunity that comes your way as you never know who you may meet, and you are more likely to meet someone useful on a job than if you are at home. Stick at it—you will have to work for expenses only at first, but you will start to build up contacts and will eventually get paid work.

PAUSE

VICTORIA POLAND'S TOP 3 TIPS

1. Take pictures. Continuity of make-up is very important. Make sure you take photographs of what the artist looks like at the beginning of the scene and at the end. Write notes about what make-up you have used on each character in each scene and what you did with their hair. Scenes are often not shot in order due to the work schedules of artists and logistics, so you may shoot "day one" in the script one day and then again a few days later, so you will need to be able to recreate what the character looks like.
2. Get rid of anything distracting. For example—shiny noses, eyelids, spots, redness, bushy eyebrows, etc. You don't want the audience to be looking at the artist's nose hair instead of paying attention to the film. Also, depending on the script, the make-up should not be the star of the show. It needs to be appropriate for the story. The best make-up is that which no one notices. It is also the most believable.
3. Be creative. If you have no budget, you can make a substance that looks like blood from golden syrup and food coloring. The most basic of kits can be used to do most make-ups. For example a grease palette can do a natural make up, a red lip or even an ageing make-up.

PAUSE

FURTHER READING

The Make-up Artist Handbook: Techniques for Film, Television, Photography and Theater (2008)
By Gretchen Davis and Mindy Hall

This full-color illustrated book is written for film, television, and theater make-up artists who need to know the basics on how to accomplish flawless make-up applications. It begins with fundamental practices and continues through more complex techniques usually known only by Hollywood make-up artists. Written by two expert authors who have experience doing make-up for television, commercials, and blockbuster films, readers will learn about beauty, time periods, black and white film, as well as cutting edge techniques such as air brushing, make-up for computer-generated movies, and make-up effects. Published by Focal Press.

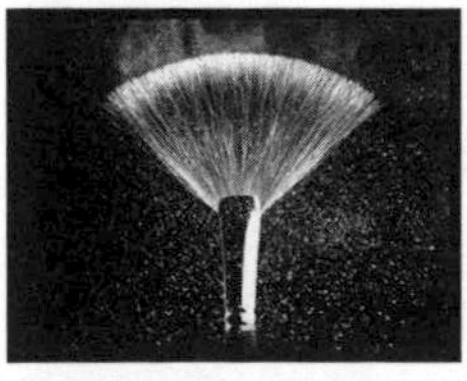

6.2 Gretchen Davis
▶▶ P.**81**

6.3 Jan Musgrove

P.81

Make-Up, Hair and Costume for Film and Television (2003)
By Jan Musgrove

This is an introductory guide for students learning professional make-up, hairdressing, and wardrobe skills and "front of camera" professionals needing an understanding of the techniques. The manual offers a step-by-step approach for the complete beginner with diagrams to show procedures for a variety of make-up effects, from corrective and character make-up, to period dramas, special effects, and prosthetics. It describes the skills required of the job, introduces special make-up products and how to apply them for different effect and sets the context for the make-up artist's role, by considering technical requirements such as lighting, camerawork, and chroma-key backgrounds. Published by Focal Press.

STOP

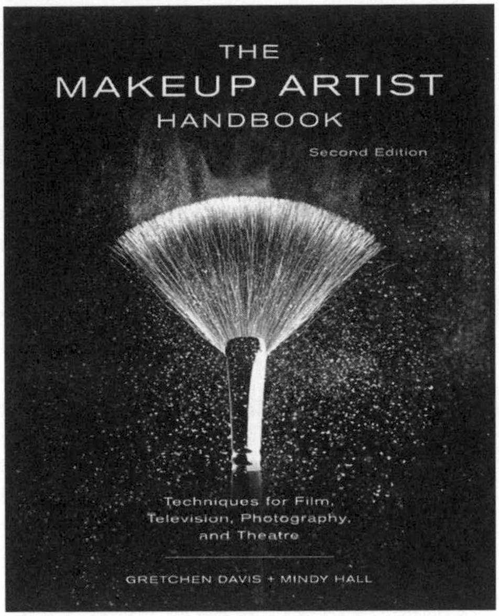

6.2 The Makeup Artist Handbook

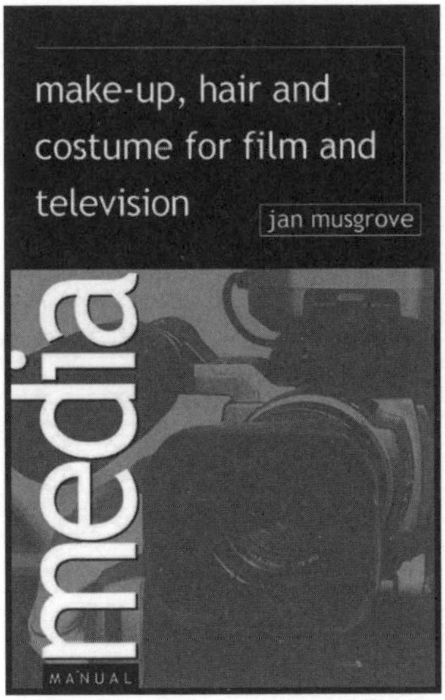

6.3 Make-Up, Hair and Costume for Film and Television

START

CHAPTER 7

Casting

A short film is a puzzle, by its very nature often more complex than a feature. Even when the script is tuned, the locations are sorted, and the producer has cut some cool deals with the facilities houses, the puzzle will remain muddled without due care and attention with casting. It is unlikely, although not out of the question, that you will have a star name in your short film, but finding the right actor for the right role is the keystone that holds all the pieces of the puzzle together.

A DP shooting his first film has undoubtedly been a focus puller and camera assistant. Sound designers serve an apprenticeship as sound editors. The sparks must survive the deadpan wit of the gaffer before they are let loose on the panoply of lights. Just as the craftsmen know the tools of their trade, trained actors who can get into the skin of the character will find the soul of the part and give more than the director expects. Dustin Hoffman as Michael Dorsey in the 1982 *Tootsie* is so desperate for a job he summons up all his power and expertise, cross-dresses for a casting and lands a female role in a soap opera that makes him/her famous.

Casting often comes at the end of the long laborious task of getting the script right, the director working alongside the writer, or the writer/director producing new drafts under the watchful eye of the producer. While the writing process continues through one draft after another, the director will also be working on a variety of other equally important details: the shot list with the DP; the storyboards, alone or with an artist; he'll be seeking out locations; thinking about costumes and liaising with the art department. After months, even years, of talking about the film, when it starts to happen, everything happens at the same time and if casting suffers during the last minute rush to production, so will the finished product.

The same care that goes into the script has to be applied to casting and, once the cast is in place, the director needs to ensure each actor understands the dreams, foibles, and motivations of the character they are going to play. The director must give clear, simple directions that are consistent and easy to follow. He must establish a trusting relationship that will get the most from rehearsals, and he needs to know how to jazz up poor performances before shooting begins. A first-time director must learn how to be firm without being a bully—if he wants a football-playing six footer to weep like a child, he will know exactly why and will inspire the tears from his actor. All aspects of mise-en-scène—set, costume, music, sound—contribute to audience pleasure and participation in the film, but it is the actors who hold our attention every moment they are on screen. Memorable performances occur as if by magic when the director casts the right actor for the role, when he feels completely comfortable with those actors, and when the actors feel comfortable with each other; what they call screen chemistry.

A director learns directing from doing it, but knowledge is power and the director will have more authority on set when he does his research. In *Directing Actors*,[1] Judith Weston describes directing film as a high-stakes occupation—"the white water rafting of entertainment jobs," and adds, "For many directors, the excitement they feel about a project tightens into anxiety when it comes to working with actors." In this practical guide, Weston explains exactly what actors want from a director; what directors do wrong; how actors work; and the director/actor relationship.

PAUSE

IN THE SPOTLIGHT

The Spotlight was founded with 236 artists in 1927, the same year as *The Jazz Singer* brought the silent era to an end. Based in the heart of London in Leicester Square, the service was formed "to give professional performers the best and most efficient exposure to casting opportunities."

There are now more than 40,000 actors, actresses, child artists, presenters, stunt artists, and dancers listed in the print version and Internet directories. As the industry's leading casting resource, Spotlight is used by most TV, film, radio, and theatrical companies in the UK, and serves to connect actors, agents, and producers worldwide.

Spotlight's website receives more than one million artist searches a year and actor CVs are viewed almost six million times. www.spotlight.com

ACTORS' AGENCIES

Short-filmmakers can approach actors' agencies directly. Agents will suggest suitable talent on their books if they like the script, and believe the exposure will both enhance their clients' careers and give them a useful addition to their showreel. The more work their clients do, and the better roles, the more valuable a commodity they become. Agents will normally negotiate a fee that, while reduced for budget filmmakers, pays for the agents' time and shows the actors they are working with professionals. Agents take on a client for the long term, each part building a career that is rewarding for the actor and economically viable for the agent.

For those working on a low-budget film in the UK, a useful organization is Castnet—www.castingnetwork.co.uk—a free service providing online CVs, photos and showreels.

PAUSE

THE DANNY RICHMAN GUIDE TO CASTING

1. Allow sufficient time to see a wide selection of actors for each role and include time for call-backs to confirm your original shortlist. Do not leave the castings until a few days before you intend to shoot.
2. actors subscribing to the casting service are required to have trained at an accredited drama school and have at least three professional credits on their CV. Use a casting service that only allows submissions from actors that meet the precise requirements of your breakdown.
3. Research the drama schools with the best reputations and attract the highest number of applicants. If an actor has graduated from a drama school, i.e. RADA, LAMDA or Central they will have already completed a rigorous and competitive audition process indicating a probable high level of talent.
4. When preparing your breakdown, try to be as specific as possible and provide as much detail as you can about the character and their situation in the film. Good actors are attracted to interesting roles that closely match their playing range and characteristics. A description of "Jim, 25–30 male" will attract only the most desperate and least experienced actors.
5. Let actors see your script prior to the casting. If they have read the script and have expressed an interest they are far more likely to show up on the day of the casting. It will also give the actors the maximum possible time to prepare for the role.
6. Make sure that you are well organized and provide actors with all relevant information about the logistics of the casting and what they will be required to do on the day. Behave professionally at all times and never ask actors to attend a casting at a residential address or hotel.
7. Try not to keep actors waiting unnecessarily at the casting and ensure that refreshments and toilet facilities are available.
8. Make the actors feel comfortable and in a supportive environment. Allow sufficient time for them to have several attempts at reading.
9. Get them to read it differently to test their ability to respond to direction.
10. If the reading contains dialogue, ensure that there is a third party present to read the other character/s with them. Do not attempt to do this yourself as you will find it far more difficult to view their performance objectively.
11. Never direct actors to read with emotive instructions, e.g. happier, angrier, more flirtatious etc. This type of instruction will only result in a contrived performance. Use verb-based direction, e.g. "Thrill her," "destroy him" and make sure the actor realizes how much is at stake for the character in the chosen scene. If there is little at stake for the character then you have not chosen a suitable scene for a reading.
12. If you have no intention of casting the actor, do not go on to ask them questions about their availability. This will only give the actor the false impression that they have a strong chance of being cast.
13. Always let the actors know as soon as possible after the casting whether they are being considered or will not be considered for the role.

DANNY RICHMAN INTERVIEW

1. How can Castnet help a short-film producer?
Producers can contact the agency directly to receive intelligent, immediate suggestions for a production. We will contact all actors on their behalf, schedule castings and let actors know the outcome. Once we have made suggestions it is then up to the director or casting director to make the final shortlist and selection.

2. What general advice would you give new filmmakers regarding casting?
New filmmakers frequently devote far too little time and attention to the casting process. An underdeveloped script and poor selection of actors are the two areas most likely to result in a poor quality film. It is vital that filmmakers understand the qualities that make a good actor, how to determine an actor's ability from their CV and learn the difference between an actor who may give a reasonable audition but fail to deliver on set.

3. Do producers come to you with fixed ideas; and if so, how do you help them make sure they get the right person for the part?
There is a huge community of actors available for even the most low-budget film productions. Filmmakers should have a clear vision of the roles they are trying to cast. The only exception is where the role requires an uncommon ethnic background, children, or those aged over 60. These categories of actors can be far harder to source for a low-budget film offering little or no payment.

4. Do you try and balance the cast; if there are two female leads, for example, would you go for a blonde and a brunette?
Although the primary consideration should be the quality of the performance, audiences will often visually identify a character on the basis of very obvious physical characteristics, e.g. blonde female. If both of your main female characters are blonde, this may cause some confusion when they appear in different scenes.

5. Do you find some actors are better adapted for stage than screen?
Many drama schools have traditionally focused more on stage performance than screen. Some actors may therefore graduate from drama school with little idea of how to adapt their performance for the camera. It is important to look at an actor's CV for evidence of screen work and to film their audition to ensure that they are able to adapt their performance.

6. How can you help short-filmmakers specifically?
Many filmmakers may have had the experience of advertising their requirements on a casting website or in a casting publication only to find themselves inundated with applications from entirely unsuitable, inexperienced, or poorly qualified actors. CastNet uses a unique process to ensure that every actor is entirely suitable for the specified role, has confirmed their interest and availability for the production and has achieved a high standard of training and professional experience. This can save stressed filmmakers

an enormous amount of wasted time and expense in finding the right talent for their production.

7. Do short-filmmakers have unrealistic hopes?
If they did not have unrealistic hopes, they would probably never have chosen to pursue a career in filmmaking! They should however ensure that their short films are realistic in what they are trying to achieve and are not overly-ambitious in terms of cast, location, and special effects. Most new filmmakers fail by trying to do too much, too soon, rather than just telling a simple story, truthfully and economically.

8. Are short films a good place for actors to hone their screen skills?
Many actors may be participating in a short film solely to gain material for their showreel. Actors gain the most by working on a well-organized production with an efficient crew and talented director who understand how to work and communicate with actors. Unfortunately, these are few and far between in the world of short-filmmaking and far too little time is devoted to working with actors in most British film schools.

THE CASTING SOCIETY OF AMERICA

A one-stop shop for casting in the US is the Casting Society of America—www.castingsociety.com—the premier organization of casting directors in film, TV, and theater. It has more than 490 members represented not only in the United States, but also in Canada, the UK, Australia, and Italy.

CSA was founded in Los Angeles in 1982 to establish a standard of professionalism and to provide its members with a support organization to further their goals and protect their interests. With less than 40 members during its first year, the monthly newsletter helped grow the organization and drew into its ranks many of the top casting directors in the industry. The creative contribution of casting directors is recognized by the Academy of Television Arts and Sciences and since 1989, casting directors have been awarded Emmy statuettes in various casting categories.

What can the CSA do for producers?

"We are diplomats; we are counselors; we are negotiators," said Mary V. Buck, former CSA President. "We are teachers; we are artists and visionaries. We are a key element in the creation and success of every theater, film, and television project ever made."

There is a huge number of sites offering similar services, so it's worth checking the costs and benefits of each. Here's a selection:

- LA Casting—www.lacasting.com
- Now Casting—www.nowcasting.com
- BackStage—www.backstage.com
- Mandy.com—www.mandy.com

- Explore Talent—www.exploretalent.com
- Actor's Access—www.actorsaccess.com

CASTING DIRECTORS

The ideal way to cast a film is to use a casting agency, or use a casting director who gathers a portfolio of CVs and glossy 10x8s. Casting directors are the go-between between actors and their agents—and little-known performers will have an agent straight out of drama school if they are serious about the business. If you have a role for seven-year-old identical Chinese twins, the casting director will know exactly where to look to fill those roles.

Once the casting director has found suitable actors, they will liaise with the production company in setting up auditions. In fact, the first audition is often with the casting director and actors need to give a convincing performance before they are even sent to auditions. The casting director wants to provide the absolute best person for the role because that reflects on their skill and justifies their fee. The cost of employing a casting director varies greatly and many will assist in casting a short film gratis if they believe the filmmakers are eventually going to make a feature, showing support for talent as well as making long-term commercial sense.

7.1 Erica Arvold

ERICA ARVOLD – CASTING DIRECTOR

www.ericaarvoldcasting.com

1. What do you do, and what does this entail?
As a casting director I am the liaison between the director's creative vision when it comes to actors, and the production or producer's vision when it comes to financial matters, or the budget. So I find that sweet spot in between the actors that will work for a certain amount of money and the creative vision and taste of the director.

2. Describe your average day.
That's a challenge to answer, as there are so many stages within the casting process. Through any project, whether it's one day or a twelve-week process, I always have the same skeleton, somewhat like a screenplay, as in the first act, second act and third act. We start with brainstorming and creative vision—from the filing cabinet in my head; the directors and producers that are creatively involved in the project and the agents' ideas. We then move into the sessions, demo reels—seeing those visions. Then there's the decision-making process, narrowing down, and when we have our top choices budgetary concerns come up. I'm given the entire casting budget, and I think that's typical of casting directors. So if I've got a certain amount for Character A and they demand more money, I can take it from another character and choose a less-known actor—in collaboration with the producer, of course. Once the choices are made there's negotiations, contracts, cast lists. It's a whole lot of very detailed paperwork that needs

to be put through production as well as a lot of discussions with unions and making sure people are paid etc.

3. Do you enjoy your job, and why?

I love that it is two ends of the spectrum: the creative vision and the big challenge. No matter how many television shows or movies or commercials I've cast, at the beginning of every project I'm absolutely terrified I'll never find a cast for it. To accomplish that in whatever time period is so much fun for me.

4. Did you always know you wanted to be a casting director?

I was actually very lucky. I grew up in a home without a television, but I was innately incredibly visual. I remember watching the television show *Square Pegs* at a friend's house and Sarah Jessica Parker was in it, and I remember seeing her face and thinking, "I need to keep track of her because I think she's really got a factor where she's going to have quite a career." I don't know where that came from as I didn't know casting directors even existed at that point. When I was in my late teens, I got an internship with Jane Alderman, and on my first day I started crying as I knew I'd found what I wanted to do. One of my goals was to find a job where I never had to wear pantyhose. This is not a nine to five bank job. Kudos to those who enjoy them, but I fall down a rabbit hole on every project, and can just enjoy the complete obsession.

5. How do you find the right actors?

I find them in so many places. I rely heavily on agents and submissions. There are all sorts of people interested in acting, but you have to have a business sense. Actors themselves really need to do their homework and understand how their business works and what an audition is and take classes constantly. The best actors—even Meryl Streep—they're always taking classes, always getting coached. There's never a point at which someone stops training. It's very sad if that happens.

6. What advice do you have for student filmmakers hoping to enter your part of the industry?

I'm not only a casting director, I've produced and worked in many other departments and exposure to everyone else's job is essential and helps you find what you really want to do within the industry and helps you with your own job. For example I did work in wardrobe for a bit and accounting and wardrobe have deadlines to meet, so they're constantly calling casting asking "who's the actor". But now that doesn't bother me, as I know where they're coming from.

7. What have you learnt along the way?

When I watch the Academy Awards, this is my little secret, my own bar is if I can recast one of the roles with another actor that I think would be phenomenal. I'm not rooting for that person to win the Award. For instance Michelle Williams from *Blue Valentine*, I cannot imagine any other person playing that role. Period. So that's my bar. Also, every casting director I've worked for or collaborated with, it's always about finding new fresh faces that will bring life to a project in an original way. For example, some big celebrity, which is fine as it balances the budget and the distribution, but when it comes to other roles that don't need a big name, especially a short film, I think the director and casting director together should really be looking under every rock for someone with that appeal. For me that's so exciting and such a fun part of casting. I remember a film I was working on—*The Horse Whisperer*. We found a normal kid who could lasso and it was gratifying that we didn't have to go with a New York Broadway actor or a seasoned commercial actor. We wanted that real quality and with kids you can really find some gems. Kids just get it. I was an associate on *Natural Born Killers,* and it was fascinating to watch. Prisoners are the only people besides kids that we discussed that had this instinct that just go into it and there's not this third person watching themselves, or this awareness, they just go. Prisoners are the same. It's fascinating. It's almost like this escapism. A lot of adults don't have this ability. They're always judging themselves. When one judges themselves as an actor, it shows on screen so you're not getting an authentic experience.

8. Can a director with a very low budget get away with not using a casting director?

I think so. One of my favorite experiences was when I was working on a commercial for a small company. After a couple of days, they looked at me and said they could never do it again without a casting director. I don't know what the difference is as I've never been on a project without a casting director, but they said it's a whole world of difference. So directors can find actors themselves, but when they start working with a casting director, it's a different level of commitment to one's filmmaking.

9. How should directors go about casting?

In my mind actors are never bad or good, they're just not right for a project. There are actors that come in for commercials and the ad agency says "oh, they're terrible, they'll never work," when in fact it's probably it just wasn't that commercial they were right for, and they're better suited for a feature film. For example John Malkovich came in for a commercial I auditioned in Chicago and the ad agency didn't see it. They thought he's the worst actor on the planet, which he's not. He's a fantastic actor! And soon enough he got feature films and off he went on his career. So especially new filmmakers, instead of judging people being good or bad, think "do they fit in this project". It's a much more healthy way to level the perceived power play when an actor comes into a room. It's much harder to perform when they feel pressure or that they're being judged. It's much easier to get the part and make the film better if it's an even collaborative playing ground and we're all just experimenting if it's going to work for this part.

10. What advice would you give to someone making his or her first short film?

No one will ever believe in your film as much as you do. It's like the accounting principle: You don't trust your accountant as much as you trust yourself to worry about your own finances. A film is the same thing—when you're passionate, you just have to go and do it. It takes an equal amount of energy and effort and connections and chutzpah to create a bad film as it does a good film, so you may as well make the best film you can. For me it's all about story—story, story, story. The word on the street is the script is somewhere between 65% and 95% of directing.

RAINDANCE FILM FESTIVAL TIP

REHEARSING ACTORS DO'S AND DON'TS

DO

Prepare in advance of casting and meeting the actors. As well as the visualization, production design, sound design, etc., spend time fleshing out the worlds of the characters. What do they want, what are they afraid of? What makes them confident? There is no need to set these choices in stone but being equipped to answer the questions about character shows everyone that the characters are more than a means to convey plot and say the clever funny lines of dialogue in your script. Characters are behavior, and human too.

DON'T

Let your decisions on who these characters are blind you to what the actors will bring to their roles. The key skill here is to let them show you what they have understood from their work on the scene and what they have understood from your direction. Slowly meld your vision with theirs so it becomes something you are both excited by and ultimately tells the story you have set out to tell.

DO

Schedule some time in pre-production with your cast. The whole purpose of pre-production is to prepare for the time when the cameras are rolling. You will spend hours and hours with your other heads of department, quite rightly, planning and developing your vision. Actors play a vital part in how well this vision comes across. Spending time now with them sharing and enriching your ideas for them will pay out later on the shoot, and actually save time.

DON'T

Talk too much. The way we communicate as directors affects the abilities of others to give us what we want. This is no more so the case than with actors. Actors re-act. That's their main goal, to react well to the stimulus provided. The more you talk the harder it becomes to react to all they have heard. Think about how difficult it is to follow a long series of verbal instructions, e.g. getting directions to a hard-to-find place from a local. Impart your thoughts in chunks (or beats, as they are often known) and then let the actors try them out. Break down the scene into bite-sized sections and work them gently, then put them back together.

DO

Spend time working on the script, paying attention to the meaning of the dialogue in simple terms of what is intended by the character that is speaking. What do they want?

DON'T
Spend hours poring through the words, sitting at a table. Try and get the scene "off the page" as soon as possible. The best way I have found is to improvise the scene, without the script in hand, maybe even not focusing on the exact dialogue. The sense of the scene is more vital to get familiar with than the words during pre-production rehearsal.

DO
Plan your rehearsal time well. Have a goal in mind for each session. They need not be long. Even an hour or two with each character, and relationship will give you a great sense of preparedness and you will have begun a rewarding collaboration with your actors.

DON'T
Overdo it. Many directors and actors shun rehearsal as, badly used, it can kill the energy of the scene or send you down a road of over-indulgence where the message of the scene gets lost and muddy. Your aim is to prepare the scene so it is clear as to what is happening, but will remain fresh enough to explore its subtleties in front of camera. Unless the scene is action heavy, such as a fight scene, or contains a complicated physical need, leave blocking until the day you are shooting the scene. You can prepare your general blocking and explore it with the actors, but don't force them into remembering it in advance.

Finally ...
Do enjoy it. Approached in the right way, rehearsal is inspiring, productive, and most of all will give you greater confidence when communicating on set with your cast. They will appreciate the efforts you have made and feel a part of the team, and so they should.

Chris Thomas

PERE COSTA—ACTOR

www.perecosta.com

7.2 Pere Costa

1. What do you do exactly?
I'm an actor, but I also work behind the camera—making videos for companies. But what I really love is acting.

2. What is your training, and is it essential for actors to go to drama school?
I started when I was 16 going to acting classes a few times a week. I then began acting in short films for friends. I did more courses in Barcelona while studying a different degree, and then went to *Col·legi de Teatre de Barcelona*, while also working in different projects—shooting commercials, a feature film, and a theater tour. I've done a number of other courses, and will keep doing more in the future. This is pretty normal for an actor. There

are actors that haven't been to school, maybe from amateur theater, but this is getting less common.

3. Describe your average day.
If I'm working I'll read over my lines a final time just after waking up. I like to "activate" my body by "clapping" or yoga—it means I work better. I'll go to the set, speak to the director. Go to the make-up department. Depending on the role, there may be a lot of waiting around. This is a good time to rehearse the scene with other actors. When my scene comes up, we just roll.

4. Describe your average day when you are not working.
This is a better question as when you're working you just do your job, but when you're not working—no one tells you what to do. Not working is a big part of the life of most actors. Bigger actors may have project after project lined up, but this is far from the norm. While looking for work, staying fit is essential. It's not necessarily about being strong, but certainly healthy. I'm a part of a few agencies, but if they don't have anything that's right for me I'll look for work myself by checking different websites. Preparing scenes or monologues is a good way to train as an actor, and at the same time you can also record it for your new showreel or you can use the text you have learnt in a casting.

5. How important is the showreel?
Along with a CV and portfolio, a showreel is essential. It allows people to see a mix of what you can do. It should be around three minutes, any longer and people won't watch it. It's also important to permanently improve your material. Your showreel, portfolio, website, and CV always need to be up to date and looking professional.

6. How important is the Internet?
It's essential. Checking different websites for castings—every day there will be new jobs posted, listed in terms of what is needed—gender, age, location etc. If one fits, you need to send over all of your information. All of your material is also online, so people can access it easily. Keeping an up-to-date mailing list is also important—casting directors, producers, other actors, and people you have worked with. Last year I was working as a runner on a TV movie—I did the job partly for the money and experience, but mainly for the contacts. When you have new material, sending it out to your list can really help. But be careful not to spam—only use this list when you genuinely have something worth sharing.

7. On a short film, who do you work most closely with?
Apart from the other actors, definitely the director. A short film is a very different experience from a feature film, where there will be so many people involved if you have a smaller part you won't have so much contact. It's very important to have a good relationship with a director. You can ask questions about the character, and it may lead to more work in the future.

8. What are important qualities for an actor to have?
One of the most essential qualities for an actor is being a good listener, being aware of the space you're in and what's around you. And not just

when you're on stage or in front of the camera, but also in everyday life. Observing the behavior of people, you take elements to create different characters. Imagination is another crucial tool—so that you can believe what you are doing. Without imagination and you're acting in a scene—let's say that your father is dead—you won't be able to do it. With imagination you can get that feeling and be convincing. And patience. The work may not arrive, but if you keep trying, casting after casting after casting, one day you will be chosen, and over the castings, you will have improved. In any job, but particularly in acting, putting time into perfecting your trade does pay off.

9. How do you choose roles?
If I'm in a position to be selective, I like to choose characters I haven't played before. This allows me to learn, forces me to investigate—which won't happen if I always play the same characters. For example Gary Oldman has played completely distinct roles, like a chameleon, and I have a lot of respect for actors that do this. I won't name the ones who don't.

10. Do you have any advice for someone who wants to be an actor?
Some people have an image of actors—of glamour and fame. But wanting fame isn't a good reason to become an actor. You have to love it. You have to be constant. You can't worry about being criticized. This will happen, and it's normal. Don't try to act well, just do every exercise. If you fail, then you learn. Risk is important. Moving outside of your comfort zone. Doing things you haven't done before. Trying something and failing is a good opportunity to learn. Always doing the same thing is a shame. Also when you are working, care about the whole process. It's not just about doing a job. Don't think "I've done my hours, and I'm not going over." If you are easy to work with, you are more likely to be called for a casting, or given a role.

PAUSE

STOP

THE MYSTERY OF THE MISSING EARRINGS

The title role in my 10-minute short *Greta May* requires the actress to go through a range of costumes—as well as emotions. Three agencies sent 40 actresses to three castings and the standard of performance was extremely high.

This was a role actresses could really sink their teeth into and they were pulling out all the stops to try and get it. One actress appeared looking scruffy and depressed and seemed perfect when Greta is in her dejected state.

The actress called that night to say she had forgotten her earrings. She had some fresh ideas about the character and, could she attend another audition to try them out. She arrived dressed to the nines as the optimistic Greta May, slipped on her earrings and gave an upbeat performance.

I didn't cast that actress because I had a clear mental image of who I was looking for (in the script notes I'd written: 25, vulnerable but with a steely core of self-preservation). The actress wasn't quite right for the role, but I admired her determination and kept her photo and CV on file.

START

CHAPTER 8

Locations

There are two location musts on budget shorts:

1. Have as few locations as possible.
2. Keep the locations close together.

That doesn't mean the story needs to adapt to the locations, but if the same story can be told by combining or cutting locations, so much the better. Take another look at Quentin Tarantino's *Reservoir Dogs*. There's a lot more talking than action. Most of the action takes place in an empty warehouse. But the odd glimpse of the outside world moderates any sense of claustrophobia.

GRETA MAY

To return again to the short film *Greta May*, in the original short story, the stranger, Richard, gives Greta his telephone number on a tube train. Getting permission to shoot on the Underground is straightforward. London Transport has a film division for that purpose. But is the train set up essential?

Later in the story, we see Greta rehearsing on stage in the theater. On a scouting expedition, we looked at the Battersea Arts Centre. Not only did it have a theater space we could use, as the story has a theatrical background, the foyer was actually a far better place for the first meeting of the two main characters. It was a bonus that the arts center is in an old town hall with a regal if faded elegance and a pair of sweeping marble stairs that would have been perfect for a Fred Astaire/Ginger Rogers movie. Being a local authority concern dedicated to promoting the arts, the rental cost suited our budget and the production company's third-party indemnity covered the insurance.

Now, without changing the story in any way, not only were we able to shoot two scenes in the same location, the sound of Greta's hollow footsteps in the cavernous foyer reflected her inner feeling of emptiness, an accidental homage to the library sequence in Orson Welles' *Citizen Kane* (see Chapter 11: Sound). The arts center had toilets (an essential) and a café where we put some money through the till at breakfast and lunch.

Another shot requires Greta studying magazines outside a newsagents. We went to the shop nearest the house where we were shooting the interiors. By luck, the proprietor had once allowed his premises to be used by the BBC and our request touched on some nostalgic nerve from his brush with that eminent institution. He negotiated a £50 fee for the two hours we needed to get the shot and was on hand in case we needed any extras. People like the movies and even on a small production, they are often keen to help. It goes without saying that a thank you letter with a copy of the DVD will make life easier for the next low budget producer seeking a location.

INTERIORS

Another important consideration is having enough physical space to shoot. If you've got a girl in the shower, à la *Psycho*, along with the actress, you're going to have to squeeze into the bathroom the DP with his camera, a tripod at least, and perhaps a grip to dolly the camera; the sound engineer and boom operator; the gaffer with his lights; wardrobe with a gown ready to wrap the starlet; the clapper boy to shout ACTION and, of course, the director—and let's hope he doesn't have the same girth as the majestic Mr Hitchcock. It is easier to make a large space look small than to operate in a small space surrounded by kit and crew.

If a film has a lot of interiors, you can try asking a real estate agent if they have an empty property; they may be persuaded to let you have a short-term lease. The property will give you a variety of rooms for wardrobe and make-up, a base for the kit, and a challenge to the set designer who, like painters with their blank canvas, generally prefer to begin their creation with an empty space.

As the example above shows, shooting in bathrooms is particularly difficult (producers should try and get them written out of the script), and if the scene is crucial, you might try asking the management at a hotel if you can hire a room for a day. Emblazon the hotel name on the credits and they may even let you have a room for free.

The great illusion in movies is to make the audience believe what they are seeing on screen is authentic. The audience is a willing party to the illusion, and what matters is the *sense* of veracity and the power of the story itself. In the French set *Perfume*, the Barrio Gótico in Barcelona becomes Paris and the old quarter of Girona stands in for the pretty town of Grasse in Provence. What may come as more of a surprise is that several principal scenes in Michael Winterbottom's emotional roller-coaster *Welcome to Sarajevo* were shot in London, a tough assignment that required all the skills of Mick Ratman, a veteran location manager and former chairman of the Guild of Location Managers.

EXTERIORS

8.1 *Perfume* (2006)

▶▶ P.**104**

Sarajevo is an Austro-Hungarian city with sturdy stone buildings from the Grand Epoch at its heart and a fringe of rundown 1960s tower blocks rising in the distance. "If you search London, you can find exactly the same," Ratman explained during an interview. "You just have to be creative."

By creative that means dressing the set: covering street signs and road markings, or paying the local authority to remove them. "You then add your own street names and markings as necessary. If it's a period film, you lay down false cobbles or straw. The location manager looks at the details, consults books of reference, steeps himself in the period and place where the film is set."

Mick Ratman has location-managed-five features and numerous shorts. His advice is: if you can afford a location manager, bring him in as early as possible. The location manager studies the script, breaks it down into locations, then breaks the locations down into how many scenes there are in each location and how many days are needed. "You cut your cloth to suit your budget," he adds. "If you want to shoot in St Paul's Cathedral, it's easy enough, but it will cost a fortune. A location manager may well suggest doing an establishing shot of St Paul's, then shooting the interiors in a lesser known church that won't cost any more than a donation to the roof fund."

8.2 Mick Ratman

The location manager is employed to save the production money, but just as important is his role of ensuring the crew behaves responsibly and leaves each location with the providers happy to welcome back other productions in the future. A code of practice can be found at the Guild of Location Managers' website—www.golm.org.uk.

PAUSE

MICK RATMAN'S SEVEN-POINT LOCATION GUIDE

1. Don't be too ambitious.
2. Plan everything, every shot, every take.
3. Don't undervalue the importance of storyboards. The more time you spend planning, the easier the shoot.
4. If you have a good idea you have to check it through, plan every detail, make sure it really is a good idea before you shoot.
5. Try to find one location that can be shot to look like several different locations.
6. Get an experienced location manager who can advise creatively—not only on locations, but how the director wants to shoot each scene. A location manager who has been in the job for a while knows what has to be done and how to do it.
7. Look outside the envelope!

THE LMGA—WWW.LOCATIONMANAGERS.ORG

The Location Managers Guild of America dedicates itself to establishing and maintaining professional standards of personal conduct and business ethics among its members. The guild states that the primary job of a location manager is to find the place that best represents the visual concept of the producer, director, and production designer, which is done through research, scouting, and photography. The skill is finding the setting that best enhances the story and character development. As well as finding the location, a location manager is also responsible for the day-to-day management of locations, and will also:

- Meet with those neighbors and merchants directly affected by prep, shoot, or wrap activities.
- Negotiate the location fees, contracts, and associated paperwork.
- Co-ordinate legal issues with company attorneys.
- Request filming permits with all pertinent authorities, listing filming activities in detail.
- Call in notification of special effects and extended hours. Notify neighbors and gather signatures as required.
- Schedule police, fire safety officers, and security personnel.
- Co-ordinate with company safety department and supervise environmental clearance and studies in an expedited manner.
- Design and implement traffic plans and street closures.
- Work closely with Transportation Dept. to ensure that parking arrangements meet both production and neighborhood needs.
- Prepare directional signage and maps.
- Act as liaison between the public and the shooting crew.

The LMGA also works closely with the California on Location Awards—created in 1994 and known as the Cola Awards, which honors location professionals and production companies for their work on location in California.

PERMISSIONS

It is the producer, production manager, or locations manager, if you have one, who will generally seek permission where necessary to shoot on location and it is their responsibility to provide the owners or local authority officers with a basic Location Release Form. These can be downloaded free from various sites; there is an example below kindly provided by EM Media, the Regional Screen Agency for the East Midlands—www.em-media.org.uk.

LOCATION RELEASE FORM

From: name of company and address
To: name of owner of premises and address
Dated: date

Dear name of owner of premises

Name of film (the 'Film')

This letter is to confirm that we may film at your property which is known as ________ (the 'Property') from **start time to finish time** on date together with a setting up period of ________ hours and a clearing away period of ________ hours.

It is therefore agreed as follows:

1. That our personnel, props, equipment, vehicles and artists employed on our production are allowed onto the Property for the purpose of setting up and filming on the dates and for the periods agreed.

2. We may return to the Property at a later date if principal photography and recording is not completed on the dates agreed.

3. We have notified you of the scenes which are to be shot on or around the Property and you confirm and agree that you consent to the filming of these scenes.

4. We are entitled to incorporate all films, photographs and recordings, whether audio or audio-visual, made in or about the Property in the Film as we may require in our sole discretion.

5. We shall not make any structural or decorative alterations to the Premises without your prior consent. In the event that we do want to make alterations and you agree, we shall properly reinstate any part of the Property to the condition it was in prior to those alterations.

6. In consideration of the rights granted in this letter we will pay you the sum of **£amount** on **date**.

7. You agree to indemnify us and to keep us fully indemnified from and against all actions, proceedings, costs, claims, damages and demands however arising in respect of any actual or alleged breach or nonperformance by you of any or all of your undertakings, warranties and obligations under this agreement.

8. This agreement shall be governed by and construed in accordance with the law of England and Wales and subject to the jurisdiction of the English Courts.
Please signify your acceptance of the above terms by signing and returning to us the enclosed copy.

Yours sincerely,
Signed.................................

STUDIOS

If you have won the lottery, rather than merely received a lottery grant, or you have wealthy parents or sponsors, you may choose to shoot in a studio. Building a set allows you to shoot at any angle, put up walls and knock them down again, throw televisions through glass windows. And you don't have to worry about the weather. Studios provide space for a production office, wardrobe, make-up and hair, catering, workshops, and a props area. You can often save money shooting a feature and, if you're working on a budget short, you can at least take the tour. Pinewood, Elstree, and Ealing have facilities to rival Hollywood, and in Hollywood, the studios guarantee a nostalgia fest recreating the memorable moments from *Jaws, Alien, Titanic*, and *Indiana Jones*. Back in the real world, Brighton has a studio attached to the film school, and in Liverpool, from about £1,400 a week, you'll be following the footsteps of Samuel L. Jackson, Robert Carlyle, Emily Mortimer and Meat Loaf, who crowded the stage in studio one to film the interiors on *The 51st State*.

SCREEN AGENCIES

There are nine screen agencies in the UK, helping filmmakers find locations and make contacts with the local authorities and police. It is perfectly legal to shoot in public areas in the UK but, if you are trailing cables over the footpaths and may potentially create an obstruction, the police and local council must be informed, and the producer will need to show proof that he has valid insurance. Many film and TV police dramas are shot in London and producers will need prior permission to shoot exteriors of police stations and other police facilities. You will also need permission to dress your actors in police uniform and for anyone to carry weapons, even if they are dummies. For a fee, a Rent-a-Bobby will remain with the crew to manage crowd control.

Film agencies also provide information on other essentials like toilet facilities and parking. If you are shooting in an area you don't know, the regional screen agencies will put you in touch with a location scout who will set up recces during pre-production. An allocation manager will do the same job and also, if required, deal with contracts, negotiate fees and stay with the crew throughout production to ensure the smooth running of the shoot. They will be knowledgeable of the practicalities of a film crew descending on a location in their area and can save productions time and money by knowing what is and isn't possible to shoot.

LOCATION LIBRARIES

There are numerous commercial location-finding companies and libraries, some holding location photographs for different countries, others specializing in particular regions or types of location: private homes, period properties, industrial sites and so on. Locations may be grand, country houses and castles in Scotland, but likewise more modest or eccentric properties, cottages, flats, lofts, tree houses, are also listed.

There is a fee for this service, but that may be offset where libraries act as agents and negotiate a fee with the owner of the location; owners listed in libraries are familiar with the disruption that occurs when film crews descend on their property. With a library's help, a deal concerning a location can often be signed and sealed just days before shooting begins. Contact information for location personnel and location libraries can also be found in a number of directories including The Knowledge, Kemps and Kays (see Chapter 34: Useful Links).

ONLINE LOCATION LIBRARIES

With the world recession leading many people and businesses to search for extra income, thousands sign up every year to allow their homes or land to be used as film sets. The following sites list every possible location, from submarines to stately homes to swimming pools:

Reelscout—www.reel-scout.com
Film locations UK–www.locations-uk.com
Shoot Factory–www.shootfactory.co.uk
Location Works–www.locationworks.com

8.3 Greg Babcock

GREG BABCOCK – LOCATION MANAGER

www.coloradofilmlocations.com

1. How did you first get into the industry?
I set up an internship with an equipment rental house in my last semester of college. After graduating, I convinced the owner to hire me full time and began working behind the rental counter. There, I met many local production people. After working at the rental house for a while, I began freelancing as a production assistant and would work occasionally as a 3rd grip. When the national jobs came to Colorado, I began working as a co-ordinator and then moved into locations.

2. How long before filming starts would you ideally get involved in a project?
As much time as they'll give me! Obviously, features and other long-format productions require more time because they usually have more locations to be secured. A scout can start on a feature months before principal photography begins. Unfortunately, budgets on commercials have dropped dramatically, so rarely do I get enough time to scout properly. Agencies award the jobs very last minute, sending production companies and scouts scrambling for any location that will "work." I used to be on the road for days scouting a job. But now, because the money is so limited, often they'll only have me scout locations within the zone so they won't have to overnight any crew. That really limits your location choices.

3. Do you ever disagree with a director about the best location based on the script, and if so how do you resolve this?
I never disagree—I make strong, valid, and well-thought-out suggestions as to an alternative location (schedule, cost, logistics, look). Experience is your best tool in these situations. If you make a suggestion, you have to merge the logistical reasons with a creative alternative. Don't suggest an alternative location just because it is easier—make sure it can satisfy the Art Director's vision, as well as the Director's. Murphy's rule: they will ALWAYS want the location they CAN'T have! Make sure the second choice isn't too disappointing for them. Sometimes they may discover it actually works better than the first choice.

4. On low budget/short films do you ever suggest re-writes to save money?
Often times when I'm approached with a low-budget film, the people involved have Rolls-Royce tastes with a Volkswagen budget. While I appreciate their enthusiasm, I try to coach them into a more realistic production plan. An example I recall, two recent NYU film grads had written a script that involved the building of the transcontinental railroad using slave Chinese laborers. It required a period railroad train & tracks, massive set building and hundreds of Asian extras. They really only had the money to shoot a film with two old guys sitting on a park bench telling the story! Most low-budget movies/short films can't afford a truly professional location manager—they have their 19-year-old cousin do it. The unfortunate thing with low-budget films is they usually hire someone with little to no experience because they can't afford the day rate a real scout needs to survive. Because of this, many times locations aren't taken care of properly and then become unavailable for future filming.

5. How do you find, and then secure locations?
Initially with research, file pulls and phone calls. Securing the location also requires some experience and knack. A good scout has to have the personality to be able to instill a certain amount of trust very quickly. Then once a location they have found is used, the scout has to manage it and do final walk-throughs to make sure the location will be willing to be used again. Getting a location agreement signed and providing insurance.

6. Do you consider websites that list locations that can be used for filming a threat to your profession?
Yes—the ones that give away too much information. I've used location services in the past, and they are very handy for the scout. However, when a client goes directly to the service, that's work lost.

7. Do you always visit a location personally, or is seeing photos ever enough?
Always in person—because you need to know it's present condition. Paint can change, remodeling can change, foliage can change, owners can change, etc.

8. How important is the LMGA?
It gives more credibility to the positions of Location Scout and Location Manager. Also, to become a member, you must be vetted to insure you have substantial experience.

9. Location management is much more than simply finding a location. What aspects do you enjoy the most/not look forward to?
Discovery. The people. I've often said the scout has the best job as he gets to meet people one on one and learn about their history and the history of the community.

10. What are your "three golden rules" for location management?
Bi-Partisanship. You're hired by the company, but also have an obligation to

the location and neighborhood. Second, *respect*. It takes a unique kind of person. You have to establish trust and not bullshit people and third, *follow up*. Leave your campsite better than you found it—you have a responsibility to the company at hand, but also to future companies using the same location. If you burn a location, no one else will be able to use it or it will take a lot more convincing for the next location manager.

11. What advice do you have for students who would like to become a location manager?

Get on the biggest set you can and either intern or PA in the locations department—it *still* is a mentoring industry. I believe that is the only way you'll learn correctly. By being involved with a locations department you can learn about all the positions.

STOP

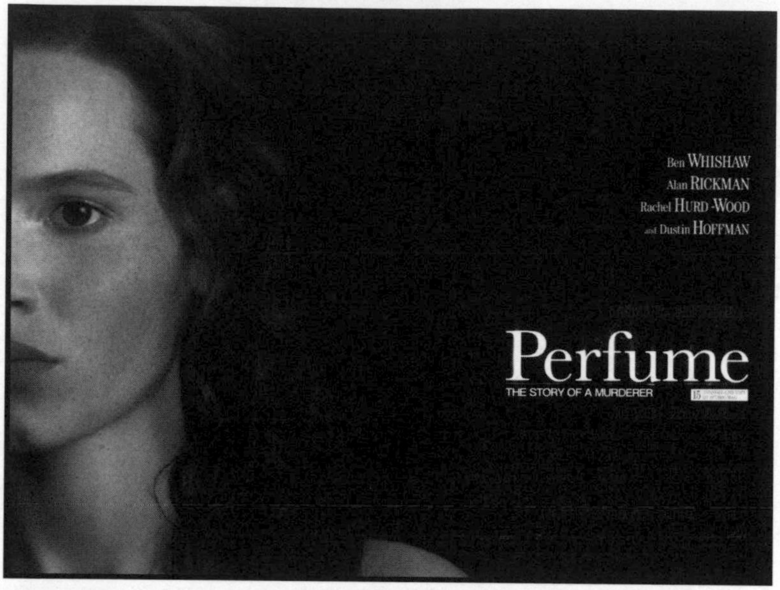

8.1 *Perfume* film poster (2006)

PART

III

TITLE

Production and kit

START

CHAPTER 9

Camera

The format you choose will affect how your film is shot, edited, and, most importantly, how much it will cost. Many filmmakers have strong feelings on the matter: Steven Spielberg has said he will never make a movie without film, while George Lucas will now only shoot in digital.

Great films can certainly be made digitally—*Slumdog Millionaire* was the first movie shot mainly in digital to win Best Cinematography at the Academy Awards. Parts of *Black Swan* were shot using a Canon EOS 7D—an affordable DSLR camera—chosen by DP Matthew Libatique because of its small size and excellent image quality. Film looks great but it's expensive and takes time to master.

Many filmmakers believe digital filmmaking has "democratized" the industry, making it affordable to almost everybody. Considering the high cost of film, and the ever-increasing quality of relatively inexpensive digital cameras, this chapter concentrates on the latter. If your heart is set on film don't let this put you off though. Where there's a will, there's a way—just get saving!

Technology is changing fast; lots of companies are competing to create better lenses, develop more powerful editing software, and capture higher quality sound. It can be hard to keep up with but as a result we have access to better equipment often at lower prices. However, don't feel that you must use the newest or most powerful piece of kit—a great film can be made for little money with modest equipment. A decent lens, for example, can last a lifetime and if it's good enough now, it doesn't matter what new models are released, it'll still be good enough in five years. Money can buy you great equipment but not talent. It's your skill that will make a film great.

PAUSE

SHOOTING ON FILM

There are three main film formats:

- **35mm—this is the most expensive. The camera comes with bulky equipment that requires a team to shift around on set and a multitude of lenses that can create the entire spectrum of mood and effects. It captures a clean, precise image and, for the purist, there is no other way to make film.**

- **16mm—the format gained in standing after its wide use in television and, though it lacks the gloss of 35, it is still used for serious productions. A slightly larger picture area can be obtained with Super 16, used by Ken Loach, who casts non-professional actors and shoots miles of film to capture natural performances. It was also chosen by the team behind the 2009 Academy Award winner for Best Picture *Hurt Locker*.**
- **8mm—the Super 8 and Real 8mm are formats for those learning their craft.**

Don't forget that shooting on film or digital needs the same discipline, the same care with lighting, the same preparation, and if this is all done, when the tape is blown up to 35mm, it will be the quality of the product that matters, not the way that you got there.

FILMMAKING ON A BUDGET: TOP FIVE CAMCORDERS UNDER $2000

By Jeremy Stamas of www.camcorderinfo.com

In many ways there has never been a better time for amateur filmmakers to go out and purchase new equipment. The rise of HD video has brought forth a wave of new products: from high-performance camcorders that sell for under $1000, to hands-free adventure cams that let you capture all the action for just a couple hundred bucks. And let's not forget all those video-capable DSLRs that offer the flexibility of interchangeable lens systems at lower costs than ever before.

So, if you're on the prowl for new video equipment, let us help you out for a moment. Here's our list for the top five camcorders for the budget filmmaker, with all of these models costing less than $2,000.

COMPACT PROSUMER CAMCORDER

9.1 Canon HF G10.

The HF G10 straddles the line between consumer and professional.

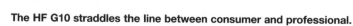

The Canon HF G10 sets the bar for compact "prosumer" camcorders. Its price tag is high compared to the rest of Canon's Vixia line, but it includes a wide range of professional-grade video features and controls. With its suite of color modes and cinema filters, as well as its native 24p frame rate option, the camcorder is ideal for those who are looking to add a film-like aesthetic to their video recordings.

Thanks to Canon's redesigned CMOS image sensor, the HF G10 was able to churn out an incredible performance in our low light image tests. The camcorder was also strong in other areas, although its images weren't quite as sharp as the top-level competition (one of the G10's few downsides). The manual lens ring, large LCD, and old-fashioned electronic viewfinder are all pleasant to work with, and give the HF G10 the look and feel of a professional device.

The HF G10 also doesn't have XLR inputs, so if you're looking to hook up professional audio equipment to the camcorder you're going to be disappointed. Canon's answer to this predicament is the XA10 camcorder, a model that is nearly identical to the HF G10 except it comes with a removable handlebar with XLR audio ports. It does cost an extra $500, though, so you may be better off getting a separate digital audio recorder along with the G10 instead.

PAUSE

CAMERA TIP 1: THE RULE OF THIRDS

The Rule of Thirds is less a rule than a guideline, albeit one of the most important guidelines in both photography and cinematography. Of course, not all well-composed shots adhere to it, but if you're going to break a rule it's best to master it first. Before you shoot, imagine the frame broken into thirds both vertically and horizontally, in effect imposing a grid over the image (whether mentally or using the built-in function available on many cameras). If you place points of interest within your shot on one of the four points at which the lines intersect, or along the lines themselves, you will create a balanced composition as the human eye is naturally drawn to these points. Sometimes it is effective to have your subject in the middle of the frame but if all your shots are like this your film will soon bore its audience. If you are shooting a landscape it is common to have the horizon aligned with the lower or upper third of the frame. This will more often than not create a dynamic, and thus interesting, composition.

9.2 Rule of Thirds

▶▶ P.**117**

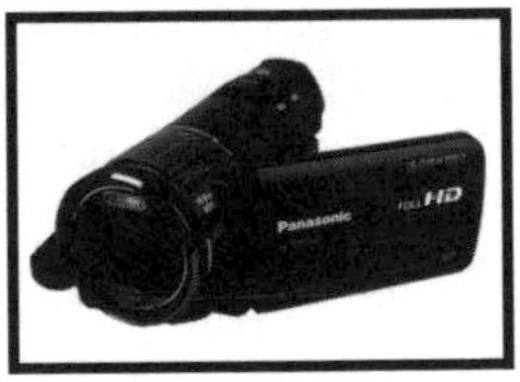

9.3 Panasonic HC-X900M.

HIGH-END CAMCORDER FOR BARGAIN HUNTERS

Panasonic's past three flagship models have offered excellent bang for their buck.

If you can't spend more than $1,000, but you still want a high-end consumer camcorder with all the bells and whistles, the Panasonic HC-X900M should suit your needs. The camcorder doesn't feel or look as professional as the Canon HF G10, but it has a near-equivalent set of manual controls as well as multiple frame rate recording options (including a 1080/60p record mode, which the Canon lacks). Additionally, the X900M has a very compact design that makes it ideal for the nomad filmmaker.

Our main issue with the HC-X900M, and Panasonic camcorders in general, is the company's apparent lack of innovation over the past few years. The HC-X900M is nearly a direct copy of the HDC-TM900 before it, which was almost identical to the HDC-TM700 before that. So, for three years now, Panasonic has sat tight, offering minor updates to its flagship camcorder design. It doesn't bode well for people who are looking for exciting new features, but it is great for anyone who wants to shop around for a good deal. A refurbished, used, or clearance-rack TM900 or TM700 would net you a fantastic camcorder at a bargain price.

PAUSE

CAMERA TIP 2: APERTURE AND F-STOPS

A camera's aperture works much in the same way as a human eye: the iris dilates in dark surroundings to allow more light to enter thereby helping us see more. Conversely, when it's bright it retracts so we're not blinded by too much light. In much the same way, the amount of light that is let into a camera must be controlled by changing the lens' diaphragm, which is made up of several blades forming an adjustable hole in the center. The size of this hole is known as the aperture (*see picture*). If the aperture is too large too much light will be let in and the image will look overexposed (washed out). If the aperture is too small not enough light will be let in and the picture will be underexposed (too dark). The size of the aperture is measured in f-stops and can range between f/1 (largest aperture) and f/64 (smallest).

Be warned, the lower the f-stop you require, the more expensive the lens. Reducing an f-stop not only lets more light into the camera but also decreases the depth of field (see Tip 3). It is for this reason that although many cameras have an auto-aperture function it is essential for you to learn how to do this manually. If you don't, you won't have control of your image.

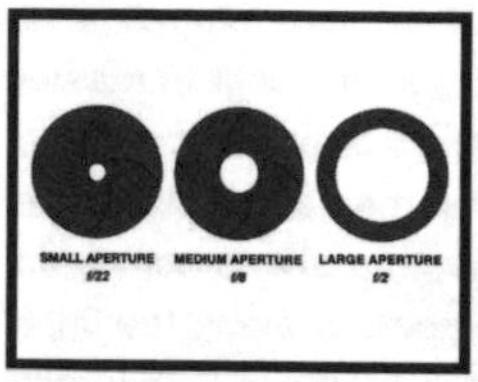

9.4a The aperture can be can be changed to adjust the amount of light entering the camera

▶▶ P.117

9.4b Aperture

▶▶ P.117

9.5 Canon 60D.

VIDEO-CAPABLE DSLR FOR THE MASSES

DSLR cameras that can record video are everywhere, and they're especially popular with filmmakers on a budget. Gone are the days where you'd have to spend upwards of $30,000 for a camcorder with an interchangeable lens system. Now you can do it for less than a thousand bucks with a video-DSLR. The Canon 60D is an older camera that hit the market a couple of years ago, but its video performance and capabilities are still impressive to this day.

It's not hard to find a 60D for under $900 these days, and usually you can find it packaged with a kit lens for around $200 bucks more. Purchasing a ton of extra lenses will obviously bloat your production costs, but good lenses can do wonders to enhance the quality of your video. In addition to its removable lens, the Canon 60D has a full set of manual exposure controls, all of which can be adjusted during recording, and it features cinema-friendly 24p and 30p frame rate options. Be warned, however, the EOS 60D doesn't have a good autofocus mechanism. In fact, it's downright terrible. If you're going to use the 60D to shoot video, you'll have to get accustomed to adjusting focus on the fly manually—that is, using the lens ring. It's not too hard to get the hang of, and it's more akin to what the pros do anyway, but it's something that people should be aware of before they purchase a 60D.

Canon makes a lot of good DSLRs that shoot video, but the EOS 60D gets you the best bang for your buck. It tested nearly as well as the EOS 7D camera, which usually retails for about $500 more than the 60D. Besides, the 60D also has the benefit of an articulated LCD, which is always something that makes the cinematographer's job easier.

PAUSE

CAMERA TIP 3: DEPTH OF FIELD

The depth of field in an image is essentially how much of that image is in focus. More technically it is the distance between the nearest and farthest objects within the frame. The human eye can only focus on one thing at a time—leaving other objects blurry. Good lenses, on the other hand, can keep everything in focus at the same time. A deep depth of field—achieved by setting the camera's lens at a wide angle and using a small aperture—may be exactly what you need in a landscape or establishing shot. But focusing on the subject while blurring out the background—if used properly, it can be a powerful tool. This shallow depth of field can help manipulate the attention of the viewer and reduce background distractions and is achieved by using longer focal lengths and wider apertures. Depth of field is connected to focus, but the two must not be confused. Focus is how 'sharp' an object is within an image, while DOF is the amount the space represented is in focus.

9.6 Depth of Field

▶▶ P.117

AFFORDABLE INTERCHANGEABLE LENS CAMCORDER

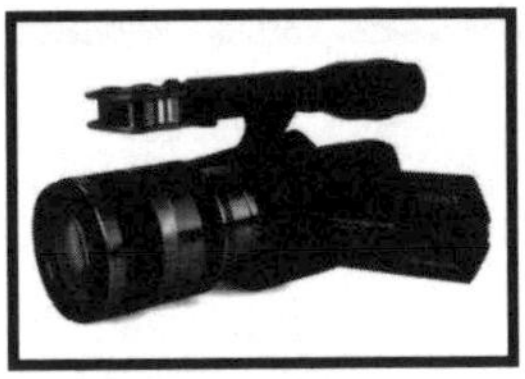

9.7 Sony NEX-VG20.

With the popularity of video-capable DSLRs increasing every day, Sony went out and did something very smart. They made the NEX-VG20; a product that combines the image quality and flexibility of an interchangeable lens camera, with the design and handling of a traditional camcorder.

From the outside, the NEX-VG20 looks just like a camcorder should. It has a rotatable LCD, a large, angled viewfinder, and a right side grip that makes handheld recording an ease. Taking a peak under the hood reveals a product that is almost identical to Sony's line of Alpha NEX digital cameras (the NEX-5N being the most apt comparison). The VG20 has an APS-C image sensor that is much larger than the CMOS chips found in traditional compact camcorders. The camcorder also has an interchangeable lens system that fits any Sony E-mount lens. A few years ago it would have been impossible to find a removable lens camcorder for less than $2,000, but now you can get the NEX-V20 for around $1,600 (body only).

Before you run out the door and swipe your credit card for a new VG20, you should be aware the camcorder does have a few problems. It has no motorized zoom control, so the camcorder is very difficult to wield with one hand. You must use a second hand to turn the zoom ring on the attached lens, and this doesn't always result in the smoothest of zooms. The camcorder also lacks some of the professional color and image controls that we'd expect to see from a model in this price range, but it does get by with the basics.

PAUSE

CAMERA TIP 4: CAMERA MOVES

Camera moves make shots dynamic, but should only be used with good reason—generally to reveal new information.

Pan—The camera itself is fixed – ideally to a tripod for a smooth pan—and is moved horizontally.
Tilt—The up or down movement of the camera, which is again stationary.
Pedestal—The camera itself is moved upwards or downwards.
Dolly—The camera is moved forward or backwards, usually on a set of tracks.
Track—The same principle as a dolly, but moving sideways, parallel to an object.
Crane—Used to follow the action of a subject or for a bird's eye view.
Zoom—Changing the focal length of the camera to make the object appear to be moving towards or away from the viewer.
Angles—A low angle, where the camera shoots close to the ground, can emphasize the power of a character. Conversely a high angle, or shooting from above, can make the same character seem weak. With a Dutch angle, the camera is tilted at a disconcerting angle, often used to show tension or unease (see picture).

9.8 A Dutch Angle
▶▶ P.118

9.9 GoPro Hero2

ACTION SEQUENCE B-ROLL CAMCORDER

We know what you're thinking. It sure looks funny to include a wearable adventure cam on a list of best camcorders for filmmakers, doesn't it? But the GoPro Hero2 is an exceptional piece of technology, and it can be a useful tool for capturing those high-cost action sequences that you have to absolutely get right on the first take. From underwater shots to POV sequences from moving vehicles, the Hero2's versatile design will likely come in handy at some point during your filmmaking process.

Let's be clear, the Hero2 is not something you can use to shoot a feature film, but it's the kind of camcorder you definitely want to have in your arsenal. For $299 bucks, you get the tiny Hero2 camcorder, a waterproof case that lets you travel up to 180-feet below the Earth's surface, and your choice of mounts and attachments.

Planning a few car chase scenes in your indie film? Check out the GoPro Motorsports Edition that comes with a suction cup mount that will hold the Hero2 to the side of a vehicle traveling at speeds up to 150 miles per hour. If you're more likely to be filming shots on the beach, the Surf Edition may be the smarter direction to go. There's also the more generic Outdoor Edition that has a few helmet mounts that are great for point-of-view recording.

PAUSE

CAMERA TIP 5: CAMERA SHOTS

A camera shot is how much of a particular scene is shown in each frame, and shots should be mixed up to create mood and add atmosphere to the story.

Extreme wide shot (EWS) is also known as the establishing shot as it gives the audience perspective as to what is happening in terms of scale, distance, and geographic location in a scene, see picture.
Wide shot (WS) typically shows the whole object or character, placing it context of the surrounding, and is also known as a **long shot.**
Medium shot (MS) often shows a character's upper-body and head and can be used for dialogue. Variations include an **over the shoulder** shot, showing a character or object from the shoulder of a second character, and a **two shot**, which includes two people.
Close-up (CU) tightly frames the character or object, usually showing little or no background. It is often the result of zooming, and can show the importance of what is being framed.
Extreme close-up (ECU) shows only a part of a character or object, filling the screen with the details. For example, an ECU of a victim's mouth in a horror film.

9.10 An Establishing Shot
▶▶ P.118

9.11 Mark Duffield

MARK DUFFIELD – DIRECTOR OF PHOTOGRAPHY (DP)

1. As a cinematographer, what areas of a film are you responsible for?

The cinematographer is responsible for lighting and camera work. The main responsibility and creative input is to create the "look" of the film. This is influenced by the story and mood of the film. The key technical responsibility is to capture the image in the best quality that serves the purpose of the film. High Definition (HD) is now the format of choice for independent filmmakers and also becoming the industry accepted medium. The cinematographer can suggest suitable camera and lighting equipment to serve the productions needs. This is obviously based on the experience of the cinematographer and the budget of the production. However the key responsibility is to work with the director and support their vision. As a cinematographer, I will read the script which, in turn, will influence the choice of camera, lenses, lights, and camera support (tracks, dolly, steadycam) and even crew to help capture the film. I will also suggest certain types of equipment for specific shots, and depending on the budget, suggest equipment that is affordable. The experience of the director may vary and I may also be responsible for blocking the scenes, that is to work out all the camera placements, suggest wide, medium, and close-up shots, and most importantly insure that the scripted scene is covered. Apart from filming the key drama, I would also suggest alternative or extra shots to make the scene work. An example of this would be suggesting close ups or cut-a-ways that can be useful in the editing stage.

2. How long does it take to set up each of these areas?
On average it can take up to 30 minutes to an hour to set up a shot. But this will depend on the scene in the script. What happens is first the director, actors, and cinematographer will block the scene. This involves walking through the scene on the set with the actors loosely performing and the director and cinematographer deciding on what camera angles, lenses and camera support will be needed to film the scene. It is also the time for the cinematographer to work out the lighting positions since it's probably the first time the actors are on set, so a clearer idea is formed on where and how to illuminate the drama. Keep in mind these decisions are rarely fixed as filmmaking requires a lot of fine-tuning and adjustments, usually right up until the camera rolls. Setting up on the first day of any film is slow, usually because everyone, crew and actors are finding their pace and working out how to work with each other as well as getting familiar with the location and equipment.

3. How did you first break into the filmmaking industry?
My first break into filmmaking happened through a friend who was also having his first break. It was our first feature film together as director and cinematographer respectively, but we had worked on many shorts as a team for several years before. You are basically judged on what you create. It is a visual (and sound) medium so your work needs to be seen and if it has potential and perhaps originality, then people in the industry will be keen to work with you.

4. Describe your average working day as a DP.
The average working day as a DP usually starts with blocking the scene, as described, with the actors and the director. The actors would go to make-up and costume and the director to deal with other aspects of the film. This would give me time to set up lights and the camera, usually with the help of assistants, gaffers, sparks, etc. Once we are all set, the filming happens. Depending on the scene, this process is repeated throughout the day. The average day usually starts early and lasts about ten hours.

5. What equipment do you prefer to use? And what is the most basic equipment someone can "get away with" on a low-budget short film?
I would say the preference for equipment can depend on the budget and scale of the production. In the HD format the preferred camera for independent filmmaking presently is the RED camera or the Canon 5D DSLR. If your budget is low, then a Canon 7D is best. The 2010 Winner at the Sundance Film Festival was a feature film called *Like Crazy* that was entirely shot on a Canon 7D.

6. How has technology changed the way a DP works, and what are your thoughts on this?
The new digital technology is giving much more creative freedom and an endless pallet that was not available before in the film world. It is possible to film using a small lightweight camera that captures true HD images now. This means that cameras can go anywhere and not be too obvious, so location filming can be much freer and more creative. It also means you don't need such a big support crew nor any crew, which may help if you

have a tight budget or don't want to appear as the "filmmaking travelling circus". The digital pallet is allowing DPs to create a whole range of new cinematic and stylish looks that were not available before or expensive to achieve in film. Trust me, I shot eight feature films on 35mm and grading was always a slow and expensive process. Now it's a press of a keyboard. I totally embrace the digital technology, and I'm no computer expert by any means, but it has allowed me to be visually creative in ways I could have only imagined a few years ago.

7. Does a good knowledge of still photography help cinematographers compose each scene?
It helps if a cinematographer has a good understanding of composition. And most cinematographers naturally have a background in still photography. I would also say a good understanding of drama and interest in actors can also help compose a scene as most films have people as the key subject, so an understanding of movement is essential.

8. What mistakes that can be avoided do you see most in people's first films?
The first mistakes people make with their first film is usually the script is not ready. The second is usually the edit is too long.

9. Are you a member of a trade organization such as the British or American Society of Cinematographers, and is it worthwhile?
No I am not a member of a trade organization such as the British or American Society of Cinematographers. I can't say if it's worth it.

10. You have moved into directing—how does this compare to DPing, and is this a normal career move?
I have directed two feature films in which I was also DP. This was a normal transition for me and has given me a lot of creative freedom. As a DP, I am working with and supporting the creative choices of a director, but when I am doing both roles there is a lot more personal satisfaction. I have no objection to working with a DP on future projects and my visual passion would make that creative working partnership very dynamic. As a career move I am keen to continue directing but will also be interested in DPing a project if it interests me.

11. With so many technical aspects, is film school essential or can people "learn on the job"?
Film school is great IF you can get in and pay the fee! And film school is great for education, motivation, inspiration, networking, and facilities. But it is also possible to "learn on the job". Remember you are judged by the physical evidence of your work. Nicolas Winding Refn was rejected by film school in Denmark and went on to independently make *Pusher* and *Drive*.

12. What advice do you have for aspiring DPs?

Watch films, watch life, read scripts, go to locations, practice lighting, and make films.

9.12 Mark Duffield in action

▶▶ P.118

Mark Duffield is a writer, cinematographer, and director. With many shorts and eight features to his credit, he won the 2006 Best Cinematographer award at the Slam Dunk Festival for the feature film *Butterfly Man*. He wrote, shot, and directed *Ghost of Mae Nak* in Thailand, the feature distributed by Tartan DVD for UK and US release. He reprised those roles in *Demon* (2013), a Gothic love story filmed entirely in London. Mark also works for Drama Centre London Central, Saint Martin's College, where he produces and supervises the MA and BA final year short films.

STOP

9.2 Salt flats in Uyuni, Bolivia pictured, adhering to the Rule of Thirds

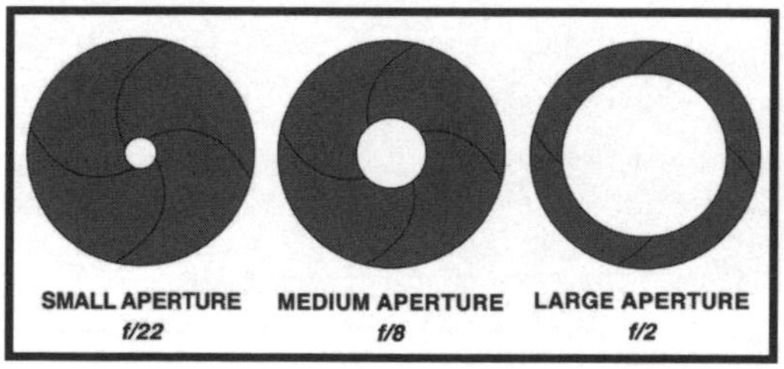

9.4a The aperture can be changed to adjust the amount of light entering the camera Image

9.4b Aperture

9.6 Depth of Field

9.8 A Dutch Angle makes Easter celebrations in Ecuador disconcerting

9.10 An establishing shot, such as this image of the Serengeti National Park in Tanzania, sets the scene...

9.12 Mark Duffield on set focusing the 5D

START

CHAPTER 10

Lights

However good the script, artful the storyboard, diligent the producer, whoever you have on board in the editing suite, if the lighting is not right not even the best camera in the world will be able to make up for it.

With a big crew comes a gaffer, an electrician in charge of all things to do with light and helped by an assistant known as the best boy. He will know how the sun will affect each shot at different times of the day, set up a range of specialist lights and use equipment such as gels and barn doors and computer programs to create different effects and in turn the mood of each scene.

Without a specialist on board, good lighting can still be achieved following some basic principles. When inside with no external light, you can have a large amount of control over how you illuminate what you are shooting.

10.1 Key light directly in front of character

THREE-POINT LIGHTING

Three-point lighting is the standard used across film and still photography. By using a **key light, fill light**, and **back light**, any subject can be illuminated with complete control of shadow and mood.

10.2 Key light at 45° to character

Key Light

The key light is the primary light source in a scene. If this happens to be outside and daytime, the sun will almost certainly be the key light. If it is inside, the key light can be placed anywhere, and its position and intensity dictates the mood of the entire picture.

Avoid placing the key light directly in front of the talent as the resulting shot will lack depth, and the subject's shadow may also be visible see figure 10.1. It's also uncomfortable for an actor to look directly at a light for a long period of time and if he is wearing glasses, the key light will be reflected back into the lens.

10.3 Key light at 90° to character

As you move the key light from directly in front of the subject to the side, less of it becomes lit and more is in shadow, figure 10.2, making the mood more dramatic. More of the surface detail is also visible. By 90° figure 10.3, the subject is half light and half dark and even surface detail becomes more

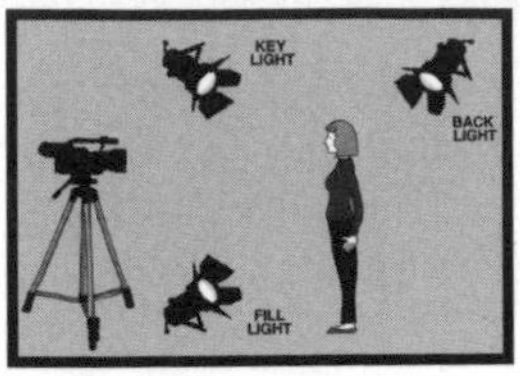

10.4 Three-point lighting

▶▶ P.127

apparent. This effect could be used in a scene where the character has a difficult decision to make.

Changing the key light's vertical position also makes a huge difference to the mood of the scene. If the key light is at a 90° vertical angle, or directly above the subject, the top of the head will be very bright, while the face and body will be in shadows. This generally produces an unflattering result, but could also be used to represent a spiritual awakening. Shining a light from below is uncommon in everyday life, and is often used to portray a character as evil or powerful.

Fill Light

Fill light is to lighten, but not necessarily eliminate, shadows created by the key light. It is usually placed on the opposite side of the key light. Using a reflector board to bounce key light back into the shadow area is also possible.

Back Light

The back light defines the edges of the subject and separates them from the background. The backlight helps draw the viewer's eye to the actress and creates depth in the composition. Adding a fourth light just on the background, usually a different color, can further distinguish the subject.

Lighting Equipment

On a Hollywood blockbuster a team of people have access to endless types of lights, stands, and gels. On most shorts making do is often the key. Having said that, lighting equipment, both to buy and rent, is generally good value and many technical items can be replaced with things around the home.

10.5 Barn Doors

COMMON LIGHTING TERMS AND ACCESSORIES

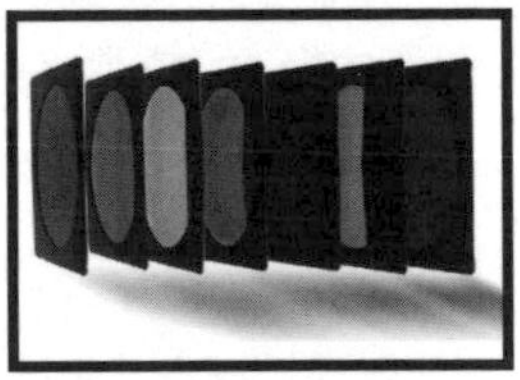

10.6 Gels

10.7 Honeycombs

Ambient: General (and often undesirable) lighting of the visual environment.
Barndoors: Metal flaps to shape a beam of light from a fixture, and stop it spilling into areas where it is not wanted.
Beam: A cone of light emitted by a Luminaire.
Burning Up: When parts of a scene or subject are overly bright, or washed out.
Color Rendering: The way surface colors appear under a certain light source.
Color Rendering Index (CRI): Measures how good a light source is at reproducing colors of certain objects faithfully. It is measured out of 100, and 85 or over can be considered good color rendering.
Cool: Light, gels, or subjects in the blue-green region of the spectrum.
Cross Light: The illumination of a subject from both sides.
Diffuse Light: Diffuse light is given off from large luminescent surfaces, producing a soft, even illumination.
Diffusing Lens: A lens used to widen the distribution of light from a source so as to increase its diffusion.

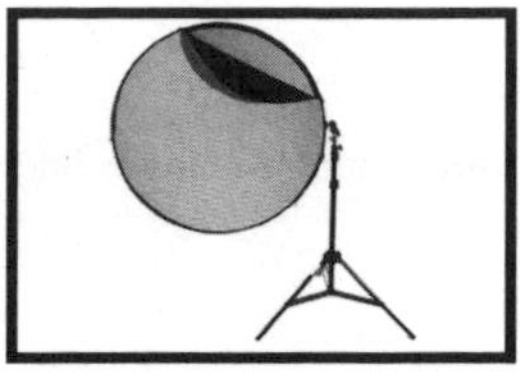

10.8 Reflector

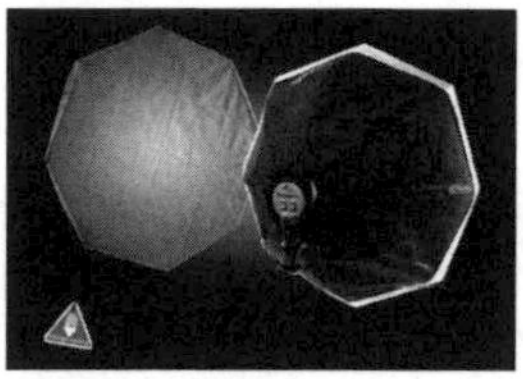

10.9 Softbox

10.10 Umbrella

Dimming: The ability to change the luminous flux of a light source. Dimming produces a great visual experience and adds flexibility to any scene.
Gels: Filters made out of a thin, heat-resistant material to alter the color of your light instruments, and are available in a huge range of colors and sizes. See iPhone app Gel Swatch Library which lists over 1,000 gel color filters.
Honeycombs: Deliver a small, soft-edged pool of light to add emphasis, for example to emphasize high cheekbones. They can also be used as a backlight that doesn't produce lens flare.
Illumination: The process of lighting.
Indirect lighting: Illumination of a point or surface where the light arrives after reflecting from a surface onto the area being lit, for example, lighting a desk using an uplight.
Luminaire: A light fixture or fitting that is an electrical device used to create artificial light by use of an electric lamp.
Luminance: The brightness of a surface that emits light, either as a light source or by transmission or reflection.
Reflection: The ability of surfaces to reflect light; the ratio of the luminous flux reflected to the luminous flux incident on it. Reflection can be specular or diffuse.
Reflector: Also known as a Bounce Card, is a reflective surface used to redirect light.
Scrims: pieces of metal screening that lower the amount of light without changing the angle or color.
Soft box: An enclosure around a bulb comprising reflective side and back walls and a diffusing material at the front of the light to create even and diffused light.
Spot lighting: Light fittings with light distribution that can be directed at any desired point by turning and swiveling.
Umbrella Reflector: Another type of reflector used to diffuse light and also as a glare shield and shade.
Wattage: The power requirement of the device being used, such as a lamp. It refers to the electricity being consumed, not the light output.[1]

RAINDANCE FILM FESTIVAL TIP

5 TOP TIPS FOR LIGHTING ON A LOW BUDGET

1) Recce

Your DP and director need to visit each location you are utilizing at the appropriate time of day for the shoot. Checking available light sources and reflective surfaces is important to planning your lighting.

2) Cast a Shadow

Lighting is as much about shadow as it is illumination, this is where both atmosphere and relief is created. Hard direct light creates strong shadows, soft diffused lights almost no shadow.

3) Conceal
Make sure you have heatproof material such as "black wrap" and aluminum flags for shaping the light and blocking unnecessary "spill".

4) Reflect
Bouncing light off different types of reflective surface will give a lot more control and texture than just pointing lights directly at the subject and set. There are many purpose-built reflectors such as the Lastolite range and even Balloons used to redirect large lights such as the Sun.

5) Know your limits
Lighting requires power and most domestic and small industrial supplies have a load limit. Your gaffer or lighting tech needs to know how much can be safely plugged in and err on the side of caution. You don't need lights going pop or worse blowing an un-reachable fuse-box in the middle of your lovely shot.

Chris Thomas

PAUSE

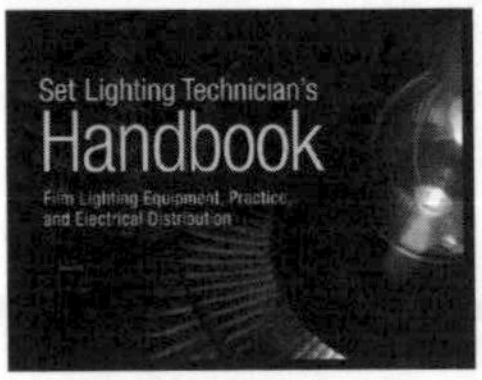

10.11 Set Lighting Technician's Handbook

▶▶ P.127

10.12 Motion Picture and Video Lighting

▶▶ P.127

FURTHER READING

Set Lighting Technician's Handbook, Fourth Edition: Film Lighting Equipment, Practice, and Electrical Distribution (2010)
By Harry Box

A comprehensive hands-on manual that covers the day-to-day practices, equipment, and tricks of the trade essential to anyone doing motion picture lighting, including the lamp operator, rigging crew, gaffer, best boy, or director of photography. This handbook offers a wealth of practical technical information, useful techniques, as well as aesthetic discussions.

Motion Picture and Video Lighting, Second Edition (2007)
By Blain Brown

An indispensable guide to film and video lighting. Written by the author of the industry bible *Cinematography*, this book explores technical, aesthetic, and practical aspects of lighting for film and video. It will show you not only how to light, but why. Written by an experienced professional, this comprehensive book explores light and color theory, equipment, and techniques to make every scene look its best.

Lighting for Digital Video and Television, Third Edition (2010)
By John Jackman

Enhance the visual quality of your motion pictures and digital videos with a solid understanding of lighting fundamentals. This complete course in digital video

10.13 Lighting for Digital Video and Television

▶▶ P.127

lighting begins with how the human eye and the camera process light and color, progresses through the basics of equipment and setups, and finishes with practical lessons on how to solve common problems. Filled with clear illustrations and real-world examples that demonstrate proper equipment use, safety issues, and staging techniques, *Lighting for Digital Video* presents readers with all they need to create their own visual masterpieces.

10.14 Peter Carrier

PETE CARRIER: GAFFER

www.carrier-media.co.uk

1. What exactly do you do?

I'm a Gaffer and the Gaffer works alongside the Director of Photography turning the theoretical design of a scene into reality. Together we will look at storyboard and graphical representations, pre-visualizations and lighting plots. The script will drive many of DP's decisions indicating perhaps that the scene is between two people sat in the front of a car, immediately this raises questions: will the vehicle be on a low loader travelling or will it be parked? Decisions which in theory would be made by the director alone will of course be influenced by schedule, the time of day, and the weather. Prior to speaking to the DP I would be thinking ahead and expect that we would shoot a wide of the car in its location, something through the windshield, then close ups of the two characters. I might also expect and allow for close ups of business inside the car (gun in the glove box kind of thing). These decisions are ultimately made by the Director of Photography, however I would want to have likely suspects standing by, not at the back of a truck.

2. And what other members of the crew do you work most closely with?

The electrical department will often be the largest single body of staff and will often have the greatest amount of equipment. Within our own team we will have a Best Boy handling the office, staff, daily equipment,and consumables, keeping an eye on the advanced schedule, working closely with me to ensure things are prepared when necessary, inline with the schedule order to keep the machine running. We will have a team of electricians working with us on the day—the shooting crew, then dailies and pre-rigging crew. Sparks may drift between those roles as necessary, depending on the scale of the location and the work to be undertaken.

Larger outfits will have a rigger attached to the department and there will be those responsible for specific roles within our team such as drivers or those with certificates for operating specific machinery. As a team we will work closely with the camera department, but we will also be involved with supplying power to any department that needs it, from simple things like providing a large flag to stop reflections on monitors all the way through to answering the concerns of crew when we encounter unusual electrical issues on location. The schedule is all-important and I work closely with the First Assistant Director who will be recording meticulously our progress through the shooting script and the day's schedule.

3. Describe an "average day".
I have found a neat little market for myself, which is perhaps slightly out of the mainstream. I'm a Gaffer who chooses to supply equipment and on the majority of jobs my clients will take me and my gear along with my own staff. That said I'm just as comfortable travelling without. A pretty average day will begin at five or five-thirty in the morning and will involve the short journey to my secure storage to load up the equipment for the day, followed by a drive to the Unit Base for the day for a spot of breakfast. With a typical call time of eight in the morning, we will crack on with the first set up of the day. Most UK productions run a standard 10-hour working day which includes a 1-hour lunch break (unpaid). Some productions prefer to run a continuous day and in that case the working day drops to 9 hours, although that must contain a 20 minute paid break. Ordinarily, I would expect to be finishing at around six-forty-five; the theory being that we're out of the door by seven, seven-fifteen therefore not incurring any overtime. Then it's back on the road and back to the lockup for me while my sparks will disband, ready to do it all over again the next day. The joy of my working life is that no two jobs are the same.

4. What was your first job and how did you get where you are today?
I suppose I should start by saying I began my life as an electrician in 1987 undergoing a four-year apprenticeship. I also worked at a stage lighting company in my spare time during my early years. I was lucky my very first job in the film industry was with Mr Roger Simmons back in 2002 on a short film. I worked unpaid, over a couple of weekends. I'm happy to say 10 years on I still work with Roger when he's back in the United Kingdom.

5. How has the equipment changed since you have been in the industry?
I would love to say there has been a revolution in technology during the ten years I've been in film and television; however when it comes to lighting equipment the pace has been slow. The world of camera equipment has been turned on its head by the introduction of domestic and "prosumer" cameras that offer the dream of stunning picture quality on a modest budget. While I'm sure there are people better placed to comment on this technology, for my part this has had a dramatic effect on budgets with the impression given by those selling the products that one can shoot with little or no lighting.

Of course the camera will record an image but I think there's some way to go convincing less experienced producers of the need to think about lighting at an early stage. I'm seeing a lot more LED panels and there are a few LED Fresnels knocking about, however their cost still prohibits them being used en-masse. The amount of power used on even the most modest production can be eye watering. I look forward to a day when one could light a whole project from a single 13A socket. This will affect the industry perhaps seeing the end of large scale use of lighting trucks with generators on board, but the craft will remain the same.

6. What does your job entail while shooting outdoors?
When in a studio we have almost complete control over the space and perhaps budget alone is our only limiting factor. Often films, drama, commercials will be shot on location and there are a great many more factors to be taken into account, including public safety concern for property, greater time constraints and the interests of other departments within our own crew with whom I will be sharing the same space and providing facilities.

As always it is the script that drives our activities when shooting outdoors and to some degree the type of shot, so a scene that includes a character running across a car park or driving on a motorway will be lit by the grace of God. Different Directors of Photography will have different ways of looking at exterior lighting. We're blessed in the United Kingdom with an atmosphere that on many occasions gives us a soft light source from the sun. In America with clear blue skies there is a need for large banks of 18K just to deal with the contrast and get some shape into the characters. When shooting exteriors, I would expect to be using large silks perhaps a half or quarter silk on a 20 by 20 frame and a 20 by 20 ultra bounce. I might expect to have a lamp like a 2.5k to pop a little something into the eyes of the actors on a sunny day. This of course will vary from shot-to-shot and will change by the minute as per the weather. The inexperienced may assume that the electricians have an easy day when shooting exteriors, but we can be just as busy as during an interior scene and of course the sun is roaring across the sky coming in and out of cloud which may require the setting up of a minute by minute weather station with a person able to see the clouds and provide up to date information on when cloud cover is due, and the length of time it will be present. Electrical power for monitors, the Grip, hair and make-up along with battery charging for camera. Often it will be necessary to provide a floppy flag for the monitor and additional sandbags as there is a danger of gusty wind at any time.

7. What is the minimum equipment a DP on a short film with a small budget can "get away with"?
I'm often asked what the bare minimum equipment is for production and understand that where budgets are modest, overall cost is a great concern. Personally I feel the gear that I carry on my truck is the bare minimum, that is perhaps more a sales pitch than useful advice. I suppose if budget were your first priority we might look at the shooting of an exterior with nothing more than a bit of Silver/White Poly. You could shoot many interior scenes using the available light and a small box of practical lamps, along with 2 3 4 foot for bank Kino-flo, 2 3 2 foot four bank Kino Flo and a 4 lamp dedo kit with individual dimmers.

8. Lighting is a huge field of knowledge and extremely technical. What are the most common mistakes first-time filmmakers make in relation to lighting, and how can they be avoided?
Sadly the lighting department is often overlooked and whereas credits on short films for Director of Photography or other department heads are valued, the role of spark does not carry the same cachet and are generally thought of in much the same way as driving vans and the like. I have joined productions as a favor to friends during a production and found things in

disarray with damaged equipment occasioning dangerous practice by the hobby filmmaker. The potential for injury or death is never more than in the Electrical Department with intense heat, mains voltage, trip and fall hazards. It is alarming to see a group of trainees muddling through, trying to teach each other with no experience or qualified persons onset.

9. What advice do you have for a student hoping to become a "spark"?
Maths and English form the basis of communicating ideas and thoughts and are both vital. I would urge students to get what they can for free at school, saving them the need to go back later in life. If you're looking to become an electrician, a degree is not necessary, although I would recommend going on some media course in order to get some basic knowledge. I would then look to a rental house, many of whom have opportunities for trainees or apprentices. Once there, you might be expected to work for two years in the yard gaining experience and knowledge of equipment and the vitally important testing practices before having the opportunity to prove themselves out in the field. I've been lucky over the years, I've seen cars blown up, police shootouts, fist fights, horrible murders—all with the reassuring shout of "cut" at the end.

10. What is the most exciting film project you have ever worked on and why?
I'm going to give two examples because I can't separate them. I was part of the build crew for *Dark Shadows*, the Tim Burton film working on the construction of the biggest set I've ever been on, the Collins Port set down at Pinewood. I sat on the dockside, my job for the day to wire up a number of little boats in the harbor. I looked up the street past the cannery, the shops, the cinema, the rows of houses all built on a massive scaffold staging and watched as a 1970s American police car negotiated its way past a pick up truck; taking just a moment out of a busy day to enjoy the sun and appreciate my life. I've been a very lucky boy. I worked as part of the construction crew and shooting crew on *Moon,* directed by Duncan Jones. Once the final wall section was in place, the only practical entrance point was the air lock on to the most inclusive film set there has ever been. I was lucky to work with the model unit for that same film. Happy days.

STOP

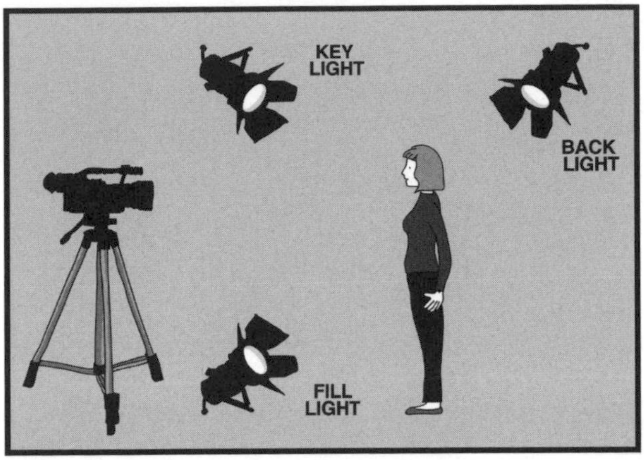

10.4 Three point light

10.11 Harry Box

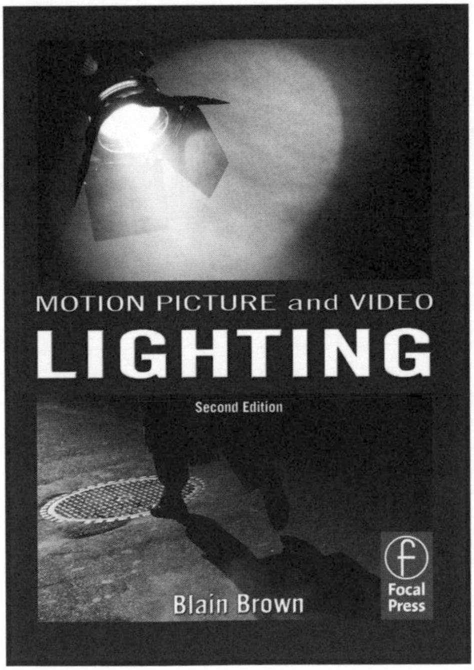

10.12 Blain Brown

10.13 John Jackman

START

CHAPTER 11

Sound

Before the turn of the twentieth century, William Kennedy-Laurie Dickson was experimenting with sound (see Chapter 31: A Brief History of Short Films). His sound version of the Kinetoscope was called the Kinetophone and, to the continuous one-reeler peep-show, viewers could hear a soundtrack through two rubber ear tubes.[1]

Dickson continued to experiment with sound at the Edison laboratories and by 1913 had devised a system to synchronize the picture on screen with sound played on a 5½ inch celluloid cylinder record. This was achieved by connecting the projector at one end of the theater by a long pulley to the phonograph at the other. Edison financed 19 talkies over a two-year period, but the system never worked that well, the film and the record were often out of sync and Edison finally abandoned sound to continue making silent films.

THE BEGINNING OF SOUND FILMS

The Jazz Singer—starring Al Jolson and released by Warner Brothers in 1927—is generally considered the beginning of sound films, although it was Orson Welles a generation later who grasped the full potential of sound and introduced a variety of new innovations. With his long experience in radio, he came to film knowing instinctively that the soundtrack could play an equal role in film narration and give balance to the three-legged stool of dialogue, music, and visuals: footsteps on the stairs, a key turning in a lock, a ticking clock, or a ticking bomb. In a Welles' film, for the first time, sound was used to warn the audience of what to expect before the visuals, an expectation that was then confirmed or, in counterpoint, surprised the audience with the unexpected.

11.1 *Apocalypse Now* (1979)

▶▶ P.138

When he came to make *Citizen Kane* in 1941, his use of light and shadow drew on the expressionistic styles of filmmakers in Germany and Russia, but it is the intricate multi-layered sound track that tells us more about mood and ambience, the hollow echo of footsteps in the monumental library; the boom of a steam boat landing; after Kane strikes his wife Susan in a tent on the beach, over the icy silence that follows a woman is heard laughing hysterically in the distance.

Welles developed what became known as the lightning-mix. In linking montage sequences by a continuous soundtrack, he was able to join what would have been rough cuts into a smooth narrative. For example, the audience witnesses Kane grow from a child into a young man in just two shots. As Kane's guardian gives him the famous sledge and wishes him a "Merry Christmas," we fade to a shot of Kane 15 years later, where the phrase is completed: "and a Happy New Year." In this instance, the continuity of the soundtrack, not the images on screen, creates a seamless narrative structure.[2]

THE BIRTH OF SOUND DESIGN

Although sound men after Welles began to play a prominent role in post, the term sound design to cover all non-compositional elements of a film only came into being when it was coined by Walter Murch[3] during his marathon 12 months in the sound studios on *Apocalypse Now*, which won his first Oscar in 1979. We can recall Colonel Kilgore's classic line, "I love the smell of napalm in the morning." Of course, we can't *smell* napalm in the cinema, but our senses are pricked by the cold gnawing whir of helicopters, the sound allowing us to *feel* the presence of napalm.

Similarly, Tom Tykwer's 2007 film of Patrick Süskind's *Perfume* is a story about the world's greatest originator of scents. The visuals alone could not convey the sensation of fragrances wafting on the air, but the sound of liquids pouring from glass vials, unguents heating in cauldrons and the extravagant intakes of breath taken by Ben Whishaw as the murderer Jean-Baptiste Grenouille allow us to imagine the secret perfume he is creating.

To return to Walter Murch, although he is best known for *Apocalypse Now*, it was his work on *The Conversation* that had first elevated the status of film sound to a new level, recognized by his first Oscar nomination in 1974. Gene Hackman as Harry Caul is a surveillance expert who can record any conversation between two people anywhere. Caul's obsession with taping, analyzing and interpreting sound is part of his being and in the intense, fixated Caul it is easy to imagine Walter Murch looking back from the mirror's reflection.

The term sound design came originally from the theater, but Walter Murch in film established the fact that the sound designer played a creative role equal to that of the editor, DP, and art director, and the credit duly appeared for the first time on *Apocalypse Now*. Coppola's 2001 *Apocalypse Now Redux* has 49 extra minutes added to the cut, and if you pump up the volume on your DVD player you get a pretty good idea of Murch's contribution to the finished film.

Murch assisted in reconstructing an old print of *Touch of Evil*, producing the sound designs Welles had noted in the shooting script before technology was up to realizing them. Murch's achievements in sound were fully recognized in 1997 when he came away from the Academy Awards with a double Oscar for editing and sound on *The English Patient*.

SOPHISTICATED SOUNDTRACKS

Before stereo, film sound was of such low fidelity only dialogue and occasional sound effects were practical. The greater dynamic range of the new systems, coupled with the ability to *place* sounds to the sides and behind the audience, required more creative decisions and sound professionals to make the most of the improved technology.[4]

The sound designer's role can be compared with the role of supervising sound editor; many sound designers use both titles interchangeably. The role of supervising sound editor, or sound supervisor, developed in parallel with the role of sound designer. As the demand for more sophisticated soundtracks on film grew, the supervising sound editor became the head of large sound departments with a staff of dozens of sound editors expected to realize a complete sound job with a fast turnaround. It is far from universal, but the role of sound supervisor comes from the original role of the sound editor, that of a technician required to complete a film, but having little creative authority. Sound designers, on the other hand, are expected to be creative, and their role is a generalization of the other creative department heads.

Just as the Internet has changed short-film distribution, the web has streamlined the work of sound designers. Rather than trawling through record stores and sound libraries, or creating their own effects, the designer has a virtually unlimited choice of crisper, more "believable" sounds at his fingertips. On my short film *Greta May*, I sat in the editing suite at True Media in Soho's Golden Square with Tony Appleton listening to thousands of doorbells and telephone ring tones trying to decide what would fit the noir mood of those moments. We had a perfectly acceptable location recording of a taxi door closing and the taxi pulling away. We listened to dozens more on the computer speakers and when we found one that sounded most suitable, we grabbed it without shame.

Computer technology has similarly revolutionized music composition and a sound designer, particularly on a short film, will often assist the composer on the electroacoustic portion of the composition.

ONLINE SOUND LIBRARIES

When searching for the right sound effect, Stephan Möbius of pdsounds has some great advice: "We *look* for information but seldom listen, because our visual senses are dominating. We like photography, don't we? With pdsounds we try to shift our mode of perception for a moment and concentrate on the information that sounds give us. Do some *phonography*. Sounds have qualities and characteristics, and they evoke reactions as much as pictures do. But we rarely really listen to the stories they tell."

Almost any sound, from mixing spices in a small ceramic bowl with a metal spoon to interference during an Internet phone conversation can be found online. Many are free, either outright or available under creative commons licenses (see box in Chapter 13: Music), while others demand a small fee. Here is a selection:

FreeSound—www.freesound.org
Pdsounds—www.pdsounds.org
Soungle—www.soungle.com
Sound Dogs—www.sounddogs.com

WHAT IS SOUND?

Essentially, sound is longitudinal waves moving through the air. A simple way to think about it is to imagine a stone falling into water. The ripples in the water move in a similar way to sound. When one of the "ripples" reaches a human ear, air molecules hit the eardrum, causing it to vibrate. This vibration is converted into electrical signals that are interpreted by our brain. Short waves of sound are interpreted as being high-pitched, such as wind chimes. Longer waves are sensed as low-pitched, such as foghorns. The number of sound waves occurring every second refers to the frequency, and is measured in hertz, or Hz. Humans can generally hear between 20 and 20,000 Hz. Lower frequency waves are less directional than higher ones, and frequencies below 150 Hz have minimal detectable directional information.

High-pitched sound waves are closer together (above in diagram), while the peaks of low-pitched waves are further apart.

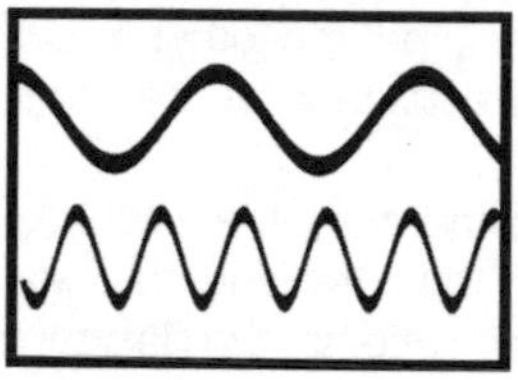

11.2 Soundwaves

RECORDING SOUND

Audio can be one of the greatest challenges for first-time filmmakers. Ironically, the better the job you do with sound, the less it will be noticed. However, many professionals agree that sound is more important than the picture. Viewers can accept shaky footage—think of *The Blair Witch Project*, or a number of viral YouTube videos—but the moment the sound is bad people change the channel. It is therefore essential to capture crisp dialogue while shooting. While libraries of sounds are easily attainable, the quality of the recording of the dialogue of actors is difficult and expensive, sometimes impossible, to be helped in post.

GEAR

Moving the camera away from the subject can be an interesting visual experience. However, if the microphone is attached to the camera, the sound will also become quieter—generally a terrible audio experience. For this reason, the mic should always be a constant—and close—distance from the subject, and to achieve this an off-camera mic is necessary. Mics have varying pickup patterns that interpret and help to record sound differently. Here is a run-through of different mics and related equipment, and their uses in recording sound:

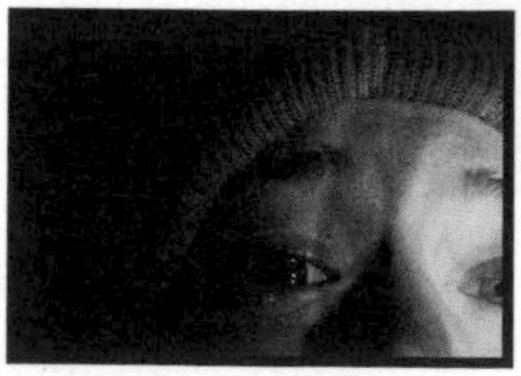

11.3 *The Blair Witch Project* (1999)

▶▶ P.138

Omnidirectional Mic: Picks up sound equally from all directions, so isn't generally that useful for recording dialogue, but is great for atmosphere recording when you don't want to on focus on a specific sound.

11.4 Cardioid mic

Cardioid mic: Picks up sound in a single direction focusing towards the front of the microphone. The name is due to the pickup pattern being heart-shaped (see diagram).
Supercardioid mic: Also known as a **shotgun** mic, is even more directional, picking up sound from the front of the mic, and rejecting the side and rear signals. They are used on booms held above the actors and are great for isolating sound from a single source.
Lavalier mic: Tiny, usually battery-powered radio mic that can be clipped onto the clothing of the actors. Great for picking up dialogue when actors are facing away from the camera.
Boom: A long pole held by the boom operator with a microphone attached to the end.
Wind jammer, or baffle: Covers the mic to protect it from wind.
Mixing board: Or just mixer, controls the volume levels and balance of several sounds.
Recording device: Until fairly recently most film sets used DAT or Digital Audio Tape, although hard disk-based recorders are now the norm on short films.

CLAPPERBOARD

The best-recognized element of filmmaking is simply made up of a slate and a clapper. The slate contains the information relevant to the shot that is about to be filmed, as well as the date, film title and the names of the director and DP. In bigger films, it is generally the 2nd AC, or assistant cameraman, who uses the clapperboard. Traditionally, this visual information, as well as the aural cue—the actual sound of the "clap"—was used to help synchronize the picture and sound in post. Today the **digital slate** performs the same function, but without the need for the "clap". The camera records the time on the board in the same way, and as the camera is synchronized with a timer, the editor can match it with the same point in the recording.

PAUSE

FILM SOUND STEREOTYPES

Sound in film often falls foul of logical flaws. Below are some examples, with a fuller list available at www.filmsound.org/cliche:

- **All bicycles have bells (that sound).**
- **Doors always squeak.**
- **Environmental sound to a shoot with the window open, are always next to a schoolyard or a construction-site.**
- **When a character pulls out a knife, even from his pants, you hear a sound of metal brushing metal.**
- **All kisses need to sound sloppy and wet.**
- **Blood will always squish when oozing from a wound.**
- **People never answer the door until the doorbell or knocking has sounded at least three times.**
- **Whenever you see a dramatic natural landscape you hear an eagle.**

11.5 Roland Heap

ROLAND HEAP: SOUND

www.rolandheap.com

1. What is your job exactly?

I've worked in a variety of roles in film sound, but started my career working at Abbey Road primarily recording film scores. We would receive a copy of the film without the final sound on it to work on; listening to the rough offline sound and then hearing the difference when the film was fully mixed triggered my fascination with the whole process of sound for picture. I left the studios and spent a while working as an assistant to a recordist on location on a TV series. The equipment and techniques had similarities with those used in the studios but also many differences—I learnt more in that short period than I could have imagined.

I moved on to doing some boom operating and before long I started working as a fully-fledged sound recordist. After a few years, I began looking at the process of sound post-production, doing sound editing and design. I now spend the majority of my time mixing and supervising the sound design for feature films.

For the purposes of this interview though, I'm going to focus primarily on my role as sound recordist, as I think it's the most important part of film sound for new filmmakers to understand.

2. Describe your average day

Getting great sound on location is all about good preparation—so ideally, long before I arrive on set, I'll have reccied the location thoroughly with the director, establishing whether there are any sound issues that need dealing with, such as nearby traffic, flight paths or even animals. One of the most common things one has to deal with, especially on low-budget shoots, is poor acoustics—if a room is really reverberant it is very difficult to get good-sounding results as you can't effectively remove reverb later.

On a shoot day I'll arrive well in advance of the start of the shoot, get my trolley or bag set up and test all my radio microphones. Radio interference is different in every location so you need to do this well before you start rolling. I try to allow enough time to have a good chat with the rest of the crew about the planned set-ups—striking a good working relationship with your colleagues is essential.

Every take presents a different challenge—there is almost always a good way to record a scene, but sometimes this will involve a lot of thinking on your feet. Many shots can be recorded very well with a single well-placed microphone, but for more complex scenes you'll need to use multiple boom, radio, and plant microphones (hidden in props on the set). A good sound recordist will have learned to spot the difference. You need to be able to work very efficiently as it's not good to keep the crew waiting. The best recordists will spot issues long before they become problems and will have fixed them by the time the camera rolls. During the shooting day I also try to keep everything organized and tidy. Labeling and keeping good notes as you go is essential. You also need to take great care of the kit, making sure it's well maintained and presented.

3. What attracted you to this side of the film industry?

Location sound can be one of the most thankless roles on a film set. The bulk of the rest of the crew are focusing on controlling the minutiae of exactly what is inside the frame—the sound recordist has to focus on that, but also has to deal with everything that is occurring outside of the frame

4. Who do you work most closely with?

A sound recordist works most closely with their boom operator. The most important thing about location sound is to ensure your microphone is pointing in the direction of the mouth of the speaking actor. A good boom operator is the person who enables this. They will have incredible stamina, fitness and poise, will know exactly who is going to speak when and will have a near-psychic link to the recordist.

5. What equipment do you usually use on a low-budget film?

It doesn't make much difference if it is a low-budget film or a large-budget film—when I'm recording I'll usually take much the same equipment. In my experience, on low-budget films the requirements are quite often even greater than on a big-budget film—the schedules are tighter, the set-up times are shorter and the shots are just as ambitious—so I think trying to achieve all that with less kit is a really bad idea.

That said, if you're a filmmaker starting out and you can't afford to pay a professional sound recordist, it is possible to get great sound without having a complete kit—but you must be willing to compromise on some shooting decisions. If you can only afford a simple boom and a recorder, you have to make sure you plan your shots so that you can always get a boom microphone close to your actor when they are delivering lines. Even a relatively cheap microphone will sound passable if it is positioned very close to your actor's mouth. Radio microphones can be great problem-solvers, but are difficult to use well—especially the cheaper ones. A boom microphone in a good position should always be the preferred option.

6. Do you have your own kit and is this necessary?

I do and, for me, as a professional recordist, it is. The reason for this is quite simply that it would be unaffordable and logistically impossible for me to hire the range of kit I require to be able to cope with unpredictable shoots, given that I am doing this every day. However, it has taken me years to build up and refine my kit piece by piece. This now saves me money, but if you are a filmmaker starting your career, then hiring all your sound kit is likely to be your best option. Professional microphones can be hired for a few pounds a day and will always sound better and be more robust and versatile than their cheap counterparts. So, you will generally be able to access better kit through hiring than buying. Buying a cheap microphone is always a false economy—and don't even consider using the microphone built into a camera!

7. What are your career highlights to date?

It's hard to pull out individual highlights. The most exciting project is always the one I'm currently working on and each film presents a new set of challenges to be overcome. That said I love travelling, so the films I've worked on abroad have been amazing—recording leopards in Thailand for an Indian thriller was certainly a highlight. I also love working on projects that have sound requirements for which you can't rely on sound libraries—recording cars, guns, and animals are especially exciting.

8. How important is sound to a film?
Turning this around, how would your film be without sound? Or with poor sound? A close friend of mine who works as a cinematographer claims that poor sound makes his images look out of focus. Another friend who works selecting films for a major festival says that the first thing that betrays a bad film is the sound of the dialogue. One thing is for certain—if you want to stand any chance of selling your film, the sound needs to be of a good standard. If the sound is done well, the audience won't notice it at all—if it is bad it will make your images look bad. For this reason sound is often neglected in the filmmaking process as new directors may not realize just how much impact it has.

9. What common sound pitfalls do filmmakers face during their first film?
Well I suggest anyone starting out in sound tries to work their way up through the ranks rather than diving straight in as a recordist. Many of the best recordists I've worked with began as assistants, working their way up to doing some additional boom operating, then becoming a boom operator and then finally becoming a recordist. Hopefully by the time they get there they have seen most of the potential pitfalls.

10. Who inspires you and why?
There have been a few people in my life who have been deeply inspiring at every stage of my career. Most of them won't have been heard of—sound people can be relatively invisible—but what makes them inspiring is the attention and dedication they have paid to honing and refining the art of sound.

PAUSE

TEN TIPS BY ROLAND HEAP

1. Get your location sound right!
2. The most important thing is not the equipment, but the person using it. If you can afford to hire a sound recordist, do. They will be the best investment you could make.
3. But they won't ask unless it is absolutely necessary.
4. Record wild tracks of any compromised dialogues as soon as possible and room tones from every location.
5. Listen back to your audio every night. If it sounds bad and you can reshoot, do. It will almost always give you better results than ADR.
6. Reccie! Assess your locations well in advance, take your sound recordist and listen to them if they say a location is unworkable.

7. Plan every shot for sound—can you feasibly record it with the equipment you have available?
8. Make sure there is always a microphone pointing at your actor's mouth. This should be obvious, but you'd be amazed at how often it is not the case.
9. Rent rather than buy—no single mic will cover you for all eventualities and a good rental company (like Richmond Film Services) will give you advice about whats best to use.
10. Never plan on fixing it later—fix it now!

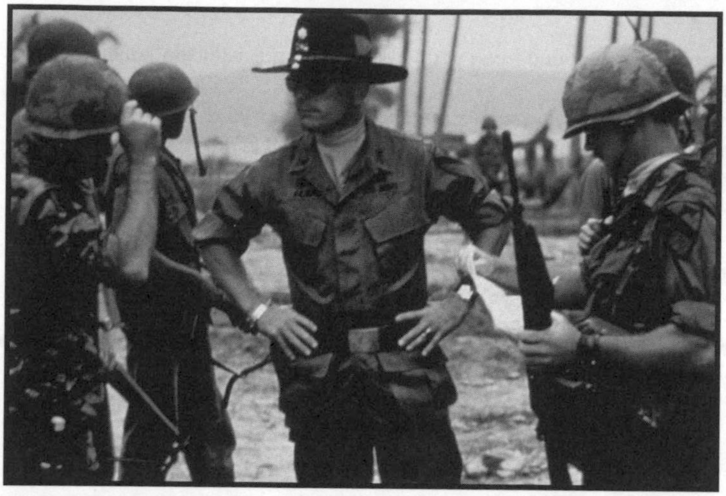

11.1 "I love the smell of napalm in the morning" Robert Duvall as Colonel Kilgore in *Apocalypse Now* (1979)

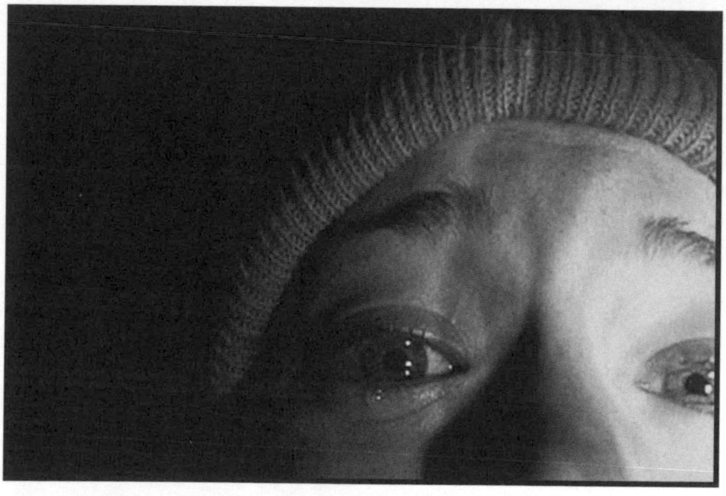

11.3 *The Blair Witch Project* visuals are intentionally shaky–sometimes just a black screen–but the audio is crisp. (1999)

PART

IV

TITLE

Post-production

START

CHAPTER 12

The Editor

Every member of the production staff has a part to play in the finished film (directors Cedric Behrel and Alexis Bicât emphasized their dependence on the Director of Photography), but the more liberated the filmmaker becomes with new technology, the more important the work of the editor.

After the director has coaxed the cast, cameraman, and crew into realizing his vision, from this incoherent, unwieldy footage, the story is reassembled. The director will study every shot in every sequence, but it is the editor who puts the puzzle together. All those miles of footage may contain not one but numerous interpretations of the same story and it is in post-production where the best way of telling the story is achieved.

It is a tense and exciting moment. Up until this time, the writer could have dashed in for last-minute re-writes, scenes may have been added or reshot; in Oliver Stone's director's cut of *Natural Born Killers* for DVD, punters can stay with the original and-they-all-lived-happily-ever-after final scene, or click on to Mickey and Mallory being blown away in a guns blazing Armageddon. Reviewers when the film premièred couldn't decide if *Natural Born Killers* was a bloody glorification of violence or a witty parody on American values; even the director must have had doubts to have shot alternative endings in the first place. Whether those doubts were aesthetic or commercial is hard to say, but Oliver Stone was fortunate to have the opportunity to experiment with his product in this way. For anyone making a short film or an indie feature for the festival circuit, the hard, make-or-break decisions must be made the first time around in the editing suite.

To help make those decisions, it is essential that the editor is just as familiar with the script as the director, and it should be remembered that few first-time directors will have seen a film being edited before. The director should have got the shots he needed, but if the budget precludes reshooting, errors and oversights will now be discreetly covered. Lighting, wardrobe, and décor will be scrutinized for inconsistencies. Where a director may want to insert whip-pans, rapid-fire cutting, and wild textural flourishes, the editor like the tutor with a child genius will exercise calm and constraint.

On child geniuses, when Orson Welles was making *Citizen Kane* he became so fascinated by editing he organized a removal truck and a gang of stage hands to haul an editing machine into his hotel room. Surrounded by his actors and hundreds of feet of celluloid, he spent hours drinking whisky and learning to juggle film. He had discovered the Frankenstein element of filmmaking. Sitting at the Steenbeck, it is really possible to assemble your own creature, and give life to it. The sense of power is intoxicating: a slow scene can be made fast, a funny one sad, a bad performance can be made good, and actors can be expunged from the film as if they had never been. To shoot is human; to edit, divine.[1] Simon Callow, quoted above, writes in *Orson Welles, The Road to Xanadu*, that Welles had discovered that in the editing process lies the ability to create as if you were God, an aspiration very close to the young filmmaker's heart.

12.1 Opening of *Citizen Kane*

P.153

12.2 The Director's Chair on set of *Citizen Kane* (1941)

P.153

Welles' use of sound was a dramatic advance for motion pictures and sound departments at all the studios studied his methods. Sound contributes enormously, but generally subliminally. "Ambient sound and sound effects can transform a sequence with the simplest of means: a clock ticking, a distant dog barking, the wind, the laughter of children. Any or all of these radically alter the sense of time or place in what is perceived by the eye."[2]

In his radio broadcast of H. G. Wells' *The War of the Worlds*, Orson Welles had terrified the nation into believing that Martians had landed. He had mastered the ability of mingling voices with effects and music and was able to apply his acute aural sense to influence the audience. "Hitherto, in film, what you heard was what you saw. In *Citizen Kane*, for the first time, you heard something—a line, a sound—and then saw where it was coming from. The audience's mind is thus kept in a state of continuous curiosity and alertness."[3]

Welles set out in *Kane* to create a documentary style and, with his big appetites, in this case for authenticity, in the *News on the March* pastiche showing the early life of the young Kane, he encouraged Robert Wise and Mark Robson, his editors, to drag the film over the cutting-room floor in order to get the scratched, grainy effect of old newsreels. Paradoxically, viewing *Citizen Kane* today, the stylization and sound effects reminds the audience that they are not watching scenes from a biodoc, but scenes from a movie. Welles had failed in his objective and made a better film as a result.

PAUSE

REJECTION!

Film festival selectors (and judges) hate being asked why a film was rejected and normally reply with platitudes. So, don't ask. Analyze your film and work it out for yourself. Here are some tips.

1. Editing

Poor editing kills the best intentions. If you edit your own film (and there's loads of great software out there to help you do just that) you are likely to fall in love with your own words, the long shot, the jump cut. A professional editor isn't wedded to the material; he's not aware of the importance of a single shot, or the back-story behind a particular performance. They see the rough material for what it is, and work with what they have to string the story together into a coherent, precise, calculated film. A 12 or 14-minute film usually works better when you cut it down to 10 minutes.

2. Length
There is a good reason why festivals like films that are 10 minutes and under. It fits with the schedules. A 20-minute film means someone else's film isn't going to get shown. That doesn't mean you shouldn't make longer films. You just need to be aware that if you are outside the pattern it's going to be that much harder.

3. Lighting
A good actor shows the audience what he's feeling and thinking by a blink of the eye, a shrug, a curl of the lips. It doesn't matter how good the performances, the subtleties and nuances will be lost without bounce boards at least, a few lights on stands better still. If you have inexperienced sparks, get an experienced DP, and vice versa.

4. DP
The DP can make or break a short film. If the director is inexperienced, the editor may be able to paper over the cracks, but it needs a skilled eye behind the camera to make sure the shots are there for the editor to work with. A good DP will talk the novice director out of his crane shots, the MTV jump cuts, the soft focus close-ups. Rehearse camera movements and lighting, just as you rehearse actors.

5. Cast
Your mates might be up for it, but although filming can be fun, it's not a joke. In every city there are drama schools and actors' agencies. Get professionals. Bad acting, no matter how good the script, kills the movie stone dead. When you've got your cast, rehearse before you roll the film.

6. The Script
Re-write. Re-write. Re-write. Don't shoot till you get it right.

7. Perseverance
Sometimes as few as 20 films are selected from a thousand or more entries. There may be nothing wrong with your film, so persevere, swallow the rejection and send it out again.

TEAM EFFORT

There are two distinct schools of thought regarding the editor's art: that it should be hidden, a device so seamlessly woven into the narrative as to appear invisible, or boldly present like a neon light announcing *MOTEL* on a darkened highway. Joining one or other of these two schools is fundamental to the film's symmetry, its *look*, and many directors will stay with the same editor once a style and a working relationship has been established. Ethan and Joel Coen have kept most of their cast and crew on side through a string of independent gems from their 1984 *Blood Simple* to the Oscar winners *Fargo* in 1996 to *True Grit* in 2010, shot by British cinematographer Roger Deakins, his *eleventh* Coen film.

Orson Welles never developed this collaborative chemistry, at least not with his editors. He would appear in the cutting room, usually late, study the rushes, fire off suggestions and down his whisky without offering the jug. Editors Robert Wise and Mark Robson had little affection for Welles, but they respected his knowledge, learned his secrets and, as revenge is a dish best served cold, both escaped the drawn out controversy that dogged *Citizen Kane* to begin their own careers as directors.

Where Welles had set out to imitate reality, Georges Méliès by 1902 had come to believe that reality is actually rather dull and it is the manipulation—in other words, the editing of film, that grips the audience. Where his historic *A Trip to the Moon* engrossed the citizens of Paris for its novelty, the first public showing of *L'Âge d'Or* a generation later caused an uproar for completely different reasons. Film had become a political tool. The left-wing press in Paris supported Buñuel's surreal affront to religious and bourgeois values, while right-wing protestors literally broke into the theater and ripped it apart. *Le Figaro* and *L'Ami du Peuple* led the moral panic accusing "Judeo-Bolshevik devil-worshipping masonic wogs" for being behind the film (Marie-Laure Noailles, who in part put up the money, was the daughter of a Jewish banker). With mumblings of "pornography" among government ministers and an official complaint by Mussolini's ambassador, it was duly banned. As Paul Hammond tells us: "The totalitarian battle-lines were drawn."[4]

Buñuel would have been well-versed in Méliès' work and was aware of the editor's key role. He may have needed Dalí's input on his early scripts, but cut his own films, importing ideas as much from Hollywood as early French cinema. For example, a scene from Buster Keaton's 1922 *The Paleface* where the hero is embracing the girl dissolves into the same scene, still in a clinch, accompanied by the card TWO YEARS LATER. Buñuel lends irony to the concept in *L'Âge d'Or* by showing a group of men in a room doing nothing in particular and dissolves into the identical scene with the intertitle SIXTEEN YEARS EARLIER. Likewise, Méliès comic use of a character falling out of a window in one place and landing somewhere completely unrelated conforms perfectly to the Buñuel/Dalí surrealist vision and was similarly borrowed. The trick, Buñuel knew, was all in the editing.

By the 1920s, film language had developed to a degree that remains virtually intact, the pace of change driven by the fact that, until 1928, film remained silent. In the theater, the playwright can sidestep tricky plot points by having his actors tell the audience what is going on. In good writing, the skill is to *show* not *tell*, and early filmmakers were impelled to use all the elements of mise-en-scène to achieve this elementary goal.

To compensate for the absence of words, silent filmmakers, from Méliès in Paris to Chaplin, Keaton, and D. W. Griffith in Hollywood, quickly mastered juxtaposition, parallel action, framing, lighting, camera angle, focus, filters, montage, and camera movement. What the audience sees is governed by the way in which the director presents the film to us. How it is cut will determine our reaction.

None of these developments, politically or technically, went unnoticed in the Soviet Union. Before the dust had even settled on the Communist Revolution, the Moscow Film School in 1919 was already a hive of intellectual debate and experiment. Lenin, who had lived in exile in Paris, was aware of the part film could make in educating the masses and intervened personally to ensure the wide release of D. W. Griffith's 1916 *Intolerance*, four interlinked stories showing intolerance throughout the ages and climaxing in a race between a car and a train.

A review in the *New Yorker* described *Intolerance* as "Perhaps the best movie ever made," and it would be studied in Moscow and in film schools across Europe for its capacity to ellicit strong reactions through the subtle cross-cutting of images. Griffith had come to see that there is no imperative demanding that film be presented from the POV of the audience. He made his camera more selective in his examination of depth of field and recognized that the insertion of reaction shots heightened drama. Griffith had thus shown that in editing, the emotional result could be greater than the sum of the visual content. He was, as Cecil B. de Mille put it, "The first to photograph thought."[5]

Griffith began making short films in 1908, created the concept of stars and trail-blazed every aspect of film technique. Frank Capra once commented, "Since Griffith there has been no major improvement in the art of film direction,"[6] and gossip columnist Hedda Hopper would recall the marks made by stars in the wet cement outside Hollywood's Chinese Theater, and declared, "Griffith's footprints were never asked for, yet no one has ever filled his shoes."[7]

Flattery from Moscow came in the form of imitation. While filmmaking was developing in Russia, Griffith's two epics, *Intolerance* and the 1915 *Birth of a Nation*, became templates for the director's craft. What Griffith devised was the convention of preparing a shooting script to plan master shots from the camera's ideal position to stage the action in each scene. Every shot that completes the scene refers back to the master shot. In this way, he had invented cinema's unique method of treating space and provided the essential elements for editing the manifold elements into cogent sequences.

12.3 Sergei Einstein

The Russians understood that truth itself can be manipulated by editing and exploited this capacity to serve the fledgling Bolshevik state. The early directors influenced by Griffith included Dziga Vertov, Lev Kuleshov and Sergei Eisenstein, whose work is studied as much in film schools today as the Russians studied Griffith in the 1920s. Eisenstein's feeling for pace and his subtle touch with actors brought a new level of quality to Russian film drama. Of his many films, he is best remembered for the 1925 *Battleship Potemkin*, particularly the Odessa Steps sequence, the sixty-second massacre of innocent civilians drawn out to more than five minutes by the frenetic cross-cutting of the 150 shots used in the scene. It has been copied many times but never bettered.

12.4 Potemkin (1925)

▶▶ P.**154**

The Russian directors were obliged to glorify the state, but if film is the most powerful form of communication ever known, the role of the modern filmmaker is more akin to the wise man in primitive societies who serves the hopes and aspirations of the community. Every anti-war story, or union struggle, or civilian massacre, is a reminder of man's need to learn tolerance and evolve to a greater state of humanity.

Today, it is more likely that an editor will be working on Final Cut Pro, an editing system that stores the rushes digitally, allowing instant access to every shot that constitutes the entire film. The director and editor can study a variety of versions of each sequence before making a selection and, as those sequences are stored electronically, there is no deterioration during the process. Another advantage is that both sound and effects can be tried, used, or eliminated at the keyboard.

The writer and director create the material, but the editor's part in shaping the scenes into a film that remains true to their vision is quintessential. Francis Ford Coppola says a film is created three times: first you write it, second you shoot it, third you edit. The pace, timing, emotional impact, the scenes that bring a tear to our eye and send icy fingers running up our spine, with music and sound effects, the editor's job is at the very heart of the creation.

Writers put into words truths we understand intuitively and, as his work goes through its metamorphosis to film, the editor is the director's conscience, the little voice that whispers when enough is enough. The finished film is in the editor's hands. Before FCP, and before sound brought new problems with synchronization, many editors shunned the Moviola editing machines and continued to cut in their open palms, judging pace and rhythm by instinct and experience. Like the midwife whose very hands enter the most intimate of all human activity, that of childbirth, and just as writers speak of their work as being their baby, an editor when he has made the final cut delivers something new and precious into the world.

Movies *are* the culture. In 2003 when *Gangs of New York* finally rolled out into British cinemas after 12 months of delay and infighting, the disputes between Martin Scorsese and Miramax chief Harvey Weinstein were already legendary and made the evening news. Scorsese had spent 30 years nursing the project and the budget had spiraled up from $50 million to $100 million. Like the street fighters depicted in the script, the diminutive Scorsese and heavyweight Weinstein slugged it out as the producer tried to prise control back from his director and the director ploughed on obsessively pursuing his dream.

Was the wildly ambitious three-hour epic going to be a masterpiece or a bloodbath for the investors? I don't know, Scorsese told Alex Williams in a *Guardian* interview. When I'm making a film, I'm the audience.

Were there problems because the producer and director had a different vision? No. Marty and I had a very similar vision, Weinstein replied sardonically. We had Marty's vision.

The exchanges are the stuff of movies and long before *Gangs of New York* even reached the cinemas, acres of newsprint drew us into the event as we followed the on and off-screen relationship between icons Leonardo DiCaprio and Cameron Diaz, every gesture and suggestion of body language as they walked the red carpet into the première in Leicester Square captured by phalanxes of cameras and an adoring public. Reviews in the quality press and radio discussions examined the film's grammar, tone, complexion, every hue and mezzotint; at the outset, Scorsese had given DP Michael Ballhaus a book of Rembrandt prints to guide the lighting, and he gave Harvey Weinstein a list of 80 films he wanted him to see including the 1928 *The Man Who Laughs*, ironically a silent movie and with the worst organ music, complained Weinstein, that he had ever heard.[8]

Just hype? Or a legitimate response to our major art form? In the final analysis, was *Gangs of New York* any good? Even with $100 million in the kitty and Martin Scorsese in the director's chair, it is only when the film is edited and on view that the question can be answered. And, then, reviewers and cinemagoers are going to differ. That's art.

PAUSE

THE BUÑUEL LAW

Director Juan Luis Buñuel has worked with many of the masters, his father Luis Buñuel, Orson Welles, Louis Malle, Claude Lelouch and Philip Kaufman. Buñuel has two basic laws regarding filmmaking.

1. The first law, and one that you cannot avoid, is that there is no fixed law—no formulas, no wise sayings, nothing.
2. The second law is that you don't know anything about a film till it comes out. You can get the best director, the best script and the biggest stars and the film can be a flop ... or the contrary, a bad director, bad actors, bad cinematography ... and the film is a huge success. Or the contrary. No laws.

PASSION IN PIECES

Scorsese's film cost a $100 million, but for the mere price of a Weinstein cigar, about a hundred bucks, editor/director Sam Small not only made his 10-minute short *Passion in Pieces*, he won the Special "Gold Remi" award at the 2003 Houston International Film Festival, and was Special Jury Selected at the 2002 New Orleans Film Festival. All you need is a domestic miniDV camera, a capture card, a cheap PC and a filmmaker's obsession, he says.[9]

That's just what I needed: an editor with passion.

Passion in Pieces is based on five Shakespeare sonnets, with modern urban settings and characters, and Small's own voiceover. If the most important element in a film is the script, wisely he chose Shakespeare—but even with just such a wordsmith on board, Small believes it is in the edit where you make the film. Be prepared for a shooting/editing ratio of at least 1:50. If you work alone, shooting is a nice day out compared to the lonely weeks and months spent in front of the computer painstakingly nudging tiny clips one frame to the left and right.

A well-planned shoot helps the editing process and before you begin, it is essential to have a good idea of what the finished film will look like. Cool, blue and slow? Red, disjointed and fast? Multicolored, madcap and fun? It may sound obvious, but the director and editor must have the same vision—and a director/editor has to be consistent.

Small advises filmmakers to *shoot everything in sight*. When on set or location, overshoot everything. If you can shoot the scene in yet another angle then do it. Actors, even if you have procured them for free, always like acting, so do another angle, another lens attitude. If you only have 15 minutes of footage for a 10-minute film you are in big trouble.

Live sound is another key element. If you are using an external mike, and not shooting dialogue, then pull the jack and use the inbuilt microphone on the camera. This is almost always a stereo mike and will have excellent digital quality. The sound can be invaluable for patching silent spots with an authentic "buzz" track, and also can be an important cue for overlaying on to dialogue tracks. Editing is a long haul: a day's shoot can produce a month of editing. Rush it and you'll ruin it. Editing live footage is in some ways akin to animation. You must fit bits of dialogue and action together second by second—sometimes a fraction of a second.

Sam Small prefers to watch all the takes over and over again, and then capture. As you can only use one take, it is best to do so while the scene remains fresh in your mind. Don't be afraid to try music or sound effects as you edit. It may help you to resolve pace and rhythm as you cut your takes. Most computer editing software has hundreds of video transitions and effects, but be wary how you use them—and never ever overuse them. Always use cut edits and very occasionally allow yourself the thrill of a dissolve or fade to/from black.

The value and importance of sound cannot be underestimated. Silent films always had a sound track, even if it was the local librarian playing an upright piano in the community hall. A truly silent film would emulate deafness for an audience and would be very uncomfortable. Half of every film is sound, sometimes more, says Small. If you find that your live sound of rain on a windowpane is inferior to a library sound, then use the library sound. Don't be proud.

In laying down sound on his own shorts, Sam Small has been inspired by Jacques Tati, the French actor and comedian who made totally original short films. To Tati, the screen was a vast canvas populated by absurd people in conflict with absurd structures. Very often a background "buzz" track is louder than the dialogue, suggesting the ephemeral nature of conversation in relation to the natural world and to that of machines. Tati's films never contain live sound. Everything was painfully dubbed at the edit, and he would take hours to find the right car horn or door squeak. For one scene, he was once observed with boxes of glasses, smashing one after the other until it sounded just right. The music often sounds banal, but he spent months looking for the music for the effect he was trying to achieve. To Tati everything made a sound, but not necessarily its own.

Under Tati's influence, Small suggests what he calls *casting against type*. Give the audience the music they are least likely to expect. Try a brass band with a sex scene. You might create a sensation, he says. And a final warning to editors: Don't edit to be interesting or clever. Audiences never find *interesting* interesting, and cleverness often looks silly. What people want is to be emotionally moved by your film. If the filmmaker is not moved by what he is looking at, the audience won't be either.

www.passioninpieces.co.uk

The films we remember best live on because of some unique, intrinsic quality that evolves through the skills of writing, directing and editing film. As cities crumble and empires fall, all that remains through time is man's art. In the architecture of our churches, in paintings on the walls in national galleries, in libraries and museums, what we create is more lasting than man himself.

The films cited in the text, *A Trip to the Moon, L'Âge d'Or, Citizen Kane, Intolerance, Battleship Potemkin*, are all carefully preserved and available for our study and enjoyment today, long after the filmmakers have gone. Whether it is that first 10-minute short or the new Coen Brothers movie shot by Roger Deakins, film's ability to change lives and minds—understood by the likes of Lenin and Hitler—is far better in the hands of artists than dictators, and in presenting truth, none play a greater role than the editor.

PAUSE

ROGER CRITTENDEN'S TEN COMMANDMENTS

1. Read the script *in advance* of cutting.
2. Become familiar with the director's previous work.
3. Read the background material relevant to the film.
4. Meet the cameraman, sound recordist and other major contributors to the film who might affect your own job.
5. Liaise with the continuity or production assistant for documentation.
6. Make yourself known to the laboratory contact.
7. Choose your assistant carefully for both efficiency and tact.
8. Find out your director's preferred working hours and eating habits!
9. Ensure that the cutting room is properly set up *before* cutting starts.
10. Make sure that reliable maintenance can be obtained for your equipment.

12.5 Gordon Burkell

GORDON BURKELL—EDITOR AND FOUNDER OF ART OF THE GUILLOTINE

www.aotg.com

1. What is AOTG?

AOTG stands for Art of the Guillotine. It is a site that was started to help organize information for film editors, film academics and students. We grew rapidly and now focus on aggregating, organizing and disseminating information for editors around the world. We teamed up with the Canadian Cinema Editors, American Cinema Editors and the Australian Screen Editors to make their videos easily accessible so anyone can enjoy and benefit from them. On top of this we've got blogs, podcasts, journals, articles, and much more. We started with around one hundred links and as of yesterday we are just under 20,000 film editing specific content submissions.

2. There are other sites that have tips for editors—how is AOTG different?

Our site is a central location to find information about film editing. We have submissions from around the world and users can now access a specially organized feed. They can customize their feed to have the content they want sent to their favorite mobile device or to their personal email. On top of that, in September 2012, we released a new "share" plugin so that editors can be browsing in Chrome or Firefox and if they find something editors should know about, they can click a button and within seconds we'll have it on the site and it will be ready to share with our users. Think of it as the quickest way to get information to your colleagues.

3. How did you first get interested in editing?

I actually started on sets as a boom operator and got fed up with waiting around for the work to begin. I moved into post sound, assisting a Foley artist, and as film post began to transition into digital I started helping the older film editors become comfortable with the technology. One editor, Alan Collins, asked if I would assist him and he's really the one who showed me that editing was more about storytelling than technology, which really interested me. Alan was originally from the UK and had worked mostly in Los Angeles on projects with Roger Corman and the two of us would always take a mid-afternoon break, go to the local deli to grab a coffee and just talk story and theory. It's one of my favorite memories from my work with him. He's since retired. But not before directing some of his own docs and hiring me as the editor for my first documentary feature.

4. Describe an average day for an editor

The average day for an editor will be different for every editor and is really dependent on what stage the film is at, for example, as a documentary editor I might receive anywhere from 100 to 1,000 hours of footage. During the dailies screening process there might be weeks of me sitting in front of a TV watching footage taking detailed notes and really thinking out the story and how to start chiseling away at the footage. If I am cutting the footage it is dependent on the relationship I have with the director. I insist on working alone as an editor, as I find the directors are too close to the footage and they slow down the editing process if they sit there for the full day. As a doc editor I usually suggest that as I am going through the footage the director do so elsewhere with their own drive full of footage and make their own notes. Then the two of us meet and begin to really bang out a rough outline/script. Where footage can go, what structure will the film take. We build a paper edit or a thorough outline and I go to work as the editor. This makes the director comfortable with the process and makes sure we're on the same page. It also saves a lot of time in the cutting room as I'm not shuttling through footage with the director.

5. How has editing changed since you first entered the industry?

Drastically. As I mentioned, I started on sets working with Nagra's and just as I was starting, the DAT tape was beginning to make an appearance on sets. So when I transitioned into post I was lucky to get a few gigs in film and experience the world through a tactile process. Watching the transition into digital has been amazing, many editors I know used Media 100 or Lightworks initially, and then transitioned to Avid and FCP. There have also been a few troubling things I've witnessed. I've watched as job postings usually stated looking for a film editor with x, y, z, experience to looking for an Avid editor or FCP editor. For me this is extremely troubling, as we are not the sum of our tools. No one would hire a writer based on whether they use Microsoft Word or Final Draft. So what is it about the editing position that has people hiring based on this aspect? The tool is irrelevant to storytelling. Know the tools but know good storytelling, that's what matters. Other than this, the future looks really exciting. I love the new interactive elements coming. The new story avenues and ways of communicating with the audience are exhilarating.

6. Is it now all about FCP, or are other interfaces relevant for the modern day short-filmmaker?
I think it should always be about the story first. Trying to know the editing equipment, the sound equipment, the camera equipment, etc. will only dilute you on set and in post. You won't have time to focus on what's important if you're constantly trying to learn everything. Find people who are passionate about their craft. People who love editing, love cinematography and want that as a life path and work with them. It's better to meet with the DP and state that you want the scene to be lit similarly to this photographic style or that painter's lighting techniques or this film that really influenced you than to try to light the set yourself and set up the camera while your actors wait for you. In post, the best directors and producers I've worked with will state the emotions they want to elicit from the audience or the particular mood the scene is to focus on and that's what I work towards.

7. Should a director try and edit his own film?
I discourage it. Not to say it can't be done, the Coen Brothers do it all the time. But as you grow beyond the short you'll notice as a director you are pulled in multiple directions, VFX, Sound, Editorial, Promotions, Distribution, learn on your shorts the art of communicating your ideas and trusting your crew. It is the best place to learn as, well, it is a short and you can make mistakes. On bigger projects, if you try to micromanage you'll burn out fast. It is also incredibly beneficial to be able to see the film from a fresh perspective. Just because you put a lot of money or time into a particular scene, doesn't mean it needs to stay in the film if it slows the pacing or derails the storyline. Your editor can see this and help you reorder scenes or pace the film to fix this issue.

8. How does an editor normally approach a film?
This really depends on the film and the editor. First things first, if it is fiction, get to know the script. On the fiction films I've done, I read the script and make notes in the margins about mood and emotions from the characters. Then I screen the rushes and adjust the mood and emotion cues based on what the actors and settings look and feel like. As a doc editor I screen all the rushes and work with the director to form an overall structure. I make sure that the character arcs are developed and fulsome and that the characters are relatable. Then I start to assemble the footage and build the scenes. Usually, for a documentary it isn't uncommon for a first cut to be 4 to 5 hours long. Then, the director, producer and I watch it and start to work on what needs to stay and what needs to go. If you are in television or in fiction films there is a different structure that usually follows union rules. So for example, in television, the editor will do the first cut, then there will be a director's cut and finally a producer's cut. The number of cuts will change depending on the broadcaster, country, and union rules.

9. How important is the Internet—and AOTG—for editors?

It is changing, it used to be just about finding out answers to tech knowledge, but with AOTG.com and our partnerships with ACE, CCE and ASE, we are really more interested in sharing information and techniques. More than simply technology. The Internet is changing everything and editors will soon be working on cloud-based systems, don't be surprised if your editing is in another country.

10. Is there ever conflict with directors about what needs to be cut, and if so how can editors deal with it?

There will always be conflicts, which isn't necessarily a bad thing. This opens up a dialogue for the editor and the director to figure out the best direction for the film, remember both want what's best for the film or short. I never allow it to rise to a shout, it should always be a discussion, a disagreement. If it gets heated, take a break, grab a coffee, and return to the discussion later. One of the benefits of the new technology. If a director wants it one way and I prefer another, we can do both and really compare and analyze them. This has made things much easier, we can see both and test them with audiences.

11. As an editor, is it possible to enjoy a film without constantly analyzing the edits?

At first I couldn't. But over time you get used to it and you find yourself able to remove your editing thoughts while watching a film. However, if it's a slow or bad film they pop right back in there.

12. What advice do you have for short-filmmakers?

The best advice I ever heard given to young filmmakers was to find a person who loves editing, another who loves sound design, a passionate screen-writer and a skilled cinematographer. Create a small group with similar goals to grow as a creative team and develop together. Then make a short film a month, one month do a comedy, a documentary, a horror, a drama etc., every month do a different genre. When the film is complete, sit down as a group. Determine what worked and what didn't. Assess the script, the editing, the lighting. Did it work, did it not work? Figure out how to improve these things as well as how each department influences the other and begin the next film. If you, as a group, all agree that the film is strong then submit it to festivals or YouTube, if not, toss it and start the next one. Don't be afraid to be extremely tough on yourselves, question each film and how to improve as a team. By the end of the first year you will be amazed at how much you've grown as a filmmaking team. Your skills will be light years ahead of where they were a year earlier. As the films get better and accepted into festivals, start working on larger projects together or attempt to get funding for bigger projects. Never stop making something, just keep going.

STOP

12.1 Opening of *Citizen Kane*

12.2 As only Orson Welles would have it. On set during the shooting of *Citizen Kane*

12.4 Tsarist soldiers march down the Odessa Steps in *Battleship Potemkin* (1925).

START

CHAPTER 13

Music

Sound plays a vital part in the overall feel of a film, but it is music more than anything that brings out the emotional heart of a scene and the director has to learn to leave *space* for music in order for it to be a part of the storytelling process. Music sets mood and atmosphere, it creates tension, and contributes in a subtle way to showing the audience about the desires, fears, even the nature of the characters. In Sergio Leone's 1969 *Once Upon a Time In the West*, with its sprawling 12 minutes of credits, composer Ennio Morricone uses a different instrument for each of the larger-than-life protagonists and, even before we see them on screen, we get to feel their presence with just a few notes whispering through the score.

An action-packed movie may need racy music, but a film with undertones and subtext requires a score that is more multifaceted, creating expectation more than thrills. In the 1970 *Five Easy Pieces*, we meet Jack Nicholson as a construction worker and only later do we discover that he is railing against his musical, middle-class family. When he goes home to visit, the score switches from contemporary to classical, and when Nicholson sits at the piano to play, he brings his two worlds together by hammering out Chopin's haunting *Prelude in E Minor* like a piece of ragtime. The metaphor is understated and not everyone will get it, but for those who do, it adds another dimension to the story and provides a deeper level of appreciation.

Most film scores are written in a style that the audience expects from the genre, the evocative cellos in a horror flick, the jazz in film noir. But in a short film the director may want to go against type and do something more original and adventurous. Composer John Williams wrote a romantic score reminiscent of Strauss for John Badham's 1979 *Dracula*, adding a feverishly sexual tone to Frank Langella's performance as the ravenous Count.

There are two distinct categories of music in a film: incidental or featured music, which is not "heard" by the actors; and background music, music they do hear and needs to be arranged to fit the feeling and location: a night club, an elevator, the song on the taxi radio; the music is never random but will be part of the emotional texture underpinning the scene.

MUSIC RIGHTS

People making their first short film, especially students, may be tempted to borrow music from their favorite bands. With music download programs it is almost too easy. But be warned: music copyright is complex and acquiring rights is generally expensive, often more than the entire budget of a short film. Clearing music rights for festivals (where copyright owners know that no profits will be made by the filmmakers) may cost just a few hundred pounds, but if the film ends up a winner and you get the chance to show it further afield, on television OR the net, the rights issue will come up again. Getting music rights isn't difficult. PRS For Music—Performing Right Society, keeps details of who owns what, and in many cases administers the negotiations and collection of money for rights—**www.prsformusic.com**

PAUSE

THREE TYPES OF MUSIC RIGHTS

Composition: **This applies to the composer and lyricist. The music is normally licensed to a music publisher and the copyright runs out 70 years after the death of the last writer involved in the piece.**
Recording: **Recording companies normally own the recording rights and those rights expire after 50 years.**
Performance: **An artist's performance on a piece of music is also protected by copyright (so you can't just take clips and put them in a documentary). Record companies normally protect performer's rights, but it is sometimes necessary to get the performer's permission as well as that of the recording company to use clips.**

For most short films, a more practical, as well as financially viable option is to steer clear of famous pieces. Using music from an unsigned local band or hiring a composer are good options. A third is to use library music, much of which is also handled by PRS For Music. There is an astonishing amount suitable for every mood and genre and also costs in the realm of about £100 for a minute of music. When contacting PRS, the BBC recommend including the following information for any enquiry:

PAUSE

CONTACTING PRS FOR MUSIC

- **The name of the company or individual applying for the license;**
- **Main contact name and address;**
- **Main contact number and email address;**
- **Song title, date of recording and the sound recording used, e.g. EMI;**
- **Film title and brief synopsis;**
- **Duration of film;**
- **Overall film budget;**
- **Context of music used (scene description);**

- **Duration of music use (clip or full version);**
- **Territory of exploitation required e.g. worldwide;**
- **Rights required, e.g. broadcast rights, film festival rights, online right;**
- **Length of license required, e.g. 2 years.**

www.bbc.co.uk/filmnetwork

If licensors consider the film as a non-commercial project, they may give a discounted or even free rate, so it's well worth including details on the project, people involved and any social angle.

CREATIVE COMMONS

Another option is using music that is *freely* available under Creative Commons Licenses. Creative Commons is built upon current copyright law, and permits, in the jargon, the use of "some rights reserved" music, as well as movies, images, and other content—all gratis. CC offers free copyright licenses that anyone can use (without a lawyer) to mark their creative work with the freedoms they want it to carry. For instance, a musician would use a Creative Commons license to allow people to legally share her songs online, make copies for friends, or even use them in other compositions.

Musicians, song writers, photographers and so on give their music away free because they want to get it out there and, if it's good, it will get noticed and lead to other things. We have used CC-licenses for the images of directors in Part X: Top Tens. Find out more at: http://creativecommons.org

Several sites offer music published under Creative Commons flexible copyright lisenses. Here are some:

ccMixter—www.ccMixter.org
Free Music Archive—www.freemusicarchive.org
Jamendo—www.jamendo.com
Magnatune—www.magnatune.com
Simuze—www.simuze.nl

There were over 400 million CC licensed works available online by 2010, and that figure is growing every day. Much of the music found on the sites in the list can be used on films, but it is important to make sure that what you want to do with the music is allowable under the terms of the particular Creative Commons license it's under. CC-licensed music isn't free for all uses, only some—so make sure to check out the terms. It's also important to still credit the author of the music in the end titles, as well as oiling the wheels on the whole indie system. Photos and videos can also be used under Creative Commons licenses, and can be found on sites such as Flickr and Picasa.

PAUSE

VIMEO AND MUSIC

Vimeo—the "home for high-quality videos and the people who love them" provides two very basic but easy to use music solutions.

1. Enhancer

Easily find the type of music you need by searching by keywords or type, including genre, mood, tempo, and instrumentations. Genre includes everything from swing to dubstep, tempos range from super slow (0-40) to super fast (160+) and moods from silly to eerie. Searches can also be filtered by price range (either "free" or "any price"), license type (with a range of creative commons licenses) and provider (including Free Music Archive, Audiosocket and SmartSound). When you've found the perfect track you can add it directly to any clip you have already uploaded to Vimeo. You can choose all or just part of the track and also control the volume levels for the audio and visual with volume faders.

2. SmartSound

Another option is to buy and add customizable, royalty-free tracks to your film. Each song is customizable in that you can choose different versions of the same song to perfectly fit the clip. Choose the mood—such as background, drums only or rhythm, as well as a variation, which, depending on the song can be anything from dance to driving. A final choice is whether you wish to buy a personal or commercial license—both of which are extremely well priced.

WORKING WITH A COMPOSER

If buying in copyrighted music is too expensive, then the indie route is a wise alternative, in every sense of the word.

When writing music for film, the composer is not entirely free to follow his own muse, but has to tune into the narrative structure. The composer writes the score, but influenced by the style imagined by the director who will, most likely, turn up at the studio with a bunch of CDs and vague memories of the films that enthused him to become a filmmaker in the first place. It is up to the composer to find the mood, the tempo, the essence, and arrange a score that is both original and, magically, the theme music to the director's dream. After the script re-writes, shooting and editing, it is the final part of the collaboration which is film and the composer really is the key piece that makes the Chinese puzzle slot into place.

If the director doesn't have a fixed notion of the music, the composer can be more creative and come up with something exciting and experimental. Just like the writer, director, and DP, the composer on a short film will often have more freedom to play with the aesthetics and it is only with this freedom that great new concepts can be explored. When the collaboration between director and composer creates a powerful piece of music on a short, there is a good chance that it will continue through further shorts and into features; to give one example: David Julyan scored Christopher Nolan's short *Doodlebug* in 1997, his breakthrough feature *Following* in

1998, the director's Hollywood début *Memento* in 2000 and three films since.

A film score is so central to film it offers a real challenge and filmmakers working on a budget need not be nervous approaching a composer with a request. They can only say no, and they may say yes. By the same token, composers who want to break into film should send out demos to small production companies, contact film tutors at colleges, and network.

PAUSE

THE AMERICAN FILM INSTITUTE'S TOP 10 FILM SCORES[1]

#	FILM	YEAR	STUDIO	COMPOSER
1	STAR WARS	1977	20th Century Fox	John Williams
2	GONE WITH THE WIND	1939	MGM	Max Steiner
3	LAWRENCE OF ARABIA	1962	Columbia	Maurice Jarre
4	PSYCHO	1960	Paramount	Bernard Herrmann
5	THE GODFATHER	1972	Paramount	Nino Rota
6	JAWS	1975	Universal	John Williams
7	LAURA	1944	20th Century Fox	David Raksin
8	THE MAGNIFICENT SEVEN	1960	United Artists	Elmer Bernstein
9	CHINATOWN	1974	Paramount	Jerry Goldsmith
10	HIGH NOON	1952	United Artists	Dimitri Tiomkin

IN TUNE WITH SPENCER COBRIN

Composers may have come through years of study in the conservatoire or, alternatively, from the hard road of rock. Spencer Cobrin belongs to the latter category. With three films in three genres behind him, a short, a feature, and a prize-winning documentary, he has a pretty good idea of the role the composer plays working with experimental and inexperienced filmmakers.

Cobrin had no formal training, except he did learn to read music as a child studying the trumpet. He played drums in several bands in the London clubs and was asked to audition for Morrissey when the controversial ex-vocalist from The Smiths set out on his solo career. This, as he says, "came totally out of left field; such is the magic of life." He worked with Morrissey for seven years, "an emotional roller-coaster to say the least."

During the long hours on the road, Cobrin began writing music, which led to several co-writing projects with Morrissey being published. When his tenure with Morrissey came to an end, Cobrin started his own band, wrote the music and licensed songs to independent features in the UK and the US.

His film breakthrough came in 2004 when he "pitched" on the short *Alice and Kitty,* a fictionalized drama based on the true story of Kitty Genovese, who was murdered in New York. The following year, he wrote the score for *Send In The Clown,* a feature comedy about a boy who awakes from a coma and pursues his childhood dream of being a clown to the disappointment of his father. His documentary début came in 2006 with *My Child: Mothers of War*, a film about the mothers of American soldiers fighting in Iraq. In 2007 he did the heist caper feature *Daylight Robbery* about a group of thieves who devise a plan to steal *easy money* using the World Cup for cover, and in 2011 he wrote the score for the crime drama *Roger's Number* for writer/director Gianluca Cavaleri.

13.1 Spencer Cobrin

1. Where do you start when scoring a short, the script or the film?
By the time a filmmaker or producer reaches out to a composer the film has more or less been assembled, unless they bring someone in at the very early stages, which I believe is kind of rare, but there are no hard and fast rules. So in my case it's the film not the script that is the starting point. If I was to base the score on the script I think I would find that misleading, firstly because by the time the film has been shot it's probably been through several significant changes, and secondly, I'm writing to the moving picture, not the written word. On the other hand, I do like to read scripts as it's fascinating to see how the words on the page are made manifest, but that's more of a directorial intrigue than a compositional one.

2. What part does music play in a film?
Music is the glue. It's like an invisible actor, it describes the narrative in sound, guiding the viewer from one point to the next, leading them along the narrative's path. Music adds emotional intensity and impetus. It can describe characters, their psychology, it creates moods, defines geography, the time period, it does so much. I would say the addition of music, if it can at all be quantifiable, probably makes up 40% of a film. The effect it has with the picture is really incredible. Music plays a very significant role, even if its role within a dramatic piece is a subtle one, it can't nonetheless be diminished.

3. Do you have a different approach with a short and a feature?
I don't think so, as a short is a condensed version of a longer form, I suppose it depends on the film itself.

4. If the director has a fixed idea on music, do you accommodate that, or convince him/her that you have a better plan?
Obviously the director, especially if they've written the script too, has a much clearer and deeper understanding of what it is they want than someone coming in cold and seeing the piece for the first time. It can also be a case of trial and error. To get inside the head of the director is very important. There could be things that may not be directly apparent

at the initial screening, so it's a good idea to give yourself time to watch the film, study it, absorb as much as possible of what it is the director is aiming for and to give it your fingerprint, that is after all why you are onboard in the first place. Maybe the film will have a temp track that has the kind of feel or direction they are looking for, but that can be misleading as it may not necessarily bring out what is inherent in the film. It's interesting to see that by trying out different pieces of music how it can alter the feel of the drama and by doing so give scenes a completely different meaning.

5. Is music useful to cover gaps in the story, places where the director perhaps has not been able to elicit the right emotions or performances from the cast?
Music has the power to bring to the fore emotions in varying degrees so that if a performance is lacking a certain something, music can certainly help support, enhance, and reinforce what might otherwise be missing.

6. And it follows, can the music be intrusive?
Oh definitely. It's important to strike the right balance otherwise it may feel that there is too much music, which might suffocate the story, or conversely, not enough could leave it a little thin on the ground and you lose impetus. Music doesn't have to be everywhere.

7. On a practical level, how do you go about writing the score?
What's the story and who are the characters? What does the director want to bring to the film by way of music? Getting the tempo and pacing right is the cornerstone of making the music fit snugly. There are other factors, like how to play a scene. Do you want to hit certain points in the performance or dialogue to emphasize the drama, or play through the scene? Diagetic sound can also spark ideas as well as improvising, intuition and just sheer grit.

8. Has technology changed music scoring?
Yes, absolutely. Not just how music is created but what kind of music and sounds can be created and manipulated. I haven't crossed any thresholds myself as I started writing solely in the digital realm.

9. What relationship do you have with the sound designer?
So far I haven't worked with a sound designer. That would be interesting though as these two fields are closely linked as sound design is used on the same level as music. The sound design I have done within my own work though is actually conceived of as part of the composition itself as opposed to seeing it as a separate entity.

10. Is it possible for filmmakers with little music experience to create their own music?
I think everyone has the potential to do anything really. So in that case, anyone can create music, anyone can make a film, but more to the point, will it be any good? If you've slaved over a project for as long as it takes to even make a short film, would you want to risk blowing it by potentially adding something that might compromise all the hard work you've poured into it?

11. Finally: list the 3 absolute essentials that music must do on a film.
I'm no professor but I would say, to set the mood/tone, support/enhance the narrative and performances, and to bring a sense of finality/conclusion.

CREDITS

While the director works with the composer, the producer should be thinking about how he is going to exploit the film at festivals, in competition, at film clubs, and with sales agents. He will be compiling a Press Kit (there's an example in Chapter 25: Greta May—The Adaptation), and working with an artist on a poster design and artwork for a DVD cover. The film has to stand up, but every detail adds a layer of gloss and professionalism to the package.

During prep and production the director has so much to do he rarely gives any thought to the credits; getting the film wrapped is a Herculean task in itself. But credits are, or at least should be, part of the story-telling process (think of the *Pink Panther* movies) and should prepare the viewer for the style and genre of film they are about to watch.

PAUSE

TOP 5 OPENING CREDITS

1. Lord Of War
Nicolas Cage shocks in his guise as an arms-dealer, breaking the fourth wall and speaking directly to the audience. The camera then follows a bullet's path, from the POV of the bullet, from its inception in a factory, its journey across the sea, into a gun and finally into the head of an African soldier.

2. Reservoir Dogs
Eight men, six in matching suits, are eating breakfast at a diner and using aliases. A slow-mo of them strutting allows each to be introduced before the action cuts to a bleeding and apologizing Mr. Orange, bringing the viewers straight into the drama.

3. Casino Royale
Trippy visuals are mixed with classic Bond themes and complemented by the alluring vocals of Soundgarden singer Chris Cornell.

4. Thank You For Smoking
Credits are written on a huge number of different vintage cigarette packaging, and accompanied by Tex Williams' *Smoke! Smoke! Smoke! (That Cigarette)*, setting the upbeat mood of the film.

5. Catch Me If You Can
The title sequence combines the chase motif with a feeling of excitement, which perfectly fits Spielberg's true story of the teenage con artist. Designed by Nexus Productions, the sequence shows stylized figures chasing each other through different scenery.

CREDIT ART FORM

From the cult classic *Reservoir Dogs*, whose gang of robbers can be seen on tee-shirts all over the world, to more stylized animations such as Spielberg's *Catch Me If You Can*, a credit sequence does so much more than simply introduce the makers and cast of a film. If done properly, the audience will understand the tone, place, and character of a film, before it has even fully started.

"A title sequence is more than just a list of credits. It can be a mini-movie which sets up the film that it's a part of. It can establish mood, period and style. A title sequence can take care of backstory. It can soothe the audience or get them agitated. Title sequences are an art form of their own."
Big Film Design, www.bigfilmdesign.com

While a short film simply doesn't have the space for a two to three minute extended title sequence, credits is an area that makers of short films often overlook, as Matthew Konz at Leapfrog Entertainment knows all too well, (see the box below):

PAUSE

STOP

BORING CREDITS

Watching the quantity of short films that I do I am disheartened at how boring and similar opening credits tend to be. So many films consist of a simple white font on a black background—usually Arial or Times New Roman. This is one of the main areas of neglect in short-filmmaking. Choose a font which suits the story, there are thousands available for free download on the net, and try to be more creative with opening credits.

Try integrating opening titles into the story and the opening shots of your film—it is actually quite rare for short filmmakers to overlay text on top of an image—most openings of short films jump between footage of the film and black screens with white text, which is almost ubiquitous and, from my point of view as a programmer, really boring and uninspired.

Ideally you should be putting the credit style under the same level of scrutiny that you place the story. First impressions mean a lot, and the font choice, size, movement, color, and style of your credits can lift the opening of your film immensely. Matthew Konz
www.leapfrog-entertainment.com

START

CHAPTER 14

Marketing

So the final cut of your film has been saved, backed up and snail mailed to a family member for safety. Unfortunately, now the hard work really begins. Even if your short is an epic in 10 minutes with game changing production values, if nobody sees it, no one will know. As Jorge Rodriguez explains in Chapter 21: Broken: "You have to learn that 50% of the creative process has to go into marketing and promotion," a statement author Jon Reiss also makes in his book *Think Outside The Box Office*.

The good news is that there are an ever-increasing number of outlets for short films, and the best of them will pick up fees when they are shown. But the traditional reason for making shorts is still for the filmmakers to get exposure and that entails applying to festivals and entering into competitions. Those that are good enough will win the plaudits and the teams behind them will be another few rungs up the ladder when they go out again in search of finance. Short films have gained new respectability and are worthy of being considered a genre in itself, but the ultimate goal will normally be to reach a wide audience and that can generally only be achieved in the long run with a feature.

14.1 *We Need to Talk About Kevin* (2011)

▶▶ P.179

14.2 *We Need to Talk About Kevin*

▶▶ P.179

One writer/director who has built her career in this way is Glasgow born Lynne Ramsey. UK Lottery money helped develop *Morvern Callar* (2002) with Samantha Morton and Kathleen McDermott, but only after her critically acclaimed début feature *Ratcatcher* (1999), and her three distinctive short films, *Kill the Day* and *Small Deaths* (1996), and *Gasman* (1998). *Small Deaths* won the Prix du Jure at Cannes and when *Gasman* won the same prize two years later, people began to take notice. Lynne's shorts are moody, atmospheric pieces where shadowy, shifting worlds are seen through the clear vivid eyes of children and innocents. She has found her own unique style, her voice, and in her idiosyncratic vision funders see an originality they want to support. Her latest accomplishment is the critically-acclaimed 2011 *We Need To Talk About Kevin*, starring Tilda Swinton.

LEGAL

It's essential to check all of the legal aspects of your film, especially that you own all of the rights, or have permission from the people that do.

Copyright owners in the UK are usually the producer and director, but if another party was involved in any aspect of the creation, especially funding, they may own some or even all of the rights. Just as important is "content clearance"—written consent for everything that features. This includes everything from the script to stock footage to music—even the font used in the credit sequence. A number of relevant example contracts are included in the Appendix.

ONLINE PRESENCE

With over two billion people now using the Internet, there are a lot of punters that may be interested in your film! While in pre-production, building an online presence may not be top of your mind. But it's worth it. Use social media to lure potential fans and keep existing ones up to date. The keyword is *engage*. With all social media, the trick is to be interesting and responsive. Share sites, blogs and articles that you find stimulating, join in discussions that other users have started, and keep shameless self-promotion to a minimum. When the time comes for marketing, these are the new friends you can call on to help get the word out. A re-Tweet, a share on Facebook or a Google+ click can go a long way.

Facebook

There will soon be one billion members on Facebook—that's one in seven people. As the world's second-biggest site (after Google), it's the best place to start your online presence. For a successful Facebook strategy, try some of the following:

14.3 Facebook logo

- Create a Page for your film that is separate from your personal page. People who "like" it will get the updates you post in their news feeds.
- Set the URL of this page as your film's title e.g. Facebook.com/MakingShortFilms. This will help SEO—people easily finding your page when they search for it, and can be used on all publicity material.
- Invite your friends to "like" the page, and ask the cast and crew to do the same.
- "Like" similar pages—they may well like you back.
- Understand EdgeRank—People are more likely to see your posts if they are shared/have comments.
- Add a Facebook link to your website and email signature.
- Think about advertising on Facebook to get noticed by relevant people.
- Check the stats—When you create a Page, Facebook shares a huge amount of relevant information about its progress. Everything from how many people see your posts every week to their virality.
- Give us a like! www.facebook.com/MakingShortFilms

Depending on how much time you are willing to put into social media, other sites that are worth checking include Twitter, Pinterest, Tumblr, LinkedIn and Google+. While they don't have the clout in terms of numbers, dedicated social networking sites for filmmakers are also worth investigating. Try

Filmkin (www.filmkin.com) and The Filmmakers Social Network (www.filmmakerssocialnetwork.com).

PAUSE

FILMMAKERS WHO TWEET

Don't expect to necessarily receive any advice, or even film-related updates, but if you're new to Twitter here are five filmmakers to follow. From Kevin's bad language to Michael's rants, if you're already on Twitter add them now!

- **David Lynch—@David_Lynch (*Mulholland Drive*)**
- **Ron Howard—@RealRonHoward (*A Beautiful Mind*)**
- **Michael Moore—@ MMFlint (*Fahrenheit 9/11*)**
- **Judd Apatow—@JuddApatow (*Knocked Up*)**
- **Kevin Smith—@ThatKevinSmith (*Clerks*)**

WEBSITE AND SEO

A website for a short is a useful tool for festival selectors and filmgoers, but also to keep the cast and crew up to date with the film's progress. The film will probably not be shown for several months after the wrap party, but those who have played a role in making the short will be keen to know how it's doing. If the shoot went well, these are the people you're going to work with on the next short.

Failing having a friend who can create a stunning website for you, or a budget to employ a professional, there are a number of easy ways to get started. WordPress is now the most popular blogging platform, but can also be used to create stunning static sites. Basic knowledge of how to use this tool is easy to learn. Alternatively, there's a large number of sites, programs, and applications—too many to list, both free and for purchase—to help with creation. Be sure to embed a trailer, display social links, and allow an electronic press kit to be downloaded (see below).

It's also worth putting effort into SEO (search engine optimization), which essentially means getting ranked highly by Google and other search engines for keywords that are relevant to your film, allowing people to find you easily or even by accident. Setting up Google Analytics on your site will give you a wealth of information about who is visiting your site, where they are from, what browsers they are using, how they find you and how long they stay on your site.

PRESS KIT

A Press Kit—both in hard (paper) format, and digitally, contains supplementary publicity material. You only get one chance to make a first impression, so be sure every aspect is professional—if not perfect. You must include:

- Name of film and director
- Synopsis (long and short)
- Stats including year of production, original format, length, copyright and funding information
- Production stills
- Director's and/or producer's statement
- Production notes and anecdotes (how the film got made including memorable moments)
- Résumés for key cast and crew, including biographies, filmographies and photos
- Links to all social media
- All other contact details, including website
- Press release and any reviews
- A CD including all of the above as PDFs or JPGs, as well as a poster—This is called an EPK (Electronic Press Kit)

Press Kits are not even looked at until a film is selected, but it is best to send it off at the same time as the film and entry form. On the other hand, some festival organizers request that you *don't* send a Press Kit with your film, but will ask you to do so if it is selected. Just follow the rules.

It is crucial to have at least one great production still, which is likely to be used over and over again. A poster, too, is useful—see below. If the film is selected, you get a real rush of adrenalin when you arrive at the event and see your poster up in the foyer. Some filmmakers try to bamboozle festival selectors with a flashy folder of photos and PR material. It doesn't work. The film has to stand on its own and, in general, it is better keeping the Press Kit simple and honest.

The time for producers to think about publicity is before the first day of principal photography. Producers normally have some down time while the director is rehearsing cast and making the shot list with the DP. This is the time to contact the local newspaper and invite the press along to the shoot; actors (and likewise directors) like being interviewed, it's good for their CV and, if you have a star on board, the more column inches you're going to get for your film. This won't necessarily put more bums on seats, unless the film is being shown to a local audience, but either way, the clippings make a positive addition in the Press Kit and shows the filmmakers are approaching the enterprise in a serious and professional manner.

EXAMPLE PRESS KIT 1

"A WONDERFULLY NEUROTIC COMEDY... HOLLYWOOD, TAKE NOTE!"

Kim Adelman, **IndieWIRE**

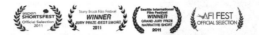

aspen SHORTSFEST Official Selection 2011 · Stony Brook Film Festival WINNER JURY PRIZE-BEST SHORT 2011 · Seattle International Film Festival WINNER GRAND JURY PRIZE NARRATIVE SHORT 2011 · AFI FEST OFFICIAL SELECTION

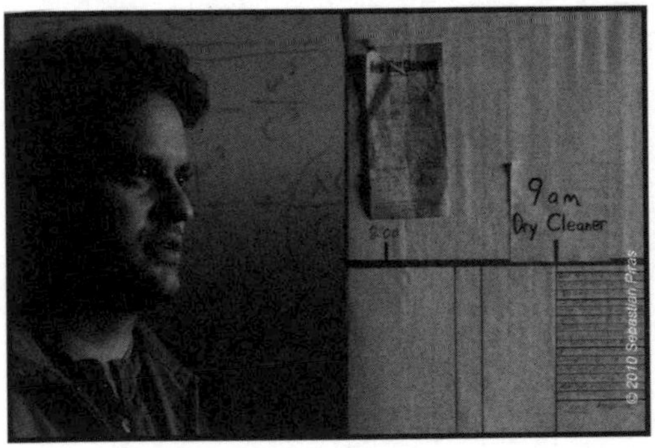

DIRECTOR: ANDREW BOWLER

PRODUCER: GIGI CAUSEY

SYNOPSIS: A neurotic inventor creates a time machine, only to get caught up traveling around yesterday.

TRT: 11 min.

ORIGIN: USA

In theaters Feb. 10, 2012
Available on iTunes Feb. 21

Facebook: tinyurl.com/3fvkgsh
Twitter: @timefreakmovie, @afbowler

Like many newlyweds, director Andrew Bowler and producer Gigi Causey turned their post-wedding energy toward making a future together. They had been saving for a down payment on a New York apartment when Andrew was struck with the inspiration for *Time Freak,* a short film comedy about a time machine and the power of nagging regret. Motivated by its theme and not wanting to face a lifetime of "what ifs", they convinced themselves that the responsible thing to do would be to abandon their plans for home ownership and make a short film instead.

The completed film was accepted to AFI Fest in Los Angeles, but a series of painful rejections, including Telluride Film Festival, Sundance and a few other notable festivals, made them question whether they had made the right decision. The tide soon changed, however, with their acceptance into the prestigious Aspen Shortsfest, where several of their fellow Nominees® screened. The film went on to win the Grand Jury Prize at Seattle International Film Festival, which qualified them to submit their film for OSCAR® consideration, and has since showcased in more than thirty festivals across the US. Their wildest expectations were exceeded when they checked THE ACADEMY'S® website at 5:30 AM on Tuesday, January 24, and learned that they were OSCAR NOMINEES®!

TIME FREAK is one of five live action short films nominated for this year's OSCAR® and is the only American film in its category. It will screen as part of SHORTS^{HD} PRESENTS: THE OSCAR® NOMINATED SHORT FILMS 2012 theatrical program on more than 200 screens across the U.S. beginning February 10 and will be available on iTunes starting February 21.

team toad

ACADEMY AWARD® NOMINATED – LIVE ACTION SHORT FILM

TIME FREAK

WRITER/DIRECTOR FILMOGRAPHY — ANDREW BOWLER

TIME FREAK (short) – writer, director

MAY THE BEST MAN WIN – writer (additional writing), cast – "Andrew Walter"

THE DESCENT OF WALTER MCFEA – writer, director
Cast – "Walter McFea"

PRODUCER'S BIO: GIGI CAUSEY

A native of San José, Costa Rica, Gigi was raised in West Texas, where she spent her adolescent years working the counter at her mother's independent video store in El Paso. After completing the undergraduate film program at UT Austin, Gigi began her filmmaking career in the art department, where she worked on George Ratliff's first narrative feature, *Purgatory County.* She went on to design projects for Bob Byington *(Olympia)* and Sandra Bullock *(Trespasses)* before moving to New York City, where she turned her creative energies toward line producing and production management.

Some of Gigi's recent film credits include Peter Sollett's *Nick and Norah's Infinite Playlist*, Amy Heckerling's upcoming comedy, *Vamps,* and Universal's *Safe House* starring Denzel Washington and Ryan Reynolds. She has a passion for indie filmmaking and often provides gratis production consulting services, recently on Dan Eckman's festival hit *Mystery Team* and Adam Fleischhacker's *May the Best Man Win.* Gigi also worked as Director of Production at RDF Media USA NY, directly responsible for the oversight of the production of multiple pilots and new series. Her other television credits include Bravo's award-winning *Queer Eye for the Straight Guy*, Discovery Channel's 13-part series, *The Detonators,* and truTV's *All Worked Up* and *Lizard Lick Towing.*

Gigi produced the Oscar® Nominated live action short film *Time Freak,* which was directed by Andrew Bowler. She has several feature films in development, including *Time Freak*; an adaptation of Tom Bissell's short story, *The Ambassador's Son;* and Jim Beggarly's award-winning script, *Donnie's Brother.*

She lives in Los Angeles with her husband and producing partner, Andrew Bowler.

DIRECTOR'S BIO: ANDREW BOWLER

A native of the Detroit area, Andrew is a director, writer and actor with ten years working in the New York film and television community. Andrew wrote and directed the award winning independent feature, *The Descent of Walter McFea,* and starred in the improvised feature comedy, *May The Best Man Win*, with Matt Walsh, Rob Riggle and Horatio Sanz.

Andrew is a graduate of NYU's Tisch School of the Arts, where he met the talented group of filmmakers (Geoffrey Richman, editor of *Murderball* and *The Cove* and Adam Fleischhacker, director of *May The Best Man Win*) that he continues to collaborate with today. He called on them once again to help with his Oscar® Nominated live-action short comedy, *Time Freak.* Recently, Andrew helmed the story department at Food Network's series *24 Hour Restaurant Battle.* His other television credits include directing MTV's High School Stories and story producing for TLC's LA Ink.

He is managed by Greg Walter at Three Arts Entertainment and represented by Frank Wuliger at Gersh. He currently lives in Los Angeles with his wife and producing partner, Gigi Causey.

PRODUCER FILMOGRAPHY — GIGI CAUSEY

TIME FREAK (short) – producer

IF I DIDN'T CARE – co-producer

SAFE HOUSE – production supervisor
VAMPS – production supervisor
NICK AND NORAH'S INFINITE PLAYLIST – production supervisor
THE LUCKY ONES – production supervisor
KEANE – production supervisor

EXAMPLE PRESS KIT 2

Metro 7 Presents

Greta May

Written & Directed By Clifford Thurlow

BACKGROUND

Produced by Metro Seven Films, *Greta May* is a contemporary, character-driven drama that tells a fully realized story in a 10-minute short. Written and directed by Clifford Thurlow, it was shot on Super 16mm on location in London.

Producer Sacha Van Spall endows the project with high production values. Maureen Murray, as the executive producer, brings a keen eye for detail, and French director of photography Jean-Philippe Gossart washes the screen in radiant light. Composer Trevor Georges provides a moving jazz score, and Jess Murphy in the title role as Greta May puts in a captivating performance.

The film stands alone as a short, indie movie and there is the additional interest of it being one of five short films studied in Clifford Thurlow's book *Making Short Films: The Complete Guide From Script To Screen.* The screenplay for *Greta May* was adapted from a short story first published in *The Dream Zone*. Then follows the Eight-Point Guide to Making Short Films devised for the book. Combined with the film, it provides an insight into the adaptation process.

GRETA MAY SYNOPSIS

Actress Greta May has lost her confidence. She has lost her boyfriend, rising star Oliver Morrell. And she has lost her big break in a major new play that Oliver has made a roaring success.

When a stranger gives Greta his telephone number it only adds to her sense of desolation until her worldly-wise flatmate Rachel tells her: "The only way to get over one man is to get under another."

Greta is uncertain about Rachel's shallow advice but, left alone, she makes the telephone call in the vain hope that an encounter with the stranger will change her life and put her back in the spotlight.

METRO SEVEN MISSION STATEMENT

Metro Seven is committed to making profitable movies that are innovative, distinctive, compelling and engaging; movies that create an intercultural dialogue; movies that make us contemplate our life's journey and touch our brightest moments and our darkest secrets.

We will endeavor to develop projects that have universal themes that embrace a wide variety of moviegoers and maintain high production values to ensure their commercial viability. This will enable us to compete with any major film studio and protect our investors while never losing sight of our main responsibility—to entertain.

Writer/Director

Clifford Thurlow received a European Media Development Award (EMDA) for his feature adaptation of the Freya North novel *Sally*. He is the author of a number of books, including *Making Short Films*.

Producer

With a keen understanding of a good story and a sense of obligation to the audience, Sacha Van Spall is ideally suited to the role of producer. His dedication and attention to detail enable the highest standard of filmmaking.

Executive Producer

Maureen Murray cut her producing teeth working with controversial film director Ken Russell. She is a member of the Production Guild of Great Britain, a former board member of Women In Film and Television, and a graduate of Media 2000's European Audio-Visual Entrepreneurs.

Director of Photography

Jean-Philippe Gossart graduated in film and journalism before moving from France to the UK in 2002. He has spent the last three years as a lighting cameraman working on features, short films, and documentaries. His passion for camera and lighting is endless and he works to translate words into visual images.

Composer

Trevor Georges began his career as a performer at Glyndebourne Opera. He moved through the music genres from Latin, playing bass for King Salsa, to being a rock trombonist, assistant musical director for *The Buddy Holly Story*, the composer for *Tapping Harlem*, and Sam in the West End production of *Casablanca*.

Editor

Tony Appleton has spent almost twenty years editing commercials, documentaries, and movies for TV and the cinema. He sees short films as the ideal training ground for new filmmakers and enjoys the challenge of working with first-time directors on projects with tight budgets, and all the constraints of creating viable drama within the limitations of the genre.

Jess Murphy

Jess Murphy brings total passion and commitment to the title role as Greta May. Before drama school, Jess graduated from the Royal Academy of Music with a B.Mus. (violin performance). She played the lead in ITV's *How Not To Find A Husband*. *Greta May* is her first film.

Produced by Metro Seven

POSTER

Ela Gancarz, writing for Filmmaking Stuff—www.filmmakingstuff.com, believes a poster should be "the starting point of your overall brand strategy," and that before beginning the design, care needs to be paid to working out the message that you want to be communicated. The three elements to consider are the style, text, and images. The mood of the film should be summed up in the style—for example a comedy needs to be funny and light. Once created, all areas of marketing—from the Press Kit to the website to the DVD cover need to have consistent design themes and elements.

14.4 *Time Freak* Poster

▶▶ P.180

We have reproduced Oscar nominee *Time Freak*'s poster, and listed Total Film's (www.totalfilm.com) five favorite posters. All five are visually appealing and striking.

PAUSE

GREATEST MOVIE POSTERS EVER MADE

1. **Metropolis (1927)**
2. **Vertigo (1958)**
3. **Jaws (1975)**
4. **Hard Candy (2006)**
5. **The Dark Knight (2008)**

THE MEDIA

Getting an honest review or being featured in an interview for a media outlet—whether print, radio, TV, or online—is a gratifying, as well as a free way to promote a film.

Journalists, broadcasters, radio DJs, and major bloggers are invariably busy and are sent vast quantities of material by PR and marketing companies, as well as members of the public. With regular deadlines, there is little time to do research, even study unsolicited material.

It is up to you, the filmmaker, to make sure your Press Kit and PR material is lively, interesting, and immediately catches the eye. Does your project have a unique selling point, something that sets it apart from all the other shorts being screened? If so, work it out and get it down in black and white. Winning an award or having a big-name star on the cast will pique media interest. Did your leading lady just row across the Atlantic single handed? That's good PR. Put it in. Send a photo.

A film publicist will have the knowledge and contacts to give your film maximum exposure. Below is an interview with the owner of publicity agency Romley Davies, but if there is no budget for the professional touch, it is important to approach relevant media in the right time frame and methodology. Consider the following:

- **Who to approach?** Think of what media may naturally be interested in your film. Local newspapers and radio stations love stories that have a local angle. If the film is shot in a certain area or key actors are from that area – that could be enough to whet the appetite of some journalists. Also consider the genre and intended audience and research websites and magazines that cover that type of story.

- **What's the hook?** What's interesting about your film compared to other stories? What's the *news* aspect? Is it covering a relevant social issue? Is it controversial? An example of a film being cleverly timed is *G.M.* (Part VI: Scripts), which was inspired by the work of Georges Méliès and was produced to coincide with the 100th anniversary of the first screening of *Le Voyage Dans La Lune*.
- **Content.** Be sure to include relevant information in every communication. The press release should cover this, but also make sure contact details are in the signature of all emails.
- **Find the right person.** Finding the relevant contact at an organization increases the chance of your material being considered. Generally look out for a critic or arts editor. If you're not sure, call the newspaper or radio station and ask who the best contact is.
- **Timing.** Content that is not "hard news" (breaking stories) is often planned and even laid out months in advance. If you hope the publicity will coincide with a certain date (such as online launch), be sure to allow at least a couple of months.
- **Organization.** Set realistic goals as to what coverage you may be able to achieve. Make a list of media to contact, the date you messaged them and who you messaged. After a couple of days, make a follow-up phone call to check the message was received.

14.5 Dave Calhoun

DAVE CALHOUN—TIME OUT FILM CRITIC

www.timeout.com

1. What exactly do you do as a critic?
I'm an editor and a critic, so I watch films and I write about them, but I also commission other people to watch films and write about them, and edit their work.

2. Do you enjoy your job, and what are the reasons?
Yes, I love my job. I love cinema and I love journalism, and my job combines the two.

3. Why do you feel your have the right to judge the work of others?
Anybody has the right to judge the work of others, in terms of offering an opinion on that work. So I have as much and no more right than anyone else.

4. How many films do you watch in an average week?
It varies. Probably three or four at the moment. Seven, eight and more at busier times.

5. What mistakes do you see in young filmmakers that really should be avoided?
Age makes no difference. Old, young, fat, and thin filmmakers do great things and terrible things. A lack of originality and a lack of passion are the things that you most wish you'd been able to avoid as a viewer.

6. Do you have any advice for students entering the film industry?
Be original, be bold, be intelligent. Listen to advice, but be careful who you listen to and don't lose sight of yourself.

7. Have you ever considered making your own film?
In the odd mad moment. But I've never had an idea I've felt worth the risk and time and blood and sweat it's necessary to employ to get a film made. I salute each and every person who has made a film, whatever it is. It's not easy.

8. Is there much interaction between critics and actors/directors? Do you think there should be more?
There's some, at festivals and socially in a city like London it's inevitable when we both work in the same industry in loose terms. It's a good thing. Dialogue and conversation always is. It's not good, though, when friendships and allegiances overshadow people's opinions of films, which does happen.

9. Do you ever feel like you have to give certain films good reviews?
Yes. I have to give good films good reviews, that is, I review a film according to what's on screen and nothing else. Luckily, I work for a publication that thrives on independent criticism. If people can't trust *Time Out* to be fair and not swayed by advertising or other commercial interests, then the magazine is doomed. I pay equal attention and try to be equally unprejudiced whether reviewing a tiny art house film or a studio's summer blockbuster. If a critic can't do his or her job properly without interference, what's the point of doing it at all?

10. Is objectivity when reviewing possible?
No, of course not. Everyone has a point of view and opinions and experience, which they bring to bear on a review. But it is possible to strive to be fair.

11. Do moviemakers have a moral obligation or should entertainment be their only concern?
If entertainment is the only concern of a filmmaker, that's fine. But it would be a sad world if every filmmaker had only that concern. Some filmmakers need to strive for more (i.e. to educate, inspire, inform etc), and many do. There's no moral obligation to be any sort of filmmaker though. It's a matter of choice. Morality only comes into play when it comes to issues of offence, but even then both taste and the law are flexible according to time and place.

VANESSA DAVIES: FILM PUBLICIST

www.romleydavies.com

1. What do you do?

I run London-based film and entertainment publicity agency Romley Davies. We work with studios, producers, and directors in regards to the publicity needs of the film during production, as well as distributors with the release of their films. This can be in the UK or globally. I was also head of production publicity on all of the *Harry Potter* films, a role which I am proud to say I held from before cameras started to roll on the first film right through to the theatrical release of the final film *Harry Potter and the Deathly Hallows Part 2*. We also run successful events, home entertainment and digital divisions working with the BAFTA Children's Awards and the Jameson Empire Awards as well as DVD releases such as *The King's Speech*, *Downton Abbey*, *Tinker Tailor Soldier Spy* and other great titles.

2. When you take on a new film, is there a general strategy you follow, and if so, what is it?

Every campaign for every film release is different or should be! There are several considerations. Firstly and most importantly, audience—primary and secondary. This may seem obvious but I see so many campaigns which are ill thought out and don't reach the audience of the film. Everything you do as part of a publicity campaign (which should also work in tandem with the ad campaign and spend) should be targeted. For instance, there is no point placing a big interview in the *Guardian* if your film is more likely to appeal to readers of the *Sun*. If your movie has strong teen appeal, they live in the online community and thus great focus should be given to that part of the campaign as they consume less print media. In other words, do your homework. Another major consideration is budget; don't spend hours brainstorming whacky stunt ideas or major promotional events when you are working on small indie release. You are wasting your time and the distributor's. The size of the campaign should be in line with potential box office. Equally, when it comes to stunts or any other ideas, really think them through. It may seem like a great idea to have a tank flanked by 100 soldiers, drive down the middle of Oxford Street to promote the release of an action/war movie, but even considering you can get the permission of the council and the police (and it won't destroy the roads!) what press are you going to get out of this? Will it justify the spend and the work? Every idea, no matter how much fun must be thought through with a guesstimate as to final publicity value. Know your target primary audience, work out how best to expand this to reach your secondary audience (with ratio of time and budget apportioned accordingly), understand the needs of the distributor and the likely size of the release and above all else ensure that every idea you come up with is on message, viable both financially and practically and that it will deliver.

3. How important is new media (blogs, social media etc) in a film's PR campaign?

Very important. It is without doubt the biggest growth area in a film's publicity release strategy. All distributors (and filmmakers) want to see a strong online presence for their films and often start to build a Facebook page and Twitter presence well before a release, even during production, as this not only helps with potential sales, but will translate into bums on seats at release.

4. Is new media more relevant than traditional press (newspapers, radio, etc.) for short films?
It really depends on the release and the audience of a release. With teens and I'd say the 14–24 age group, a campaign should focus heavily on new media and although it will be supported with activity offline, i.e. with print and broadcast, that is where you are most likely to reach your audience. Every release will be supported by a social and online campaign, but perhaps this would be less of a priority with older audiences who are less likely to live in this community and more likely to consume print and broadcast, i.e. traditional media. But, then again, let's not forget silver surfers!

5. Film PR sounds very glamorous—is this the case?
Noooo! It does sound very glamorous, but it is a job like any other and involves a huge amount of work. Look at the person stood behind a famous actor on any red carpet coverage be it Oscars, BAFTAS or whatever, I mean the person talking into a radio or mobile, that is the publicist. They will probably have been up since 6am, have taken at least 100 phone calls whilst simultaneously juggling 100 emails, have been shouted at by a pack of paparazzi, an actor, several security guards and probably a few angry fans who didn't manage to get the autograph they'd been queuing for—and their day is only half way through. It is not glamorous.

6. What's the biggest campaign you have worked on, and how did it go?
Without doubt, it is of course the *Harry Potter* films. I was there when Dan, Emma, and Rupert were told they'd first got the roles, until the day they walked down their final red carpet, it was an incredible learning experience, a ten-year-plus long campaign and one of which I am incredibly proud.

7. What advice do you have for people looking to work in film PR?
Don't go into it if you think it's about glamour and meeting famous people. That will be 1% of your time. It is about hard work, strategy, organization, creativity, the ability to work with all sorts of people, enduring patience and a never failing sense of humor. If you really do want to get into it, start by making a list of all the film publicity companies, find the name of the person you should address your email or letter to and offer your services free of charge in order to get some work experience, be it a week or a summer holiday. You have nothing to offer them in the first instance other than a willing pair of hands and you will learn invaluable experience. It is a very small industry (both in the UK and US) and we all know each other and recommendation is everything. And for goodness' sake don't start your letter dear sir or madam, in this day and age and with all information available online, there is no excuse not to do your research!

8. Can "stunts" ever backfire?
Yes, of course. And that is true in any area of publicity. But, they shouldn't if you've done your homework and thought of every eventuality. There should be no risk to the public or animals, or any chance of the stunt failing (e.g. mechanical or otherwise) and you need to ensure you have all the permissions necessary. But, the biggest problem with stunts is that the cost can be disproportionate to the publicity the stunt garners. And that again comes down to ill-thought-out ideas and inexperience.

9. Does a filmmaker at his first film festival really need a publicist, or is it more relevant for Hollywood films?
It really depends on why he/she is going and what they are trying to achieve at that festival. If you don't have a film in that festival then there is no reason for any journalist to want to write about you, so you would be wasting your money. They will want to focus on the films in the festival and particularly those in competition. You may also find that if your film already has a distributor then they will cover the cost of the publicity effort. If you have a film in that festival but no distributor or sales agent as yet, then it may well be worth getting publicity support as you will want to make as much noise as possible both in the trades such as *Screen* and *Variety* as well as consumer press.

10. What is a realistic target in terms of PR for a decent first short film?
That really does depend on the film. The trouble with short films is that unless your short film is being played somewhere that the public can go and see it, then the consumer media will not want to cover it as the simple rule is that it has to appeal to their readers/viewers etc. Why write about something their readers can't go and see or access in some way (even via download)? However, if there is a real buzz about the short and possible inclusion at an Awards ceremony then there is a level of publicity that could potentially be achieved in so much as positioning the director as someone to look out for in the future.

11. What advice do you have for a filmmaker about to attend his first festival and who is "going it alone"?
Assuming that the film is actually in the festival, then the first thing is to decide why you are going and what you intend to achieve. A lot of meetings are set up before the festival begins. Make sure you do the same.

STOP

14.1 Tilda Swinton struggling as Kevin's mother in *We Need to Talk About Kevin* (2011)

14.2 Ezra Miller playing the disturbing Kevin

14.3 *Time Freak* Poster

START

CHAPTER 15

Festivals and Distributors

With an online presence and the Press Kit and poster ready to go, it's time to consider what strategy is best for your short film. Feature movies have had a fairly standard distribution route for some years:

1. Festival circuit
2. Cinema release
3. DVD rental and then sales
4. Pay-per-view TV
5. Premium TV and then free TV
6. Internet distribution

A short film is more than likely to skip stages 2–5. Some indie short-filmmakers are beginning to lose interest in the "festival circuit," but do not underestimate the value an award can have for the film's (and your) future success, and more importantly, the invaluable contacts that can be made. Depending on the festival in question, everyone from talent to distributors, producers to industry bigwigs will be looking for fresh talent.

Festivals used to be free, now most charge for entry—anything from $10 upwards. Those that encourage mass applications may merely have found a lucrative way to finance their festival, so select with prudence. There are now over 5,000 around the world, but many are for specific genres so may not be appropriate for you. There are no shortcuts for choosing the right ones—just time and research.

We've included a list of our favorite festivals, with contact details, at the back of this book. But up-to-date and comprehensive lists can be found in numerous places. To start off, check:

- FilmFestivals—www.filmfestivals.com
- Without A Box—www.withoutabox.com
- Indiewire—www.indiewire.com

The number of festivals you apply to will be limited by time and money. When you've selected a realistic number, go about the process in an organized way. For every festival you want to apply to keep a database of:

- What, where and when
- Submission deadline
- Formats accepted and other relevant information
- Dates you applied, entry fee charge and receipts

PAUSE

WITHOUTABOX – WWW.WITHOUTABOX.COM

Withoutabox will make life a lot easier. More than 900 festivals use it to receive submissions electronically, making it much faster and easier to submit a film to multiple festivals. There's also no charge—users just pay the standard entrance fees. While submitting there's an automatic Qualify Engine to check the film fits in the right category, and once submitted there's the option to check the status of the application. The site also features daily deadline updates and an active message board for networking. Since the company was bought by IMDb in 2008, there's also increased collaboration between the sites. For example when you submit a film through Withoutabox, you'll automatically be offered promotional opportunities and the chance to create a Page on IMDb.

The deadline for submissions at festivals is generally at least three months before the event, but all festivals have slightly different rules, and each much be checked thoroughly. It would be a shame to be rejected for a small error such as sending your film in the wrong format. As an example, we've listed the main entry requirements for Sundance 2013.

Sundance 2013 entry requirements for short films—at a glance

- **ENTRY FEE:** Between $40–$80 depending on the genre of film and the time it is sent (the earlier the cheaper).
- **SUBMISSION CATEGORIES:** There are two short film categories, the difference beingwhere the funding was sourced. For the "U.S." category, at least half of the financing must have come from the States, while "International" can be from anywhere.
- **LENGTH:** Less than 50 minutes, including credits.
- **PRIOR SCREENING RESTRICTIONS:** None. It can have been played anywhere already—from a theater to the Internet.
- **AGE OF FILM:** Film must have been completed in or since 2011.
- **PRIZES:** Prizes within categories US Fiction, International Fiction, Non-Fiction, and Animation, as well as the coveted Grand Jury Prize.
- **PHYSICAL SUBMISSION REQUIREMENTS:** A single DVD-R or DVD+R disc in a paper sleeve, compatible with standard set-top DVD players (not QuickTime or AVI) with a Withoutabox tracking number and film title on the face of the DVD. NTSC, Region 1 or region free (Region 0) is preferred, but PAL and SECAM are also accepted. Other formats including Blu-Ray, VHS, Beta, Mini-DV, HD-CAM, 16mm and 35mm are not accepted at this stage.
- **DIGITAL SUBMISSION REQUIREMENTS:** In place of a DVD, upload file with a Secure Online Screener system via Withoutabox or IMDb. Must be in Flash or QuickTime and less than 2GB.

- **NOTIFICATION:** In 2012 Sundance received 11,777 films, so allow one month for submissions to be processed. It will appear on your Withoutabox account, or you can include a self-addressed, stamped postcard, which will be returned when the submission has been processed.
- **ACCEPTABLE FORMATS IF SELECTED:** Film prints in 16mm or 35mm format, digital video on Sony HDCAM tape and DCP.
- **OTHER NOTES:** Subtitles if not in English. No fancy packaging/printed promo material—it is a waste and will just be thrown away. All submissions must be registered online at the Sundance or Withoutabox website before posting.
- If accepted, a waiver must be signed stating the film doesn't violate any copyright.

15.1 Elliot Grove

ELLIOT GROVE – HEAD OF THE RAINDANCE FILM FESTIVAL

www.raindance.co.uk

1. What were your reasons for starting Raindance?
When I started the Raindance Film Festival in 1993 the British film industry was in the depths of despair, so I thought I'd start a film festival to celebrate British talent and try and get things moving again. Being a native Canadian, I didn't realize how suspicious of outsiders British people were, and I was pretty much ignored. Who came those first few years were the Japanese, the French and the Americans. It took about seven years before Brits started to realize what a great idea it was to have a film festival dedicated to celebrating independent cinema on their doorstep.

2. What are the biggest challenges you've faced?
I don't view anything in the film industry as a challenge or a problem. Years when we had practically no money or industry support I viewed as a series of challenging creative opportunities

3. What is the single biggest achievement you have made with Raindance?
Surviving twenty plus years has been my achievement. When I started most people gave me, at most, three years. And here we still are.

4. Do you consider film school as being worthwhile for young people looking to enter the industry?
Film school is a great place to meet potential collaborators and use cheap or free equipment. Film schools teach filmmaking. They can't teach HOW to become a filmmaker. This can only be learned in the work place. Learn craft at film school. Making films is how you become a filmmaker.

5. What advice do you have for people making their first short film?
Keep short films short. Under fifteen minutes, or even under ten. If your film is destined for the Internet, under five minutes is a good length. And please, please, please tell a story.

6. How many submissions do you receive, and how do you select the best?
Each year Raindance receives about four thousand submissions from over seventy countries. We pick the ones we like—it's one of the benefits of running a film festival: You show the films you like. At Raindance film is extreme. By that I mean three things: Extreme topics, extreme filmmaking and because it's Raindance, an Oscar-qualifying film festival, extremely good.

7. What are the pitfalls you have noticed people making when they enter their film, and how can they be avoided?
Most new filmmakers submitted to a festival the first time don't properly read the festival rules and guidelines. All festivals post these on their website. A second failure is a filmmaker's inability to provide a decent press kit. The biggest single mistake you can make is putting a sticky label on your DVD screener—it really mucks up one's hard drive!

15.2 Elliot Grove in action
▶▶ P.194

8. How can filmmakers get the most out of a festival if their film is selected?
Being selected into any festival is tough. Once you are selected the work has just begun: filmmakers need to promote their screening to local industry and potential partners. If you are able to attend make sure you network with other filmmakers: swap tales from the trenches and learn from their successes and noble failures.

9. Is it worth a filmmaker going to a festival even if their film has been rejected?
I can vouch from personal experience that being rejected from a film festival is an ego-shattering experience. It's important to realize why you were declined. Was it because your film was lousy? Almost certainly not. Your film was turned down because someone on their selection committee didn't like it. If the film festival has events and parties that you think you would enjoy, then by all means attend. But don't show up all bitter and twisted. Their decision isn't personal to you. Remember there are thousands of film festivals around the world. Surely there will be one that loves your film.

10. What advice do you have for someone who has created a great film and is about to go on tour?
Making a great film is a rare and wonderful thing. A filmmaker fortunate enough to have such a film will need to figure out what they hope to gain from it: is it fame or fortune he or she seeks? Once you have decided, you will most likely need to engage the services of a great publicist and a lawyer to help you negotiate the pitfalls likely to confront you.

11. Do film festival awards help a filmmaker's career?
Filmmakers go to a film festival to win awards, to get reviewed and interviewed and to try and sell their films. Festivals are an important first step in creating the buzz around a film career.

12. What advice would you give to short-filmmakers developing their first feature?

A great feature is always based on an excellent script. Without a script, you will waste your time. Shorts are a great way to develop story, filming techniques, and to explore character development. Making the leap from shorts to features is not always an easy one. Some filmmakers are expert at short form and fail miserably at feature-length movies (and vice versa). Many filmmakers I meet through Raindance are exploring other forms of longer storytelling: transmedia, web series, and so on. Think of yourself as a visual storyteller. Get really good at this, and then it will be obvious what format your skills are best suited to.

ONLINE FILM FESTIVALS

Not as glamorous as a Palme d'Or, but a win at an online film festival can help you get noticed as well as win some decent cash prizes and other incentives. New online film festivals seem to appear every month, but here's a small selection:

Vimeo Festival + Awards—www.vimeo.com

Launched in 2010, the first year saw nine categories judged by big names including David Lynch and Morgan Spurlock with a $25,000 grand prize for the overall winner. The New York-based festival also has workshops and screenings.

YouTube's Your Film Festival—www.youtube.com

YouTube launched its own online festival in 2012. They ask for a short, story-driven video in any genre and in any format—whether a short film, web-series episode or a TV pilot. Entering is also free. YouTube users voted on the films, with ten finalists being flown out to open the Venice Film Festival. The overall winner will gain a $500,000 grant for a new project, produced by Ridley Scott and Michael Fassbender.

FilmOneFest—www.filmonefest.org

Started in 2008, this New Jersey-based festival screens one-minute films shot in any format.

The iPhone Film Festival (IFF)—www.iphoneff.com

There are a number of online festivals where content has to be shot entirely on mobile phones. As the name implies, the IFF is only for iPhone/iPad users, but similar ones exist for smartphones. Using a phone to create a short film will certainly test your innovation and creativity.

ATTENDING A FESTIVAL

So all of the hard work has paid off and your film has been selected. Congratulations! It's worth preparing for each festival to make sure you, and your film, get as much out of it as possible. Festival staff will generally be super busy, so your enjoyment, networking and publicity for your film will largely fall to you. If it's a major festival and you're likely to be mobbed by the press, it may be worth hiring a publicist. Professional film PRs will be able to use their skills and contacts to give you and your film maximum exposure, introduce you to handy contacts and deal with any problems. An interview with world-leading publicist Vanessa Davies, packed full of insider-information, is included in Chapter 14: Marketing.

If you decide to "Go it alone," it's worth considering media well before the screening date. One or two months before the festival opens, the marketing manager will be happy to provide a list of all media that is covering the festival—TV, radio, print, and online. Send an email to relevant publications describing the short with links to your website, and also offer to send a screener and EKP (Electronic Press Kit).

Although you will be trying to push your film, it's important to think ahead and about future projects. Valuable introductions can be made with people who may be interested in working with you or providing funding in the future. Many festivals publish a guide of delegates that are present. Researching who you are interested in, or who may be interested in you, can make networking far more productive and less stressful. As you're likely to meet a large number of people, be sure to pack business cards (more than you'd think) as well as DVDs to hand out to relevant people.

15.3 Matthew James Reilly

MATTHEW JAMES REILLY: FESTIVAL EXHIBITOR

www.abigailthefilm.com

1. What festival did you attend and what film did you show?
My film *Abigail* was selected for the 65th Festival de Cannes.

2. How did you go about applying for festivals?
I finished a working cut of the film, which I had been preparing for a class screening at New York University. My professor was very fond of the work and he, along with my Mom, urged me to submit to festivals. I didn't know much about the festival circuit at the time. I was only familiar with the major and most prominent (Cannes, Sundance, Berlin, Tribeca, SXSW etc.). I figured I might as well start at the top. The deadlines for most of the aforementioned had passed except for Cannes and Tribeca. Tisch (NYU) had sent out an email forwarded from the Cannes Film Festival, inviting film students to submit their work for the Cinéfondation selection. Every year roughly 2,000 films are submitted from 320 institutions. Only 15 make the selection. I decided to submit to the Cinéfondation as well as Tribeca. Unfortunately I was very late in my submission. The deadline was less than a week away. One thing they always tell us at school is never wait until the last minute to submit, because it's when the programmers are the busiest and likely less focused. I had to pay a very expensive postage fee just to get the film to France in time.

3. How did you cope with rejection at festivals where you weren't selected?
I was quite fortunate to only have a very short period of grief when it

came to festival rejection. Late one night, a few weeks after submitting to the two festivals, I received an automated rejection email from Tribeca. I was a little crestfallen, as every filmmaker should be upon his or her first rejection. The next morning, however, I awoke with a nice surprise. I got an email from the wonderful Dimitra Karya (The programmer for the Cinéfondation selection) informing me of my acceptance into the forthcoming Cannes Film Festival. Needless to say, I easily forgot about my rejection from Tribeca.

I think mine was a very rare case, but what I've come to realize regarding festivals and rejections is that it is truly all about personal taste. I think each festival reflects a certain taste in all their selections. What may be right for one festival, might not work for another. Everyone has different opinions about what a film's "quality" consists of. I feel it's important to keep that in mind when dealing with rejection.

15.4 *Abigail* (2012)

▶▶ P.194

4. How did you feel at the screening with so many people watching your film?
I felt pride, exhilaration, and a palpable sense of completion. Whether they be intimate little shorts or sprawling big-budget epics, we make our films to share with others, preferably on the silver screen. After spending six to eight months in a small dark editing room, it's easy to forget that.

5. Do you have a press agent, and if not, do you think you may have benefited from one?
I did not have a press agent. Thankfully the festival was able to provide me with one, which was great. She arranged all the interviews for me, and made sure I kept up with my schedule. It definitely would have been a lot harder to keep track of everything without her.

6. Did anything happen that you weren't expecting/didn't prepare for?
I suppose the biggest surprise was winning. It kind of made the excitement and craziness jump tenfold. Aside from that, I don't think I was expecting to have so much fun. You go into it with the mindset that you are a working artist, and presenting something in the festival, but just because you're a part of the festival doesn't mean you're not still an attendee.

7. Was it useful for networking?
Absolutely. I probably met 30 to 40 different people a day, most of them shared the same passion and taste for film that I do. Cannes did an amazing job in creating forums to mingle. However, the most creative and rewarding people I associated with were definitely my fellow filmmakers in the selection.

8. What one thing will you do differently at the next festival you screen at?
I'm really happy with how my experience turned out. I don't know if I would change much. If I had to do one thing a little differently it might be watching less movies. As a film lover, it's difficult not to spend an entire day going to screening after screening. Next time, I may be a bit more cautious about keeping time available for networking.

9. Did you follow up on any new contacts, and is anything happening as a result?

A few months after the festival I'm still in the process of following up. I'm starting to realize just how many business cards I actually handed out. Something really awesome that came after Cannes was several invitations to other festivals. Just recently my film screened at the Melbourne International Film Festival, and will be doing a lot more traveling by the end of the year.

10. What advice do you have for someone who is going to go to his or her first festival?

First and foremost, have fun. At the end of the day, it's a "Festival" you're attending. It is a place of opportunity and possibility, but don't forget that you've already achieved a tremendous goal. Your acceptance should be celebrated before you move on to the next big thing. Definitely be prepared. Bring business cards, make a website, but don't get too hung up on promotional materials. Your film is one of a handful of others that will be selected. People who are there to watch short films will already know about it. It's a difficult feat to try to get someone more excited for your short film than they are for the new Michael Haneke film. Embrace the shorts enthusiast.

PITCHING

If you set up a meeting with someone, it's time for the all-important pitch—a skill requiring the same verbal dexterity as the street trader hawking perfume outside Bloomingdale's.

Pitching has a long tradition in Hollywood—deftly satirized in Robert Altman's 1992 *The Player*—and what happens in Hollywood crosses the globe with the certainty of the tide. Whether at a festival, or at a meeting set up elsewhere, the concept for pitching is the same. Executives will be drowning in a sea of words, memos, outlines, new scripts, second drafts, text messaging, and machine gun spray over the email, making a verbal pitch an efficient way for filmmakers to get their message across to potential funders in as short a time as possible—often as little as three minutes, the so-called "elevator pitch."

At film festivals, a more generous ten-minute pitch is common. Producers will suffer repeated rejection, but it at least gives them a chance to hone the pitch, as well as the concept, until they do find interest—or conclude that the idea just isn't going to hack it after all. One problem for producers is that ideas are sometimes "in the air" and while what they are pitching may be completely original to the writer, it may already be yesterday's good idea to the rushed exec behind the desk.

At one crowded pitching session we attended, independent producer Daniel San (*Understanding Jane*) hosted a panel discussion with screenwriting tutor Phil Parker, independent producer Phil Hunt (*Fast Food*), Parallax producer Sally Hibbin (*Land and Freedom, Carla's Song, Liam*) and former Film Council executive Himesh Kar.

They had all been through the mill both pitching and hearing pitches and they didn't always agree on how to approach the process, but if there was a common denominator it was this: *don't* tell the story, get people interested in the idea, the lives of the characters and the hurdles they face.

"What really matters is the power of the concept," stresses Himesh Kar. "If you can get people's eyes to light up, you've got them. If they want to know more, they'll ask, don't worry."

"Make your story grounded in reality," advises Phil Hunt. "When a story comes from the real world, or grows from a life experience, it's something everyone can identify with."

Kar was nodding thoughtfully. "Be careful, though," he adds. "Pitches that come from people who say it's a personal story, that they have lived this life, it can be interesting, but I often find it off-putting. I strongly believe in the force of the idea. That's what affects me."

What they did agree on is the need for research: "If you know about the guy you're talking to, it is less intimidating. It will be easier to find out if you have things in common," says Sally Hibbin. "Find out what people are looking for. Speak to assistants and secretaries. They are the first point of contact. They often have an overview and will know if you are wasting your time—or worse, wasting the time of the person listening to your pitch."

They dismissed the suggestion from a member of the audience who asked whether a $50 note in a birthday card for a secretary was a good way to reach the boss. Kar turned his thumbs down. "Absolutely not. There's a bullshit detector that goes off when people try and manipulate the system or exaggerate, when they say they have credits when they don't, or they have stars attached when it's just a wish list. If the person you're pitching to is interested in the idea, the first thing he'll do is go on the web and check the Internet Movie Data Base to check your credits. And if you say you have a star on board, they'll ring the agent. Everyone knows everyone in this business and if you're making your way in, you have to be honest and plain speaking. That's the way you earn respect."

As an experienced producer with Ken Loach and a dozen films to her credit, Sally Hibbin has come to rely on the Six Degrees of Separation theory. If you really need to reach an actor or an actress, there is always someone who knows someone and you follow the trail until you get to them. In the end, actors want to work, and if they are right for the role, and if the project interests them, they'll want to be involved.

For those setting out in their career, it is not going to be as easy as that. In a former incarnation, Himesh Kar represented writers and directors at the William Morris Agency and in his experience, agents and their assistants are very cynical. They have seen it all and heard it all and they are always on their guard. "In the end, it's very difficult to get talent involved unless you already have the money."

Phil Parker makes the point that it is often more important in the early stages of a filmmaker's career to find allies than to find money. If you are able to get an Executive Producer attached to a project, it may help a lot more in the long run, first to complete the package, and then to find finance. "A pitch rarely gets your film financed, a short or a feature, but it may get your foot in the door. It may seem strange, but most people in the film industry are amazingly generous. There is a core of people willing to be mentors. They are bombarded with projects and whether or not they decide to help you will really depend on the way you approach them."

Chair for the event, Danny San, points out that if you are going into the film business, you are there for the long haul. You will tend to meet the same executives again and again. You will get to learn what people are looking for, how to approach them—and when to approach them. "You have to be so passionate about a project that even if everyone turns it down, you are still passionate. That passion is infectious. It will get you noticed."

PAUSE

THE PITCH

How exactly do you approach a pitching session? Phil Hunt outlines his own ten-minute plan:

1. Introductions and greetings: give your full name, company name and a business card. Don't expect people to remember you, even if you have been invited to pitch a project.
2. Tell them what you are going to talk about: a short film, feature, documentary, TV series.
3. Clarify exactly what you want: development money, funding money, to read a script, to read a new draft.
4. Briefly outline your credentials and achievements.
5. Give them a chance to ask you questions.
6. Present the main elements of the story, the characters and conflicts, and why do you believe the story is unique. *Do not* tell the story. Describe target audience, any similar films and how much money they took.
7. Give an idea of the budget, funds attached, if any, and potential sales. Point out the benefits to the company you are pitching to.
8. Summarize important aspects of the package: cast, director, department heads.
9. Leave supporting material: synopsis and/or script, details of the package.
10. Thank the exec for listening to you, shake hands, and it's time to go.

GRAVE DANGERS

Danny San points out that there are grave dangers in going to a pitching session two handed. "If there is not a unified vision, they will know straight away," he adds. "I find it best to go alone the first time and, if I am called back, I will take the director with me. Whichever way, you should practice a pitch like an actor with his lines. Collar friends and pitch a film like you were telling a true story. You have to get so familiar with the subject, you can tell it in thirty seconds or in ten minutes, and retain the same essence."

In the same way that the $50 in the birthday card ploy is ill-advised, the panel counsels against over-packaging projects, filling pages with pictures or graphics. Many ruses have been tried. The producer Paul Trijbits (*Brick Lane, The Wind that Shakes the Barley*) admits to having once delivered a horror script to a production company in a miniature coffin. But while this might be mildly amusing, the script will have to stand up to the hype.
Parker drew everyone's attention to the importance of the written outline

or synopsis that is crucial to supporting the verbal pitch. His advice is that it should be no more than four pages, and better still just one or two, and suggests dividing it into four brief sections:

1. Premise statement, setting out the characters and what the story is about.
2. Address the needs or dilemmas faced by the central characters.
3. Deal with the central crisis of the drama, leaving enough space for the executive to get involved—don't reveal the plot.
4. Finish by stating this will be this type of film, this will attract this type of audience—something totally positive.

Finally he explains that the major weakness he comes across is that projects are rarely what they claim to be. "A film has to be unique *and* familiar, a mixture of both, and that is very hard to achieve."

PAUSE

COMPETITIONS

Competitions are also worth checking. We have listed just two, but there are often one-offs sponsored by corporations such as phone companies or production schemes, so keep up to date with the film news.

- **48 Hour Film Project—www.48hourfilm.com**

You will be given a character, a prop, and a line of dialogue at the last minute. You then have 48 hours to create a short film—from script to screen. In 2012, the Project will visit 119 cities around the world with the winner receiving $5,000.

- **Straight 8—www.straight8.net**

Make a short film on a single cartridge of super 8—without editing. The first time the creators see their work is at its premiere.

SALES AGENTS

Sales agents look after distribution deals for films, negotiate contracts, and if the film makes a profit, pays royalties. To keep their catalog of films fresh, sales agents will be at festivals looking for hot new releases, or can be contacted directly.

Sales agents generally take 30%–50% of each sale they make for a short film. If a sales agent expresses an interest in your film, they will ask you to sign a license giving them—probably exclusive—rights to sell your film for a certain amount of time, in certain places, and in certain formats. These are the three main points to consider when negotiating with a sales agent:

- Time—How long is the license?
- Territory—What countries does the license cover?
- Media—What outlets are covered? (Theater, online, etc.)

All sales agents work differently—some pay advances, some will only consider a finished product and all work in slightly different markets. Finding a good sales agent can be tough, but researching what they have already achieved—even contacting their current clients asking how they are doing—can pay off.

Unfortunately most of the bigger agencies don't work with short films, but some exist exclusively for this market:

SND Films—www.sndfilms.com
An international sales agency running since 1994, selling award-winning shorts, TV-movies and documentaries.

Future Shorts—www.futureshorts.com
Their distribution service sells to an international network across multiple platforms including broadcast, online, IPTV, and airlines.

Dazzle Films—www.dazzlefilms.co.uk
See Below

PAUSE

DAZZLE FILMS—INDEPENDENT SHORT FILM LABEL

After spending several years watching shorts while working for Buena Vista, among others, Dawn Sharpless launched Dazzle Films for the sale, distribution and exhibition of shorts in what she describes as a "selective, bijou company."

With her many years of experience, she knows what she wants to put in her catalog and the buzzwords are quality and originality. "If a film engages me then I will work with the filmmakers and do everything I can to help them. It's not a financial question: I don't think, yeah, this film is going to make a lot of money. No. I have to love it. Comedy and light drama are an easy sell, but that's not necessarily what I'm looking for."

Dawn receives dozens of spec films a month. On average, less than five of them are worth seeing more than once; about one a month makes it into the catalog. The best films, or at least those that Dazzle take on, still tend to reach Dawn after doing the festival circuit. For a short film to make cinema sales, they need to be ten minutes maximum and, again, comedies sell best. Dazzle distributes a wide range of material, from 15-second digital micro movies to 35mm mini-masterpieces. The criterion for becoming a Dazzle film, says Dawn, is very simple: they have to be good.

Now, how about the money: are short-filmmakers going to make their fortune?

Dawn Sharpless shook her head and waved a warning finger. "Filmmakers ask: how much am I going to make? But that's not really the question. What they should be asking themselves is: how can I get shown? How can I make sure my little darling gets screened? If you make any money, you should see that as a bonus."

Licensing fees vary, and Dazzle takes a commission of 40%, and earns its money by first helping the filmmaker get their film commercially finished, they help clear music rights and then resell the films as many times as they can.

One of the biggest costs can be acquiring music rights. Young filmmakers want to use current stars to create the mood they imagine, but the cost of clearing Rihanna or The White Stripes can be more than the entire cost of making the film. "They come to me with this kind of sound track on their films and say, don't worry, no one will notice. But they will notice. If you make a film for your own amusement and show it to friends, no one will bother you, but if you want to see it screened on TV and in the festivals, you have to be professional and do everything the right way."

Dawn suggests using original music. Composers just starting out in their career will often at little or no cost be willing to sit down with the filmmakers and create the music they have in mind, even the music they admire by their rock heroes. "But don't get too close to the original, or you'll still end up facing Madonna or Eminem across the court room."

STOP

In Dawn's opinion, short films in the UK are falling behind those in the US and Europe and advises filmmakers to get an education by going to every screening possible. "There are festivals all over the country, the Soho Rushes festival is free, so there's no excuse. Learn the techniques, study what makes a good story and only then should people be thinking about making a film."

15.2 Elliot Grove in action

15.4 Still from *Abigail* (2012)

START

CHAPTER 16

Hybrid Distribution

If a sales agent or distribution company is not interested or not right for your film, distributing a short yourself is easier than ever before. Dawn Sharpless at Dazzle, the short-film distributor, has told us that "money should be seen as a bonus," while "getting your film out there" should be the priority for creators of short films. While this is still the prevailing creed, not everyone agrees.

Hybrid distribution has been hailed as the final "democratization of film," as it gives filmmakers full control over how the film is released and marketed, allows filmmakers to find and build relationships with fans, and allows direct sales to the public—all of which is limited when contracts are signed with a sales agent.

Most of the industry now agrees that digital distribution is the future for all film, and the trick is to get your film into as many distribution channels as possible, or at least the right ones for your film. Keri Putnam, Executive Director of Sundance Institute, said: "Audiences are accessing independent films via a range of platforms and storefronts, which speaks to the need for filmmakers to make their work available in a variety of ways."[1]

Even with a distributor on board, hybrid distribution can be applied to geographical areas not covered by the contract since geofiltering allows sales to be limited to particular territories. Creating a sophisticated strategy is the only way to get noticed. While some general principles apply, every short film needs its own strategy geared to achieving its own goals. Prioritizing goals is essential. These can include: reaching as large an audience as possible; expanding awareness of your work among festivals, distributors, and critics; maximizing revenue; gaining funding for future projects, and building a personal core audience.

POD TECHNOLOGY

Having DVD copies of your film professionally printed and packaged for sale and to show potential future collaborators is rewarding, but expensive. The more you have made, the less each individual copy costs, but there's a risk of having boxes of your film left in the garage several years later—a truly disheartening experience. Thanks to POD, or "print-on-demand" technology, this is no longer an issue. There are a number of companies that offer this service, our favorite being Amazon's CreateSpace—www.createspace.com.

Using the footage and artwork you provide, CreateSpace creates the DVD and color prints the disc and DVD cover. If someone wants to order a copy, they can do so either through your site or through Amazon. CreateSpace will then create a single copy; post it to the buyer and save a share of the profit for you. The major downside is the "per unit" cost is significantly higher than if you were to have a 1,000 copies made. The plus side is all aspects of the creation, distribution and payments are taken care of.

CreateSpace charges a fixed rate of $4.95 per unit, as well as 15% of sales through your site, and 45% of sales through Amazon.com. Ordering copies for yourself just incurs the fixed cost, and discounts apply for bulk ordering—over 100 copies receive a 40% discount, bringing the price down to $2.97 per disc, plus postage.

DVD content and cover artwork must be supplied in certain formats, but CreateSpace provides extensive support material. Once they have the content, they also offer the opportunity to add it to their VOD service—giving fans more choice to access your film. They also offer a non-exclusive agreement, leaving other distribution channels open.

VIDEO HOSTING SERVICE

People have a hunger for watching short clips on the net, and as a result there are a dizzying amount of video hosting services—places we can upload video, and everything else will be taken care of. By far the biggest is YouTube, with 1.2 billion daily views. At the time of writing, the most watched clip is Justin Bieber's *Baby*, having been played over .75 billion times. The latest statistics reveal that 48 hours of video are uploaded every minute, resulting in nearly 8 years of content uploaded every day on YouTube alone.

In second place is Youku Tudou—the result of a merger between two of China's largest sites—which receives 150 million views every day.

Other big players include Dailymotion, iFilm, Metacafe and Vimeo. Some video hosting services have ads, some censor content, some allow videos to be downloaded and others offer ad revenue sharing. Choosing the right place or places for your film will need some care and research.

ONLINE/VOD DISTRIBUTION—MAKE MONEY STREAMING

Film Annex—www.filmannex.com

A free platform for self-distribution and funding for filmmakers and other creatives, where content is monetized through advertising. After joining, users get their own "Web TV" channel where they upload content, and then receive 50% of all revenues from ads that are shown. Revenue depends on traffic—the more page views a Web TV receives, the more money. Film Annex has 260,000 registered users and gets 1.5 million daily visitors.

IndieFlix—www.indieflix.com
A "filmmakers first" marketplace and distribution company designed to empower filmmakers as well as to make works selected at all major film festivals available to the largest possible online audience. To qualify, films must generally have received an "official selection" at a film festival. Contracts are non-exclusive and filmmakers get 70% of all net profits. Some films will also be distributed to other platforms including Cable VOD providers, Hulu, and iTunes.

YouTube Partner Program—www.youtube.com/partners
Not always the best place for an indie short, but it does work for some people. After uploading, opt your channel in for monetization. Partners can upload videos in higher quality, brand channels and access comprehensive analytics to learn about their audience and work out how to increase the number of viewers. Royalties come from various types of advertising.

ONLINE DISTRIBUTORS

Online distributors will make your film available in different places on the web where people can pay to see your film and either charge an up-front fee or share royalties. It's a competitive industry that is likely to change rapidly, so be sure to check the pricing structures of each company.

Egg Up—www.eggup.com
Post in the film and trailer, Egg Up will then make it available on MAC, PC, iPad, and IPhone. Every time someone pays to stream or download your film, your PayPal account will be automatically credited. Egg Up is a pay-as-you-go service, so there are no long-term contracts or commitments on your part. The price of the film and country restrictions can also be easily changed. Analyzing who is buying your film, and where they are buying it can also help focus marketing activity—and increase sales.

Dynamo—www.dynamoplayer.com
Add a film to Dynamo, and it can then be embedded anywhere on the web. Set the price and access period. Before streaming the video, users must pay through PayPal or Amazon. Video owners receive 70% of every sale.

Distribber—www.distribber.com
A one-time charge to place your film on various platforms including iTunes, Netflix Watch Instantly, Amazon VOD, Hulu, and Cable/Satellite/Telco VOD services. Generally it can only be made available in the United States. The charge may seem high ($1,295 for iTunes), but all revenue is then paid directly to the creator. Sales stats are accessible at all times.

Distrify—www.distrify.com
Film trailers can be embedded in any site or social network, where fans can pay to watch the films and also be shared by email, Facebook, Twitter, etc. There's also an affiliate scheme for fans who share.

PAUSE

THE 6-POINT PLAN

Following the festival circuit, DVD, and paid-for streaming, the time will come when your short is ready to be made publicly available for free. The dream is for it to go viral, or circulate rapidly on the Internet through people sharing and searching for your film. Uploading to YouTube, sitting back and waiting for the call from a studio is the easy option. It's also unlikely to happen. Instead a planned blitz using multiple platforms can work a treat.

Andrew Allen, editor of Short of the Week—www.shortoftheweek.com—has a six-point plan that worked wonders for his award-winning short *The Thomas Beale Cipher:*

1. **Go Vimeo.** It has a stronger filmmaking community than YouTube, which may hit more viewers, and Vimeo will attract the right viewers—those more likely to pass it on to others.
2. **Post early.** Upload the film early Monday morning (12AM EST) to give the film a full 24 hours to rack up views and keep it relevant all week.
3. **Use Short of the Week as a springboard.** Feature the film on our site and use our social media outlets to get the word out.
4. **Harness the crew.** Make sure everyone associated with the film knows the plan, and shares it with their social networks. With even 8–10 people sharing on Twitter and Facebook (even if no one individually is Mr. Popular) it is not hard to get over 1000 impressions, which can be enough to reach a critical mass.
5. **Target key influencers.** Email a few major blogs and news sites that share an interest in the film's topic or technique. A key consideration is crafting a good email. As curators of a site with a submit button, we know it is important to look pro. Have a well-designed email with well-written teaser description, something about the context of the making of the film, a blurb about the filmmaker and a hi-quality image. Make it easy for a blogger to turn around and publish without any further follow-up with you.
6. **Keep at it.** All day, all week if needed—continue reaching out to new people.

To target the right people, Andrew asked himself, "what is interesting about the film and to whom might we target it to?" He started by seeking interest from relevant blogs and media outlets, and before long, was being approached by larger publishers including Fast Company and Wired. After several weeks of hard promotion, *The Thomas Beale Cipher* had been viewed 170,000 times on Vimeo, it received over 1,300 blog reviews or mentions, 2,000 tweets and 5,000 shares with 500 extra fans on Facebook. For a point of comparison, on the festival circuit it was viewed 3,000 times and had 12 media mentions. The online campaign cost $0 and received interest from both the industry and distributors compared to the $1,200 spent at festivals, which received no solid interest.

Following the online campaign, Andrew says he realized "the online video world is not a meritocracy." People won't find a film just because it's good. A surge of traffic is needed to get noticed. Perhaps more importantly,

16.1 *The Thomas Beale Cipher* (2010)

P.204

the industry does take notice of what happens on the web—Andrew was contacted by studio execs, production houses, and people looking to collaborate on other projects.

He concludes by stating: "I've come to think of a festival run as more of a preview screening—a fun experience with a large audience to share with your cast and crew. The wide release—where a short film can make its biggest impact—happens online."

PIRACY AND THE MPAA

In the USA over two million people work in the film and television industry, which is worth $175 billion annually. It's an industry that's worth protecting, and the responsibility falls to The Motion Picture Association of America (MPAA), whose members include: Walt Disney Studios Motion Pictures, Paramount Pictures, Sony Pictures Entertainment, Twentieth Century Fox Film Corporation, Universal City Studios LLC, and Warner Bros. Entertainment. The MPAA champions intellectual property rights and works with content protection groups around the world.

We are all aware that almost anything can be downloaded illegally, for free, from BitTorrent sites. Filmmakers are likely to feel angry if they see their content being stolen, and most people agree that illegal downloading damages major studio films. While still the highest-grossing movie of all time, James Cameron's *Avatar* has been illegally downloaded an estimated 21 million times according to weblog TorrentFreak.

How much illegal downloading effects indie, or short films, is a contentious issue, but some people see the positive side as distribution and promotional tools. Science fiction fantasy film *Ink* went viral when it was released in 2009, with 400,000 illegal downloads in a single week. This was after creators Jamin and Kiowa Winans had been told by studios that there was no audience for the film. They then self-distributed through their own company Double Edge Films.

Producer Kiowa said that the torrent community spread the film everywhere, helping build an audience more successfully than could have been achieved by even a large budget ad campaign. It reached number one on torrent site Pirate Bay and number 14 on IMDb's MovieMeter—which collates what users are searching for. Sales for *Ink* were low before the piracy started, but then started to increase. Moreover they also received donations from all over the world after adding a PayPal support link.

Producer Matt Compton has a similar story. He was annoyed when his independent film *Midnight Son* appeared as a torrent three weeks before his official release date in 2011. He posted a comment on The Pirate Bay asking anyone that enjoyed the film to either buy the DVD or offer a donation. Like *Ink*, a number of people did so.

16.2 *Midnight Son* (2011)

P.204

However, while there are some success stories the majority of downloaders do not donate. Creators of Christian independent thriller *Suing the Devil* even received a nasty online backlash. Their film was illegally downloaded over 100,000 times in just two days in 2009, and when the creators asked for it to be removed, 400 illegal downloaders co-ordinated to rate it with a "1" on IMDb, reducing the score from "7" to a "4".

The amount of revenue that is lost to piracy is also debatable. Freakonomic bloggers Kal Raustiala and Chris Sprigman argue that many "pirates" wouldn't have bought the film anyway, so many illegal downloads cannot be seen as "lost sales". New York's New School professor Vladan Nikolic, who also created indie thriller *Zenith*, believes piracy should be harnessed and considered as an extra element in a hybrid distribution strategy, and film buff website IndieWire considered if "piracy might be a filmmaker's best friend."

Generally the quality on file sharing sites is low, and cannot compete with the cinema experience. Theft in any digital form—from peer-to-peer (P2P) to online streaming—is illegal and can be reported on the MPAA's website—www.mpaa.org. Whatever your feelings are about online piracy, at the moment it is a fact of life and it is worth considering how to approach it.

PAUSE

VODO

A legal and profitable way to embrace file sharing technology is VODO—www.vodo.net – launched in 2009 to help independent media to be promoted and distributed using Peer to Peer technology. The creators believe there is an "immense untapped potential for creators," and the site states it can: "promote and distribute new creative works all over the world and enables those enjoying shared media to make donations to creators."

Downloaders have the opportunity to sponsor the films in return for incentives such as credits in a future production, or a downloadable soundtrack. In turn, filmmakers receive 70% of all donations. "Culture jamming" activist duo The Yes Men's 2009 title *The Yes Men Fix The World* earned $25,000 in its first month on VODO. As the film was being sued by the time by the US Chamber of Commerce, the creators claimed, "p2p is the only way that this film will get seen."

VODO's biggest success so far is *Pioneer One*, which has been downloaded almost four million times since its launch in 2010. Funds were raised entirely through crowd sourcing (see box in Chapter 5: Finance), and in the summer of 2012 it was close to reaching its "donation target" of $100,000.

16.3 Peter Broderick

NEW WORLD DISTRIBUTION

Consultant Peter Broderick helps filmmakers design and implement customized strategies to maximize distribution, audience, and revenues. He believes directors and producers need to "apply the same creativity to distribution as production." As one of the leaders of the distribution revolution, he coined the term "hybrid distribution" to describe splitting rights between a filmmaker and distributors. Certain rights are granted to a distributor (or several distributors) and the filmmaker retains the right to sell DVDs, downloads, and streams directly from his or her website and at screenings.

During a Skype conversation Peter explained that instead of turning over complete control of your distribution to one company, you can partner with a distributor giving them some rights and retaining others. If you effectively promote your film online, this should increase the distributor's sales as well as your direct sales. In what Peter calls the "New World of Distribution," hybrid distribution is Plan A not a "fall back" strategy. Plan B is giving all the rights to one distributor—the reverse of how filmmakers approached things in the Old World of Distribution.

Peter has written ten guiding principles of New World Distribution that apply equally to fiction features and documentaries as well as shorts and are listed below. They are also available on his site, along with a free Distribution Bulletin on independent film distribution and marketing which is well worth subscribing to—visit www.peterbroderick.com.

PAUSE

WELCOME TO THE NEW WORLD OF DISTRIBUTION

1. Greater Control

Filmmakers retain overall control of their distribution, choosing which rights to give distribution partners and which to retain. If filmmakers hire a service deal company or a booker to arrange a theatrical run, they control the marketing campaign, spending, and the timing of their release. In the OW (Old World), a distributor that acquires all rights has total control of distribution. Filmmakers usually have little or no influence on key marketing and distribution decisions.

2. Hybrid Distribution

Filmmakers split up their rights, working with distribution partners in certain sectors and keeping the right to make direct sales. They can make separate deals for: retail home video, television, educational, nontheatrical, and VOD, as well as splitting up their digital rights. They also sell DVDs from their websites and at screenings, and make digital downloads and streams available directly from their sites. In the OW, filmmakers make all-rights deals, giving one company all their rights for as long as 25 years.

3. Customized Strategies

Filmmakers design creative distribution strategies customized to their film's content and target audiences. They can begin outreach to audiences and potential organizational partners before or during production. They often ignore traditional windows, selling DVDs from their websites before they are available in stores, sometimes during their theatrical release, and even at festivals. Filmmakers are able to test their strategies step-by-step, and modify them as needed. In the OW, distribution plans are much more formulaic and rigid.

4. Core Audiences

Filmmakers target core audiences. Their priority is to reach them effectively, and then hopefully crossover to a wider public. They reach core audiences directly both online and offline, through websites, mailing lists, organizations, and publications. In the OW, many distributors market to a general audience, which is highly inefficient and more and more expensive. Notable exceptions, Fox Searchlight and Bob Berney, have demonstrated how effective highly targeted marketing can be. *Napoleon Dynamite* first targeted nerds, *Passion of the Christ* began with evangelicals, and *My Big Fat Greek Wedding* started with Greek Americans. Building on

their original base, each of these films was then able to significantly expand and diversify their audiences.

5. Reducing Costs

Filmmakers reduce costs by using the Internet and by spending less on traditional print, television, and radio advertising. While four years ago a five-city theatrical service deal cost $250,000 to $300,000, today comparable service deals can cost $50,000 or even less. In the OW, marketing costs have risen dramatically.

6. Direct Access To Viewers

Filmmakers use the Internet to reach audiences directly. The makers of the motorcycle racing documentary, *Faster*, used the web to quickly and inexpensively reach motorcycle fans around the world. They pulled off an inspired stunt at the Cannes Film Festival, which generated international coverage and widespread awareness among fans. This sparked lucrative DVD sales first from the website and then in retail stores. In the OW, filmmakers only have indirect access to audiences through distributors.

7. Direct Sales

Filmmakers make much higher margins on direct sales from their websites and at screenings than they do through retail sales. They can make as much as $21 profit on a $29.95 website sale (including a $4.95 charge for shipping and handling). A retail sale of the same DVD only nets $2.50 via a typical 20% royalty video deal. If filmmakers sell an educational copy from their websites to a college or university for $300 (an average educational price), they can net $290. Direct sales to consumers provide valuable customer data, which enables filmmakers to make future sales to these buyers. They can sell other versions of a film, the soundtrack, books, posters, and t-shirts. In the OW, filmmakers are not permitted to make direct sales, have no access to customer data, and have no merchandising rights.

8. Global Distribution

Filmmakers are now making their films available to viewers anywhere in the world. Supplementing their deals with distributors in other countries, they sell their films to consumers in unsold territories via DVD or digital download directly from their websites. For the first time, filmmakers are aggregating audiences across national boundaries. In the OW, distribution is territory by territory, and most independent films have little or no foreign distribution.

9. Separate Revenue Streams

Filmmakers limit cross-collateralization and accounting problems by splitting up their distribution rights. All revenues from sales on their websites come directly to them or through the fulfillment company they've hired to store and ship DVDs. By separating the revenues from each distribution partner, filmmakers prevent expenses from one distribution channel being charged against revenues from another. This makes accounting simpler and more transparent. In an OW all-rights deal, all revenues and all expenses are combined, making monitoring revenues much more difficult.

10. True Fans
Filmmakers connect with viewers online and at screenings, establish direct relationships with them, and build core personal audiences. They ask for their support, making it clear that DVD purchases from the website will help them break even and make more movies. Every filmmaker with a website has the chance to turn visitors into subscribers, subscribers into purchasers, and purchasers into true fans who can contribute to new productions. In the OW, filmmakers do not have direct access to viewers.

THINK OF THE NEXT PROJECT

The way consumers behave and what they demand around the world is changing rapidly. Most of the sites listed in the second edition of the book—researched in 2005—either no longer exist or have been bought and rebranded. New sites for watching film, ways of paying for it and places to watch it—such as phones and tablets—are evolving at an exponential rate. It is an exciting time to hybrid-distribute a short film, with huge potential of getting noticed internationally, building up a long-term fan base and even making some cash.

Perhaps the most important aspect is building a large, and genuine, online fan base. People you can call on when your next project is ready, rather than starting from scratch again. Peter Broderick said: "The most important thing for people trying to have a career in this crazy world is having a serious mailing list, a personal core audience they can take with them to their next films. These filmmakers have the best opportunities." As a result he insists having access to the names and email addresses of people who watch the film should be paramount—information most distributors won't share with you, but that can easily acquired on your own site. In addition to buying your films, fans can let other people know about the work, write a review and give feedback—essential to your growth as a filmmaker.

With so many platforms and options for distribution, ways to connect through social media, tools for analyzing who is buying your film and opportunities to market, this final stage of the filmmaking process can be a full time job in itself. But if you're serious about being a filmmaker, paying serious attention to distribution and marketing is becoming a realistic way to fund the next project. While you really want to be making movies, putting time into learning what works, how to go viral and how to get noticed will pay off.

STOP

16.1 A still from *The Thomas Beale Cipher* (2010)

16.2 A still from *Midnight Son* (2011)

PART

V

TITLE

Interviews with filmakers

START

CHAPTER 17

Paul Andrew Williams

Writer-Director

Making a movie is like the plot for a movie. It begins with a call to adventure. There is a moment of doubt, a meeting with mentors, there are setbacks and ordeals, magical gifts, vital turning points, a triumph against the odds and the seizing of the prize: the film in the can.

This is the plot of Paul Andrew Williams' journey into celluloid. He started out as an actor. He directed numerous pop-promos and viral ads before writing and directing his first short, the 13-minute *Royalty* in 2001, first shown at the London Film Festival, shortlisted for the Kodak showcase and later screened at BAFTA.

Two years later, he was the only UK-based director chosen by the Fox Searchlight Director's Lab (the gift). With new knowledge from this program, he developed his second short *It's Okay to Drink Whiskey*, honing the script and cutting the footage to 10-minutes, the preferred length for festivals. The short was duly selected and first shown at the 2004 Sundance Film Festival.

Now it came for the big leap over the chasm from shorts to write, develop and direct his own feature.

He sat down and wrote *London to Brighton*, the plot inspired by *Royalty*. Old friends Johnny Harris and Lorraine Stanley reprised their roles as Derek and Kelly, while Chloe Bale and Nathan Constance, who appeared in the short, took new roles in the feature. Pulling in favors and promises from everyone he had met in the industry, he raised £500,000, arranged the script to fit the budget and found immediate approval with the finished film winning the New Director's Award at the 2006 Edinburgh International Film Festival. The film went on general release in December.

It had taken five years to turn a short into a successful feature. The end result garnered overwhelmingly good reviews, Total Film wrote: "Taut début from talent-to-track Paul Andrew Williams. Compassionate as well as steely, it's one of the year's surprises. Terrific performances, too."

"Talent-to-track" Paul Andrew Williams has since gone on to write and direct the £2.5 million horror *The Cottage* (2008); he co-wrote (with Tom Shankland) *The Children* (2008); and wrote and directed the drama *Cherry Tree Lane* (2010). He co-wrote (with Udana Fonseca) *Train to Kandy* (2012); and wrote and directed the life-affirming comedy drama *Song for Marion* (2012), with Gemma Arterton, Christopher Eccleston, Vanessa Redgrave, and Terence Stamp.

At the time of writing, he is in pre-production as director and co-writer (with Morwenna Banks) of the generously-budgeted comedy-drama *Miss You Already* with Jennifer Aniston and Toni Collette, due out in 2013.

17.1 Paul Andrew Williams

1. They say the three things that matter most in a film is the script, the script, and the script. Do you agree—and if so, why; and if not, why?
It's obviously very important but it's only one of the elements. You can have the best script in the world but if you've got Donald Duck reciting it then it's not going to work. The script is the solid base that you should have to start with, and like a magnet, it should attract equivalent solid elements to make the rest of your film. The trick is managing all the elements once you have them.

2. When you were writing *London to Brighton*, were you aware that this had the potential to be a great film?
Not at all, I wrote it in 4 days so there was no time to think ahead. It is a very hard job to concentrate on what you are doing and control the thoughts of possible success or the failure of what you are doing at that moment. Best to have as little expectation as possible.

3. In a low-budget film, when there's no spare cash for big crowd scenes or helicopter crashes, what's the key to holding the audience attention—the theme, the plot, the characters; what combination of these?
To an extent, all of them. However, the main thing to get right is the characters. As I think I would watch interesting and engaging characters on plots that otherwise I might be bored with. But you could have the greatest plot and story in the world but if the characters are one dimensional and dull then you don't invest in them, and you don't give a sh*t about them.

4. Should new filmmakers be trying to break into the home market with clearly defined local product, or thinking about the international market—or, in essence, are all stories universal?
Just concentrate on making the best film possible. If you're too busy looking at the pavement 200 feet ahead of you, you are more than likely to trip over what's directly in front of you.

5. Is it essential to have a star name in order to look for finance?
It depends on what you are trying to raise and from whom. And also what star, as you could get some glamour model who wants to act and features in *Heat* magazine, therefore having a public profile, but she could be sh*t and ruin your film. It can help, it can hinder. It can also take a very long time to get a response from someone so if you go down that route be prepared for a ton of problems.

6. Once you have your script and your package, where do you start to look for finance?
On a short film, I would look privately. On a first feature I would look privately also. I would just make sure you are making the right film for the right budget. Cut the right corners and spend the money on the film. If you

go the legitimate route, be prepared for a sh*t load of waiting and possible unwanted interference.

7. How much do you think about the market when you make a film?
I try not to. The only thing I try to keep in mind is that if I want to make a film I believe won't be that commercial, I know not to try raising millions. It will be much harder to make it back and therefore unappealing to investors.

8. More than half the people who make a feature never go on to make a second. You have broken that paradigm. How did you achieve this?
Being determined, being prepared to go back and make a film for nothing if I have to. I believe if you want to make a second film, you will make a second film. There are a lot of not-so-talented filmmakers who have made a few films.

9. What advice would you give people writing their first film? If there's a secret ingredient, what is it?
Make it interesting and don't write scenes you can't shoot, i.e. the less dinosaurs you have, the more likely you will be able to afford to shoot the film.

10. How much of being successful comes from just working hard?
I never believe or would say I was successful, I have had some successful moments which is different. You need to work hard, you need luck and you need to never give in.

11. The print book market is imploding with downloads. Is cinema threatened in the same way, or will people always want to have a night out at the movies?
I think there is nothing better than watching a film on the big screen. You can't beat it.

17.2 *London to Brighton* (2006)

▶▶ P.210

12. What's your favorite film and why?
Aliens. I think it is a master of all things. Design, story, energy, and music and great characters. The tension is fantastic and the action scenes are superb. I will watch that forever.

13. Who is your favorite director and why?
Again, Cameron. He may not be the best at everything but he is better at most things than most people. He makes massively commercial movies that break boundaries every time. He knows who he is making films for and that is everyone. He is a master craftsman and a perfectionist. And I am envious of those traits. I think he is a genius.

14. What actors would you like to work with and why?
Actors who know how to make their own bed and live in the real world.

STOP

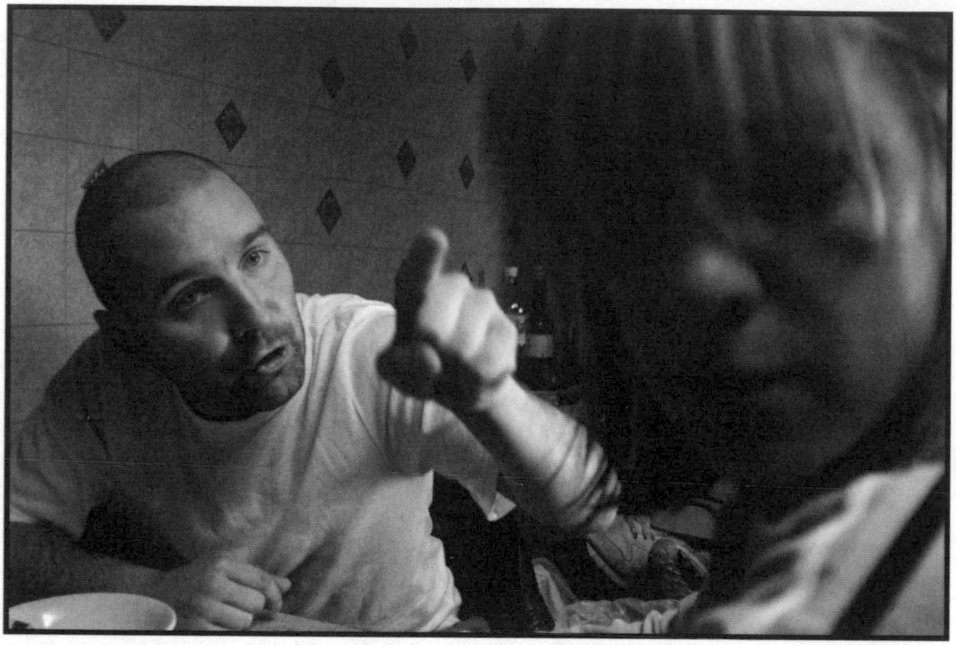

17.2 Aggressive behavior in *London to Brighton* (2006)

START

CHAPTER 18

Daniel Mulloy

2010 *Baby*—Best British Short Edinburgh Film Festival; nominated at Sundance and many other prizes.
2007 *Son*—Best Short, California Independent, Edinburgh, Lille, Chicago, Slamdance and more.
2007 *Dad*—best director Orense, best director Sapporo, premièred at Sundance.
2006 *Antonio's Breakfast*—best short BAFTA, best short Aspen, best short Indianapolis, best short Kansas, best short Newport, Youth Jury Award Clermont-Ferrand, Onda Curta Award, premièred at Sundance.
2005 *Sister*—best short, BAFTA Wales, ARTE Award Hamburg, Tamashi Award Japan, best short Concorto, best short Pol-8.
2002 *Dance Floor*—best newcomer BAFTA Wales.

18.1 Daniel Mulloy on set (left)

P.214

18.2 Daniel Mulloy working with children

P.214

Daniel Mulloy studied fine art at the Slade School in London and came to filmmaking by chance. At nightclubs in his early-twenties, he was often appalled by the way some clubbers treated the toilet attendants. It was a subject he wanted to explore, but oil and canvas in this case was too limiting. He got hold of a video camera and, without training, shot a short film about the life of a Nigerian woman who looked after the toilets in a club.

It was 2002 and *Dance Floor* won the BAFTA prize for best short film. He followed this "surprise success"—his words—with *Sister*, winner of the BAFTA best short in 2005, and *Antonio's Breakfast*, the 2006 best short at BAFTA and Clermont-Ferrand, and selected at Sundance. At the time of writing, *Dad*, made in 2006, is winning prizes from Spain to Japan. *Son* (2007) and *Baby* (2010) have both scooped up more awards across the world.

It's an impressive record. Tall and slender, a former athlete, Mulloy seems almost embarrassed when I ask him to reveal the key to making a great short film?

"There's no money in shorts, so filmmakers can be experimental. I don't mean technically, with clever angles and wild cuts, that only draws attention to the process. I mean you can experiment with where you take the audience emotionally. More than a feature, where there are so many other concerns, including other people's money, short films can be intimate, personal, concise little gems that show a unique perspective, moments from someone's childhood, or their favorite food. They don't need to deal with grand subjects and are often most successful when they tackle simple themes that everyone can in some way relate to."

"I believe it helps if you have something to say about the world. You can't just put a lot of emotive ingredients together—like people living in poverty, or children being mistreated, and expect to have a great film. The film needs veracity. It has to be your understanding and your connection to the material. You travel the world and there is a zeitgeist with certain films that have an appeal to people everywhere—and all those films, in my experience, have one thing in common, they all have integrity. The films can be comic, ironic, dramatic, but it is the passion behind the story, the feeling the viewer is left with, that lifts the film. For me, this seems to be a common factor in what makes many films popular with audiences."

When Mulloy gets an idea for a new short it is usually a simple scenario. *Antonio's Breakfast* is about a man looking after his elderly father. It could be set anywhere in the world and he tells the story from his viewpoint, a British citizen who has grown up in London. "Little things that seem insignificant can be life-changing and hold the germ of a story. It is finding beauty in the mundane and expanding on it, digging into its essence. In a short film, what I try to do is explore experience, my one or other people's, and translate that experience into a brief glimpse of someone's life."

Should films contain a message?

"I have tremendous respect for filmmakers who tackle difficult subjects. It's not easy and the results are often disappointing. Directors have massive power because they are able to talk to the audience through the first person, almost one to one. They should not abuse that power by relinquishing responsibility. If a film encourages debate it serves a valuable purpose, but it's not your job to spoon-feed people with your message."

What is the main mistake made by new filmmakers?

"I think it's concentrating on style. Too many shorts look like pop videos. People get obsessed with format. They want to shoot on 35mm rather than video. It is the emotion that's captured, not what it's captured on. When you are putting something into the public arena, a film, especially a short film, should express something you think is worth being expressed."

Filmmaking should be fun and, in Mulloy's opinion, it is up to the director to "lead from the front" and make sure everyone enjoys the process. "All the people surrounding the director are there to make sure his or her vision is realized. The director is responsible for how the finished film is going to play, but he/she cannot make the film without the good will and hard work and talent of those that he/she has chosen to collaborate with."

Mulloy in his films has until his current production avoided using music. "It is such a powerful tool. It can so easily tell the audience what to feel and, if you are learning the craft of filmmaking, it seems more appropriate to stick to the language of film. It's the same with technical feats and great camera movements. They really aren't necessary and a great treat to savor for feature length films."

Like many filmmakers, Mulloy finds writing a new script an intense and emotional experience. "When I have an idea, I think about it for a long time, try and work out what I am trying to say. When the idea is solid in my mind,

I go to the British Library when it opens at ten and stay there at the desk until six. For the first two hours it's very quiet and you can plan out what you are trying to do, then I just write the draft straight through."

One problem he sees for first-time filmmakers is that they often take too long to make their film, and then wait too long before they make their next film; Mulloy found this himself, taking three years between *Dance Floor* and *Sister*. "Don't stop after one. Carry on making films. You learn the process by working. It is a continuing process. If you are going to be respected as a filmmaker it will most likely come from having a body of work."

Daniel Mulloy's shorts are a masterclass in low-budget filmmaking. They can be found on the Sister films website.

www.sisterfilms.co.uk

STOP

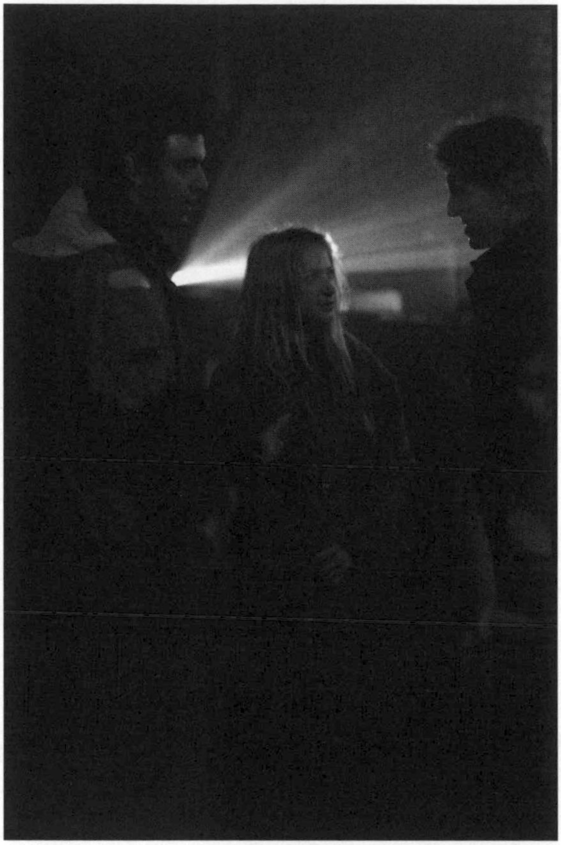

18.1 Daniel Mulloy on set (left)

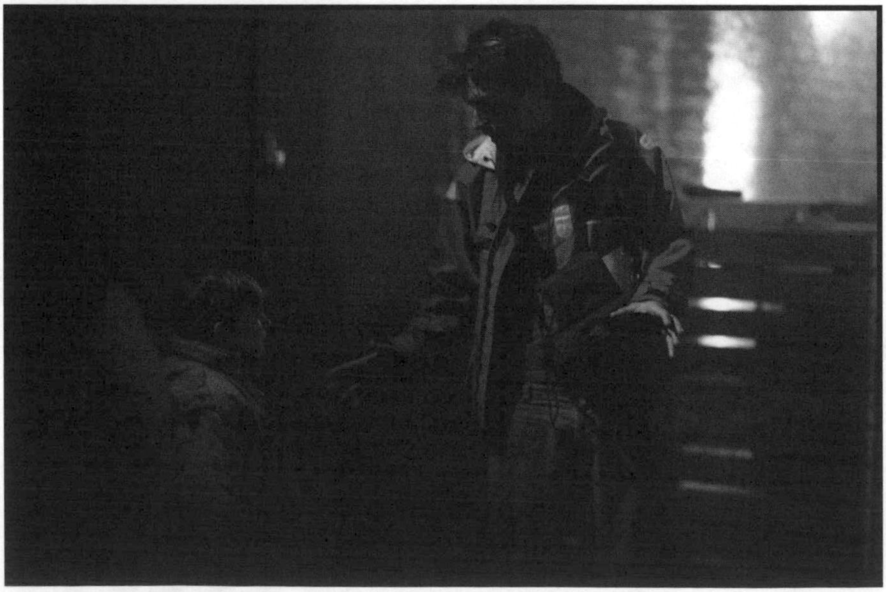

18.2 Daniel Mulloy working with children

START

CHAPTER 19

Jack Pizzey

Documentary Filmmaker

19.1 Jack Pizzey

A middle-aged man sits on a train gripping a bottle of Nembutal pills in his fingers. His features are immobile. He stares out the carriage window as the landscape turns grey in the setting sun.

Sitting opposite the man is Jack Pizzey. A young navy officer, he has been trained to recognize the signs of men under stress and how to deal with it. He knows, too, that Nembutal is a potent tranquillizer.

When Pizzey draws his fellow passenger into conversation, the man tells him that everything he has ever done has gone wrong. His life isn't worth living. When they arrive in London, he's going to swallow the pills and end it all. Pizzey persuades the man to seek help and takes him to St Mary's Hospital, close to Paddington Station. He is shocked to discover that as the suicidal man hasn't actually taken the tranquillizers, they will do nothing to help him.

Pizzey sits there until four in the morning trying to convince the man that there is always a solution to life's problems. The man, obviously unconvinced, puts his bottle to his mouth and swallows all the Nembutal pills. Pizzey raises the alarm and the nursing staff finally go into action, "Oh now we'll *have* to treat him." They race the man into the theater to pump the pills back out of his stomach.

Jack Pizzey was outraged by what he saw as a heartless way of dealing with a suicidal patient and, ultimately, an inefficient use of public money. During his weekend leave, he wrote a feature article about what had happened, phoned all the newspapers and his piece appeared the following week in The *Guardian*.

Pizzey had found his calling. He was shortly to leave the navy, he joined the training program at the BBC, and has made more than 100 documentary films since. "The lesson I learned from meeting the man on the train is that you must follow your instincts and idealism," he says. "You must question what you believe is wrong—and try to put it right."

Not long after completing the BBC training course, Pizzey found himself with a camera crew in the headquarters of a major pharmaceutical company in Basle interviewing company bosses on charges that they had organized a cartel to keep the price of the vitamin C artificially high. One of their own executives had reported them to the European Court, which had fined them, but then the drug company victimized the whistle-blower to the point where he was prosecuted for treason by the Swiss government; the charges were dropped, but the man's wife committed suicide and he left his homeland never to return. Pizzey conducted the interview surrounded by the drug company lawyers and when he brought the story back to London, the BBC's legal team had to go through every frame and every word before they would screen the film. "This is grim, meticulous work, but when you believe what you are doing is worthwhile it gives you a high and you can't imagine doing anything else."

Pizzey quotes the dictum of Lord Reith, the former director general of the BBC: the corporation's mission is to Educate, Inform, and Entertain. To pin down all three, says Pizzey, requires "the talent"—a protagonist who can carry the story, and the antagonist/s who are preventing the protagonist getting what they want or need or deserve. "Writing a story is about structure and re-writing. A documentary is about research," he explains. "Spend as many days and weeks as it needs to find someone who has a story to tell, or a wrong to be righted. One person leads to another, one thing leads to another. Even if you know nothing to begin with, you learn the subject through your research."

Like fiction filmmakers, Jack Pizzey believes in the maxim: Don't tell me. Show me.

"The non-commentary documentary always works best for me, stories that the people who are involved in tell in their own voice. These stories come from the heart. They have passion and immediacy," he adds. "A non-commentary documentary is more difficult, but they *show* the audience what is happening without a voiceover *telling* them. If you do need voiceover, it is always best to use someone involved in the story, the director perhaps. Even if you can get David Attenborough, unless he is connected to the film, the commentary will be detached."

Pizzey advises documentary-makers to do the recce themselves. "You must meet all the people you are going to use in the film. You must get to know them. If they know you, and learn to trust you, they will open up and give you what you want on camera," he says, and adds: "But when you get to filming, whatever you've planned, be open to what actually happens and how you may use the surprising and accidental."

He gives the example of a time when he was co-directing and presenting a co-production with the BBC and an Israeli broadcaster. They were on a small plane flying over the Middle East. Pizzey was sitting beside the aisle doing a piece to camera—what in Israel and the US they call a "stand up." A passenger pushed between him and the camera, so Pizzey stopped. "My co-director was stunned: Jack, that's reality," he told me. "You just carry on. The film is more real when it is not poised and posed to the camera."

The incident taught Pizzey a valuable lesson he took with him in a more precarious career as a freelance. One of his first commissions was from ABC in Australia to make eight 60-minute documentaries he called *Sweat of the Sun Tears of the Moon*—an Inca phrase for Gold and Silver—covering the history and politics across the length and breadth of South America—which he did after six weeks of intensive Spanish and which served him well enough to later interview King Juan Carlos of Spain for BBC 2.

"We were filming one time in a small pueblo high in the Andes in

Ecuador when suddenly the houses started shaking around us. Everyone was shouting *temblar, temblar! Earthquake!* I glanced at the cameraman, he shrugged, and we carried on filming," he says. "I had already learned my lesson from the Israeli director, you have to be open to what's happening: reality works best when it's real."

Looking back, Pizzey believes he was lucky to get on the training program at the BBC. He did bring to the course other life experiences, but what tilted the balance was that article in The *Guardian*. "I think these days, if you want to get into the business you have to make a film. If fifty people go for a job and six of them have made a film, they are the ones who are going to get an interview."

Pizzey advises making a 7—10 minute film that tells a structured story with a central point, a believable protagonist and a unambiguous conclusion.

"We look to documentaries to right wrongs," he adds. "But it is also a pleasure and a privilege. A film is the best toy you can be given to play with. The editing process is pure magic. When you put one image against another you get eureka moments and that's thrilling."

For most of his career, Jack Pizzey has made campaigning documentaries, but admits "inside every documentary-maker there's a moviemaker trying to emerge." While developing another Peking to Paris car rally, this time using "green" cars, Pizzey has written a screenplay for a feature with the working title *Nail'em*—a comic vengeance on the bankers. "After much advice from LA script consultants and two encouraging opinions from veterans of the business, I've embarked on the yellow brick road that leads to Hollywood."

With his fondness for the arts, he has also set up Films for Artists, a company that does just what it says on the label and makes films for and about artists—www.filmsforartists.com.

JACK'S FAVORITES

During his career, Jack Pizzey has received four BAFTA nominations and won numerous prizes for his films. In the selection below are some of his personal favorites.

Viva Nica!—a 50-minute film about Nicaragua's campaigning artists, writers, and singers on the barricades, Channel 4.
Sweat of the Sun Tears of the Moon—eight 60-minute documentaries covering South America for ABC; winner of the Australian Logie Award.
King Juan Carlos—60-minute BBC 2 interview.
Hussein the Survivor King—60-minute BBC 2 interview.
Peking to Paris—twenty 30-minute films following 85 antique cars around the planet, the History Channel and Sky and Star's Travel Channels.
Slow Boat from Surabaya—six 50-minute travelogues, A&E and Discovery, ABC and BBC 2.

STOP

PART

VI

TITLE

Scripts and insider tips

IV

START

CHAPTER 20

Time Freak

Producer Gigi Causey's story is what you might call a movie morality tale, the story of following your heart's desire, not your accountant's advice.

Married for three years to writer Andrew Bowler, both had been working in unfulfilling jobs on the fringes of the movie industry and saving all the while to buy an apartment in New York. The moment they had the deposit in the bank, Gigi felt as if a lead weight had been lowered on her shoulders. She saw a decade of high payments and dull work stretching out before them and their dream of making movies fading over the horizon.

"Let's make a movie instead," she suggested, and Andrew instantly agreed. He'd been feeling the same kind of weight pressing him down.

They now needed an appropriate subject. Andrew recalled an old joke among friends discussing what they might do if they had a time machine—as in, "What did you have for lunch?" "Oh, I had a sandwich, but if I had a time machine, I'd go back in time and have a salad."

With that as the basis, he wrote *Time Freak,* the story of a neurotic inventor who dreams of peeking in on Ancient Rome, but gets stuck in a time warp traveling through his own yesterday. They shot the film in four days with $25,000 and began to regret not buying that apartment when their film was rejected at festivals including Sundance, Telluride, and Tribeca.

20.1 Speaking at the Oscars

▶▶ P.237

Undaunted, Gigi submitted the short for the Oscars. When news came that they had been selected, she burst into tears, wept with joy, and burst into tears again, the celebration filmed by Andrew and trailed on the web. There was the usual fuss over what to wear on the red carpet alongside Brad and Angelina. Andrew chose to rent from Mr Tuxedo—renting's the new buying, he said—and Gigi, in true indie fashion, found a dress at a thrift store.

The big night came and Gigi recalls seeing her mother and Meryl Streep in an embrace, "That's Meryl Streep, she's hugging my mother, I'm thinking, and then my mom turns around, 'Gigi, this is Meryl Streep,' and I'm like, 'I know it's Meryl Streep! What are you doing hugging her?' "

20.2 Academy Awards

▶▶ P.237

Time Freak didn't win the 2012 Oscar for best live-action short, it went to writer-director Terry George for *The Shore.* Do they regret not buying the apartment? "Not for one second. We are now working on a feature." If they had a time machine and could go back and fine-tune *Time Freak*, would they? "No," said Gigi, "We wouldn't change a thing."

20.3 Gigi Causey

1. Briefly describe your job
As a short-film producer, my focus is primarily on making sure that the creative elements of the project are prioritized and made achievable. Because money and resources are so limited on an independent project (and in the case of *Time Freak,* the funding came directly from our savings account), my job is to make sure that every penny possible winds up on the screen. My background is in film production management, and those skills are exercised to their maximum potential when I produce a short.

2. How do you find good projects?
I am fortunate to be married to a very talented writer and director, so I don't have far to look. That said, there were several good ideas that didn't make the cut. For me a good project is finding the perfect combination of an excellent story that hasn't been told paired with the general "doability" of the project for the money that we have to spend. A great idea that isn't executed well due to a lack of resources will fall short on the screen. If the end goal is to have a film that has a chance of distribution on any sort of larger scale, then there is no room for not creating the best version of the project.

3. How important is the script?
The script is critical. The writing and development phase of any project is, essentially, free. Any doubts that you have during the script phase will only be amplified once you go into production. Script flaws will become screen flaws.

4. Do you make edits, suggestions and work with the writer?
Absolutely. I see my job as a collaboration with the writer and director. That said, I make it my mission to understand the creative intent behind the project, and I tend to tailor my edits and suggestions to help the director communicate that intent.

5. Was it hard to set up your production company/how did you do it?
We run a mom and pop operation. I'm married to my producing partner, and we didn't go through the cost of setting up a company. We still operate more as a family than a business.

6. How do you find funding?
Time Freak was funded by money that we had personally saved. We have yet to seek out external funding for a project.

7. What producers do you look up to, and why?
I have tremendous admiration for Lauren Shuler Donner [*X-Men* film trilogy]. She has an incredible knack for finding and nurturing emerging talent.

8. Is getting big names involved in the project important?
Yes and no. I think that a short film can certainly benefit from having a big name attached, and it is certainly easier to find funding for a short when it can be tied to that big name. However, the most important thing is to make a good film. Short films are an opportunity to showcase unknown talent.

9. What are common pitfalls you have faced, and how did you overcome them?

Write, write, and re-write. Don't shoot before the script is ready. Think carefully about what you are spending your money on, and make sure that the money you are spending goes on the screen.

10. What advice do you have for wannabe producers?

Trust your gut. If your gut tells you that something isn't working … It probably isn't. The same is true in the opposite direction. Do it because you love it. Filmmaking takes tremendous time, energy, and dedication. The process is grueling, frustrating, and often unpleasant and terrifying. It is also very rewarding!

You'll find Time Freak at:

`http://itunes.apple.com/us/movie/time-freak/id501240303`

20.1 Andrew Bowler and Gigi Causey at the 84th Academy Awards®

20.2 84th Academy Awards Poster

START

TITLE

Time Freak

Script/direction by Andrew Bowler
Produced by Gigi Causey

1 EXT. BROOKLYN - DAY 1

Subways pass on the elevated tracks overhead.

EVAN purposefully walks past the subway entrance, along the streets of the rougher looking parts of the borough.

2 EXT. STREET - DAY 2

He quickly walks down the sidewalk, checking the addresses as he goes.

3 EXT. GATE - DAY 3

Evan stops in front of a metal gate pulled 3/4 the way down. He checks the addresses on either side and BANGS on the gate.

4 INT. LAB - CONTINUOUS 4

We see the semi - closed gate from the dark inside. Evan bends down and peeks his head inside.

EVAN

Stillman?

Evan stands up again and continues to BANG, still calling out.

EVAN (O.S.)

Stillman?!

5 EXT. GATE - DAY - CONTINUOUS 5

Evan looks around, unsure. He BANGS once more.

6 INT. LAB - CONTINUOUS 6

After a moment, Evan reaches his hands under the gate and pulls it up.

He steps into the dark space looking around.

EVAN
Stillman? Are you here, dude?

He slowly walks into the lab looking for his friend.

He walks around a massive blast door to see STILLMAN, slumped over a desk, lost in thought with a wild look in his eyes.

2.

He's wearing a jumpsuit which is pulled down around his waist.

EVAN
Oh my God.

Now just a few feet away, Evan calls out to his friend again.

EVAN
Stillman?!

Stillman snaps out of his daze and looks up at Evan like a long lost friend. He leaps up and gives Evan a hug.

STILLMAN
Evan!

EVAN
Hey man.

Evan breaks away from the hug.

EVAN
Are you okay?

Stillman becomes self conscious about his exuberance and tries to act casual.

STILLMAN
Sure. Why do you ask?

EVAN
Well for one, you haven't been at the apartment for three days.

STILLMAN
Oh right.

EVAN
And you look like hell. Is everything alright?

STILLMAN
Sure, sure. Of course man.

Evan looks at his friend, skeptical. Suddenly Stillman darts off.

JUMP CUT TO:

7 INT. LAB 7

Evan is once again outside, BANGING on the gate.

3.

EVAN (O.S.)
Stillman?

Evan lifts the gate and walks in.

EVAN
Stillman? Are you here, dude? Oh hey.

Stillman finishes an equation on a chalkboard and turns around. His hair is combed and his jumpsuit is fully on and clean, he generally looks much more put together.

He tries his hardest to seem normal.

STILLMAN
Hey Evan, what's going on!

EVAN
Dude! Didn't you hear me banging?

Stillman is caught off guard by the question.

STILLMAN
Oh...

JUMP CUT TO:

8 EXT. GATE - DAY 8

Evan walks up to the gate but before he can knock, Stillman pops his head out, looking put together.

STILLMAN
Hey Evan!

Stillman lifts the gate.

STILLMAN
Come on in.

Evan walks inside. Stillman looks up at the sky.

STILLMAN
Look at that, daylight.

9 INT. LAB - CONTINUOUS 9

STILLMAN
Okay, enough of that.

Stillman closes the gate.

4.

EVAN
Dude!

STILLMAN
I know, I know. I'm really sorry I haven't responded to your messages.

EVAN
Yeah, what happened to you? Have you been working for three days or what?

STILLMAN
Evan, I have discovered something really amazing.

EVAN
Awesome, let me see.

Stillman tries to stop Evan who just walks past him and towards a light coming from around a corner.

STILLMAN
No wait!

EVAN
Holy cow! What is that!? It looks like a time machine or something!

We stay with Stillman who looks like a kid who's just had his surprise ruined.

Stillman slumps his shoulders, enters something on the keyboard in front of him and pushes past Evan towards the light.

JUMP CUT TO:

10 INT. LAB 10

Stillman closes the gate.

EVAN
Dude!

STILLMAN
(calm)
Evan, I have discovered something really amazing. But...

Stillman stops just inside the lab turns around to Evan.

5.

STILLMAN (CONT'D)
(on edge)
You need to stay right there!

EVAN
What's going on?

STILLMAN
I have something to show you.

Evan and Stillman walk over to the light source which is now covered by a white sheet.

Stillman YANKS off the tarp to reveal...

A homemade time machine. Four electromagnets made of copper wiring flank all sides of the metal platform wit a rubber mat. A multi faceted prism wired into a control box is suspended overhead. A laptop computer seems to be engineering the whole device.

EVAN
Is that your time machine?

Stillman beams back a smile.

EVAN
No way.

STILLMAN
Here, I'll show you. Step up here.

EVAN
Is it safe?

STILLMAN
Of course it's safe. Come on.
Let's take a quick trip.

EVAN
(hesitant)
To where?

Stillman just smiles.

JUMP CUT TO:

11 INT. LAB 11

Stillman is holding Evan's shirt as he was minutes ago.

Evan is stunned. Stillman pushes on the bridge of his nose.

6.

STILLMAN
Do this.

Evan rubs the bridge of his nose and regains himself.

EVAN
Dude... whoa!

STILLMAN
Pretty cool, huh?

Evan looks around.

EVAN
Amazing. So where is the me from
now?

STILLMAN
It doesn't work like that. You and
I went back in time but there is no
other us. That's why we are
standing where we were two minutes
ago. Here, I'll show you the
equation.

Stillman walks over to the blackboard realizes what's there, gets self conscious and flips it over the board revealing a fresh sheet of paper.

EVAN
Wait, what's that stuff?

STILLMAN
It's nothing. Let me explain time travel to you.

EVAN
I get what happened, dude. What is that other stuff you don't want me to see?

Stillman reluctantly pulls down the original sheet of paper. There is a long time line written across it. Dashes indicate significant events and times of day across the line.

EVAN
What is that?

STILLMAN
It's the time line I've been traveling along.

EVAN
Oh wow, where have you been so far?

7.

STILLMAN
(embarrassed)
Uh, just to... yesterday.

EVAN
(confused)
What?

STILLMAN
That's the only place I've been so far, okay?

EVAN
Wait, you invented a time machine and you've been traveling around yesterday?

STILLMAN
It's complicated.

EVAN
What does 9am dry cleaners mean?

STILLMAN
Well you know I've been working non-stop on this idea for a long time.

EVAN
Of course.

STILLMAN
And this week I could tell I was getting close. Which is why I never came back to the apartment. Finally, super late Tuesday night I cracked it. So I was planning on doing my first real trip on Wednesday morning.

EVAN
Ancient Rome.

STILLMAN
Exactly. That's always been the dream. I went to the dry cleaners in morning to pick up my nice shirt, so I could look presentable, ya know, for pictures and whatnot. And the dude at the dry cleaners was a real jerk.

EVAN
Okay.

8.

12 INT. DRY CLEANERS 12

Stillman walks in with a ticket in his hand.

Evan and Stillman's discussion narrates the following scenes.

STILLMAN (V.O.)
He told me the shirt would be ready by Monday and it wasn't. This was Wednesday and he wasn't even cool about it.

The MAN behind the counter gives Stillman an indifferent shrug.

STILLMAN (V.O.)
So I flipped out on him.

Stillman starts yelling.

STILLMAN (V.O.)
Maybe it was the lack of sleep but I really went off... bad. And so when I came back here I felt so awful about how I had treated this guy.

13 INT. LAB 13

Stillman enters the lab shaking his head.

EVAN (V.O.)
So?

STILLMAN (V.O.)
So I went back in time to do it over.

14 INT. DRY CLEANERS 14

Stillman walks in again holding the ticket.

EVAN (V.O.)
How'd that go?

STILLMAN (V.O.)
I finally got it after a few trys.

Stillman yells again.

9.

EVAN (V.O.)
(mildly concerned)
A few trys?

JUMP CUT TO:

15 INT. DRY CLEANERS 15

Stillman walks in again.

STILLMAN (V.O.)
It was harder than you'd think.

EVAN (V.O.)
Why?

STILLMAN (V.O.)
(defensive)
The shirt is never ready, okay!

The man at the cleaners gives the same indifferent shrug.

STILLMAN (V.O.)
No matter how many times you go back in time he still never has it even though he told me it'd be ready, ya know, back in the original timeline. I was just trying to change my reaction to the situation.

16 INT. LAB 16

We are back to Stillman and Evan in front of the board.

EVAN
(off the board)
So what's Debbie 9:45?

STILLMAN
I ran into Debbie on the way back here.

EVAN
Oh God.

17 EXT. BROOKLYN - MORNING 17

Stillman is walking through a section of Brooklyn, similar to the location of the lab. The streets are mostly empty as Stillman runs into DEBBIE, who is holding a yoga mat.

10.

STILLMAN (V.O.)
Yeah, I had a really funny line as soon as I saw her...

Debbie LAUGHS at something Stillman says.

STILLMAN (V.O.)
...but the conversation got terribly awkward after that.

Debbie shifts uncomfortably as she listens.

EVAN (V.O.)
So you did that one over too?

JUMP CUT TO:

18 EXT. BROOLYN - MORNING 18

Stillman runs into Debbie again.

STILLMAN (V.O.)
Dude, I really like her. I wanted to get it right.

EVAN (V.O.)
But you had to keep that opening line.

Debbie LAUGHS again.

19 INT. LAB 19

Back to Stillman and Evan in the lab.

STILLMAN
Exactly! It took a while, though. Debbie is a tough audience, man.

FLASH OF:

20 EXT. BROOKLYN - MORNING 20

A CU of Debbie's face JUMP CUT through many reactions from her, some smiles, some laughter and a lot of painful nods.

11.

21 INT. LAB 21

STILLMAN
But after a few hundred tries Debbie and I had a pretty meaningful conversation.

EVAN
(a little more concerned)
A few hundred!?

STILLMAN
Yeah. It was a nice talk though. She even...

EVAN
What?

STILLMAN
Well, she convinced me how important it was that I stand up to that dry cleaning dude.

FLASH OF:

22 INT. DRY CLEANERS 22

Stillman marches into the dry cleaners again.

CUT BACK TO:

23 INT. LAB 23

EVAN
Oh no.

STILLMAN
Yeah. You don't even want to know about my phone call to my parents.

Stillman walks over to his desk and sits down.

EVAN
You have to let some of this stuff go.

STILLMAN
I want to! But it's a snowball effect. Conversations get really awkward after you've had them 25 times. It takes a lot of work just to get them back to normal.

12.

EVAN
So you haven't made it to ancient Rome?

STILLMAN
Dude, I haven't made it past 2:30!

Evan looks at the board.

EVAN
So wait a second. I haven't seen you in three days but it's been longer for you...
(turns to Stillman)
How long have you been doing this?

STILLMAN
Let's see, um...

Stillman looks at his watch and reluctantly shares his secret.

STILLMAN
About a year and half.

EVAN
Stillman. This is crazy!

STILLMAN
I know.

Evan walks towards the machine.

EVAN
Well you have to go back in time and not invent this or something.

STILLMAN
No!

EVAN
It's killing you. It's gotta stop.

STILLMAN
Don't say that! I can fix this. I should have never told you what's happened.

Something occurs to Stillman and Evan sees it.

EVAN
Don't you dare!

Stillman eyes the time machine and then looks back at Evan. Evan slowly moves his body to block Stillman's path.

13.

Stillman makes a break for it. Evan shoves his friend back and runs towards the machine, leaving Stillman far behind.

STILLMAN
No!

JUMP CUT TO:

24 INT. APARTMENT 24

CLOSE ON: A slightly younger looking Evan looks around, wide eyed.

He is sitting next to a slightly younger Stillman. They are at a kitchen counter in junky apartment. Evan is working on a lap top. Stillman is sorting through brochures.

STILLMAN
What do you think? Quantum
Mechanics or Oceanography?

EVAN
Oceanography!

CUT TO BLACK:

STILLMAN
Yeah?

EVAN
Absolutely. Oceanography. No
question.

STILLMAN
Yeah, okay.

STOP

START

CHAPTER 21

Broken

Broken is a 20-minute film written and directed by Alex Ferrari and produced by Jorge F. Rodriguez. The full script appears at the end of this chapter.

- budget: $8,000
- running time: 20-minutes
- shot: on mini-DV
- festival screenings: over 140 with many prizes
- 3 hours of special features on the DVD and 6 commentary tracks reviewed and interviewed by over 250 international press outlets and entertainment websites

What's the film about? Here's what it says on the DVD cover:

A gun blast, a flash of light, and a young woman awakens to the comfort of her own bed. Bonnie Clayton has It all, a great relationship, a challenging career, and the burden of a dream that grows more vivid and disturbing with each passing night. But when Bonnie is abducted by a sadistic stranger and his colorful entourage, she discovers that the key to her survival lies within the familiar realms of her recurring dream.

When Alex Ferrari and Jorge F. Rodriguez shot *Broken* as a promo for a feature they re-wrote the rule book and showed filmmakers and Hollywood studios what could be done with a tight budget and total commitment. With their 8,000 bucks and, it has to be said, a lot of dedicated assistance from amigos, actors, and crew, they shot a calling-card masterwork with the gloss of 35mm and the look and feel of a big-budget flick like *Sin City*or *Batman*. *Broken* explodes on the screen and through 20 nerve-jangling minutes we are dazzled by more than 100 visual EFX created, not in a digital post-production studio but, incredibly, on an Apple Computer.

Dispensing with the standard 10-minute-and-under imperative, hundreds of festivals selected *Broken* including the influential Los Angeles International Short Film Festival. The filmmakers traveled the country picking up awards, networking and selling DVDs of the film which they show with more than three hours' worth behind-the-scenes footage and how-to tips from the team. As Jorge Rodriguez explains: "You have to learn that 50% of the creative process has to go into marketing and promotion."

Horror is one of the most successful genres in filmmaking and from the DVD extras we encounter the art of creating scars, tattoos, shotgun blasts, burnt eyes, there's even a useful recipe for making "brain matter." Just as important: there are insights into acquiring and using weapons, stunt work, the rehearsal process, and insurance. Rodriguez gives advice on producing shorts; Angel Barroeta has some useful ideas on indie cinematography; and Megan Graham goes step-by-step through the ways of attaining high quality make-up special effects at little or no cost.

21.1 Concept art

▶▶ P.244

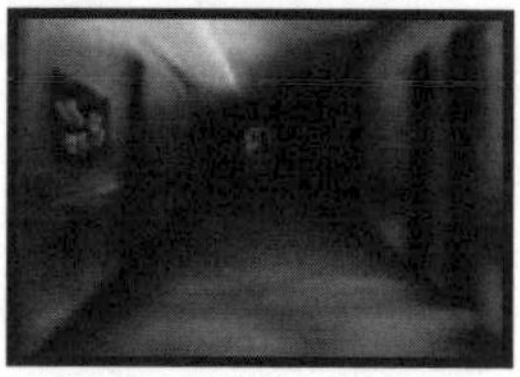

21.1 Concept art

▶▶ P.244

Broken was made by Rodriguez's Fortuity Films and Ferrari's The Enigma Factory. To date they have sold thousands of DVDs through the production website WhatIsBroken—www.whatisbroken.com, Amazon.com, and at Comic Book fairs, earning back the initial investment and putting this $8,000 short film into profit. Comic Book fairs? The book, *The Art of Broken*, was published in March 2007 with 100 pages of illustrations of visual effect breakdowns, sets, on-set photographs, character designs, and storyboards by artist Dan Cregan, Ken Robkin and director Alex Ferrari.

Broken is the perfect example of how to exploit every aspect of a project, to push and keep pushing, to find new angles and give a short film legs. After making the film, marketing is fundamental: it is the gasoline that drives the car. Ferrari and Rodriguez went everywhere and wrote to everyone, including Roger Ebert on the *Chicago Sun-Times:* a kind word from the celebrated film critic is enough to launch a thousand careers. This is what he had to say:

"Broken is essentially a demonstration of the mastery of horror imagery and techniques, effective and professional. Looking forward to *Broken: The Feature*."

Interview with Jorge F. Rodriguez

1. How do you make a great short film?
First off, you have to have a clear purpose of what you are trying to accomplish with your short. Are you doing it for experience? Is it a vehicle for a larger project, and so on. After that, it is all about the planning. What kind of budget do you have? And how can you take the majority of that budget and get it up on the screen. Most importantly it's about surrounding yourself with a team of people who share your vision and desire to see your project cross the finish line.

2. What was the development process on the script of *Broken*?
Alex approached me with a short script that he wanted me to read. I liked the story and began working on the dialogue and giving it a bit of my own spin. He had a clear idea about where we were going to shoot and what we had at our disposal there, so it was just a matter of constructing the story around what we had at the location.

3. You had lots of great actors and obviously a good crew. How did you assemble these people?
The talent was acquired through open casting calls in our area as well as

working with smaller local talent agencies. Over the course of two weekends we had over 350 people show up for the parts we were casting. We just had to find the right combination of talent and attitude that worked for us.

4. And the crew?
Florida is home to some of the best and hardest-working crews around. For some positions it was just a matter of calling the people we already trusted and checking their availability. With other positions we put the word out and met with dozens of people until we found the skills we needed.

5. Broken is very high energy. Did that come from the atmosphere on set?
The script was filled with tension and energy that was definitely palpable on set. Everyone from cast to crew had a level of anticipation, a kind of "how the hell are we going to pull this off in five days" vibe. We had lots of setbacks, but the mood on the set was always positive. It was my job to make sure that everything ran as it was meant to and that Alex didn't have to worry about anything but directing the movie. We had a lot of fun and a real sense of accomplishment when it was all said and done.

6. You managed to make this film for $8,000. How is this possible?
When you know you only have $8,000 you don't create a budget for your film, you back into it. Reverse budgeting is a skill every indie filmmaker learns one way or another. You can't stick a round peg in a square hole. What you've got is what you've got, and if that means you have to production design, stunt co-ordinate, and do the catering yourself, then that's what you do. You also find people who can multi-task. In one case I trained our set PA to become the prop master and gun wrangler. He rose to the job and handled it brilliantly. Even my wife Michelle was co-ordinating craft services and supplies from her hospital bed just hours after giving birth to our third daughter, Jessica. You do what you have to do to get the job done and you don't keep score.

7. The locations were stunning. How did you get these places?
We shot on location at AG Holley State Sanatorium, one of the oldest standing Sanatoriums left in the entire US. The facility is mostly abandoned, although it is still staffed and carries a census of about 30 to 60 tuberculosis patients, mostly people who are HIV positive, who populate one private floor of the main hospital building. We were allowed the use of the entire facility with the exception of the infected floor. We negotiated a reasonable rate to rent the facility for prep and production and got insurance to cover us and them for the time we were there.

8. How long was the shoot?
Five days, but just before we were scheduled to shoot, the facility, as well as the rest of South Florida, was hit by a massive hurricane. The buildings withstood the storm but suffered extensive damage. Enough damage that we had to postpone the shoot for two weeks. By the time we were ready to go in again we were informed that during the week we would be shooting the facility would be used as a federal aid station. We said no problem, but

little did we know that for the next five days we would be sharing a usually abandoned site with 200,000 people. Considering the massive traffic jams, the late starts, the later nights, and the condition of the facility, it was amazing that we got the whole thing shot in the original five days.

9. What part did the music composition play on Broken?
Mark Roumelis' contribution through *Broken*'s score and sound design was one that gave the project a genuine authenticity and provided the audience with a glorious feast for the ears.

21.3 Costume design
▶▶ P.244

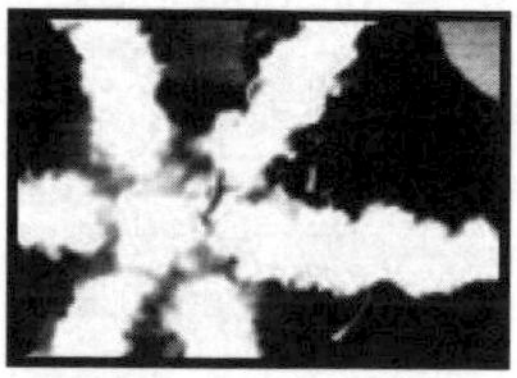

21.4 Poster designs
▶▶ P.244

10. What advice would you give someone wanting to get into the film industry today?
Be clear on what you want to do, and be prepared to take the long way around to get there. It takes more than just talent to get somewhere in the industry. The world is filled with talented people who didn't have the balls to hang in there. Another route is to become a student of the business side, not just the creative. You need money to make movies, learn how to get it, and get to the people who have it; then dazzle them with all your wonderful ideas. Fill your quiver with as many arrows as you can, so that when the opportunity presents itself you are prepared to take advantage of it. And another thing: be kind to everyone you meet, because those people you meet on the way up will most likely be up there soon as well, and if they are not you will most certainly see them on the way down.

11. Broken looks like a promo for a feature. Was that the intention?
Always. It was only meant to be shown as a part of the package for the feature script, but after people saw the trailer it took on a life of its own. That is when we decided to put together the DVD and Alex came up with the ideas of all the extras for the DVD.

21.4 Poster designs
▶▶ P.244

Two questions with director Alex Ferrari.

1. How do you like to work?
Fast! I like to move the camera a lot. I'm a technical director so I love to move the camera and compose the shot. Every shot is storyboarded before I walk on set. It's the Hitchcock in me. My major influences for *Broken* were Robert "The Man" Rodriguez and David "screw the studio" Fincher—among others. Those guys make films their way and do it with a great amount of style and control. *Se7en* and *Fight Club* are on my top five of all time, and almost all of Rodriguez's films as well. Also, comics like *Sin City* and *100 Bullets* had an influence. They have fun telling stories ... this is supposed to be fun. If not, we would get real jobs. Also, I admire Akira Kurosawa, Marty Scorsese, Steven Spielberg, Sergio Leone, and Quentin Tarantino.

21.6 Screen capture
▶▶ P.244

2. The efx on Broken are exceptional. What hardware did you use?
Sometimes I look back and forget how I got there. I just play around A LOT with the tools. Many independent films do not take the time to design their stories. I did not want to fall into that trap. It also took about 35 hours of rendering all the filters to get the final look for *Broken* (on an Apple G5 Dual 2 GIG, w/4 gigs of RAM and 1 terabyte of storage). I was an AVID editor

for over six years but when I was introduced to Apple's Final Cut Pro, I was hooked. The power this little program has is amazing. It gave me the ability to open my own Post facility (Numb Robot) and for the price there is nothing on the planet that can come close. The transfer modes that FCP has is amazing. I'm able to get very unique looks that you could never get on an AVID. It's like having Photoshop for a moving image. I also love the speed and scalability of the program. For a little bit of cash you can have FCP editing HD footage and you can scale up at your own pace. Also, since Apple purchased Shake, we can transfer files with the greatest of ease. Bottom line, even if we get $20 Million to make the feature version of *Broken*, it will be edited on Final Cut Pro ... NO DISCUSSIONS!

21.1 Concept art

21.2 Concept art

21.3 Costume design

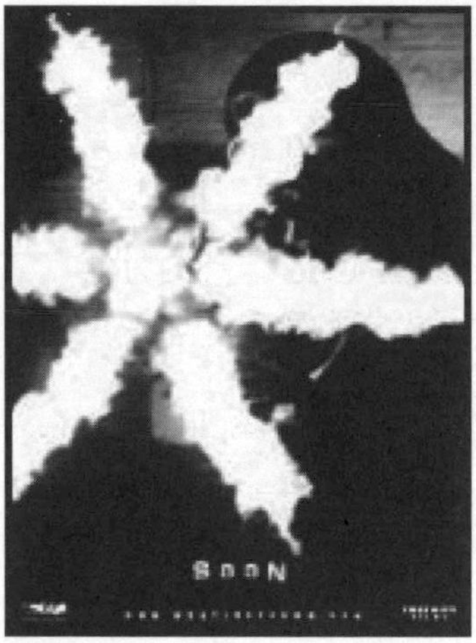

21.4 Poster designs

21.5 Poster designs

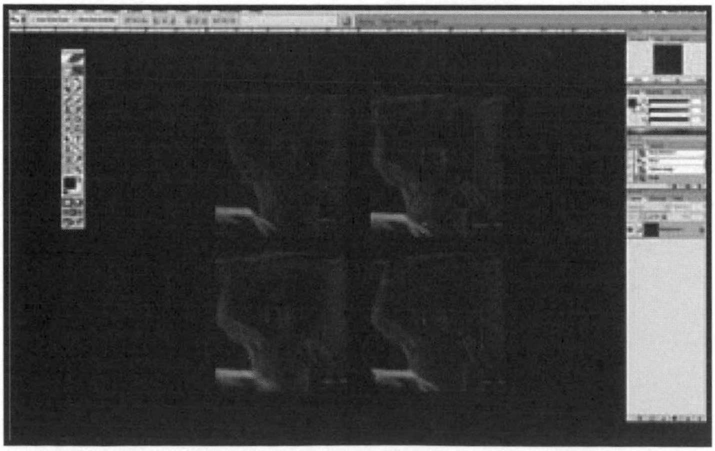

21.6 Screen capture

START

TITLE

Broken

Story by Alex Ferrari
Screenplay by Alex Ferrari & Jorge F. Rodriguez
Produced by Jorge F. Rodriguez

FADE IN:

1 INT. ABANDONED MEDICAL FACILITY - EVENING 1

Petrified eyes fill the frame. We pull back to discover a young woman leather-bound to a vintage wheelchair, only wearing a "Dabbit" (an old Looney Toons-type cartoon) nightshirt.
A gun barrel is aimed at her. The trigger is pulled and a bullet ERUPTS out of the gun.
Every detail of the bullet's exit from the gun is seen.
Sparks fly as the bullet SLICES through the air toward its target.
Just as the bullet is about to find its victim, we slam into an ECU of her face. She lets out a HELLISH cry.

2 INT. BONNIE'S APARTMENT - BEDROOM - NIGHT 2

The woman wakes from her nightmare. Her eyes are an unnatural blue but they slowly change to a realistic brown.
Her back is soaked with sweat. She was the woman in the dream and it's not the first time she's woken up like this.
The alarm clock is flashing 3:15 a.m.
The bedroom is well manicured. Clothes and shoes are laid out for her work day.
BONNIE CLAYTON, a young twenty-something woman, gets up and sits on her bed wearing only her "Dabbit" nightshirt.
She reaches over to her night table and grabs a pill bottle marked "for sleep." Then she pulls the last pill out. She places the bottle back on the night table and we see a frame with pictures of her and her boyfriend Christian.

3 INT. BONNIE'S APARTMENT - KITCHEN - NIGHT 3

She stumbles in the dark toward the kitchen and stubs her toe as she navigates her way to the fridge. She cracks it open. Nothing but health food, soy this, and tofu that.
The light from the fridge slightly illuminates the darkened living room. She is not alone; the light exposes the boot of someone who is sitting in the living room, watching her.

She grabs the soy milk and moves over to the counter. As she is about to drink from the carton, someone starts playing a HARMONICA in the living room.
The sound startles her and she almost chokes on the pill, which she now has coughed out. She drops the milk carton and spills the milk on the floor. Slamming her hand on the counter...

BONNIE

Jesus Christ! Christian. You scared the shit out of me. When are you going to stop sneaking up on people?

She turns and sees a silhouette of a man sitting in her boyfriend's favorite chair. She grabs a towel and starts to clean up the spilled milk.

BONNIE (cont'd)

Was your trip cut short?

DUNCAN

No ... but your trip is about to begin.

Bonnie jumps out of her skin. She slips and falls on the milk as she tries to get up. She attempts to flip the kitchen/living room light on but things are not going her way.
DUNCAN is a thirty-something man who is wearing an outfit as unique as his harmonica. The man has style. He is calmly sitting in the living room with his face lost in the shadows.
Half a glass of red wine sits on the end table. He smiles lewdly at Bonnie as he notices her nightshirt.

DUNCAN (cont'd)

Long time no see, little girl.

A chill runs down Bonnie's spine. She slowly crawls against the wall toward the doorway.

DUNCAN (cont'd)

I wouldn't ...

Then she makes her move and jets for the only exit.
Before she can reach the door Bonnie is FRONT-KICKED IN THE FACE by an imposing redheaded woman, MARQUEZ. Bonnie's head is whipped back as blood flies out of her lip and mouth.

DUNCAN (cont'd)

... do that.

Marquez sweeps her legs out from under her and Bonnie slams onto the floor. Still dazed, she looks up, Marquez is over her and the last thing that Bonnie sees is her fist.

TITLE SEQUENCE: B R O K E N

4 INT. ABANDONED MEDICAL FACILITY - ELEVATOR - EVENING 4

The sound of a BLUES HARMONICA fills the air. The door of an old freight elevator opens as a vintage wheelchair exits.
BONNIE has her arms and legs bound by leather straps to the wheelchair.

4A INT. ABANDONED MEDICAL FACILITY - HALL - EVENING 4A

Her mouth is duct-taped. She is completely unconscious as she is pushed by Marquez down a long hallway.
Once used to care for tuberculosis patients, the corridors of this abandoned hospital are now overgrown with out-of-date medical technology and bear the scars of a fire that licked through the entire facility.
Patterns of permanent shadow decorate the walls and rooms of this medical graveyard.

4B INT. ABANDONED MEDICAL FACILITY - ROOM - EVENING 4B

Bonnie is rolled into a cavernous room, where DUNCAN sits calmly with his back to her. He is the source of the evening's soundtrack.
Marquez walks over to him and whispers in his ear and he stops playing. He makes his way over to Bonnie. His face is cloaked by the shadows cast across the room. He inspects her for a moment, then pinches her nose with his hand.
She wakes with a gasp, trying to breathe air. Her eyes are still blurred from being knocked out by MARQUEZ.
Duncan speaks. His voice has a hypnotic quality to it.

DUNCAN
(eerie Mr. Rogers vibe)
Rise and shine.

He begins to circle Bonnie, walking in and out of the light, much like a tiger circling its prey before devouring it.
Now fully awake she finds herself strapped down and her mouth taped shut. As she FIGHTS for air you can see the tape on her mouth going in and out.

DUNCAN (cont'd)
Relax darling.

For the first time we see Duncan's face, which is decorated by a deep scar running from the front of his cheek to the back of his ear. Bonnie is repulsed.
He notices that she doesn't seem to recognize him.

DUNCAN (cont'd)
Do I look familiar?

Bonnie shakes her head, no.

DUNCAN (cont'd)
Does anyone in this room look familiar to you?

Duncan's motley crew, six men and one woman (Marquez) in all, start to come out from the shadows.

SNAKECATCHER: A killer with Aztec roots. A tribal tattoo decorates his arm as he swings his cane.
GABRIEL: Duncan's large and silent clean-up man. An old case sits by his feet.
SHA-MON: His outfit is as flamboyant as his personality. He's wearing alligator couture as his .45 dances in his hands.
RUNT: A large gentleman wearing a pair of Uzis. The bulldog of the bunch; when cornered he usually blasts his way out of situations.
PENANCE: Ex-missionary from South America. He sits quietly behind Duncan.
UKYO: A bald Buddhist with issues. Sanskrit protection tattoos are engraved in his head. He stands behind PENANCE, waiting.
All of them give her a knowing look. Bonnie looks around and shakes her head, no.

DUNCAN (cont'd)
Then we have a problem.
(beat)
Marquez, inform management.

Marquez nods and quickly leaves the room.

5 EXT. ABANDONED MEDICAL FACILITY - EVENING 5

The sky is lit up by lightning cracking open the dark veil of night as a storm rolls in.
Another flash reveals a MAN wearing black walking rapidly past an old air conditioning unit the size of a small space station. A FAMAS F1 assault rifle is in his hand; an impressive piece of weaponry.
He jumps some pipes and heads for an old maintenance door, which he breaks open with little trouble and makes his way into the hospital.

6 INT. ABANDONED MEDICAL FACILITY - EVENING 6

Duncan moves closer and slowly runs his hands through her hair. Then, quick as a rattlesnake, he savagely rips the duct tape off her mouth.

DUNCAN
Better?

She takes in a few mouthfuls of air as her lips and mouth begin to burn.

BONNIE
(almost hyperventilating)
Please ... let ... me ... go.

DUNCAN
I can't do that.

Bonnie is searching her mind for answers to this whole thing. A nervous smile comes across her face.

BONNIE
(hysterically)
This is a joke? Right?
(beat)
Right!

DUNCAN
Yeah, it's all one big joke
(beat)
... and you're the punchline.

Marquez walks back into the room. She smiles at Bonnie as she whispers into Duncan's ear.

7 INT. ABANDONED MEDICAL FACILITY (OTHER SIDE OF ROOM)- EVENING 7

Moving like a cat, the man in black makes his way through the room.

8 INT. ABANDONED MEDICAL FACILITY - EVENING 8

His face turns serious.

DUNCAN
Thank you.

He turns to Bonnie and begins to circle her again as he pulls the harmonica out of his coat pocket.

DUNCAN (cont'd)
(sarcastically)
Bonnie, right? Well Bonnie, do you know what this is?

She nods her head, yes.

BONNIE
It's, it's a harm ...

He cuts her off.

DUNCAN
Marvelous little thing really. It completely transformed the face of Western music.
(To himself)
Why can't I come up with something like this?

Bonnie feels that the right leg strap of the wheelchair is loose and starts to discreetly tug on it.

DUNCAN (cont'd)
Anyway, the reason I'm so fond of this awkward little tin sandwich is because like you, its complexity lies within its simplicity.
(beat)
Dozens of little reeds working together to make the perfect note.

He blows into it.

DUNCAN (cont'd)
Perfection attained ... Or is it?

He takes the harmonica and slams it violently on the wheelchair. Then blows again. This time a distorted note, sounding like nails across a chalk board, leaves the wounded instrument.

DUNCAN (cont'd)
Perhaps a reed has split.

Duncan begins to fiddle with the harmonica as he moves closer to Bonnie.

DUNCAN (cont'd)
When something like this happens, we have a choice to make. One can either ...

Takes the harmonica and runs it down from Bonnie's face and shirt using the harmonica as a scalpel.

DUNCAN (cont'd)
... open her up. Checking every ... single ... reed ... till we find the broken one. Or you simply ...

Pulls away from her, drops the harmonica on the floor and crushes it with the heel of his boot.

DUNCAN (cont'd)
... replace it.

Duncan hugs her head in a lovingly sick manner and strokes her hair.

DUNCAN (cont'd)
Management is no longer concerned with your ... lack of progress. Now they just want "you" ...
(whispering)
... replaced.

9 INT. ABANDONED MEDICAL FACILITY (OTHER SIDE OF ROOM)- EVENING 9

The man quietly screws a scope on his assault rifle and takes aim. We see the crosshairs on Duncan.

10 INT. ABANDONED MEDICAL FACILITY - EVENING 10

Bonnie's scared shitless.

DUNCAN
But let me let you in on a little secret.

Duncan is about to whisper in Bonnie's ear when a large man in a Kangol beret bursts through the door.

GUARD
Duncan, the men have ...

Without missing a beat, Duncan pulls out his hand cannon and nails the guard in the head. Blood squirts onto Bonnie's face as the man slams against the wall and drops.
The other associates barely move; some even smile. GABRIEL quietly opens the case next to his feet and pulls out a rubber smock and gloves.

DUNCAN
I detest interruptions.

He puts them on and walks toward the new stiff. GABRIEL grabs his feet and pulls him out of the room.

DUNCAN (cont'd)
Thank you Gabriel.

11 INT. ABANDONED MEDICAL FACILITY (OTHER SIDE OF ROOM)- EVENING 11

The man's crosshairs switch to the back of Bonnie's head.

12 INT. ABANDONED MEDICAL FACILITY - EVENING 12

Bonnie's face is SLACK-JAWED, frozen in fear. Duncan cleans off the small squirt of blood with his hand.

DUNCAN
(whispers)
Where was I?
(beat)
Ah yes. Everyone here – even the fellow wearing that ridiculous little hat – came here for a reason and one reason only: to kill you.

Takes the gun and rubs the eyes of her Dabbit shirt.

MARQUEZ
Duncan we don't have time for ...

Duncan cocks his weapon, abruptly ending any objection Marquez may have had. She retreats slowly into the shadows.

DUNCAN
Now me on the other hand, I came for two things.

Duncan moves the gun slowly down Bonnie's shirt. Her fear is being replaced by anger.

DUNCAN (cont'd)
To get one last look at your eyes ...

He takes a deep whiff of her hair. His breath stutters in excitement.

DUNCAN (cont'd)
... and to give you a little something to remember me by ...

Duncan moves in close. Bonnie stops breathing and pulls back.

DUNCAN (cont'd)
... you know, return the favor.

A smile, razor-thin, curls the corner of his lips as he begins to breathe down her neck.

DUNCAN (cont'd)
(whispering)
I love this part.

Her pupils constrict and her eyes change to a vivid shocking blue.
Then, like a whip, she SLAMS her forehead hard into his face.
Blood erupts from his mouth. No one else is going to touch her tonight, not if she can help it.
The men move in; Duncan waves them off. He grabs his mouth and wipes the blood.

DUNCAN (cont'd)
Look at those baby blues. This bitch is furious. I just had to see it for myself.
(pause)

Bonnie says nothing.

DUNCAN (cont'd)
And now that I've seen them ...

He draws his weapon and points it right at Bonnie. That's all this situation needed.

13 INT. ABANDONED MEDICAL FACILITY (OTHER SIDE OF ROOM) - EVENING 13

Muffled fire shoots out of the man's weapon.

14 INT. ABANDONED MEDICAL FACILITY - EVENING 14

At the sound of the trigger, Bonnie flinches from a sharp pain in her head. She feels the action before it happens.
Just as Duncan is turning to see what is happening, the first bullet hits him in the leg, and the other slices his cheek and rips through his ear, sending him flying into a group of barrels and out of commission.
The bullet that hits Duncan in the ear now punctures PENANCE, standing behind him, spits out of his back, and tears through a large mirror, shattering its pieces all

over the floor.
The darkness of the cavernous room cloaks the sniper as what is left of the crew fire blindly toward the far side of the room.

14A INT. ABANDONED MEDICAL FACILITY - UKYO DEATH - EVENING 14A

Before UKYO can react, another group of bullets puncture his body. His protection tattoos were no help to him today.

14B INT. ABANDONED MEDICAL FACILITY - RUNT DEATH - EVENING 14B

RUNT turns the room into the Wild Bunch; he aims blindly and starts to spray the room. THE MAN changes his focus and takes RUNT out. Gun smoke thickens the room.

14C INT. ABANDONED MEDICAL FACILITY - MARQUEZ PT #1 - EVENING 14C

MARQUEZ notices where the last shots were fired from and grabs an old surgeon's lamp. Faster than a snake spits, she whips it toward the action, slamming it on and exposing the cause of the evening's excitement.
She pulls her hand cannons from her back holsters and opens fire. There is no wasted movement.
THE MAN returns fire and hits the lamp, sending sparks out, burning MARQUEZ's face. She falls and takes cover behind a loose wall in the middle of the room.

14D INT. ABANDONED MEDICAL FACILITY - SNAKE DEATH - EVENING 14D

SNAKECATCHER jumps into action and starts to blast away.
THE MAN fires and shoots the gun out of SNAKECATCHER'S hand.
THE MAN is out of bullets and tosses the rifle.
He rolls on the floor, jumps up and opens his cane to reveal a sword. He whips the sword at THE MAN.
The sword just misses THE MAN and lands four inches from his face. As SNAKECATCHER is about to pull another gun from his back, THE MAN grabs his side arm and takes him out.

14E INT. ABANDONED MEDICAL FACILITY – SHA-MON/ GABE DEATH - EVENING 14E

SHA-MON comes out from behind a wall and grabs BONNIE'S wheelchair and uses it for cover as he fires. THE MAN pulls out his hand gun but can't get a clear shot.
GABRIEL comes back into the room, guns blaring.
THE MAN changes his focus and pins GABRIEL down by the gate door. SHAMON tosses BONNIE'S wheelchair over to GABRIEL for cover as he finds new accommodations.
The bullets crisscross each other. Bodies are flying everywhere. Bonnie is smack in the middle of a John Woo film.
GABRIEL slowly walks over to where SHA-MON is and uses BONNIE as cover. THE MAN is empty. He fired his last bullet. GABRIEL gives BONNIE a look. She returns the favor but also bites down on his shooting hand as he yanks it back.
SHA-MON comes out. In a blink, THE MAN pulls out two surgical steel knives, which he whips in one motion at the men.
The knives SLOW DOWN as they pass Bonnie's head; she turns and sees her reflection

and a strange insignia carved in the blade.
The knives ramp back to speed and nail both GABRIEL and SHA-MON in the neck and rip out the back. The knives stick in the wall behind them. They fall faster than Pauley Shores's career.

14F INT. ABANDONED MEDICAL FACILITY - MARQUEZ PT #2 - EVENING 14F

MARQUEZ sees her comrades go down and loses her mind. She jumps out and begins to shoot, her hand cannons raging against the weaponless MAN.
THE MAN runs quickly for SHA-MON'S gun, which is lying next to his dead body. He dives and grabs the gun, whips around and fires a bullet at MARQUEZ, who is still screaming and has just run out of ammo. The bullet flies right into MARQUEZ's mouth and explodes out of the back of her head as she drops hard.

14G INT. ABANDONED MEDICAL FACILITY - DUNCAN'S RETURN - EVENING 14G

He is now behind Bonnie's wheelchair. Feeling the coast is now clear, he starts to move toward her but is stopped in his tracks by the sound of clapping.
Duncan rounds the corner, bloody gun in hand, taunting the MAN.

DUNCAN
Bravo kid, B R A V O.
(pause)
They said you were dead.

The MAN in disgust tosses the gun aside and slowly gets up, hands raised.

CHRISTIAN
They talk a lot, don't they?

DUNCAN
Guess that makes them liars.
But then again, aren't we all?

The legrest strap of the wheelchair is almost completely loose now. The Man gets up from the ground and walks unarmed toward Bonnie and Duncan.

DUNCAN (cont'd)
You can take the mask off now.

THE MAN takes his mask off to reveal CHRISTIAN, Bonnie's boyfriend.

DUNCAN (cont'd)
And while you're at it, set the sword down
too, Samurai.

Christian smiles, surprised that Duncan remembered.

DUNCAN (cont'd)
You didn't think I'd forget, did you?

He slowly reaches behind his head, pulling out a STOCKLESS SAWED-OFF SHOTGUN from his back. As he places it down, we see the word "KATANA" engraved on the barrel.

DUNCAN (cont'd)
Kick it over here. I taught you better than that.

"KATANA" slides over to Duncan's boot. He picks it up off the floor, looks it over and cocks it with one hand.

DUNCAN (cont'd)
I always hated this thing. It has no style. No panache.

Duncan taunts Christian by placing the shotgun along the side of Bonnie's face.

DUNCAN (cont'd)
Much too crass to use on such a delicate face.

CHRISTIAN
Come on man, this is business. Stop making it personal.

DUNCAN
Oh, personal ...

Duncan shoves KATANA down Bonnie's shirt.

DUNCAN (cont'd)
... hold this, will you?
(pause)
You know my therapist says the exact same thing.

He starts to run his hand down the gun and her shirt.

DUNCAN (cont'd)
... can't let go of the past, can't move on. I need closure.

Duncan's breath stutters as he steps back aiming the gun at Bonnie. Her look expresses the anger and hatred that she has for this man.

DUNCAN (cont'd)
Which reminds me.

Without warning, Duncan fires a shot. Bonnie flinches and realizes she is still alive. But over her shoulder, Christian falls to his knees.
A smile dances across Duncan's face.

DUNCAN (cont'd)
(To himself)
I'm starting to feel better already.

The man's thigh is torn open and blood flows from the gaping wound. He painfully strains to get up, but can't. He looks up and sees Duncan's barrel now aimed at

Bonnie.
Duncan stands back and aims his gun at the side of Bonnie's face.

DUNCAN (cont'd)
Now, don't move. I wouldn't want to kill you.

A piece of broken mirror dangles and twirls, reflecting the scene. It breaks loose and falls, causing Duncan to turn for a split second.
Bonnie rips the leg of the wheelchair completely loose, and slams her body back into the chair, simultaneously pushing off with her foot. Seeing this, CHRISTIAN grabs hold of the chair, SLAMMING it to the floor.
Her leg kicks the gun out of Duncan's hand.
Christian falls over Bonnie and grabs KATANA, which is still resting in her nightshirt, and zeros in on Duncan as Bonnie sees the man's face for the first time.

BONNIE
Christian!?

Christian pumps a shot into Duncan's chest, which sends him flying back into the pieces of broken mirror. His body lies motionless.

<u>14H INT. ABANDONED MEDICAL FACILITY - CHRISTIAN - EVENING 14H</u>

The man limps around and places the wheelchair upright.
Her eyes widen as they return to normal at the sight of her lover.

BONNIE
But how ...?
(relieved but confused)
Honey, what the hell is going on?

CHRISTIAN
Shh.

Christian looks back; he thinks he hears something.

CHRISTIAN (cont'd)
We don't have much time.

BONNIE
(screaming)
Time? What the hell are you talking about?
Get me out of this thing!

Christian covers her mouth with his hand. He moves the hair covering her face away and looks into her eyes. They exchange a look only two souls in love are capable of.
He passionately kisses her. For her it's a kiss hello; for him a kiss goodbye.
He pulls away as he hears the sounds of glass breaking and footsteps outside come closer.
Christian limps over to the gun on the floor, which he dropped in the firefight.

CHRISTIAN
I did all I could to protect you, but now I'm out of options.

He takes a small case from his back pocket, places a strange blue bullet into the gun and slowly turns, raising the weapon to Bonnie.

BONNIE
Christian, what are you doing?

CHRISTIAN
Trust me Bonnie, you're better off forgetting the whole thing.

He takes aim.

BONNIE
God, I just want my life back!!!

CHRISTIAN
I'm sorry honey, but it was never your life to begin with.

He fires. The strange bullet ERUPTS out of the gun toward Bonnie. Every DETAIL of the bullet's exit from the gun is seen.
Sparks fly as the bullet SLICES through the air toward its target.
The bullet RIPS into her arm; we SLAM into an ECU of her face as she lets out a HELLISH cry.

15 INT. MENTAL INSTITUTION HALLWAY - NIGHT 15

We snap back from the HELLISH cry to reveal Bonnie being injected in the same arm by a nurse. Two huge orderlies are trying to restrain her. She begins having convulsions.
We are now in a mental institution and Bonnie is a patient.
She gets pulled up from the floor, kicking and screaming. When she sees her psychiatrist, she loses her mind.

BONNIE
(frantically yelling)
Who are you? Where am I? I loved y ..!
(turns to the doctor)
You bastard! You—you did this to me!

ORDERLY #1
We were walking her back to her room and she just snapped Doc.

NURSE
We found this next to her bed.

The nurse has multiple blue pills in her hand. The doctor turns to Bonnie. She is still mumbling incoherently.

PSYCHIATRIST
(To Bonnie loudly)
Bonnie, you have to take your medicine. We want you to get better.

Bonnie takes her last breath and spits in the doctor's face. He wipes his glasses and turns to the nurse.

PSYCHIATRIST (cont'd)
Alright then, let's keep her sedated and confined to the quiet room till this episode subsides. Up her dosage until she is back to a manageable level. Short of that ...

He looks back at her as they carry her off.

PSYCHIATRIST (cont'd)
... I don't know what else to do.

NURSE
Yes doctor.

As Bonnie is being pulled down the long hallway, her sedative begins to take effect.
She makes a few last mumbles, not distinct enough to be called words.
As her vision goes blurry, the last thing she sees is a janitor pushing a cleaning cart.
They pass the janitor, he turns, looks up, tilts his head and smiles at us. He has a striking resemblance to DUNCAN, and you can't help but notice the "DABBIT" hat he is wearing and the bandage on his ear.
He pulls out his trusty "TIN SANDWICH" and begins to play. As he LIMPS down the hall the sound of HARMONICA MUSIC fills the corridor.

FADE TO BLACK

STOP

START

CHAPTER 22

Noise Control

Noise Control is an 8-minute film written by Terence Doyle, directed by Alexis Bicât, and produced by Danielle Anneman and Terence Doyle. The full script appears at the end of this chapter.

Movies are magic. But to make the magic work, the coincidence of opportunity needs the backing of preparation.

That was the experience of writer Terence Doyle.[1] He was lamenting the state of his various feature projects in a pub one night when TV director Peter Chapman mentioned that he could get hold of a jet plane—for free. By the time his glass was empty, Terence had made two promises: to write a feature with "the pace of *Top Gun*, the poignancy of *Local Hero* and the humor of *Withnail and I*," and to get the project rolling with a short.

22.1 Nick Moran

▶▶ P.262

22.2 On location

▶▶ P.262

22.3 Framing the shot

▶▶ P.262

Such are pledges *in vino veritas*. But he knuckled down, wrote the short version of *Noise Control* over the coming weeks and at the Cannes Film Festival showed it to *Lock Stock and Two Smoking Barrels* star Nick Moran. The short, to quote the synopsis, is an action comedy about "a TV crew doing a story on the problems from low-flying jets in the Welsh valleys meeting its match in the shape of a single parent family on the ground and a heroic fighter pilot in the air."

Nick Moran just happened to be learning to fly single engine Cessnas in his spare time. Would he take the role of the pilot in the short?

"Just try and stop me," he replied.

That's movie magic.

Terence had joined the London Filmwriters Workshop five years before to learn screenwriting. He had written several features, and sold options on some of them, but believes he truly got to grips with the writer's craft by working on the short.

"You come to understand the complexity of the film-writing process by seeing what actually works and what doesn't. There are things on the page that seem funny—that are funny—but they're just not funny on the screen. On the other hand, we found humor where it had not been planned on the page but it appeared out of thin air on set," he says. "So much goes into setting up each scene and you take this knowledge with you into future projects. I now look at all my past scripts in a different light and, of course, the feature based on the short embodies everything that I've learned."

Terence Doyle's initiation into screenwriting coincided with the increase in new production companies and, even if the number of features being made has remained static at around a hundred a year in the UK, the growth in outlets for short films has been exponential.

Most commercial shorts are self-funded and Terence Doyle had deliberately set out to write something that was commercial. "When people go to the movies they want to be entertained; they want to see something humorous, colorful, light in tone. That's what we were striving for in the short because we wanted to keep the cast on board when we set out to fund the feature."

Top actors make short films because they like the exposure. Everyone wants to get out and work and, if it's an interesting script, they would rather be working for nothing than not working at all. "I imagine," says Terence, "the time will come when you will need a big-name just to get your short film shown."

Not only actors, but technicians who work on features as the assistant to the assistant come into a short as the head of a department and finally get the chance to put their hard-earned skill into practice. Standards are constantly improving. More shorts are being shot on film stock with full lighting kit and high quality sound equipment. "You can learn a lot at film school but there's nothing quite like being out there and actually doing it."

22.4 Alexis Bicât and Nick Moran

P.262

By the time *Noise Control* was ready to roll, Peter Chapman, the man with the spare fighter jet at his disposal, was working on a new project. Alexis Bicât switched hats from co-producing to directing, and Danielle Anneman came on board as producer. At just 21, the Texan ex-model already had seven years experience working on film sets in Los Angeles and London and showed, according to Doyle, the organizing genius required for the tight budget.

With Nick Moran already at the party, Danielle went through her contacts at the casting agents and signed up Gail Downey, Nigel Hastings, Sarah McNicholas, Thomas Myles, Daniel Macnabb and Søren Munk. A crew of 23 was assembled and moved en masse to the countryside for four days on location.

22.5 Alex Bicât directs

P.262

"Everyone's heart sank—including mine—when we rolled up at the youth hostel," says Danielle. "When actors and crew agree to work on a low-budget film they know what they are letting themselves in for, but it was pretty bleak and, if we'd had more money, I would have put it into decent accommodation."

Doyle continues: "The first day was the brightest April day I had ever seen. It was a miracle. Then, when we set out to drive to the airport at Kemble, the road vanished as we were consumed by fog. We weren't shooting a movie. We were in a movie. It was so bad," he recalls, "they had to send out a rescue team to bring us in. We stood around in the hangar until about two o'clock in the afternoon, when the fog finally lifted and we started our day."

22.6 Bicât directs on set

P.262

After the ill-starred beginning, the rest of the shoot went according to schedule and "we began the nightmare of post." Unlike a feature, as Terence Doyle was to learn, about half the budget on a short is required for post-production. The blow up from 16mm to 35mm is expensive, as are digital effects and the use of blue screen. *Blue screen?*

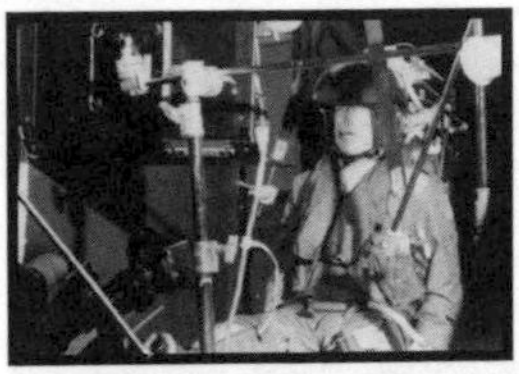

22.7 Nigel Hastings

▶▶ P.262

"The blue screen is literally that. You shoot against a blank screen on to which you can later project images as background. For example, you may have a couple talking in a car. You shoot that in the studio with a blue screen, then superimpose the landscape."

There were problems with the digital effects which caused a knock-on effect in post. The company making the blow up from 16mm failed to print the edge code numbers aligned to each frame, which means when you add the digital effects, you can just refer to the number. Since that had not been done on the 35mm print, the special effects technician had to do it by eye. This requires looking at every frame individually—and at 24 frames a second, that's a long and complicated business. Terence and Alexis had been fortunate to secure downtime in an editing suite at Remote Films in Battersea, and editor Brad Watson patiently cut the film together during spare weekends over many months.

Just as the budget for Martin Scorsese's *Gangs of New York* doubled from $50m to $100m, the cost of making *Noise Control* went up by the same proportion from £5,000 to £10,000. There are always hidden costs, according to Terence, even short films need end credits, then there's the cost of making videos for festivals, the press kits and postage. When you think it's all over, there are yet more unforeseen costs: in the United States, for example, they charge around $30 as an entry fee to festivals, whether the film is shown or not.

Was it all worthwhile?

There was a reflective pause, the sound of Doyle's fingers scratching his chin. Then his Irish eyes lit up. "Absolutely. It's worth it to see your characters transforming into people, hearing them speaking your lines. Seeing the story you wrote come to life is an enormous thrill, it's an education and, for me, many of the scenes look better than I had ever hoped."

What Terence took away as a final lesson from *Noise Control* is that the writer and director have to work closely together and understand exactly what they are trying to achieve, what each thing means, the subtext, the humor, and pathos. The writer and director must have the same vision and a good producer will make sure they are looking through the right end of the telescope—and at the same time.

www.parent.co.uk/noisecontrol

22.1 Nick Moran

22.2 The cast and crew of *Noise Control* fake Wales in a Gloucestershire garden.

22.4 Alexis Bicât and Nick Moran

22.5 Bicât (standing) readies his stars for the next take.

22.3 DP Simon Dinsel (left) frames the shot with director Alexis Bicât

22.6 The cast and crew look on as Bicât (far left) directs the action on the set of *Noise Control*.

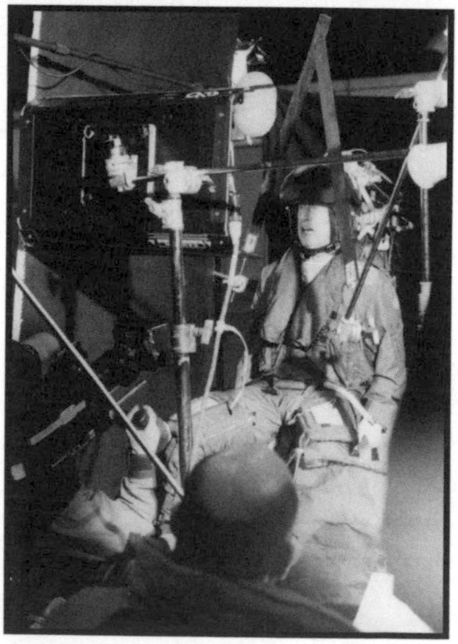

22.7 Leading man Nigel Hastings (center) readies himself for his final cinematic moment.

START

TITLE

Noise Control

A Bicât / Doyle film
Directed by Alexis Bicât
Screenplay by Terence Doyle

1. EXT - FOREST - DAY

FADE IN:
A three-man TV crew - INTERVIEWER, CAMERAMAN and SOUNDMAN (nickname BIG EARS) - is rushing through a dense forest. They can't be seen clearly. Close ups only of the branches ahead and their pounding feet as they run puffing and panting and swearing. Suddenly the Interviewer breaks out into open sunshine. He struggles to make himself stop - there is obviously some kind of drop.

INTERVIEWER

Whooaa. (he turns) Careful ... There's a cliiii ...

The cameraman thunders up behind the Interviewer and doesn't manage to stop in time. He bumps into the Interviewer. The Interviewer falls off screen with a yelp. The crew stop at the top of a precipice and look up, wondering where the Interviewer is. The cameraman admires the sheer drop, he holds the camera over the edge, then moves it back and forth, admiring the stomach churning effect. No sign of the interviewer yet.

CAMERAMAN (O.S.)

Nigel ... ???Nigel ... ???? Nigel ????

INTERVIEWER (O.S.)

(ruffled) Will someone give me a hand ...!!?

The camera whip pans right to reveal the interviewer pulling himself back to safety. The Cameraman hurriedly puts his camera down facing in the opposite direction into the woods. We see a beautiful "Chinese Angle" view of nature. Dappled sunlight streams through the forest canopy and the delicate chirping of birds is set against the gentle movement of the trees. Off screen we hear the crew helping the interviewer up

INTERVIEWER (O.S.)

Alright. Alright. Get off. Get off. (Panting) (beat) Okay, this is good. We'll set up here ... (Breaks off, with a chunky throaty smokers cough) ... I've got to give up these sodding nature gigs ... (More coughing)

The cameraman has started to fiddle with the camera, which affects our beautiful view of the forest. He straightens up the shot, zooms slightly, focuses and perhaps tries a different filter.

BIG EARS (O.S.)
Gotta give up the fags first.

INTERVIEWER (O.S.)
Alright genius. (Pause for cough) (Calls to Cameraman) Fred. (Beat) Hey, Fellini. (sarc.)
Finally the camera jerks around from the forest to focus on a full body shot of the Interviewer, an ageing media "still-trying-to-be-star" looking ridiculous in the latest tracksuit.

CAMERAMAN (O.S.)
(Faking Italian accent)
Pleasea, you cana calla me Fedrico.

The camera crash-zooms in on Interviewer's face to focus and crash zooms out to frame him in a very media friendly and convincing manner.

INTERVIEWER
Sure ... (fake Italian accent) ... when you starta bringa me zee women ... (Beat, normal voice) ... Ready, Ears. Sound check ... (Beat, exaggerated "presenter" voice) ... Good morning, this is ... (Clears his throat, tries again) ... Good morning, this is ... (Another pause, more coughing, really throaty) ... Good morning, this ... Okay, that's good. (he snaps into presenter mode) We have come to this pristine North Wales valley to report on one of the great evils of our time. Listen for a moment to the incredible silence around me ...

He pauses to allow his audience to hear, and for a moment, there is absolute silence

INTERVIEWER (CONT'D)
(To the crew) Scary, isn't it, lads?

Then there is a shrieking sound in the distance

INTERVIEWER (CONT'D)
What the ...
He breaks off as a low flying jet rips past, its engines shaking the microphone.

2. EXT—COCKPIT VIEW OF THE VALLEY SWEEPING PAST—DAY

PILOT (O.S.)
There is an adrenaline rush. (beat) That's not why I fly ... the buzz, the thrill, whatever ... It's there but ... this is serious business. Simulated Attack Profile.

3. EXT—BACK GARDEN, FAMILY HOME—DAY

Laundry on a line—white in the wind. The sound of a **BOY** and a **GIRL**, eight and ten, playing idyllically with simple toys while their **MOTHER** sorts clothes. The TV crew arrive and dodge through the laundry.

INTERVIEWER
Excuse me ... Hello, good morning ...
Yes, hello.

The camera shocks the woman. She backs away and fusses with her hair.

INTERVIEWER (CONT'D)
Don't be embarrassed. You look ... you look ... (Beat) We're doing a program on the effects of low flying jets on the valley. I wonder if you would tell us about their effect on your life?

The woman looks around confused. The kids begin to chatter in the background.

WOMAN
The jets?

INTERVIEWER
The low-flying jets. Listen, right now, it is blissfully quiet here.

He pauses to take in the silence ... and the air is filled with shrieks as the kids suddenly start yelling.

LITTLE GIRL (O.S.)
No he's not.

LITTLE BOY (O.S.)
Yes he is.

LITTLE GIRL (O.S.)
Shut up you're a little prat.

INTERVIEWER
Hey, can you keep it down for a minute?
(beat) Hey . . .
Can somebody get those kids . . .

The kids are suddenly quiet, smothered by the crew.

INTERVIEWER (CONT'D)
(sigh) That's better. Now . . .

It is beautiful again, the laundry flapping in the breeze.

INTERVIEWER (CONT'D)
(Mock enthusiastic) It's wonderful, isn't it?

WOMAN
What?

INTERVIEWER
(Impatiently stressing) The peace. The quiet. The tranquility.

WOMAN
Are you from a television station?

INTERVIEWER
(Laboriously explaining) That's right. We're doing a piece, on the impact of modern life in the valley.

The woman starts primping again.

INTERVIEWER (CONT'D)
You look er . . . You look . . . (Beat) Now can you please tell me about the negative effects of these jets on your simple lifestyle?

The woman looks at him for a long time as if she has no idea what he means; then.

WOMAN
The jets?

INTERVIEWER
That's right

Another long moment of waiting.

WOMAN
(Finally) You're right, of course. There are jets . . .

Again there is the hornet's shriek of a jet in the distance, growing rapidly louder.

WOMAN (CONT'D)
There are . . . (her words are drowned out)

INTERVIEWER
(Overlapping, screaming) Ohhh. Not now . . .! (Even he is drowned out)

Then the plane is past and there is silence again.

INTERVIEWER (CONT'D)
Ears, did we get any of that, Ears? . . .

Ears shakes his head solemnly.

INTERVIEWER (CONT'D)
Bloody hell . . . (To woman) Could you say that again, please?

WOMAN
I said, there are planes but you get used to them. They become part of the background. They don't bother us.

4. EXT—VIEW FROM THE COCKPIT AGAIN—DAY

More scenery sweeps rapidly past.

PILOT (O.S.)
I know some people aren't happy. But when you're doing Mach 2 at a hundred and fifty feet you don't start worrying about peace in the valley.

5. EXT—BACK GARDEN, WELSH FARMHOUSE—DAY

Close-up on the beautiful little girl in a pink dress, smiling.

INTERVIEWER
Can you tell me about the effects of these low-flying jets on the valley?

The girl smiles beguilingly. Suddenly we hear the Soundman make an impression of an approaching jet.

INTERVIEWER (CONT'D)
(Believing the sound to be real) No.

The interviewer realizes it is Big Ears playing a prank. He leans into shot and looks off screen left. We see his face clearly.

INTERVIEWER (CONT'D)
(frustrated) You think that's funny?

The interviewer walks across the shot and exits frame left, we hear a thump and the boom falls through the shot, crashing to the ground in front of the girl, completely unfazed. The interviewer walks back to his first position.

INTERVIEWER (CONT'D)
(to girl) I'm so sorry about that. (to Ears) Ears. Come on. Come on. Pick it up.

The boom slowly rises up through the shot shaking as it goes. The girl smiles sweetly all the time.

INTERVIEWER (CONT'D)
Right. Going again. (to little girl) Would you say that the jets are a negative influence on the quality of your idyllic life?

The girl has been waiting for this interview all her life and she knows how to use a camera.

GIRL
I want to be a supermodel. And I want to live in a big house in the city.

Interviewer laughs artificially.

INTERVIEWER
How sweet ... (aside) Give me a call when you get there ... (beat) But, can we talk about the jets for a moment?

The girl pauses, smiles beguilingly.

GIRL
I want to make a lot of money and travel around the world and have men at my feet.

Interviewer chuckles again. Then lets out a sigh.

INTERVIEWER
But the jets ... Can we please ...

There is the hornet's shriek of a jet quickly approaching.

INTERVIEWER (CONT'D)
(Continues, looking skyward) Oh ... for Christ's sake ...

The jet drowns him out. And he walks off screen fed up.

6. EXT–TARMAC, JET AIRPORT–DAY

The pilot approaches his jet and about-faces to speak to camera. His helmet is off, held under his arm. He is a handsome twenty something, smiling and ingenuous.

PILOT
There's no permanent damage. We come. We go. A couple of seconds. Ba-Boom. We're gone in a flash. Who can complain about that?

7. EXT–BACK GARDEN, WELSH FARMHOUSE–DAY

Close-up on the second child, an impish little boy with red hair and freckles.

INTERVIEWER (O.S.)
(Tiring now) Can you tell us about the effects of these low-flying jets on your life?

A long hold on the little boy's face, as if he is never going to speak.

INTERVIEWER (O.S.) (CONT'D)
(Continues, an edge to his voice) Go on. Say whatever you like.

The boy pauses as if forever.

INTERVIEWER (O.S.) (CONT'D)
Well yes well ...?

The boy hesitates, then finally.

BOY
I can say whatever? Really?

INTERVIEWER (O.S.)
Yes. (Beat, irritated) ... Just get on with it.

His silent face again. Again we hear the screech of an approaching jet. The interviewer gives up.

INTERVIEWER (O.S.) (CONT'D)
Right that's it. I've ... (breaks off)

The jet gets louder.

BOY
(Screaming, excited by the sound) I want to be a pilot. I want fly a jet plane. And touch the stars ...

The jet roars by overhead, drowning him out.

8. EXT—VIEW FROM COCKPIT AS PLANE FLIPS UPSIDE DOWN—DAY

The plane flips upside down. The landscape is inverted.

PILOT (O.S.)
You want to know what I really think?

INTERVIEWER (O.S.)
(strained by being upside down) Yes. Yes. Please.

PILOT (O.S.)
You want to know where I really stand?

INTERVIEWER (O.S.)
(about to puke) Please tell me. Please. Quick.

PILOT (O.S.)
I'll tell you ... Up here it's you and the machine. In combat ...

Suddenly there is an ominous rattling sound.

PILOT (O.S.) (CONT'D)
What the ...?

INTERVIEWER (O.S.)
What was that?

The plane rights itself.

PILOT (O.S.)
Pan, pan, pan. This is Blackjack five. I've got a problem. Engine down.

INTERVIEWER (O.S.)
Is that a bad thing?

PILOT (O.S.)
Requesting 'Nearest Suitable', over.

The landscape flashes by, but in an oblique, jerking manner now.

CONTROL (O.S.)
Blackjack Five. This is London Control. 'Nearest Suitable' Five four two seven North. Zero six three four East.

PILOT (O.S.)
Copy that.

The Pilot looks at the cockpit indicators to see them all turn red one by one.

PILOT (CONT'D) (O.S.)
This is very bad (beat) Mayday, mayday, mayday. Blackjack five preparing to eject.

INTERVIEWER (O.S.)
I don't want to eject.

PILOT (O.S.)
Blackjack five going down right now. Altitude 500 feet and falling. 400. 300. (to interviewer) ... We're gonna eject mate. Just like the drill ... Are you ready. (beat) Ready. (beat) Now!

PILOT
Eject! Eject! Eject!

INTERVIEWER (O.S.)
Eject! Eject! Eject!

The canopy blows off and there is a sudden swoosh ... but something is wrong ... the Pilot has ejected but the Interviewer is still in the cockpit. He holds his broken ejection cord.

INTERVIEWER
(frantically) Eject! Eject! Eject!

The interviewer looks incredulously at the broken chord from his ejection device that has come away in his hands leaving him stranded.

INTERVIEWER (CONT'D)
Hey. (looks up) Come back here. My seat is stuck. Hey.

9. EXT–BACK GARDEN, WELSH VALLEY–DAY

The little boy is standing in the garden, looking skywards, frozen in horror as the jet falls towards him. MS contra zoom of the little boy.

LITTLE BOY
Oh Muuuuuuuu ...!

10. INT–COCKPIT

ECU of Interviewer's face shaking violently with the jet. He sees the little boy through the windscreen. He utters his last words.

INTERVIEWER
Oh no it's that family again! (he screams) Nooooooo . . . !

CUT TO BLACK . . . A SINGLE BIRD CHIRPING . . . MAIN END CREDITS . . . THEN

11. EXT–SOMEWHERE NEAR BACK GARDEN–DAY

The little boy (blackened by the explosion) staggers into a shot from a camera positioned in a tree. There is some smoldering wreckage . . .

LITTLE BOY
(Yelling excitedly) Hey . . . Mum, Sis., Over here! Come on. Quick. The pilot's stuck in a tree . . .
The little boy looks up admiringly into the tree.

LITTLE BOY
Can I have your autograph?

START

CHAPTER 23

G.M.

G.M. is an 8½-minute film written and directed by Martin Pickles, and produced by Kate Fletcher.

This surrealist film in which an Edwardian gentleman is tormented by spirits who appear through holes in his sitting-room wallpaper was inspired by the work of Georges Méliès and was timed to coincide with the hundredth anniversary of the film pioneer's first screening of *Le Voyage Dans La Lune (A Trip to the Moon)*.

23.1 *G.M.* director Martin Pickles

P.277

Though a period drama, it makes use of the latest digital post-production techniques to create "a modern silent horror film about birth, sex and death,"[1] and bridges time from the artisan magic of Méliès's short films to the digital magic of today. *G.M.* was made with a £15,000 grant from the London Production Fund, Martin Pickles' first film to receive formal industry backing.

It had taken a long time for Martin to get funding because his wonderfully eccentric films are neither dramas in the conventional sense, nor work suitable as gallery installations. Pigeonholing projects is clearly more an obsession in the UK and, up until the time when *G.M.* started to get noticed, his shorts found better response elsewhere in Europe.

Martin came to filmmaking after studying classics and, following a childhood enthusiasm for drawing cartoon strips, went from Oxford to art school to study fine art. In his mid-twenties he was still unqualified to do very much at all—he comes, he says, from a long line of late starters—and finally did something practical: a course in computer art that led to a job as a designer. By then, he had started experimenting with a super 8 camera and discovered his passion for film.

With a borrowed camcorder, he made the 5-minute *Shaving*. Inspired by surrealist painter René Magritte, it shows a man getting up in the morning, putting on shaving foam and carefully shaving off his face. He sprays on a suit with an aerosol, places a bowler hat on his head and goes faceless through his day. In order to achieve this effect, Martin and graphic designer Jonathan Mercer had to repaint the film frame by frame on computer, using the PhotoShop program, a task performed in their spare time and which took nine laborious months to complete.

Shaving had cost £500 (as an artist, Martin Pickles didn't factor time in the budget); the film won a prize at the Arts Digitalis Festival in Berlin, was screened on Channel 4, on ITV, at various festivals and was acquired by Canal Plus in France for £1,600 (around $2,500) putting the project suddenly into profit. A shortened version was taken by the Berlin metro to amuse passengers between stations in a scheme launched in 2003, giving the film an unexpected new life and commuters the chance to save their daily papers for the coffee break.

After *Shaving*, Martin stayed his course with experimental films. He shot a pair of short, commercial comedies, but climbed straight out of the mainstream, dried himself off and concluded that, for him, it was more important to make the sort of films he wanted to make, surreal, eclectic, and without compromise. He also came to realize that, paradoxically, by keeping the day job and self-funding his films, he had been taking the easy option, and validation of his work, particularly at home—often the hardest market—would require proper funding, a professional shoot, trained crew and actors, and a more businesslike approach.

THE DREAM

While thinking through this conundrum, Martin happened to be reading a book about the working methods of Georges Méliès. He dreamed that night that he was at a film festival and saw snatches from a short silent film. He woke up feeling annoyed that he had not seen it all and, as if guided by the hand of Freud, jotted down what he remembered. The next day, he wrote the first draft of *G.M.* "I don't want people to think I'm completely mad, but it really happened like that, in a dream, and I knew it was the one."[2]

Martin had already discussed his ideas with Angie Daniell and Kate Fletcher at the pop-promo production company Momentum Video. They had advised him to research what funding schemes were available, locally and nationally, and to make a habit of applying to them regularly. He still doubted that a funder would back this off-the-wall project but, remembering Kate and Daniell's advice, started sending out proposals anyway. One important thing he discovered was that when you have to justify why your film is good enough to deserve public money, the discipline crystallizes the concept, you start to see it from the audience point of view and, if there are holes in the script, you're more likely to find them.

G.M. is in fact full of holes, characters and objects appearing and disappearing through holes, characters seeing themselves through holes, but the point is clear. Martin knew he wasn't nursing a slick, commercial idea and put as much effort into writing the proposal and drawing the storyboards as he had previously put into the entire productions of his guerrilla films. His former modus operandi had been to get out and start shooting from the hip, but when the award finally came through from the London Production Fund, a scheme run by the LFVDA, now Film London, he controlled that urge and asked Kate Fletcher, who'd liked the idea from the outset, to nurture the project (read: Martin P.) as his producer.

While Kate began to organize the crew, cast, equipment, studio hire, "and the entire universe of logistical issues," Maggie Ellis at the LFVDA worked with Martin to further develop and refine the script. "Even if the

23.2 Neil Edmond takes to the streets

▶▶ P.277

23.3 Isabel Rocamora in *G.M.*

▶▶ P.278

23.4 *G.M.* set

▶▶ P.278

23.5 Tracking shot

▶▶ P.278

whole thing is in your head, the rewrites and discussions clarify the concept and make it easier when you get on set."

They had enough money for a three-day shoot at the Bow Road Studios. Pete Nash was brought in as DP, John Pattison wrote the music score, and actors Neil Edmond, Leslie Cummins, and Isabel Rocamora filled the three roles. Martin was free for the first time to concentrate on his work directing and came to realize that when you move away from low-budget productions, the specialized skill of a producer is not just advisable, but essential.

The film required a number of trick shots, including the lead actor playing two characters at the same time. With only three days to shoot, they got behind on the first two days and Martin had to work out what shots he could afford to sacrifice on the third day in order to wrap with the film complete. "Even if my film is not to everyone's taste, it has the production values I wanted and it is at least the best possible film I could have made."

G.M. was shot on Digi Beta, and was transferred to VHS for the rushes. The VHS copy was burnt with the timecode reference from the mastertape visible on screen, allowing Martin to select the takes and make a preliminary edit on paper with the timecode references. Editor Brian Marshall digitized the rushes using the computer editing system Discreet Edit, and made an assembly edit based on Martin's paper edit. Martin used After Effects, another useful program, for the special effects and to retint the frames.

In the editing process, they had used similar effects and stylization to those pioneered by Méliès, albeit in a different form. Méliès would have teams of people hand-painting his film. Martin painstakingly tinted his film digitally in order to get a feeling of being removed from the real world, without merely creating a pastiche.

The film, after months of slow, intricate work in post, was completed in summer 2001. Kate Fletcher and Maggie Ellis then had to persuade Martin to take a minute out of the center of the film to give it more pace. "I would probably not have seen the need to do this myself, but they were right, and I did it."

It required another grant to get the film blown up on to 35mm before starting the festival circuit, first at the London Calling screenings at the London Film Festival in November 2001. The British Film Institute added *G.M.* to its listings as sales agent and took it to the festival at Clermont-Ferrand; it was shown at the Dalí Universe, at the old County Hall on the South Bank, and several more festivals across Europe. Cut to 8½ minutes, the film is the perfect fit for festival and TV schedules.

A FILMMAKER'S VISION

Drawing on inspiration from Méliès, Buñuel and the painters Magritte, De Chirico and Dalí, Martin Pickles has stuck to his own vision. He has come to see filmmaking as a multi-skilled pursuit and, if you haven't been to film school, it is useful when filmmakers bring other life experiences to their work. In Martin's case, reading classics, studying art, drawing cartoons, and mastering computer techniques combined in a surreal way with his Méliès dream for him to find a story that Joseph Campbell would have said was always there, waiting to be found.

If you track Martin's course through the firmament, as an astronomer may track the orbit of a new star, it is his single-pointedness and a belief in his own vision that has got him noticed. When the TV production company Talk Back was making a series of sketches in a Victorian style, Martin got his first industry commission as a director.

He is still, however, creating shorts, animation, and new media work. He sees the short film as an art form in its own right and his style of filmmaking suits the genre.

"Short films can pursue one topic, be single minded; they can be experimental, which is hard to sustain over 90-minutes."

I caught all the enthusiasm of the perennial university student in his tone and guessed that a feature was now on the agenda.

"It's the inevitable next step. I am working on a comedy with another writer," he explains. "I have always made films to please myself and could not work on a film that I didn't completely believe in. All my sensibilities are contained in the feature, but it is my co-writer who brings me back into the real world."

www.gmfilm.co.uk

23.1 *G.M.* director Martin Pickles

23.2 Neil Edmond takes to the streets

23.3 Isabel Rocamora in *G.M.*

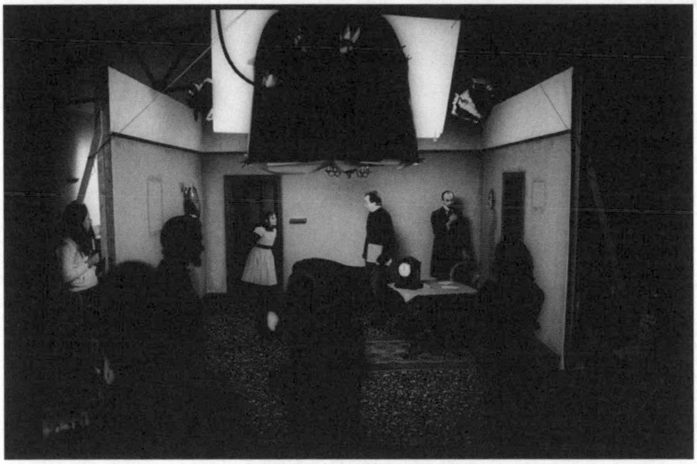

23.4 *G.M.* set

23.4 Tracking shot

START

TITLE

G.M.

Script/summary by Martin Pickles
Storyboards drawn by Martin Pickles
Stills photography Kalpesh Lathigra

Please note: the film has no dialogue so this is merely a list of stage directions

Interior. Edwardian Sitting Room. Day.

A man ("G.M.") sits at a table reading his correspondence. The remains of a light lunch sit in front of him.

His HOUSEKEEPER enters the room and walks over to pick up his breakfast tray. They exchange pleasantries, after which she leaves the room.

G.M. gets up for a pace around. The clock on the back wall stops ticking with a clunk. G.M. compares the time on the clock - two minutes to twelve - with his pocket watch, which reads ten past one.

He goes over to the clock takes it down off the wall very carefully and puts it on the table. He turns back to the wall to get the clock's key and finds, where the clock was hanging, is a hole in the wallpaper (hole 1) through which a human eye is looking out. G.M. does a shocked double take and then turns back to the wall: the eye has gone and the hole is empty.

G.M. looks into the hole.

G.M. sticks his fingers in the hole: it moves slightly along the wall. He continues and pushes it right the way across the wall and eventually it passes the face of a GIRL inside the wall. She has a serene expression with both eyes closed.

G.M. looks on in amazement. The GIRL's face disappears as a shadow covers her.

G.M. tears at the hole (hole 2) until it becomes large and tattered. Inside the wall is an array of figures draped across each other, wearing the clothes of decades earlier. They all have their eyes closed and move only slightly, like figures in their sleep. The sides of the hole grow back slowly until the hole is as small as it was to begin with.

G.M. turns away in shock and flops onto the chaise-longue. He thinks for a moment and notices the mirror on the right-hand wall. He looks from the mirror to hole 2 on the back wall and gets up, walks over to the mirror and takes it off the wall.

G.M. takes the mirror off the right-hand wall and reveals a much larger hole (hole 3) through which an evil version of his own face: "M.G.", stares back at him. The surprise makes G.M. drop the mirror which lands at his feet and breaks. He looks down at the mirror, which nearly hit his toes, and as he does so M.G. shoots out of hole 3. By the time G.M. looks back at the hole, it is empty. G.M. sticks his head into the hole. Unknown to him M.G. is hiding behind the table behind him.

As G.M. stares into hole 3 the GIRL appears out of hole 2. She skips around the room, unconcerned by her surroundings and then exits via the left-hand door.

M.G. rushes G.M. from behind and pushes him into hole 3. He grins triumphantly at the imprisoned G.M. and places the mirror back over the hole.

M.G. prances across the room to the left-hand wall and takes down a small ornamental sword. He tests its strength and shoots a grin at the camera. He walks back to the right-hand wall where G.M. is trapped, brandishing the sword as he goes. He carefully pushes the sword into the wall just under the mirror.

As he does so the GIRL reenters the room via the left hand door. The sight of M.G. stabbing the wall brings her out of her thoughts and she stares at him in terror before turning on her heel and running out of the room. M.G. chases after her through the left-hand door. A moment later he reappears through the right-hand door. The GIRL is nowhere to be seen.

M.G. thinks for a minute. He looks over at hole 2 and grins at the camera.

Some time later: the GIRL reenters the room through the left hand door. She finds the room empty but looks around cautiously. She goes over to the left-hand wall and takes down the remaining ornamental sword which she secretes in her dress. She runs towards hole 2 in the back wall and jumps into it.

As she does so, inside the wall M.G.'s jaws slam shut, devouring her. He wipes his mouth gleefully.

Outside the room is quiet once more. The sword which is still stuck in the wall under the mirror is slowly pushed out and drops out onto the floor. G.M.'s eye appears at the hole. Inside the wall we see him alive but in considerable distress.

Hearing the sound of the sword, the HOUSEKEEPER reenters the room calling for G.M. Surprised that the room is empty she looks around and sits for a moment on the chaise-longue. She gets up to go out, notices the clock on the table as she passes it and puts it back on the wall. She exits.

Inside the wall G.M. sees her so near to him, yet oblivious to his cries. As she leaves he sinks into despair. The room is empty once more.

The clock on the back wall starts to tick again. The paper on the back wall becomes stained with blood.

Over on the right hand wall we can see the hole and G.M.'s downcast eye. A shadow falls across the wall. A blade starts to cut upwards through the paper below the mirror. G.M. is revealed through the expanding gash in the wall paper. He looks up at his saviour: it is the GIRL, holding an ornamental sword.

She holds out her hand and helps him to his feet. Serenely he follows her into the room. He looks around at the back wall: it has a huge bloody gash in it and the deflated remains of M.G. lie in a pool of blood on the floor. The GIRL smiles at G.M. who smiles back, unconcerned, even amused, by the gory scene.

The clock strikes twelve. G.M. and the GIRL look at the clock and each other and laugh. They kiss.

G.M.

or 'The Sitting Room'

A proposal for a short film
by Martin Pickles ©1999

G.M. Storyboards

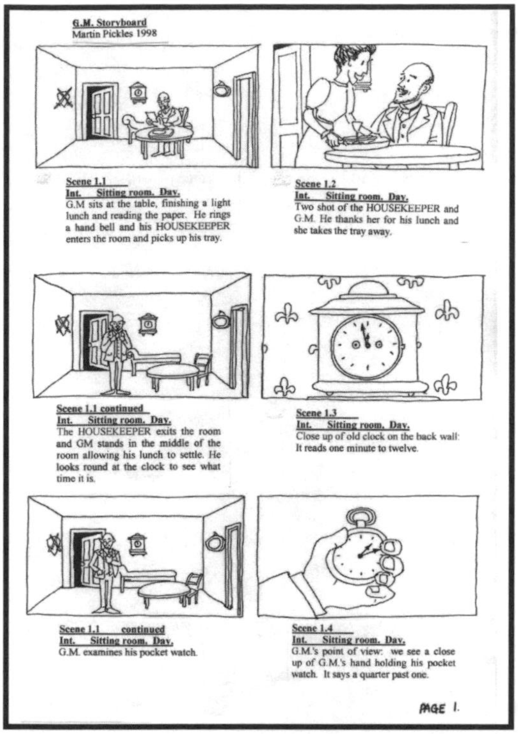
G.M. Storyboard
Martin Pickles 1998

Scene 1.1
Int. Sitting room. Day.
G.M sits at the table, finishing a light lunch and reading the paper. He rings a hand bell and his HOUSEKEEPER enters the room and picks up his tray.

Scene 1.2
Int. Sitting room. Day.
Two shot of the HOUSEKEEPER and G.M. He thanks her for his lunch and she takes the tray away.

Scene 1.1 continued
Int. Sitting room. Day.
The HOUSEKEEPER exits the room and GM stands in the middle of the room allowing his lunch to settle. He looks round at the clock to see what time it is.

Scene 1.3
Int. Sitting room. Day.
Close up of old clock on the back wall: It reads one minute to twelve.

Scene 1.1 continued
Int. Sitting room. Day.
G.M. examines his pocket watch.

Scene 1.4
Int. Sitting room. Day.
G.M.'s point of view: we see a close up of G.M.'s hand holding his pocket watch. It says a quarter past one.

PAGE 1.

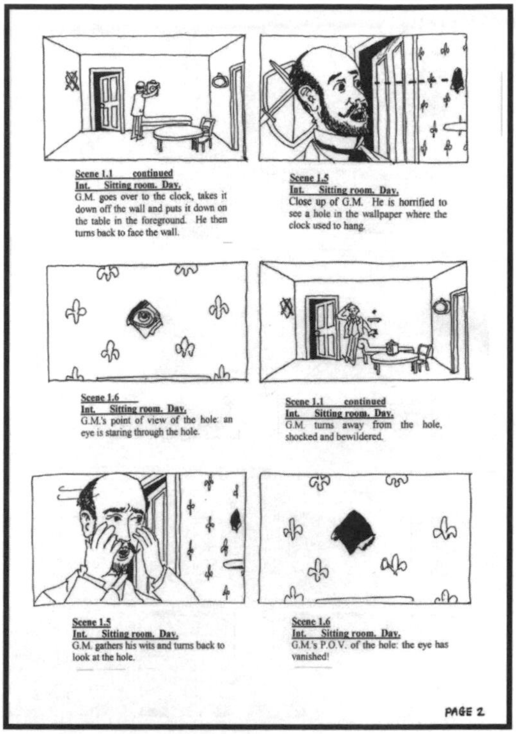
Scene 1.1 continued
Int. Sitting room. Day.
G.M. goes over to the clock, takes it down off the wall and puts it down on the table in the foreground. He then turns back to face the wall.

Scene 1.5
Int. Sitting room. Day.
Close up of G.M. He is horrified to see a hole in the wallpaper where the clock used to hang.

Scene 1.6
Int. Sitting room. Day.
G.M.'s point of view of the hole: an eye is staring through the hole.

Scene 1.1 continued
Int. Sitting room. Day.
G.M. turns away from the hole, shocked and bewildered.

Scene 1.5
Int. Sitting room. Day.
G.M. gathers his wits and turns back to look at the hole.

Scene 1.6
Int. Sitting room. Day.
G.M.'s P.O.V. of the hole: the eye has vanished!

PAGE 2

Scene 1.5 continued
Int. Sitting room. Day
G.M. tries to look through the hole.

Scene 2.1
Int. Inside wall. Day.
View from inside the hole looking out: we see G.M. looking into the darkness.

Scene 3.1
Int. Sitting room. Day.
Close up of the hole from G.M.'s point of view. We slowly zoom into the hole.

Scene 3.2
Int. Sitting room. Day.
Over-shoulder shot: G.M tries to tear at the sides of the hole to make it bigger.

Scene 3.2 continued
Int. Sitting room. Day.
G.M. doesn't enlarge the hole but instead pushes it along the wall.

Scene 3.3 (as 1.1)
Int. Sitting room. Day.
We return to the wide covering shot of the room: G.M. pushes the hole right along the back wall.

PAGE 3

Scene 3.4
Int. Sitting room. Day.
G.M.'s P.O.V.: close up of the hole. G.M. sees a GIRL's face inside the wall.

Scene 3.5
Int. Sitting room. Day.
Close up of G.M. from the hole's point of view. We see his shocked reaction.

Scene 3.6
Int. Sitting room. Day.
A wider shot of the hole: the GIRL's face disappears into the darkness as a shadow passes in front of her.

Scene 3.5 continued
Int. Sitting room. Day.
G.M. leans forwards to look deeper inside the hole: he is very distraught.

Scene 3.7 (similar to 3.6)
Int. Sitting room. Day.
G.M. tears the hole open with his hands.

Scene 4.1
Int. Inside wall. Day.
We see G.M. as seen from inside the wall. He rips at the wallpaper and stares inside.

PAGE 4

Scene 5.1
Int. Sitting room. Day.
G.M. sees that inside the wall are dozens of people crammed together. They move only slightly as though disturbed in their sleep.

Scene 5.2
Int. Sitting room. Day.
Close up from G.M.'s point of view of the people in the wall.

Scene 5.3 (as 5.1)
Int. Sitting room. Day.
The sides of the hole start to heal up of their own accord....

Scene 5.3 continued
Int. Sitting room. Day.
...until the hole is no bigger than it was to start with.

Scene 5.4 (as 1.1)
Int. Sitting room. Day.
Wide shot of sitting room: G.M. sits down on the chaise longue in shock.

Scene 5.4 continued
Int. Sitting room. Day.
G.M. looks over to the right hand wall and sees the mirror. He looks from the mirror to the hole: he has an idea. He gets up and goes over to the mirror to take it off the wall.

PAGE 5

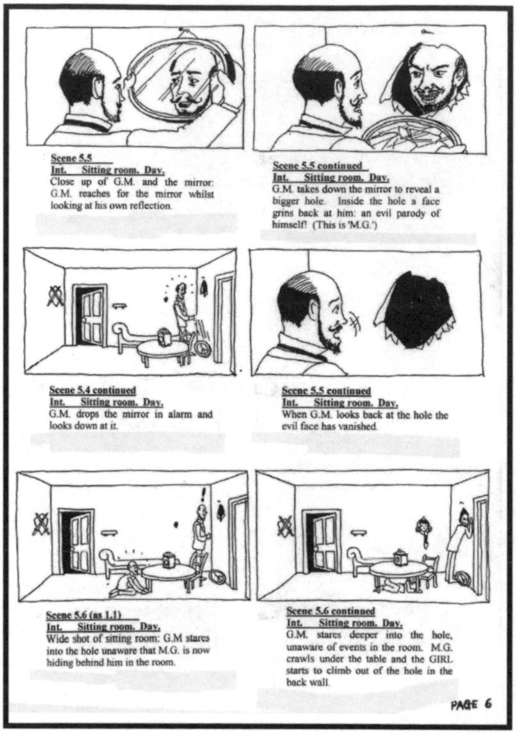

Scene 5.5
Int. Sitting room. Day.
Close up of G.M. and the mirror: G.M. reaches for the mirror whilst looking at his own reflection.

Scene 5.5 continued
Int. Sitting room. Day.
G.M. takes down the mirror to reveal a bigger hole. Inside the hole a face grins back at him: an evil parody of himself! (This is 'M.G.')

Scene 5.4 continued
Int. Sitting room. Day.
G.M. drops the mirror in alarm and looks down at it.

Scene 5.5 continued
Int. Sitting room. Day.
When G.M. looks back at the hole the evil face has vanished.

Scene 5.6 (as 1.1)
Int. Sitting room. Day.
Wide shot of sitting room: G.M stares into the hole unaware that M.G. is now hiding behind him in the room.

Scene 5.6 continued
Int. Sitting room. Day.
G.M. stares deeper into the hole, unaware of events in the room. M.G. crawls under the table and the GIRL starts to climb out of the hole in the back wall.

PAGE 6

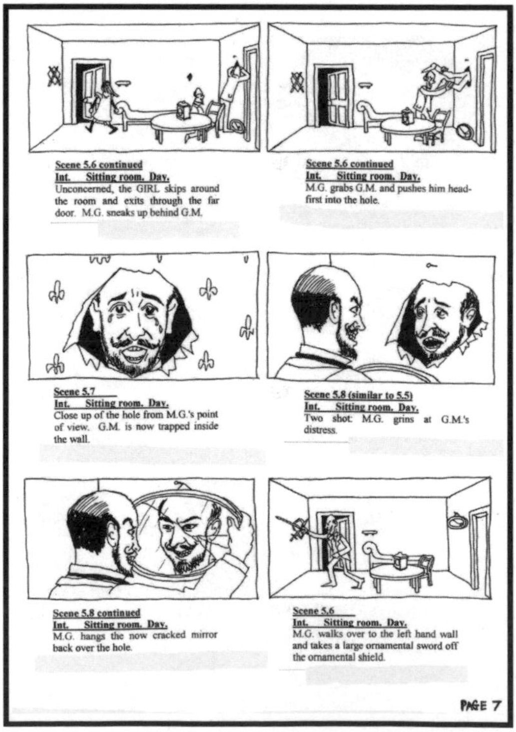

Scene 5.6 continued
Int. Sitting room. Day.
Unconcerned, the GIRL skips around the room and exits through the far door. M.G. sneaks up behind G.M.

Scene 5.6 continued
Int. Sitting room. Day.
M.G. grabs G.M. and pushes him head-first into the hole.

Scene 5.7
Int. Sitting room. Day.
Close up of the hole from M.G.'s point of view. G.M. is now trapped inside the wall.

Scene 5.8 (similar to 5.5)
Int. Sitting room. Day.
Two shot: M.G. grins at G.M.'s distress.

Scene 5.8 continued
Int. Sitting room. Day.
M.G. hangs the now cracked mirror back over the hole.

Scene 5.6
Int. Sitting room. Day.
M.G. walks over to the left hand wall and takes a large ornamental sword off the ornamental shield.

PAGE 7

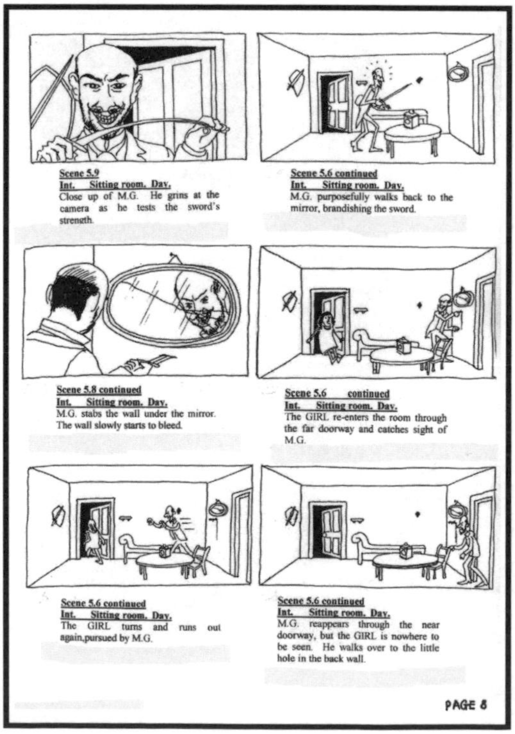

Scene 5.9
Int. Sitting room. Day.
Close up of M.G. He grins at the camera as he tests the sword's strength.

Scene 5.6 continued
Int. Sitting room. Day.
M.G. purposefully walks back to the mirror, brandishing the sword.

Scene 5.8 continued
Int. Sitting room. Day.
M.G. stabs the wall under the mirror. The wall slowly starts to bleed.

Scene 5.6 continued
Int. Sitting room. Day.
The GIRL re-enters the room through the far doorway and catches sight of M.G.

Scene 5.6 continued
Int. Sitting room. Day.
The GIRL turns and runs out again, pursued by M.G.

Scene 5.6 continued
Int. Sitting room. Day.
M.G. reappears through the near doorway, but the GIRL is nowhere to be seen. He walks over to the little hole in the back wall.

PAGE 8

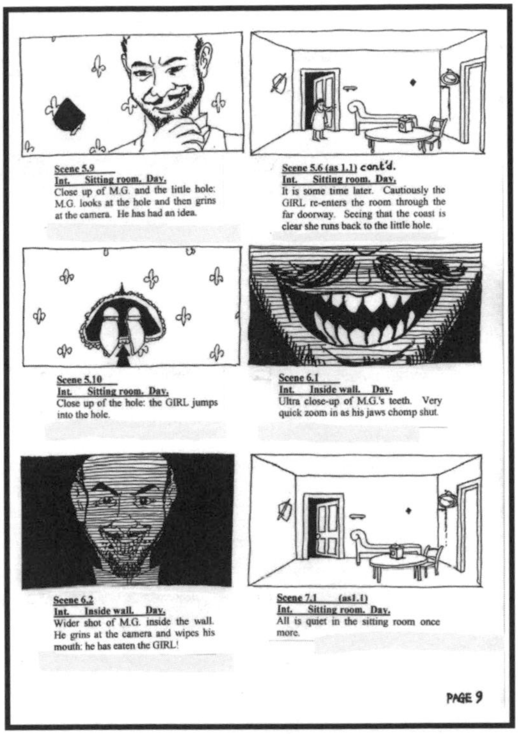
Scene 5.9
Int. Sitting room. Day.
Close up of M.G. and the little hole: M.G. looks at the hole and then grins at the camera. He has had an idea.
Scene 5.6 (as 1.1) cont'd.
Int. Sitting room. Day.
It is some time later. Cautiously the GIRL re-enters the room through the far doorway. Seeing that the coast is clear she runs back to the little hole.
Scene 5.10
Int. Sitting room. Day.
Close up of the hole: the GIRL jumps into the hole.
Scene 6.1
Int. Inside wall. Day.
Ultra close-up of M.G.'s teeth. Very quick zoom in as his jaws chomp shut.
Scene 6.2
Int. Inside wall. Day.
Wider shot of M.G. inside the wall. He grins at the camera and wipes his mouth: he has eaten the GIRL!
Scene 7.1 (as1.1)
Int. Sitting room. Day.
All is quiet in the sitting room once more.
PAGE 9

Scene 7.2
Int. Sitting room. Day.
Close up of the corner of the room. Slowly the sword is pushed out of the wall until it falls onto the floor.
Scene 7.3
Int. Sitting room. Day.
Close up of the hole left by the sword. G.M. is still alive! He stares out of the hole.
Scene 7.1 continued
Int. Sitting room. Day.
G.M.'s HOUSEKEEPER enters the room.
Scene 7.4
Int. Sitting room. Day.
Close up of the HOUSEKEEPER looking around the room.
Scene 7.5
Int. Sitting room. Day.
The HOUSEKEEPER sits on the chaise longue and notices the clock sitting on the table.
Scene 8.1
Int. Inside wall. Day.
Close up of G.M. trapped inside the wall in distress. He tries to call out to the HOUSEKEEPER.
PAGE 10

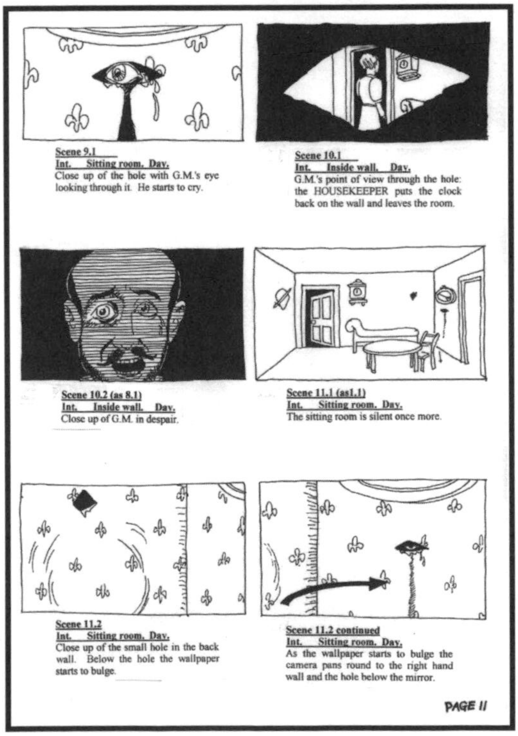
Scene 9.1
Int. Sitting room. Day.
Close up of the hole with G.M.'s eye looking through it. He starts to cry.
Scene 10.1
Int. Inside wall. Day.
G.M.'s point of view through the hole: the HOUSEKEEPER puts the clock back on the wall and leaves the room.
Scene 10.2 (as 8.1)
Int. Inside wall. Day.
Close up of G.M. in despair.
Scene 11.1 (as1.1)
Int. Sitting room. Day.
The sitting room is silent once more.
Scene 11.2
Int. Sitting room. Day.
Close up of the small hole in the back wall. Below the hole the wallpaper starts to bulge.
Scene 11.2 continued
Int. Sitting room. Day.
As the wallpaper starts to bulge the camera pans round to the right hand wall and the hole below the mirror.
PAGE 11

Scene 11.3
Int. Sitting room. Day.
Close up of the hole below the mirror. We can see G.M.'s downcast eye. A shadow falls across the wall.
Scene 11.4
Int. Sitting room. Day.
Close up of a gruesome knife cutting through the wallpaper.
Scene 11.5
Int. Sitting room. Day.
Close up of G.M.'s face appearing through the slit in the wallpaper.
Scene 11.6
Int. Sitting room. Day.
Two shot of G.M. and his saviour.
Scene 11.7
Int. Sitting room. Day.
Two shot from a low angle. It is the GIRL! She has escaped and has come back for him.
Scene 11.8 (as 1.1)
Int. Sitting room. Day.
The GIRL helps G.M. to his feet.
PAGE 12

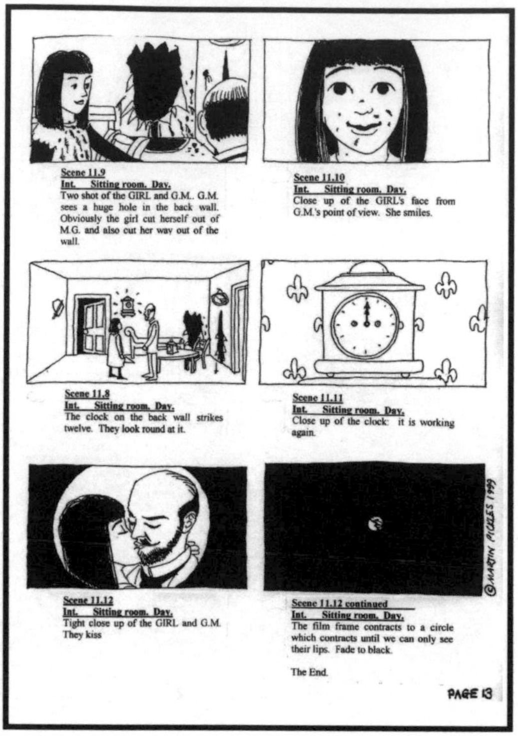

Scene 11.9
Int. Sitting room. Day.
Two shot of the GIRL and G.M.. G.M. sees a huge hole in the back wall. Obviously the girl cut herself out of M.G. and also cut her way out of the wall.

Scene 11.10
Int. Sitting room. Day.
Close up of the GIRL's face from G.M.'s point of view. She smiles.

Scene 11.8
Int. Sitting room. Day.
The clock on the back wall strikes twelve. They look round at it.

Scene 11.11
Int. Sitting room. Day.
Close up of the clock: it is working again.

Scene 11.12
Int. Sitting room. Day.
Tight close up of the GIRL and G.M. They kiss

Scene 11.12 continued
Int. Sitting room. Day.
The film frame contracts to a circle which contracts until we can only see their lips. Fade to black.

The End.

PAGE 13

START

CHAPTER 24

Room Eleven

Room Eleven is a 15-minute film written by Eoin O'Callaghan, directed by Clive Brill, and produced by Tom Treadwell and Maureen Murray. The full script appears at the end of this chapter.

Room Eleven is a horror pastiche where the slaughter of an innocent child may or may not have occurred and the Hitchcockian twist provides the essential intake of breath that comes with the unsettling ending. Here the dead return, not as zombies revived by radiation, as in George Romero's low-budget *Night of the Living Dead*, but as an obsessive memory that moves as if by osmosis between the minds of the principal characters.

At fifteen minutes, the film breaks the ten-and-under barrier self-imposed by producers faced with the usual twins of evil: cash constraints and an eye for the bite-sized time slots in typical festival and broadcasting schedules.

These considerations were secondary in green-lighting *Room Eleven*. Pacificus Productions was in the process of developing a horror script with Clive Brill attached to direct and needed to show potential backers that their established radio, TV and theater director could leap the gap to a feature.

The production company dropped £30,000 in the kitty and engaged Maureen Murray to make it happen. After ten years working with *enfant terrible* Ken Russell and another ten as an independent producer, Maureen had the web of friends and favors needed to bring in a crew of experienced technicians, hire the equipment, catering, make-up and wardrobe, and shoot in five days a short film with the feeling and style of a feature. Impossible?

"It's like skiing blindfold. I wouldn't recommend it, but yes, it's possible."[1]

Maureen began where the process always begins: with the script. Working closely with writer Eoin O'Callaghan, she helped trim out the fat and encouraged the writer to ensure that every word and gesture carried its weight. "Writers often resist this, their darlings cast into the abyss, but when the job's done and you read through the new draft—it always reads better."

With the script more sharply in focus, director Clive Brill had to be convinced that the very scene he cherished most, where one of the characters throws herself out of a window, needed a hard cut from her climbing up on the sill to the body lying spread-eagled on the ground below, just as dramatic, if less spectacular, and a whole lot of saving in terms of time: the most expensive commodity on set. On a feature, it is normal to get about 2½ minutes of cut and finished film a day. On *Room Eleven*, they were aiming to get at least 3 minutes a day and still maintain feature quality.

Another crucial decision was to hire Roger Tooley and his Steadicam for a day. This 80 pound piece of equipment that straps on to a body harness, and looks a lot like a military flame thrower, can chase through gardens and upstairs, as ghosts are wont to do, and avoids rolling the DP over miles of track on a dolly. Garrett Brown had developed the gyro-stabilized camera for the film industry and when Stanley Kubrick tried it out in 1977, he discovered that the operator could "walk, run and climb stairs while retaining a rock-steady image."[2]

Kubrick had just purchased Childwick Bury, a remote manor house in rural Hertfordshire, and tested both the camera and its inventor to their limits on *The Shining:* the story of a man coping with writer's block. Kubrick wanted the Steadicam to do things it had never done before and Brown was employed to make it possible. "I realized by the afternoon of the first day's work," Brown was to observe phlegmatically, "that here was a whole new ball game, and that the word *reasonable* was not in Kubrick's lexicon.'[3]

It is probably why Kubrick's films remain memorable and why the camera movements envisaged for *Room Eleven* were inspired by *The Shining*.

Like all good ghost stories, the script required a gothic mansion with turrets, towers, and macabre gargoyles for intermittent close-ups and reaction shots, not cliché but *de rigueur* for the genre. First assistant director Simon Hinkley had become attached to the project and he recalled just the place: Chenies Manor House, a Tudor pile that began life as a settlement mentioned in the Domesday survey of 1086 and where "the sepulchral footsteps of a lame man are occasionally heard on the staircase . . ." The lame man is said to be Henry VIII, who visited the house with Katherine Howard, the fifth Queen; she was having an affair with royal aide Thomas Culpepper at the time, so haunting footsteps are hardly surprising.

Chenies is open to the public from spring until autumn and the present owner, Elizabeth MacLeod Matthews, agreed to allow the house to be used for the shoot with a generosity that extended to her taking part as an extra in the dining scene. I do not know who suggested this, but can safely assume it was Maureen Murray, who knew we were writing this book and called me, Clifford, suggesting that I fill another of the vacant seats at the table.

STRETCHING THE BUDGET

With the cast, extras, and crew in place, Maureen began calling hire facilities for equipment and film stock. There had been a surge of projects greenlit at the same time, but having brought in the bucks on numerous features, Maureen used her long-standing contacts to acquire everything needed for the five day shoot at about a quarter of book price. "You always have to bargain with the hire companies. No one pays list price and, with a short film, they tend to be generous," she adds. "There was the usual Friday frenzy and everything finally arrived at the last minute."

I was able to observe how the budget is stretched from my POV as an extra, and discovered that the crew were working that week for nothing, or next to nothing, for many diverse and complicated reasons: a gaffer wants to partner with a particular DP; a 3rd AD gets the chance to be a 2nd; assistants in set design, wardrobe and make-up graduate to heads of department; camera loaders and focus pullers exchange jobs, assist the sound man by holding the boom, or the props department by sticking something on to something. The film set is hierarchical, the master in each department taking on acolytes much like teachers in Eastern philosophy and training them to one day replace them.

On a short film, everyone pitches in, scurrying around with determined expressions and silver wheels of gaffer tape hanging from their belts. There are two things that hold the film industry together: gaffer tape and networking, who you know—as in most fields—as important as what you know, the result being an odd blend of the egalitarian and nepotistic. On *Room Eleven* when we broke for lunch, Tom Treadwell queued up in the biting cold for his chicken green curry and rice, the same as everyone else.

Another reason for taking on a short film is that top technicians use the opportunity to experiment. "It's like going back to film school and being tested," says DP Philip Robertson. "You don't have this lens or that piece of equipment—so what are you going to do about it? And what you do is make do. It's good not to become too spoilt. On a short film resources are scarce so you have to stretch yourself and make things work."

The DP has an assistant, loader, and operator, each with their own vital functions and serving the long apprenticeship that leads to becoming a director of photography. The DP will often be asked to choose the lighting chief and head of props—the gaffers and grips—because the producer knows that when people have worked together before, like formation dancers they have learned how to move in harmony.

A producer or director will often contact a DP because they admire the lighting and camera work on a particular film. It should not be forgotten that, experimentation aside, with *Room Eleven* being shot with high production values, the crew and cast would have at the end of the week a further credit, a valuable showreel and an extended loop on their web of industry contacts.

Philip Robertson had long ago learned that some directors want you "to light up and shut up." Others, he adds, want a little bit more, and his calm presence on set was ideal for Brill's début. They discussed shots and tried alternatives, listened to suggestions from 1st AD Hinkley, and bowed always to Brill's final decision. Glenda Jackson once told a *Guardian* interview at the National Film Theater on London's South Bank that a good director listens to everyone—"unlike a politician." It's an unwritten law: the director's always right, even when he's wrong.

Roger Tooley puts it another way. "With inexperienced directors you are walking a tightrope. Some are arrogant, but most ask: what do you think, and when they do, you can insert your own artistic vision, which is what it's all about." He adds: "As a cameraman, you have to extract the shot the director wants and, if they are new to the game, you have to understand what it is they are trying to achieve when they don't actually know how to achieve it."

Tooley describes the film business as an addiction worse than any drug. Once you start, you can't stop. He spent two months working on a French film set in the desert. There were sand storms on a daily basis, the hours were long, he hated every minute he was there and looked back with nostalgia the moment the plane touched down back at Heathrow.

"You would think that a big budget film would be more organized, but that's not the case," says Tooley. "On a short film you have to be organized, and after the intensity of working on a feature, there's nothing like the close atmosphere and the sense of working as a team you get on a short."

COSTUME

I had joined the team a few days before on a rainy bleak Wednesday when Maedhbh McMahon arrived like a glimpse of sunshine with sparkling eyes, a shooting script under her arm, and a camera in her bag. A quick kiss on the cheek and she was bounding upstairs to poke around in my wardrobe. She pulled out various shirts and decided on pale blue, some fawn cargo pants, brown docksiders and a light jacket with a faint check. She uhmed and aghed over the jacket and took some photo stills to show the director. My big scene was being shot in a room rich in patterns, so the cast were being dressed in solid colors.

As the costume designer, Maedhbh (pronounced Maeve) had been poking into quite a few wardrobes during the hectic days prior to shooting. She had worn her heels flat walking around Camden Market and had popped into the National Theater's warehouse in Brixton in search of a sixties' outfit to be used in the flashback sequence. Renting from Hire Houses isn't cheap, anything from £60 per week per costume, but the National does special deals for budget filmmakers.

Maedhbh starts out by breaking down the script in order to relate the costumes to the characters and figures out what costumes are going to be needed for each day's shooting. As films are not shot chronologically, all the costumes have to be ready in case the shooting schedule changes. Sometimes, the director may decide a character doesn't look right in a certain color, it throws out the entire design, "and everyone," says Maedhbh, "ends up running around like headless chickens."

When the budget permits, the costume designer will need at least two sets of clothes for each character, but even that is rarely sufficient. If a scene is shot in pouring rain, a dry jacket becomes wet, and while the actor wears the spare costume for the second take, the wardrobe department is anxiously drying everything with a hair dryer ready for the third. If a scene requires characters wading through mud, the problem is easy to imagine, more "headless chickens."

And then there's the nightmare of squibbing—the bloody patches that explode when characters are shot and, of course, it looks far better on a nice crisp white shirt. In gangster movies and war films, the costume department spends all night in the laundry like a clean up party for the mafia.

Are there any tricks to the trade?

Maedhbh McMahon would only give away two: new clothes are soaked in cold tea to take out the stiffness and age them; and that by the end of a film, costumes are held together by safety pins and gaffer tape. "What the eye can't see, the director's not going to worry about."

Maedhbh began her career after studying art history and spent five years working as a milliner. She helped make props as an assistant on *Captain Corelli's Mandolin*, the big budget Nicholas Cage/Penelope Cruz feature shot in Greece, and moved straight on to making hats for the extras in the *Harry Potter* films. "To become a costume designer it is important to make contacts," she said. "I was lucky because there were seven different designers working on *Captain Corelli*. When I returned to London, they were all preparing different films and I was offered work straight away."

Even though she now has wide experience on features and TV drama, Maedhbh enjoys the intimacy of short films. "The atmosphere is always very friendly," she says, echoing Roger Tooley, "and you get this nice feeling that you are working as a team."

THE SHOOT

The following day I received a four-page fax from production manager Sam Holt with directions to Chenies, a map, and final instructions: wear warm clothes. I understood why as we approached the house. Horses were galloping through the low-lying mist clinging to the fields and the brick chimneys and towers had the look of enormous props below the leaded vault of the sky. It only needed a flash of lightning and we would have been in a Dracula movie. I was brought down to earth by the piquant, early hour smell of frying bacon.

It had just gone seven and the caterers were serving robust portions of egg, bacon, sausages, hash brown potatoes, and beans. "Heart attack on a plate," said the 1st AD, leading me from the cold courtyard with my laden dish into the dining room where there were urns of coffee, boxes of cereal, and plates of Danish pastries. It was Tuesday. The crew had worked a solid 12 hours the previous day and was stoking up for the day ahead. Like an army going into battle, a film crew marches on its stomach. In fact, as Simon Hinkley pointed out, when the film business was reviving after the last war, a large number of sergeant majors joined the profession as first assistant directors.

It was easy to see why as Hinkley managed the schedule, barking out orders to the crew, protecting his officers: the director and DP, while they considered performance and the visual realization of Eoin O'Callaghan's script.

THE FIRST ASSISTANT DIRECTOR

The 1st AD's role is to ensure that the director's vision is accomplished with the minimum of fuss or delay. He will make sure the extras are ready when they are needed; he'll tell make-up to bring a shawl for the scantily clad actress to keep warm between takes. If a horse is going to be sent galloping across the misty fields, he'll be behind the groom making sure the beast is saddled and biting at the bit. A good 1st AD—and that's why Simon Hinkley was brought into *Room Eleven*—will see problems before they happen, and stop them happening. It is up to him, finally, to see that the director gets through his day's schedule and is prepared for the next day. In this respect, the assistant director also has one eye on the money; if a film does fall behind, he's likely to get the blame.

After the 1st AD has ensured everyone is ready for a take, on set he directs the extras and controls crowd scenes. While the director is concentrating on his leading players, the 1st must capture the same vision from the rest of the cast and, in this way, the assistant director is in training for that day when (and if) he wants to move up the greasy pole. The 1st AD is assisted by a 2nd AD, who runs around on the First's instructions and fills out the production reports with the aid of the script supervisor's notes. The 1st AD needs eyes in the back of his head: the 2nd is that pair of eyes.

After breakfast, I watched Roger Tooley strapped into his Steadicam running through the drifting mist among the pruned rose bushes in the garden, capturing the movements of the unseen poltergeist. Andrew Ellis, another extra, had turned up with a camera and was quietly wandering around the set taking photo stills. Sisters Helena and Lottie Rice, two more extras, were wisely using the day they had skived off school to do some exam revision. An extra's day is long and, if directing is death by a thousand questions, for bit-part players it's death from waiting.

MY SCENE

It was almost noon when Simon Hinkley finally rounded us up, rushed us through make-up and readied Andrew Ellis, Helena, Lottie, and myself for the dining scene. The skyscraper tall American producer Tom Treadwell sat at the head of the table and Elizabeth MacLeod Matthews appeared from the warren of rooms at Chenies to join us.

We sat sipping apple juice from crystal glasses and imagined—with little success on my part—that it was Chardonnay, and invented *polite* conversation as we waited for Avril King, our host. We turned *with courteous interest* on hearing her voice, but the moment she entered, she was hurrying out again, distressed by the vision seen by her, though not we extras. We now looked suitably astonished—so astonished, in fact, Clive Brill called a quick cut and we did it all again, with slightly less awe.

The scene was repeated several times until Clive and DP Philip Robertson both nodded judiciously, a quiet understanding reached between them, and the process was repeated with Celia Barry floating through the dining room, a ghostly presence all in white, unseen by us, but terrifying for Avril King.

We controlled our gasps, looked surprised rather than shocked, and in little more than an hour the two twenty-second scenes were in the can. While the grips started dismantling the kit, we following the smell of curry out to the parking lot and stamped our feet as we queued before the catering van. It was lunchtime. I was starving, a big breakfast always does that, and I sat down with Maureen Murray curious as to why she was producing a short film, her first, after being involved in various capacities with more than 20 features.

"I wanted to work with the writer and director," she answers without hesitation. "Eoin O'Callaghan and Clive Brill have a strong synergy between them and this was an opportunity to see them in action. Often you are invited to work on a project that has already started, it's like a moving train. This one was waiting at the station." She continues, warming into the metaphor: "Often, the rails have already been laid and you know the train's going to derail before it gets to the next station. On *Room Eleven* I had the chance to get in at the beginning and set the film up properly. Keep it on track."

For Maureen, the most important aspect of a short film is preparation. The producer must ask two key questions at the outset: why are we making this film? And what is the market for it? If both questions can be answered positively, it is then essential not to compromise when it comes to finding crew, hiring equipment and casting experienced players, in this case the well-known actors Anton Lasser, who plays the psychiatrist, Susan Brown, as Avril King, and Poppy Miller in the dual roles as Sophie Calder and Celia Barry.

"Making a short film shouldn't be really that different from making a feature. You need to keep everyone involved, from the runner to the star, and set up a thoroughly professional level of production."

THE DIRECTOR

A sympathetic and flexible editor was needed to allow Clive to immerse himself in the editing experience. Maureen signed up Xavier Russell, who has both the quick turnaround flare fundamental to television and the more measured proficiency brought into 35mm features. Even from rough cut to fine cut, a few nips and tucks were required, and Xavier she knew had the artistic and technical skills, as well as understanding how to achieve the pace and character development visualized by the director.

Clive was completing the process when I called to ask him about his experience directing *Room Eleven*. This was his response:

The first thing that hits a new director is the sheer number of aspects of the film he has to take responsibility for whilst simultaneously respecting the art of those he has chosen to work with. Actors will give you a whole range of performances you hadn't necessarily thought of; learning how to shape, accept, and sometimes reject what they have to offer is key. But from the script up—everyone and everything is offering you an almost bewildering range of choices. The budgets on short films are tight, so you simply don't have the luxury (as in say theater or radio) of trying quite a few things out before committing to a decision. It suddenly hits home that decision-making—from placement of props to choice of wigs, to placement of camera to interpretation of lines, all require a rapid and committed response.

Looking at the rushes, I can see all the places where I allowed my judgment to be slightly compromised by being focused on something else I thought more important. Watching a scene unfold on a monitor requires a hundred eyes. How's the frame? How was the move? Does the color of the picture behind draw the eye away from the actor? Is the camera moving in a way that organically compliments the scene? Above all: are you telling the story, and making the audience understand the way you want them to?

It is impossible to say how closely the finished product resembles the initial picture in your mind. The dreams I had before I started shooting were a mixture of interpretation of script—other film moments I had seen—and knowledge of what I thought the actors and key crew might bring to the set. But inevitably nothing is quite as envisioned. A new, fresh, sometimes alarming perspective is flickering before me.

The editing process is like a new buzz of electricity after the film is exposed. All this mass of material sometimes appears limiting. But the joy of working with a new pair of eyes—and amazing Avid technology—suddenly gives you myriad choices you hardly dared suspect were there. More choices equals more decision-making of course ...

I had always known starting at the beginning of my career in radio that sound played a hugely significant role in film-making. I mean, the combination of fx, speech and music. A few days before the final dub we have a locked off picture, with luck the best performances and the most imaginatively edited version of the material we shot. And yet—the music's not on, the well-placed shut door is unheard—even the speech is woolly. I won't know if the film's any good until the final sound effects are added. And I feel instinctively that, without sound, the pictures will never completely work. I think like all directors I wish I'd had four times the shooting time I was given. To me, every scene shouts a missed camera angle, a lost CU, a slight mis-emphasis, a head turned a fraction too far. I pray the audience doesn't notice.

The whole experience has confirmed to me what I always suspected. With all the frustration of never being completely in control of everything—of always feeling that the picture might slip away from one's grasp—of hoping that the art at the end will justify the process of getting there—it's the most exhilarating job on the planet.

START

TITLE

Room Eleven

Screenplay by Eoin O'Callaghan
Directed by Clive Brill
Produced by Tom Treadwell and Maureen Murray.

Ext. Mayfield House, Entrance aND GRAVEL PATHWAY. EVE.

Immense pillars topped with stone cherubs support a distinctive wrought-iron gate, leading onto A GRAVEL DRIVEWAY. We follow the drive way around to the right.
C/U of cherub

EXT. Mayfield House, Entrance aND GRAVEL PATHWAY. EVE.

A GATE leading onto the garden. Through this we discover a second GATE – which leads us past the nursery garden and which sweeps up to a gloomy TUDOR PILE with hooded eaves and heavy with ivy. It is forbidding and uninviting – a Mervyn Peake drawing.
The front door creaks open and yields to black. O/S we hear a baby's insistent CRYING.
C/U of cherub

INT. MAYFIELD HOUSE. EVE.

We travel along a corridor and into the main Reception area. This in turn leads onto an ante room and then a dining room. 5 GUESTS are seated for dinner. We pass them and swing hard right into a corridor, past a sitting room with another guest, and up a spiral staircase. Establish: photos of boy and girl and yellow cross on window of the stairwell.
Now onto the upper floors. Paneled corridors lead left and right. We head to the left past the tapestry room. The crying MORE SHRILL now -Straight ahead is ROOM 11 – an ornate bedroom. We enter. In the corner of the room a small wooden door stands ajar.
C/U of cherub

INT. ANTE ROOM & ARMORY. EVE

We follow the source of the crying up some stairs.
Through a small ante room to a long wooden corridor: the armory. Through the gloom at the end we pick up SOPHIE CALDER, 30s, by a window – her face bleak

and tear strewn. A bottle of TRANQUILIZERS lies half spilled on the table at which she is seated. In another corner is a CRIB.
The baby's crying is now unbearable.
ANGLE ON the anguished face of SOPHIE as she hauls herself to her feet. She almost sleepwalks to the crib.
She takes THE PILLOW from the cot and without emotion places it over the baby's mewling mouth.
HEART THUMPING exertion fills SOPHIE'S face as she presses downwards.
At last THE NOISE CEASES. There is a moment of absolute calm.
SOPHIE walks to the window and presses her hands against it.

EXT. MAYFIELD HOUSE. EVE

PU shot from EXT below
Sophie pressing against the window. Is she going to jump?

INT. ARMORY. EVE

Angle on Sophie as she turns back to face the room and catches sight of herself in the mirror beside the crib.
The mirror smashes in a tremendous explosion of sound.

INT. ARMORY. EVE

POV from the window.
Sophie's broken body on the gravel below.

EXT. HOUSE. EVE

POV the ground.
Sophie's broken body.

INT. HARLEY ST. OFFICE OF THERAPIST PAUL LAVELLE, 47. DAY.

SOPHIE sits opposite LAVELLE in a leather chair. She looks stricken.
LAVELLE is lean and intellectual, a man born to listen.

LAVELLE
(gently prompting)
And?

SOPHIE
(nonplussed)
That's it. That's all there is.

LAVELLE
Do you think you killed the baby?

SOPHIE
Yes. Of course.

LAVELLE
(pressing her)
And why do you think you did that?

Silence.

lAVELLE (CONT'D)
Might it have something to do with the termination?

SOPHIE
(Losing patience)
Look, I know why I keep having this dream. I just want it to stop.

LAVELLE picks up SOPHIE's file.

LAVELLE
When did you last have a holiday - I mean a complete break from work?

SOPHIE
I haven't the time.

LAVELLE
Don't you and - er ... Danny get out of London occasionally?

SOPHIE
Danny's not around any more ...

Silence.

LAVELLE
If I were to recommend a quiet country house, where you could take time alone, read a few books, walk in the fields, what would you say?

SOPHIE
I'd be bored out of my brain.

LAVELLE sighs.

LAVELLE
Let some air at the wound, Sophie.
Make some space.
Will you at least think about it?

He hands her a card with the legend:
Mayfield House - Country House Retreat. Prop: Avril King.

SOPHIE
Is this one of those Harley Street scams

where the analysts get a percentage on referrals?

LAVELLE
You've been working in the Media too long.

He rises and she takes the card.

SOPHIE
I'll think about it.

As the door closes behind her, LAVELLE experiences a flash image of SOPHIE smothering a child.

RESUME SCENE 2

Shocked at the vividness of this image, he puts his head back in his chair and shuts his eyes.
FADE OUT.

EXT. THE A1. Sophie's car. day.

Up and past.
She passes a sign for The North.

INT. SOPHIE'S CAR. DAY

Angle on SOPHIE driving intently. The rain beats down on the windscreen. She punches out LAVELLE's number on her hands-free mobile.

INT. LAVELLE'S OFFICE. DAY.

Lavelle's phone buzzes and he picks it up.

LAVELLE
Hello. Paul Lavelle.

INT. SopHIE'S CAR / LAVELLE'S OFFICE. DAY.

We cut between the two:

SOPHIE
(Jokily)
Hi. I wanted you to know I'm on my way to your "country house retreat".

LAVELLE (O.S.)
Hey. Good for you.

SOPHIE
It's not a health farm, is it?

lavelle
God, no. Guaranteed heart attack on a plate.

SOPHIE
Great, soon I'll be clinically depressed and overweight.

LAVELLE (O.S.)
You are not clinically depressed.

SOPHIE
(sarcastic)
Right, I forgot. I'm just having bad dreams . . .

LAVELLE
Sophie. Stop it. Relax.
I'll talk to you next week.

She ends the call and drives on through the lashing rain.
FLASHBACK TO SC. 1: As the windscreen wipers deal with the rain, each wipe presents SOPHIE with a quick succession of flashbacks to her dream:

ROOM 11, THE BABY, THE PILLOW pressing down

RESUME SC. 5: She shuts her eyes on these images.
The blast of an air horn makes SOPHIE suddenly open her eyes.
Rear View as Sophie veers dangerously.
Close up as she regains control of the car and herself.
The air-horn crosses to:

INT. Lavelle's office. DAY

LAVELLE's eyes open suddenly. Disconcerted, he gathers his notes on Sophie Calder and puts them in a drawer.

INT. SOPHIE'S CAR. EVE

Sophie as she spots the stone cherubs atop the immense gate posts. The House's familiarity begins to register.
The rain has abated. The sun shimmers off the wet tarmac. Mayfield House looms imposingly.

INT. MAYFIELD HOUSE. EVE. POV from window.

Sophie's car is seen entering the driveway, the car makes its way round to the right of the house and towards the rear.

EXT. MAYFIELD HOUSE. EVE.

Sophie now on foot. A wooden door leads onto the garden. Through this we discover a second door - which leads past the nursery garden and which sweeps up to the great house.
By the time she reaches the front door it has dawned on Sophie that Mayfield House is, indeed, the house in her nightmare.
Her first instinct is to ring LAVELLE again, but her cell phone has "no service".
A moment of apprehension. Then a decision to press on.

Int. Mayfield House. RECEPTION. EVE.

SOPHIE enters cautiously. She rings a BELL and studies the somehow familiar surroundings. She tries the bell again. She calls out.

SOPHIE
Mrs King.

There is movement in the office behind reception.

SOPHIE (CONT'D)
Sophie Calder. We spoke on the phone.

The proprietor, AVRIL KING, emerges cheerily from an office.

AVRIL
You made good time.

SOPHIE
Yes, struck it lucky on the motorway.

AVRIL stops short - stunned when she sees SOPHIE's face.
An awkward silence. The color drains from AVRIL's face.

SOPHIE (CONT'D)
Mrs King. You alright?

AVRIL steadies herself without answering.

SOPHIE (CONT'D)
(pleasantly)
Room 11? Isn't it?

AVRIL, struggles to regain her composure. She reaches for a room key.

AVRIL
Yes, that's right. Room 11.

SOPHIE
Second floor.

How can she have known that? AVRIL regards her with fear.

AVRIL
(Abruptly)
Dinner's at 8.30.

SOPHIE
(taken aback)
Thank you.

SOPHIE lifts her case and heads for the stairs. She drinks in the details of the house.
Avril watches her. Sophie appears to know exactly where she is going.

INT. MAYFIELD HOUSE. CORNER OF RECEPTION. EVE.

AVRIL shakily pours a long stiff drink. She is extremely agitated.

INT. MAYFIELD HOUSE. EVE

As if by instinct, SOPHIE heads for ROOM 11 through the empty dining room.

INT. MAYFIELD HOUSE. STAIRWELL AND SECOND FLOOR CORRIDOR. EVE.

Sophie climbs the stairwell, passes though the tapestry room and reaches

THE DOOR OF ROOM 11.

She notices her hand is trembling. The door opens to reveal the room exactly as she had seen it in her dream. She goes rigid as if a blast of ice-cold air has taken her breath away. She proceeds cautiously into the room.

INT. MAYFIELD HOUSE. CORNER OF RECEPTION. EVE.

AVRIL draws hard on her cigarette. She catches sight of herself in a mirror in the corner of the reception. She is not pleased at her appearance.
Now suddenly beside her face in the mirror there appears the face of SOPHIE - or rather, someone very like SOPHIE. It is Celia Barry, (as we will discover) the previous owner of Mayfield House - now dead.
CELIA - bleached hair and 1960s dress - produces a lipstick and touches up her heavy carmine make-up. She dabs her lips then gazes resentfully at AVRIL. The image disappears. AVRIL shudders, drains her drink in one and lifts the phone.

INT. LAVELLE'S OFFICE. EVE.

LAVELLE sits quietly at his desk. The answer machine clicks on.

AVRIL (O/S)

(sotto and full of anxiety)

Dr Lavelle. That woman you sent to me, Sophie Calder . . .

INT. RECEPTION MAYFIELD HOUSE. EVE.

AVRIL (O/S Cont/D)

. . . it's Celia Barry – it's her to the life . . . Please . . . please call me as soon as possible -

INT. LAVELLE'S OFFICE. EVE.

Lavelle regards the answer machine impassively.

EXT. SHOT OF MAYFIELD HOUSE. LIGHTS BLAZING. NIGHT.

INT. MAYFIELD HOUSE. ROOM 11. NIGHT.

SOPHIE sits at the dressing table. Every corner of the room is familiar to her. She turns and sees the wooden door ajar in the corner. She rises and moves towards it.

INT. MAYFIELD HOUSE. DINING ROOM. NIGHT.

AVRIL, dressed for the evening with considerably more make-up, greets the dinner guests. She is suddenly distracted.
We follow AVRIL's terrified line of vision and see the ghost of CELIA BARRY seated at the table, staring at her.
AVRIL is now oblivious to the guests. Her gaze is fixed on CELIA, who heads for the second floor. AVRIL follows her.

Int. MAYFIELD HOUSE. The armory. Night.

SOPHIE moves along the long wooden corridor as in her dream towards an object she recognizes with horror:
A CRIB in the corner.
It is as though she has lost the capacity to breathe. A pain sears through her temple. She sits unsteadily on a chair by a table.
Shakily, she pulls out a bottle of tranquilizers, spilling them onto the table. She sits back in terror and despair.

Int. Mayfield house. Stairwell and second FLOOR CORRIDOR. night.

Avril glimpses Celia through the stairwell window and follows her.
AVRIL moves silently but briskly along the maze of corridors. It is the same journey we traveled at the very beginning of the film.
We hear a baby crying.
AVRIL momentarily freezes. But the baby's insistent crying compels her forward towards ROOM 11. The baby's crying from inside the room is now much louder. Light spills through the half open door of Room 11. AVRIL pushes open the door and enters Room 11
C/U OF STONE CHERUB

INT. MAYFIELD HOUSE. The ARMORY. Night.

AVRIL moves quickly through the wooden door up the final steps towards the armory.
As AVRIL enters. The crying suddenly stops.
CELIA is removing an embroidered pillow from the crib where a baby now lies smothered. SOPHIE is nowhere to be seen.
ANGLE ON AVRIL: She looks in horror at the dead infant and screams.

AVRIL
Whose child is this?
WHOSE CHILD IS THIS!

A movement attracts Avril's attention.
Angle on the mirror by the crib, in which Avril sees Celia pressing her hands against the window panes - as if attempting to force her way through the glass.
C/U The Mirror
Suddenly the mirror shatters explosively.
Resume Sc 19
Instinctively Avril raises her arms to cover her head.
She whips round to look at the window. The window is intact. There is nothing there.
AVRIL rushes to the window and looks down.

Int. Mayfield house. Night.

AVRIL's POV: CELIA lies broken on the driveway below.

ext. Mayfield house. eve.

Angle on Celia's broken body on the driveway. POV the ground.

Int. Mayfield house. THE ARMORY. Night.

AVRIL reels back from the window shocked and appalled - but as she turns back into the room she has the second, more awful, surprise. There is SOPHIE sitting by the table looking at her, questioningly.

AVRIL holds her gaze. Neither is going to flinch.
As the camera pulls back we see both window and mirror intact.

INT. LAVELLE'S OFFICE. DAY.

SILENCE except for a ticking clock.
AVRIL turns to look at LAVELLE's benign, all-comprehending face.

AVRIL
You don't believe me.

LAVELLE glances at a card for Mayfield House on the table between them.

AVRIL (CONT'D)
She was there.

LAVELLE
I believe Sophie was there.
Celia Barry died in 1964.

AVRIL
(definitely)
It was the same woman.

The clock ticks. LAVELLE makes a note.

LAVELLE
Why did Celia Barry kill herself?

AVRIL
She'd murdered her child. She was driven to distraction, I presume.

Silence.

LAVELLE
Do you have many friends, Avril?

AVRIL shakes her head almost imperceptibly.

LAVELLE (CONT'D)
How much are you drinking at the moment?

Silence.
She sees him glance at the clock on his desk.

AVRIL
Is it time?

LAVELLE
Has Celia gone?

AVRIL considers this remark, then announces simply.

AVRIL
I think she has.

LAVELLE stands and ushers her to the door.

LAVELLE
Then you'll call me. If you need me.

She leaves and LAVELLE shuts the door behind her.
FLASHBACK TO SC. 20 -in Lavelle's head - to the body of CELIA lying dead on the driveway of Mayfield House, exactly as AVRIL described it earlier.
The image fades.
RESUME SC. 22: LAVELLE breathes heavily and considers.
The telephone rings. He snatches it up.

LAVELLE (CONT'D)
Hello.

SOPHIE (O.S.)
You've heard, have you?

LAVELLE
(non-committal)
Sophie. No. How was it?

<u>INT. SOPHIE'S CAR / LAVELLE'S OFFICE. DAY.</u>

We cut between the two:

SOPHIE
Avril King went berserk - burst into my room and attacked me - then had to be sedated. It was a nightmare.
Has she got a drink problem?

LAVELLE considers this version of events.

LAVELLE
God . . .

Just then LAVELLE glances into an office mirror. He sees a flash of CELIA staring straight at him.

SOPHIE
And, that house - Mayfield House is the house in my dream. I mean like the same in every detail. I'm dreaming about the house of one of your patients.
How do you explain that?

LAVELLE
(distracted)
Ley-lines, crop circles - Psychokinetic transference . . .

SOPHIE

(emphatic

I don't know what kind of voodoo you're at - it's very, very scary - but I haven't had the dream since I went there.
Bizarre, eh?

Another flash of CELIA in the mirror. Followed by:
FLASHBACK TO SC.19A. A flash of CELIA's image shattering in the mirror.
RESUME SC. 23: LAVELLE cries out, involuntarily.

SOPHIE (CONT'D)

Dr Lavelle? What's happened?

Shaking and sweating, LAVELLE places his back against the wall, shuts his eyes tight.

SOPHIE (CONT'D)

Paul.

Another glance in the mirror. There is NOTHING there.
But sweat is running down LAVELLE's face.

SOPHIE (CONT'D)

PAUL. Answer me ...

LAVELLE

Yeah ... yes ... it's OK. Yes. Look, I'm sorry ... I can't seem to ...

SOPHIE (O.S.)

What's wrong?

LAVELLE replaces the phone. His hands are trembling. He wipes the sweat from his face with a handkerchief and breathes deeply. But:

INT. LAVELLE'S OFFICE. DAY.

In the mirror LAVELLE sees images of SOPHIE CALDER then AVRIL KING, seated on his patient's couch. They stare at LAVELLE derisively from within his imagination. He breathes deeply. He begins to calm down. The images begin to fade.

INT. LAVELLE'S OFFICE. DAY.

The intercom sounds. The images evaporate. LAVELLE answers. It's his receptionist.

LAVELLE

Yes?

MARY (O.S.)
You know your last patient is here. It's ten past now.

LAVELLE
Just two minutes.

LAVELLE goes to the mirror and peers in it. He glances back at the couch: NOTHING.
He smoothes his hair and presses the intercom.

LAVELLE (CONT'D)
OK, Mary.

MARY (O.S.)
She's on her way.

He takes a deep breath, dabs the sweat from his face with a handkerchief. We hear the door open.

CELIA (O.S.)
Paul?

A young woman in a 1960s dress and bleached blond hair walks in. We just see her face. LAVELLE's face freezes in terror. He is barely able to articulate her name.

LAVELLE
Celia?

CELIA
I've been having such dreadful nightmares.

The camera pulls back as CELIA stretches out to LAVELLE a tightly wrapped bundle - containing a child.
She smiles. Now she is his nightmare.

START

CHAPTER 25

Greta May

The Adaptation

Greta May is a 10-minute film adapted from a short story first published in *The Dream Zone*. Written and directed by Clifford Thurlow, it was produced by Sacha Van Spall and Maureen Murray. The complete script appears at the end of this chapter.

Francis Ford Coppola with the three *Godfather* films became one of the most acclaimed filmmakers of modern times. The scripts were adapted from Mario Puzo's books about the mafia, and what Coppola learned from the adaptation process was that where the writer has already labored over his narrative, the key elements of characterization and the story's major turning points are already in place. With Hollywood filmmakers in intense competition to option the latest high profile novel, Coppola in 1998 took the original step of launching *Zoetrope: All-Story*,[1] a literary magazine that publishes innovative new fiction, and gives Coppola first rights to option the story for film. What Coppola had discovered was that in the neglected world of the short story there is a gold mine of precious material.

Short stories by their very nature contain no wasted words, every scene is necessary; a good story has pace and rhythm, every gesture and nuance driving the narrative to a climax that is often both satisfying and unexpected: just what filmmakers are looking for. If the short story writer has done his job well, the script won't exactly write itself, but the foundations are already in place.

It is a common complaint that the film is never like the book; more frequently, not as good as the book. But the forms do not bear comparison, and each must be as good as they can be within their own medium. The scriptwriter may decide to make the climax his opening scene and let the story unfold as a long flashback. Perhaps he will see a story about twin brothers better told as twin sisters. The possibilities are limitless, but the elements are already there like cards to be reshuffled and dealt in endless new patterns.

Greta May began life as a short story published in *The Dream Zone*, a small press magazine edited by Paul Bradshaw. When it came to adapting the story as a screenplay, I had three objectives in mind:

- To test the Eight-Point Guide to writing short scripts created for this book (See Chapter One: The Writer).

- To analyze the adaptation process.
- To make a worthy short film independent of the first two objectives.

A short film must stand alone as an accomplished piece of work, and that was certainly the prerogative of Sacha Van Spall when he agreed to come on board as producer. For the writer, the producer is like a strict parent, there to encourage but also to discipline. It is easy for writers, especially when directing their own screenplay, to get carried away with visions of street riots and crashing trains. The producer, with the line-producer or executive producer, prepares a budget and if your crashes don't come within its confines, you'd better go back to the script.

We sat at the kitchen table with a pot of coffee most afternoons for several days and went through the incessant finesses that mold each draft of the screenplay that comes before the final draft is ready to be presented to what we called the "3 Cs": cash, cast and crew.

25.1 Lighting check

▶▶ P.320

Film is sometimes described as a cottage industry in the UK. It is certainly not huge and networking is invaluable. With a recommendation from screenwriter Terence Doyle, we were joined by French DP Jean-Philippe Gossart, who studied the script and saw the story washed in muted color. It was his opinion that the best way to capture *Greta May* both in the darkness of a theater and the moody light of London's nighttime streets was to shoot on film, not tape. Our decision to switch to Super 16mm required both a new budget and the expertise of a production manager. With 20 years in film, including a decade at the side of the iconoclastic director Ken Russell, Maureen Murray was ideally placed to shepherd us in gathering the team and would also keep an eye on the ticking meter.

Now we were shooting on film, we had to think through every aspect of the process to see where we could streamline the production and cut corners. It is only in preparation and scheduling where money can be saved: perfecting the script, but also considering locations, rehearsing cast, having the right equipment at the right time, getting permission to film exteriors; knowing where to park vehicles, having change for meters, knowing where the loos are. Everything must be thought through and planned for.

The chief concern of an executive producer on a big-budget film is usually putting the finances together. On a short, they are more likely to serve as mentors: travelers who have gone on the journey from script to screen many times and know the pitfalls and precipices that mark the way ahead. Maureen Murray, serving in the dual role as production manager/ executive producer, passed a judicious eye over our 10-page screenplay yet again: scripts are like a detective novel, every word, gesture, and shot are clues that must contribute to the final film, the audience experience. And once the script is locked in place, you try to change one word and, like a dropped stitch, the entire fabric can unravel. The importance of the script can never be overemphasized: it is the foundation upon which the entire project rests. Give a bad script to a great director and at best you can hope for is a mediocre film. Give a great script to a bad director and the quality will try and force its way through.

25.2 Jess Murphy

▶▶ P.320

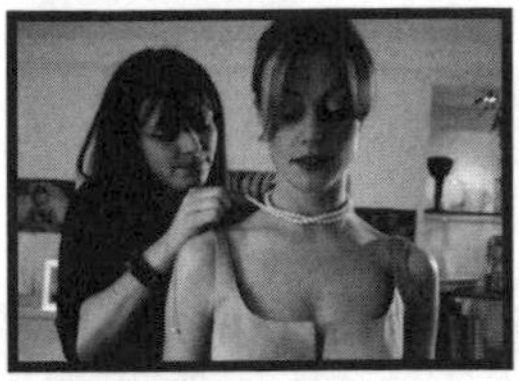

25.3 Emma Rand advises Greta

▶▶ P.320

25.4 Jean-Philippe Gossart lighting Philip Desmeules

▶▶ P.321

25.5 make-up artist Jenny Spelling works the clapper

▶▶ P.321

CASTING

After Maureen Murray had expunged a few superfluous lines, casting agent Susie Bruffin looked over the screenplay and recommended us to various actors' agents. We were seeking first to cast Greta May, the title character, and those agents who liked the script sent back files of CVs with glossy 1038s. Jean-Philippe filmed the auditions and each actress brought a different vision reflected in her performance, Greta May becoming posh with a plummy accent; a working-class girl struggling in the middle-class environment of the theater; a chaste virgin and a *femme fatale*.

Greta May appears in every scene and it is her dilemma that is portrayed and resolved in the drama. Each of the actresses we auditioned were trained, eager, and good at their job. Each would have brought a different interpretation, and we would have had a different picture, not necessarily better or worse, just different. Imagine Gwyneth Paltrow rather than Renée Zellweger in the title role as Bridget Jones. As I had based the script on my own story, Greta May had lived in my mind for a long time. I had fixed notions of her appearance and characteristics, which is not necessarily a good thing, and I wouldn't advise it, but Jess Murphy satisfied these pre-conceived ideas the moment she appeared at the casting. It was fortunate that she happened to be a fine actress as well.

Having found Greta May, we went through the same process to cast a suitable Rachel Gold, the mentor/friend who guides the story to its first turning point with her no-nonsense advice: *The way to get over one man is to get under another!* Emma Rand had the worldly-wise air demanded of the character and, as a blonde in contrast to brunette Jess, was perfect for the role. The girls instantly seemed like old friends and believable as flatmates. Emma and Jess came from the same agency, Roger Carey Associates, as did Philip Desmeules, tall and gentle, the ideal Richard Bates, the new love interest in Greta's complicated life. Big Management's Thomas Snowdon, with his set jaw and steady gaze, was a shoe in for the driven actor Oliver Morrell. (He had longish hair at the casting and showed up on set first day with his hair butchered for his part in a First World War movie, a challenge for Jenny Spelling heading up hair and make-up).

With our young performers assembled, we needed the "voice of authority" in the cameo role as the theater director. Although David Sterne had been busy the previous several months in *Vanity Fair* with Reese Witherspoon and Gabriel Byrne, as well as his regular TV spot as Professor Dust in *The Mysti Show*, he had worked with Maureen Murray on a number of occasions and agreed to join us for the one day the part required. Finally, we needed a black taxi; Tim Pierce supplied his cab and, though unseen, drove with the conviction we have come to expect from a London cabbie.

CREWING

Jean-Philippe provided a mixture of passion and professionalism at the casting sessions and brought his regular camera crew with him to film *Greta May*. After casting, we toured the locations making a video storyboard.

Jean-Philippe and I were in agreement on how the film should look, but my shot list turned out to be inadequate with missing elements from most scenes when it came to the shoot. In future, I will draw traditional storyboards with matchstick men to illustrate each shot. The video version is better than nothing, but pencil on paper has yet to be supplanted and I learned from experience that it is vital to draw a detailed study of each shot, the angle, camera movement, lighting, point of view, background, choice of lens, what the audience can see in the frame and how you want the audience to interpret the scene. The more the director and DP map out the shoot, the less time you lose in discussion on set.

For Jean-Philippe, the director and his DP are like lovers. "You are a couple. The director supports his actors and the narrative. The cinematographer is loyal to the aesthetic. Sometimes they clash. If the narrative is weak, the DP will cover the weakness by making the film flashy or glossy. He will leave space for the narrative. The DP must learn to adapt to the director, but this is not a one-way street. It is a shared experience. Each half of the partnership must have great respect for the other but, in the end, the director has the final word."[2]

The DP and director must also work closely with the production designer, the look and feel and texture of the film relying on all the departments running in harmony. The cinematographer invites the director into his world of lenses and filtration. He is the eyes of the director. "They must connect. Ideally, they will be people who share the same tastes and envisage the same aesthetic."

Jean-Philippe had worked with Maja Meschede on another film and she was duly engaged to bring her flair and visual talents to the wardrobe department; her last job had been with the Royal Opera House, so I knew we were in safe hands. Likewise, Maja recommended Julian Nagel as production designer and together they gave the costumes and sets a coherence that enhances the film. J-P's camera team consisted of grip Pete Nash, camera operator Renee Willis and gaffer Pete Carrier, all skilled craftsmen who enjoy the sense of adventure making a short.

The rest of the crew came to us through notices on Shooting People, the essential indie and short film internet exchange operating in both London and New York. Through Shooters we found soundman Daniel Rosen and boom operator Daniel Owen; Jenny Spelling, who makes a living with stills photographers but prefers to work in the make-up department on film; continuity supervisor Susan Hodgetts, who had given up a career as an economist to retrain for the film industry; stills photographer Alexander Atwater; runners Max Thurlow, Nick Burgess, Adam Greves, Charlie Lass, Igor Degtiarev, Adam Partridge, and Luc Tremoulet. Sydney Florence came to assist Maja, and Julian Nagel's usual assistant John Pearce not only put in many long hours as our art director, but created some great graphics for the theater flyer, the magazine cover used in the film and the DVD artwork. Assistants in the various departments, camera, set design, wardrobe, sound, make-up, will often get more responsibility on a short and the experience will help them rise up the ladder to be the head of department; the head honcho on a successful short is more likely to get the same role on a feature.

25.6 Sound man Daniel Rosen wires up Emma Rand

▶▶ P.321

STILLS PHOTOGRAPHER

When films were silent, the stills photographer on set could click and flash to his heart's content. When sound came, the snap of a shutter would ruin a take and the stills man was reduced to restaging scenes, much to the annoyance of the actors. Directors flexing their muscles, after banning the writer from the set, would then often pick on the stills photographer.

In 1959, the Los Angeles photographer and inventor Irving Jacobson had come up with the cordless battery pack, a design—sold later to Nikon—that saved many a photographer from choking himself on his own cables at the worst possible moment. In the mid-sixties Jacobson designed and built the first sound blimp, which effectively silenced the camera's shutter and finally allowed the set photographer to shoot while the actors were performing.

On *Greta May*, Alexander Atwater used two Nikon film SLRs, one camera with black and white film, the other with color. He carried a 20mm lens, a 50mm and a 28-105mm lens. Since the shoot he has switched to Leicas, which are quieter and more discreet.

Atwater views set photography as being similar to reportage. "Readiness is probably the most important thing because the actors and the rest of the crew won't wait around for you to take pictures. Like reportage, you never know what's going to happen or when. There is a lot of waiting around but you still have to be constantly alert. The best time to photograph a scene is before and after a take—never during."

Does the stills photographer try and disappear into the background?

"I try and be unobtrusive, move slowly and take my time. The best shots come when the actors aren't really aware of your presence and are therefore not too posed. It helps to be *in the background* and stay out of people's way."

Does the stills photographer ever make suggestions?

"If I want a specific shot I might ask the actors to play the scene again for my camera. Regarding the shooting of the film, I don't think it is the photographer's place to make suggestions, except in an extreme situation."

What kind of shots is the photographer trying to get?

"Shots that relate to the narrative of the film. Portraits of actors in character (and out). Scene shots. Behind the scenes, for example: make-up, filming, various technical aspects of the set. Shots that capture the essence and the atmosphere of the film. One of the easy things about set photography is that you don't have to worry too much about lighting, everybody is already beautifully lit. For set photography it is important to be able to work with available light. Flash ruins photographs. Also it is very important to be able to build good relationships with the director, actors and crew so they feel comfortable and have trust in you. This is when you get honest and occasionally intimate pictures."

www.alexanderatwater.com

BUDGET

When Sacha and I first sat down with our coffees, we were planning to make the film for about £4,000. Many short films are made with everyone taking part working for nothing but a credit. Once we had employed professional cast, the budget had to be re-written. There is a special arrangement with Equity in the UK, the actors' union, that allows members to work for a minimum fee of £100 a day on low-budget projects, and we set that as the benchmark for everyone working on *Greta May*.

The cost of cast and crew, coupled with the added expense of shooting on Super 16mm, resulted in a final budget of £10,000, and it would have been about 50% more had Sacha and Maureen not cut some amazing deals for the hire of camera equipment and the panoply of lighting the DP needed to give the sets the desired high production values we had envisaged.

THE SHOOT

We had started planning *Greta May* in the spring of 2004 and finally did the shoot in four days in November, when the weather was particularly kind, and the team gathered for Day 1 at the Battersea Arts Centre. On a big-budget movie, the production team would be expected to get an average of about 3½ minutes of finished film a day; about 3½ pages of script, 5–6 weeks to shoot a feature. In that time, the crew becomes a team and learns to work quickly and efficiently. On *Greta May*, we only managed to get 2½ minutes of film in the can on the first day and overran by about five hours. Was everyone a perfectionist, or just too slow? Time would tell.

25.7 Clapperboard

▶▶ P.321

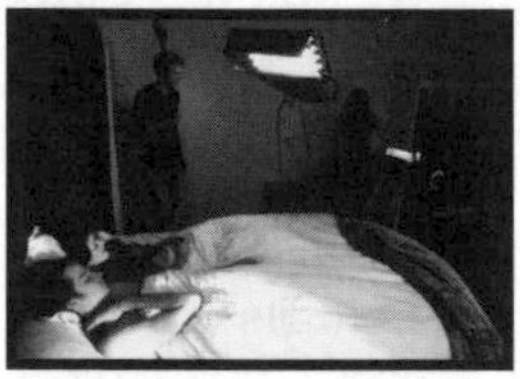

25.8 Bedroom scene

▶▶ P.322

25.9 Philip Desmeules gets slapped

▶▶ P.322

The film was developed overnight at Soho Images[3] and when we looked at the rushes next day, we were satisfied with what we had and no one seemed to mind when that pattern set on Day 1 continued late into the night on the next three days of the shoot. At least at Battersea Arts there is a good café and the army had been well fed.

Day 1 had been demanding for Jess Murphy, who spent about eight hours in her underwear being slapped around by Thomas as Oliver Morrell and growled at by the theater director David Sterne, who brought such authority to the role, even I as the director had to think twice when he roared: *No, no, no. For heaven's sake. Do it again.*

The mood remained buoyant and at midnight we were still unloading the lighting into the house where we would be for the next two full days shooting interiors. I have tried to bring to mind any dramas, beyond the drama of *Greta May*, and really can't remember any. I can recall nostalgically Maureen Murray screaming at Jean-Philippe that if he tweaked the lights one more time she would close down the set. But he kept tweaking, she kept on urging him on, and the film got made at the same slow rate of 2½ minutes a day.

Twenty or so people in a small house for 48 hours tends to become cramped, and it was a pleasure to do the exteriors on the last day. It is the final reel of Greta May's drama, where she goes to the apartment of Richard Bates as if there she will resolve her dilemma. The scene requires

25.10 Greta May dressing for a stranger

▶▶ P.322

a long corridor (the tunnel from one state of being to another) and Niccoló Gioia, who had been following our progress, not only volunteered his home for the night, we used his kitchen to prepare the last feast for the cast and crew.

Jess, as *Greta May*, arrives in a taxi in a breathtaking black dress made by couturier Breege Collins especially for the production; Breege gave Jess the dress after the shoot and Jess duly modeled for Breege when she prepared her spring collection, a marvelous example of the indie aesthetic. Greta steps out of the cab and paces assertively along the pavement. At the blue painted door, she hesitates, changes her mind and dawdles back along the street to the newsagents. It was an unseasonably warm evening. Jean-Philippe, Pete Carrier and the runners labored for hours to give the street a film noir feeling that justified J-P's extravagance with the lights (we'd rented enough for a feature!) and when I got the rushes back next day, I knew even if we had made a lousy picture, we did have some super night shots of London. Jean-Philippe brings a French sensibility to his camera work. With sets by Julian Nagel and costumes by Maja, both from Germany, *Greta May* has the European flavor faithful to the original short story.

We finished around 4.00 a.m. I was home at 6.00 a.m., and back at the rental houses at 9.00 a.m. to return the gear to avoid having to pay for an extra day. It was sad to see the team break up, although now the production was over, the long journey through post was about to begin.

When you make a film, you should draw up a budget and stick to it. Sacha had been reminding me of that every day and it was through my excesses that the river had run dry, regardless of all the people who had donated their time, flats and expertise to the production. Along with the rest of the crew, we had three associate producers helping along the way: Gerardo Silano, Cedric Behrel, and Keith Eyles.

POST-PRODUCTION

We were fortunate that Trevor Georges agreed to compose an original score, a moody jazz piece that brings out the tone I'd been aiming for, and as final proof that filmmakers are the most generous people in the world, Ron Lloyd at True Media let us loose in his facilities in Soho's Golden Square during his editor's downtime on *The Constant Gardener,* directed by Fernando Meirelles with Ralph Fiennes and Rachel Weisz. I worked odd hours, late afternoons and late nights for a month with editor Tony Appleton, who covered the inevitable gaps left by me as the director and teased out the emotional heart of *Greta May* with his adroit grasp for rhythm and timing. After adding sound effects and music, I came to appreciate Coppola's oft-quoted remark: "A film is created three times: first you write it, second you shoot it, third you edit."

Greta May premièred at the Curzon in Soho at the launch of the first edition of *Making Short Films* in 2005. It was shown at various screenings in the UK and at CinéGuernsey; it was audience selected at the Savannah Film Festival, Georgia, and was runner-up for best short film at the Marbella Film Festival, Spain, in September 2006. *Greta May* was selected at Leeds Film Festival and got its first broadcast credit on Sky on 31 March 2007 in the First Film series produced by Propeller TV, and can now be seen on YouTube.

Jess Murphy went from *Greta May* to appear on stage with the Mexican actor Gael García Bernal in *Blood Wedding* at the Almeida Theater, London, and scored a role in Tim Burton's *Sweeney Todd* with Johnny Depp and Helena Bonham-Carter. Emma Rand was cast with substantial roles in two TV shows, *Casualty* and *Judge John Deed;* Philip Desmeules has appeared in the movies *Trafalgar Battle Surgeon*, *Twice Upon A Time* and *Gracie!*, released in 2009. Thomas Snowdon joined the cast of EastEnders in 2012.

I had set out with *Greta May* with the lofty goal of writing and directing a short film that would win major prizes. It makes sense to aim high and, while the mega success was not realized, I learned so much through the hands-on experience I am optimistic that my next effort will put some silverware on the shelf. You learn by doing. A mistake made by many first-time filmmakers is that they compare their first efforts with *Star Wars* when they should be looking at George Lucas's film school shorts. In making a film you run the risk of being criticized or appearing foolish. All creative work runs the same risk and only when you take the risk, and keep taking risks, do you cut through the cliché and the formula to create something truly original. Like good wine, filmmakers mature with time. The secret is to keep going.

PAUSE

The short films selected for this book represent different genres and were not chosen for any inherent qualities. Each have their strengths and flaws. By studying them, new filmmakers should draw inspiration from the strengths and try and avoid the flaws. The films can be seen at: www.making-short-films.com

THE SHORT STORY

It will be a useful exercise for filmmakers to study the short story below and make notes before reading the script. Decide how you would adapt the story, and compare it with my own adaptation. There is no right or wrong way, but it will be interesting to see how I've done it, and how similar or dissimilar your own take on the story.

GRETA MAY

She was glancing at the night's TV listings in the *Standard* when she became aware of the man staring at her. Studying her. It's something that just isn't done. Not on the tube. It's so intimate. While your body's rubbing against other bodies the last thing you want to do is make eye contact. She looked away. There was a movie with Jack Black, Channel 4, nine o'clock. Shame about the commercials. She'd microwave something during the breaks. Drink a glass of wine. Or two.

She glanced up. He was looking still. He smiled. Good teeth. She frowned. If she'd been in a pub she would have liked his brown eyes and broad shoulders. She looked down, then back up again, instinctively, as if against her will. He was writing something in a notebook.

He tore out the page and gave it to her as the train slowed at Gloucester Road.

"My stop," he said, and squeezed through the sliding doors before they closed.

His name was Richard. His number was 05557 757 777. She wondered how he managed to get so many sevens. Was it lucky? For him? For her?

She screwed up the piece of paper and let it drop to the floor among the fast-food bags and abandoned newspapers. She'd grown to despise the tube in the two years she'd worked in the shop. A shop assistant. How did it happen? Why? Two years at drama school. Two on the boards. Two in a shop. And another birthday in June. She didn't even bother to read the trades anymore. Twenty-five. That's almost thirty. She'd be looking at comfy slippers next.

She picked up the piece of paper again. Richard. 05557 757 777. Black jacket. Blue shirt. Dark jeans. Media: television, advertising, web-design.

The train pulled in at Hammersmith. As she stumbled along behind two girls in gray veils she thought about the crowd at Gloucester Road. Well-heeled. Closer to the action. London was a chessboard. Blacks and voids.

As soon as she got home she spread the slip of paper flat on the kitchen counter. She called the number. She let it ring twice. Then hung up. It was ridiculous to call a total stranger. Then, it was ridiculous not to. What did she have to lose? She lit a cigarette and poured a glass of wine. The first drag and the first sip are the best. Life's like that. An unfulfilled promise. She'd played at the *Royal Court* in Sloane Square when she was nineteen. She was Polly in *The Raw Edge*, a pilot for a soap that had never got made. There had been hundreds of girls up for it. But she'd got the part. At twenty she could play fifteen. They liked that. She looked like the girl next door who gets raped and murdered.

She lifted the receiver and phoned again. Her sister.

"Alison. It's me."

They talked: Alison's child. Alison's partner. Alison's stiff joints; she was learning to be a yoga teacher. Alison was about to hang up. Then remembered.

"How's things with you?"

"A man gave me his telephone number on the tube."

"How exciting."

"I know." Greta paused.

"Well?"

"Nothing. He was a stranger."

"What was he like?"

"Mmm. Tall, dark, nice accent."

"Lucky devil."

They talked some more. Said goodbye.

Greta finished her wine and started to pour a second glass, stopping herself and adding just a touch. She had decided to make the call while

Alison was going on about her aches and pains and was bracing herself to actually do it. What would she say? What if she got an answerphone? No problem. She'd hang up.

There was no answerphone. He answered.

"It's me."

"I knew you'd call."

"How?"

"Nothing ventured ... "He trailed off. 'Come over."

"What for?"

"I could say a plate of spaghetti."

"Why don't you then?"

"Okay. A plate of spaghetti." She knew he was smiling. He gave her the address.

"Do you need to write it down?"

"I have a trained memory," she told him.

"I'll put the water on."

She replaced the receiver. A chill ran through her. This was insanity. He was an axe murderer. A madman. *American Psycho!*

It wasn't her that went through to the bathroom and took a shower. Shaved her legs. Perfumed her parts. It wasn't Greta May. It was someone like Greta May, a mirror image that stared from the mirror as she slid into black underwear. She cleaned her teeth. Lit a cigarette. Smiled at the absurdity of it. Of everything. She put on a black dress, looked down at her breasts, and took it off again. She tried blue jeans and a shirt. Good hips, she thought, took off the jeans and put on a skirt instead. Clothes help you find the character. Then, when you're up there, out there, you're no longer you, but then you are, even more so. Yes, they really were someone else's eyes peering back as she did her mascara. Someone who didn't work in the shoe department in a big store. She removed the skirt, slid back into the black dress, then swiveled round just quickly enough to catch a glimpse of Polly in *The Raw Edge*.

A taxi stopped as she was about to enter the tube and she stepped in the back. She despised London taxi drivers. But she loved their cabs. It was like returning to the womb. You were coddled. Luxuriated. You learned how to love yourself, your reflection opaque and vaguely surreal in the dark glass, amber streaks of light crossing the sky. She imagined dying and being carried to her funeral in the back of a taxi. Nirvana on the radio.

He lived in a red brick building divided into five flats. His bell was the bottom one. She stood there on the threshold, her finger hovering before the shiny brass button. This really was madness. The taxi had gone. The street was silent. She marched off back the way she had come and only slowed her pace when she reached the newsagent's on the corner. She studied the magazines. She flicked through the pages of *The Stage* and put it back in the rack. If she hurried she'd get home in time to see the movie on Channel 4.

She lit a cigarette and blew a long stream of smoke into the sky. The night was clear. Full of stars. She had every intention of going home and watching the film, but found herself crushing the cigarette below her heel, cleaning her teeth with her tongue, and setting out again for the red brick building. She took a deep breath and hit the bell. The door buzzed open almost immediately. She heard his voice.

"Come in."

It was hollow. Like an echo. She heard the sound of her shoes tapping over the black-and-white tiles in the hall. There was a table piled with letters, a gilt mirror reflecting an image of herself she didn't recognize. Richard stood in the doorway to his flat. He was wearing jogging pants, a polo shirt. Bare feet. It's very familiar. Bare feet.

As she stepped into the hall he pushed the door just hard enough for it to catch. They stood motionless in the half-light. He leaned towards her, placing his two palms flat on the wall, her head trapped in the space between them. He wasn't smiling. He just stared. And she stared back. He had dark eyes. Jet black hair. She wondered if he would ever be cast as a leading man.

The slap came as a complete surprise. It stung her cheek. It really stung, and so loud in the silence. It was hard. Not so hard as to bruise, but hard enough for her teeth to cut the inside of her mouth. She tasted blood. She slapped him back, just as hard. Her breath caught in her throat. She would have screamed, but his lips were on her mouth, sucking at her and she responded to his kiss. His hands slid down the wall, across her back, over her bottom. He pulled up her dress and ripped the side of her knickers. They fell to her feet. She remembered reading in *Cosmo* that women got wet when they were excited. It had never happened to her. Never. But it did now.

She could feel a dampness inside her stomach. She felt that dampness grow liquid and leak from her, wetting her thighs. The feeling was ... *luxurious*. The sound of the word ran through her mind as he turned her round and pulled her down on the floor. He entered her in one swift movement. The cheek where he'd hit her was pressed against the coarse floor covering. Her breath came in short gasps. She could feel his breath, hot against her ear. He rammed deep inside her, harder and harder, and when he came the warm feeling in her stomach filled her whole body and that feeling was ... Luxurious.

Now that he'd finished she imagined he was going to open the door and toss her back out again. But he didn't. He turned her over and did something she had not been expecting. He kissed her cheek. He lifted her awkwardly into his arms and carried her through to the bathroom. He didn't say anything. He turned on the taps, filled the big bath and added blue crystals to the flow. She was reaching for the zip on her black dress automatically, her fingers doing the thinking for her. He turned off the taps and she stepped out of her dress into the foaming blue water.

He was about to go, but leaned back through the door: 'What kind of pizza do you like?" he asked.

"What about the spaghetti?"

"Takes too long."

"Spinach with an egg."

"Anything else?" he asked her.

"Yes, you can get this week's *Stage* at the newsagents."

"You're an actress?" he asked and she nodded. "I thought so. What's your name?"

"Greta May."

"Nice one."

He closed the door and she held her breath as she sunk for a moment beneath the dark blue water. Luxurious.

25.1 Lighting check, DP Jean-Philippe Gossart with actress Jess Murphy

25.2 Jess Murphy doing her Audrey Hepburn impression

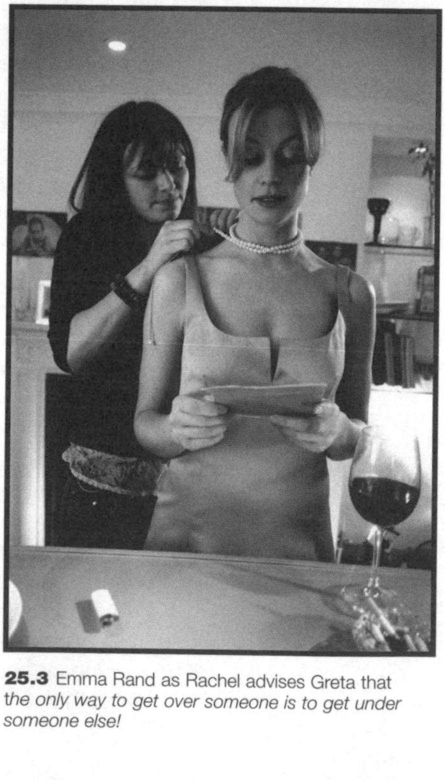

25.3 Emma Rand as Rachel advises Greta that *the only way to get over someone is to get under someone else!*

25.4 Jean-Philippe Gossart lighting Philip Desmeules

25.5 Make-up artist Jenny Spelling steps in to work the clapper - making short films is a it's a multi-tasking pursuit

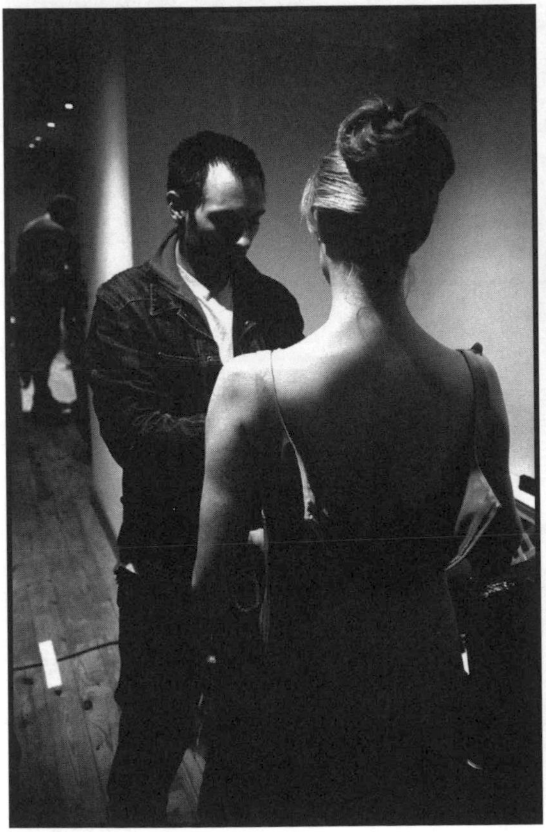

25.6 Sound Daniel Rosen wires Emma Rand up for action

25.7 Clapperboard

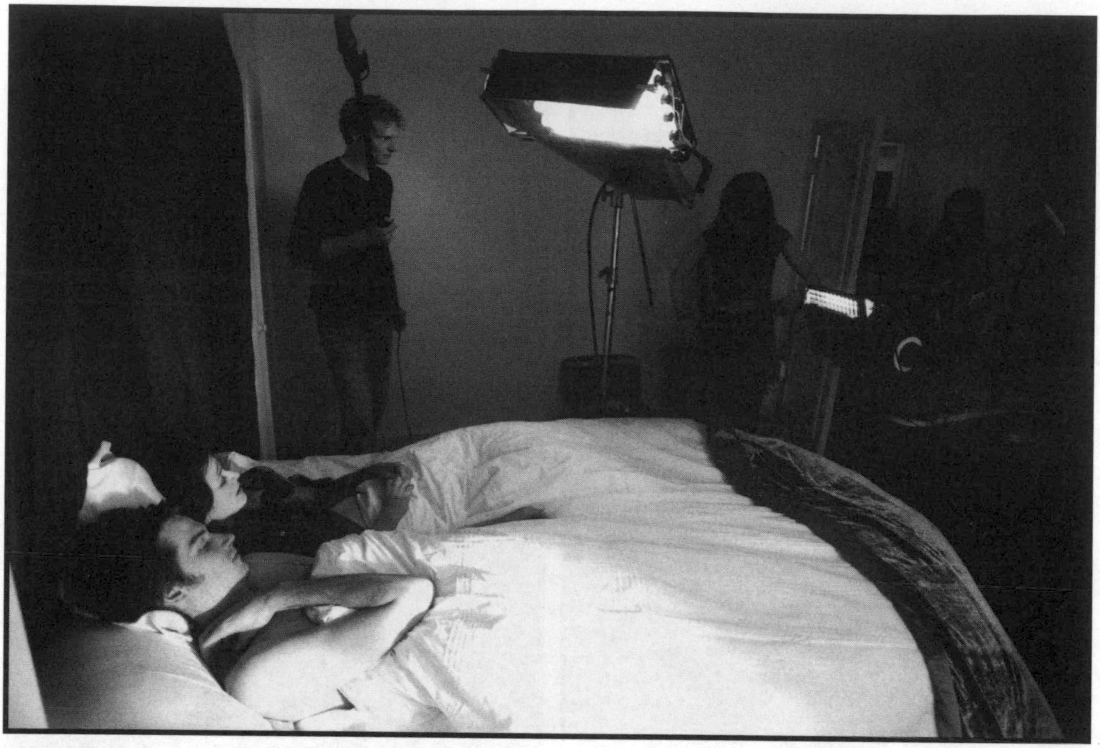

25.8 Bedroom scene, a big crowd in a small room

25.9 Philip Desmeules gets a good slapping

25.10 Pensive Greta May dressing for a stranger

START

TITLE

Greta May

Script/direction by Clifford Thurlow
Produced by Sacha Van Spall
and Maureen Murray

1 INT. THEATER FOYER – EARLY EVENING

Greta May descends the stairs and peruses the flyers in a theater foyer. She is 25, attractive, down in the dumps. **5**
She removes a flyer with a picture of a powerful handsome guy below the play title: ***You're Not Alone***. **4**
Richard Bates, 25, confident, but not pushy, carries a newspaper. He recognises Greta and approaches.

RICHARD
Hi, it's Greta May.
She tries to place him . . .

RICHARD (CONT'D)
Richard. Richard Bates.
She acts like she's kind of remembering him. He doesn't press.

RICHARD (CONT'D)
I saw you in your last play, *Hope Express* . . .
(notices the flyer)
. . . with Oliver Morrell. Of course. You were terrific.

GRETA
But I'm not in this one, though.

RICHARD
It's not that good. What are you doing now?

GRETA
I'm sorry?

RICHARD
What are you in?

GRETA
I'm reading scripts, considering things.

RICHARD
Listen, do you want to have a coffee or something?

GRETA
Another time. I've got to ...

Greta moves past Richard.**50**
Richard scribbles his name and number on his newspaper: *Richard* 05557 757 777. He tears off the corner and hurries after Greta.

RICHARD (CONT'D)
Next time you're in something, you know ...

Greta reluctantly takes the scrap of paper, and glances at it. **20**
Richard watches her wander towards the exit, shoulders slumped, and sees her shove the piece of paper in her pocket.**5 (1.24)**

2 INT. GRETA'S KITCHEN - NIGHT

On the kitchen counter there is a half eaten chocolate cake, an ashtray with a smoking cigarette, a glass of wine, a bottle of wine, a mobile phone and the theater flyer from *You're Not Alone*.
Greta sips wine. Wine drops in red tears down her front.
She studies Oliver's face on the flyer, wipes away the wine with her fingers and real tears well up into her eyes ... **8**

FLASHBACK
There is a fleeting image of Greta dressed in an ultra-sexy outfit consisting of a red bra and pants, teetering heels, and sheer nylons. She looks terrified ... *3*
Greta's name called off-screen shakes her from her reverie.

RACHEL (VO)
Greta. Greta.

Greta cuts and takes a big slice of cake.**4**
Rachel Gold, Greta's flatmate, enters: same age as Greta, sophisticated in a slinky dress and ready for an evening out. She carries a pearl necklace which she twirls around her finger. Greta remains silent and looks shaken. Rachel ignores her, arranges the flowers. Greta breaks off a piece of cake and shoves it in her mouth. Rachel approaches, picks up the flyer and puts it back down again.

RACHEL
You know something, I've been dumped more times than you've had hot ...

GRETA
(cutting in)
... sex?

RACHEL
... tell me about it.

GRETA
I was chatted up today. Some bloke saying he knew me. What a jerk.
9

RACHEL
Handsome jerk or an ugly jerk?

GRETA
You're so shallow, Rachel. "Shallow Rachel!" Sounds like a bad play.

RACHEL
Yeah, you should be in it. You're not doing anything else. Can you? Rachel releases the necklace like a conjuring trick from her palm. Greta stands to help.

GRETA
I'm resting.

Greta hooks the necklace in place. Rachel turns and looks at the cake.

RACHEL
Is that what you call it?

Greta straightens Rachel's sleeve. She's looks great.
Greta looks sad.**1.02**
Rachel grabs the flyer and screws it up.

GRETA
Rachel ...

Rachel crosses the kitchen ...

RACHEL (CONT'D)
Oliver would step over his own grand-mother to get a part. He's just a bastard.

GRETA
Don't ...

... and drops the flyer in the pedal bin.

RACHEL(CONT'D)
The way to get over one man is to get under another.
Rachel kisses Greta's forehead and makes her way to the door. Greta sits

and cuts into the cake. Rachel turns and holds her own slender waist as she nods towards the cake.

RACHEL
Cake is not the answer. **35**

Rachel exits. Greta speaks to the cake.

GRETA
Depends on the question. **4**

A door slams from above. **(2.18)**

3 INT. GRETA'S KITCHEN (LATER) - NIGHT

Greta spins her mobile. She stares thoughtfully at the keyboard, then stabs in a number. It rings and she hangs up. She takes a sip of wine. Then presses RECALL.
INTERCUT TELEPHONE CONVERSATION: **(15 jumps)**

4 INT. RICHARD'S LIVING ROOM - NIGHT

Nice pad. Richard reads the Evening Standard (corner is torn).

RICHARD
Yeah . . . Richard.

GRETA
So what about that coffee?

RICHARD
What . . . Greta . . . You kept my number.

GRETA
Nooo. I've got a trained memory.

RICHARD
You didn't remember me.

GRETA
I'm sorry. Where do I know you from?

RICHARD
I work in the theater. I've seen you in the spotlight.

GRETA
Agh, that's right, in Hope Express. Why don't you ask me over and you can tell me why Oliver Morrell was so amazing!

RICHARD
Yeah! ... I'll give you the address.
Are you ready?**40**

Greta listens. Hangs up. She stands, takes the whole cake and slides it in the bin on top of the flyer. **5 (45)**

5 INT. GRETA'S BEDROOM - NIGHT

Greta stands in front of the mirror in modest underwear -moving to her own music.**2**
The same fleeting image of Greta dressed in the sexy red underwear crosses the mirror and for a moment she sees Oliver standing behind her. ***2***
She shakes away the image. Quick cut to: **2**
Greta dressed in blue jeans, tee-shirt and a leather **3** jacket, hair carefully scruffy. She faces CAMERA and spins round to catch her reflection in the mirror - very James Dean with the fag in the corner of her mouth.

GRETA (VO)
Biker Girl ...

She wriggles out of her clothes and tosses them on the bed. She gazes at her image and combs her hair.
Quick cut to Greta dressed in a formal black dress - a demure Audrey Hepburn. She poses for the mirror. **9**

GRETA (VO)
Socialite ...

Greta undresses and stands staring into the dark wardrobe. Car lights flicker over the ceiling. **5 (21)**

GRETA (VO)
Femme fatale ...

6 EXT. BLACK CAB - NIGHT

A black cab going around Hyde Park Corner, lights streaming by, Greta's reflection in the black glass flickers into a momentary flashback:

7 INT. THEATER STAGE - NIGHT

Greta wears the sexy red outfit from Sc. 4 flashback. She looks panicky as **Oliver Morrell** crosses a darkened room, empty but for a sofa.
Oliver slaps her across the face. He enjoys abusing her. Oliver kisses Greta violently, and as she struggles to get away he pushes her roughly down on the sofa.

GRETA
You bastard, what are you doing?
What the hell ... **10**

The voice of the dissatisfied **Director** intervenes from the darkened auditorium. We see now that the action is not "live" but is taking place on stage.

DIRECTOR (VO)
No, no, no, Greta, for heaven's sake.
Let's try again. **8**

Oliver bends and touches Greta's shoulder in a sweet way. He raises his eye-brows as if to say he can't understand what's wrong with the Director and takes Greta's hand to pull her up from the sofa.
Greta smiles ... **5**
Close Up on Greta becomes her reflection in the cab window as the cab plunges into the tunnel at Hyde Park Corner and disappears.**7 (30)**

8 EXT. RICHARD'S HOUSE - NIGHT

Greta crosses the pavement, climbs three steps and her finger hovers over the doorbell. The sound of the taxi disappears into a silence that is deep, oppressive.**3**
Greta reads the nameplate: Richard Bates. Her hand trembles, and she backs away. The cab has vanished. Greta's shoulders drop. She dawdles along the street in her heels, turns the corner ... **10(13)**

9 EXT. NEWSAGENTS - NIGHT

... and stops at the rack of magazines outside the late night newsagents. It's gloomy inside, the dim yellow light casting an insipid glow over the pavement. She slips a cigarette into her mouth.
Greta notices *The Stage*.
She pulls *The Stage* out of the rack and Oliver Morrell is staring from the front page below the heading: *"**You're Not Alone - Oliver Morrell Strikes Again**."*
She shakes herself and takes a deep breath.
She pushes the magazine back in place, removes her unlit fag and stamps it out anyway.
(20)

10 EXT/INT. RICHARD'S HOUSE - NIGHT

Greta marches back to Richard's building and gives the bell a decisive press.

GRETA (VO)
Femme Fatale
The door buzzes open. **4**
Greta enters the darkness. As she opens the interior doors, the door to Richard's flat opens.**5**
Richard is in an open doorway at the end of the hall in sharp silhouette, the light behind him.**2**
Greta walks the long corridor towards him.
(11)

11 INT. RICHARD'S LIVING ROOM - NIGHT

Greta is composed, ostensibly in control. Richard, unsure of himself, while trying to conceal his pleasure that's she's there.**4**
She studies Richard: his polo shirt, jogging pants, bare feet. She looks from his feet to his dark eyes and down to his feet again.**4**
It's difficult to know who is going to look away first - but it is Richard.

RICHARD
Coffee? Drink ...

Greta glances around the room, taking everything in. Looks back over her shoulder, seems bored as she answers.

GRETA
Red wine.

He produces a bottle, glasses, corkscrew.**4**

RICHARD
I didn't really think you were going to come. I mean, I'm glad you did ...

GRETA
Don't they all come? The girls you give your number to. **10**

Greta glances at the photos on the shelf: they show Richard as a little boy, in school uniform, getting into a car, with mummy: family snaps, all very normal.**5**

RICHARD
I don't make a habit of it.
As Richard points out something in one of the photos, he places his hand gently on her bare shoulder (the same action as Oliver when he was being sympathetic on stage).

RICHARD (CONT'D)
Look that was ...
Greta flinches, as if she has woken from a dream, and with the jerk of the movement wine spills down her front.**5**
Richard puts his glass down. So does Greta. Greta's hand is covered in wine.**3**
Richard goes to take her hand, and Greta slaps him across the face in exactly the same way that Oliver hit her on stage.

RICHARD (CONT'D)
What the ...**(52)**

As Greta goes to hit him again ...
Quick Cut:

12 INT. THEATER STAGE - NIGHT

... Oliver hits Greta across the face. He kisses her violently, and as she struggles to get away he pushes her roughly down on the sofa.

GRETA

You bastard, what are you doing?
What the hell ... No.
Oliver slides his belt out of his trousers and roughly ties Greta's hands. He hits her again.

OLIVER

You're going to enjoy this, you little bitch.

GRETA

What? Why are you doing this ...

INTERCUT **(20)**

13 INT. RICHARD'S LIVING ROOM - NIGHT

Greta moves towards Richard, grips the side of his head, and kisses him violently, the action mirroring Oliver kissing her.
As Richard moves back, he stumbles over a chair and lands on the floor. Greta falls on top of Richard, straddling him. She kisses his neck. She pulls off his shirt, her actions frantic, violent. She slides out of her dress, revealing the red underwear from the theater costume.

(20)

As Richard goes to embrace her, she pushes his hands away.

CUT BACK TO SCENE 12

DIRECTOR (VO)

He's not going to do anything.

The Director's voice brings the action to an end.
The Director comes into view, a ghostly figure in the dark auditorium. He sits in an end seat beside the aisle.

He is a middle-aged man in black trousers, a turtle neck and distinctive polished black leather shoes.

DIRECTOR (CONT'D)
Oliver, a word please.

Oliver makes his way off stage. The Director stands as Oliver approaches. His voice like an echo inside Greta's head.5

DIRECTOR (CONT'D)
I know you've worked together before, but this isn't doing it for me. I'm going to use the French girl ... **12**

The Director turns and his footsteps recede up the aisle. Oliver looks back at Greta for a moment, then follows the Director. **6**
Close-up on Greta lit by a single spotlight. **2**
Close-up on Richard: the lighting operator working in the control booth.3
(28)

14 RICHARD'S LIVING ROOM - NIGHT

Greta has tears in her eyes.

RICHARD
It's okay ... I understand ...

Richard caresses Greta.
At first she is unsure. Then she returns his caress, truly focusing on him for the first time.
The caresses become more passionate. Richard gently rolls Greta over and kisses her eyes, kissing away her tears. Their lips meet. They kiss, discovering each other.
(17)

15 INT. RICHARD'S BEDROOM - MORNING

Sunlight streams into the room. Greta is in bed wearing Richard's polo shirt. Her eyes adjust to the light. 3
She snuggles up to Richard and the movement wakes him. He opens his eyes and they look at each other for a long moment.

GRETA
Where's that coffee you promised?

Richard still can't quite believe she's there. He smiles ...

GRETA (CONT'D)
What did you really think of me In *Hope Express*?

RICHARD
You were adorable ...

She pulls him towards her, pulling his ears, and kisses him tenderly. Richard is about to get up, but she pulls him back.

GRETA (CONT'D)
There's no hurry.

They kiss.**30**
(33)

FADE OUT
30 seconds end credit
Total 10 minutes

PART

VII

TITLE

Software

START

CHAPTER 26

Final Cut Pro

By Zach King

26.1 Final Cut King logo

▶▶ P.339

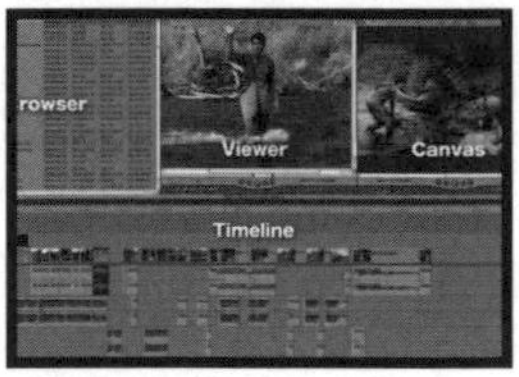

26.2 Final Cut Pro

▶▶ P.339

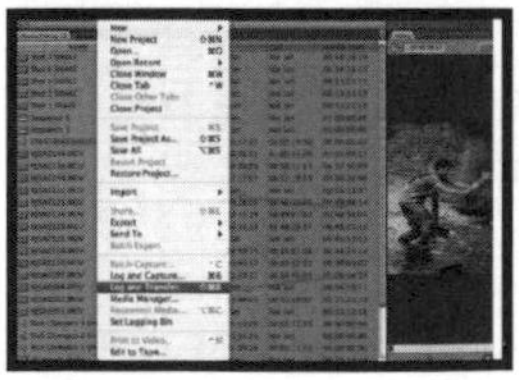

26.3 Log and capture

▶▶ P.339

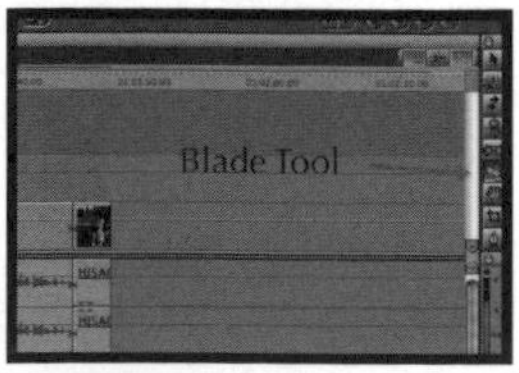

26.4 Blade tool

▶▶ P.339

For the beginner, editing for the first time in Final Cut can be a daunting experience. But let me assure you, it is well worth the investment of your time. This chapter will give you a brief overview of how the editing process works in Final Cut Pro 7. As you dive more deeply into the topic, you can check out my website, www.FinalCutKing.com for more free tutorials and training. But for now, let me run you through the basics.

Below you can see a picture of a working Final Cut Pro project. This is taken from a new video I am working on called the *Fish Olympics*. The upper right hand window is the media browser, which allows you to store and organize all the media that will be used in your video. It can be photos, music, footage, etc. You also have items called sequences and these are the actual projects that you will be editing in your timeline.

Before you can get started on a project you need to be able to import footage. It's pretty simple. If you have a camera connected via USB or Firewire you can use the importer called "Log and Transfer" which is found under the FILE menu.

If you already have the video or photos on your computer you can go to File > Import > Files or Folders, or drag them directly into the browser.

Once you have the media desired in your browser you can prep them in the preview window which is on the right of the browser window. When you double click a clip or drag it in to the preview window you can trim it to the desired length. Using the "I" and "O" keys (In and Out Points) you can select a beginning and ending point. Once that is trimmed, drag it below to your timeline.

The timeline is where you will open your sequence by double clicking on it in the browser. If you don't have a sequence yet, you can create one by right clicking in the browser and hitting: New Sequence.

You can begin splicing the clips in your timeline by using the "B" tool, which is the blade. In the picture below you see the blade tool in the tool panel.

Let's talk about the playback bar. As you view your project in the canvas you can scrub through your timeline with this playback bar. When you hit the space key, the playback will begin playing forward. To play backwards you can hit the "J" key. In the shortcut section at the end of

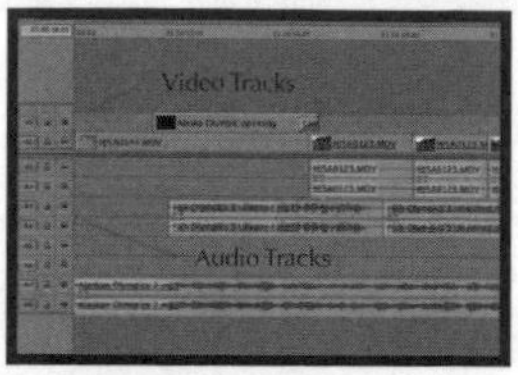

26.5 Audio tracks

▶▶ P.340

26.6 Render window

▶▶ P.340

this chapter I have more details about how you can use these keyboard shortcuts in the timeline for an easier playback.

You can see that both video and audio tracks are in the timeline. There can be up to 99 tracks of video and 99 tracks of audio. Right now, this project is only using 2 tracks for video and 8 tracks for audio.

If you mix various frame rates, video formats, or add special effects, your computer will need to render them. If you see any red lines in the timeline, this means those sections will need to be rendered before you can have a real time playback.

Hit "Command R" on your keyboard and that will allow you to render the video. It may take a while depending on the amount of effects you have in your video. The more RAM and processing power your computer has, the faster the video will render. On my secondary machine I use 64GB of RAM so that I can bust through some pretty intense renders more quickly.

I like to think of editing like painting. The software is a tool like a paint-brush, but the real art comes out after a lot of experience and practice. I always tell people that the best way to get into editing is to dive right into the deep end and get as much exposure to it as possible. Final Cut Pro may look complex and difficult, and it is at first, but pretty soon, it will be second nature.

KING'S TOP 10 KEYBOARD SHORTCUTS

Option > Window > Arrange

The top way to store a custom layout is to hold down the option key.

J-K-L

The coolest playback method that is available in Final Cut is using these three keys. J plays the video backwards, K is pause, and L is forwards. You can also click J and L several times to speed up the video playback in increments.

Shift Z

"Fit to Window" allows you to fit your video into the largest size possible within your window constraints for the viewer, canvas, and timeline.

Command 3

This brings back up the Timeline window when you accidentally close it. It's a lot quicker than trying to look through your project bin to re-open the sequence.

I and O

These are the best ways you can create In and Out Points in the viewer, canvas and timeline. Realize that an editor can use the In and Out points in the timeline to help speed up editing.

Option D

Duplicate—comes in super handy.

Option R
Render all video, yup it's that simple!

V
This selects the edit point that is closest to the playhead in the timeline.

Option + or –
This is a great way to zoom in or out of the timeline in the viewer, canvas, or timeline.

Tool > Keyboard Layout > Customize
You can head over here to set up your own shortcuts in this window.

STOP

26.1 Final Cut King logo

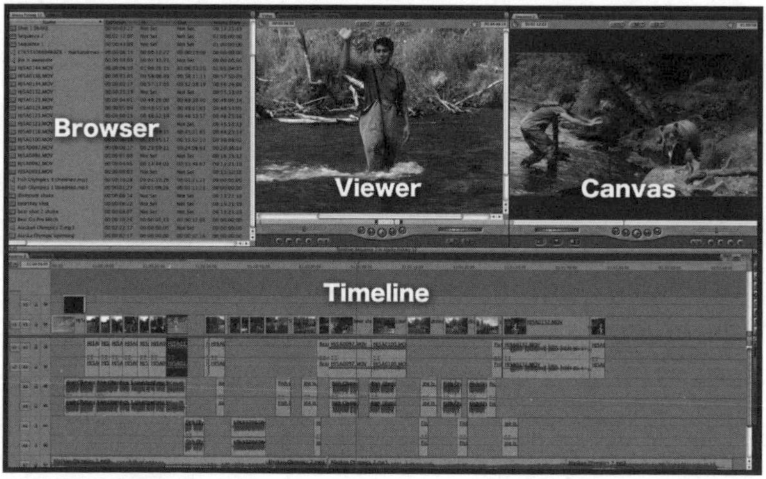

26.2 Final Cut Pro

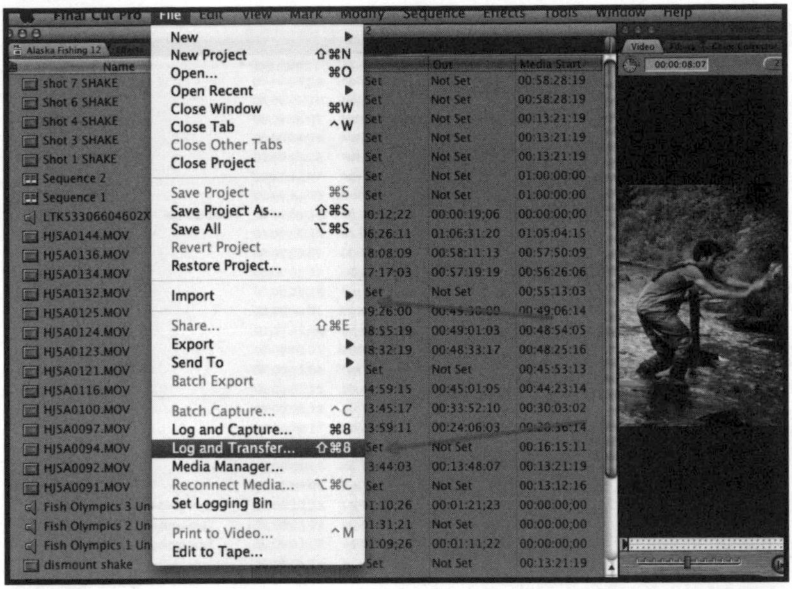

26.3 Log and capture

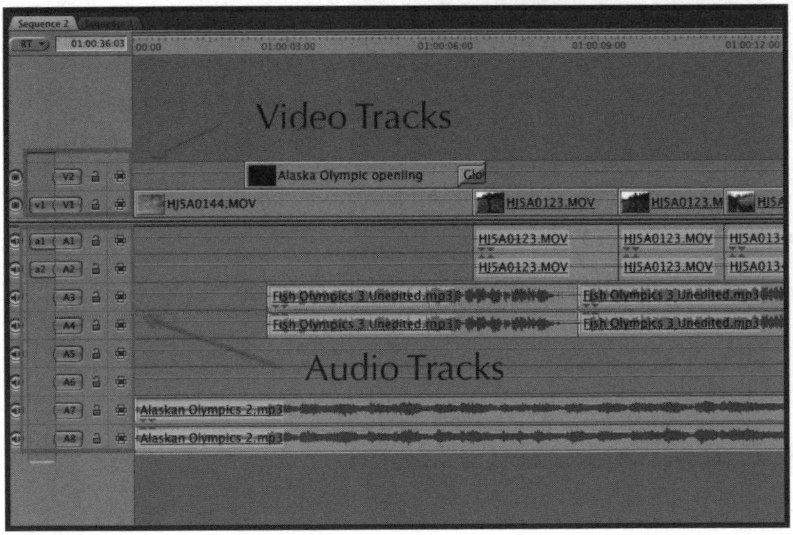

26.4 Audio tracks

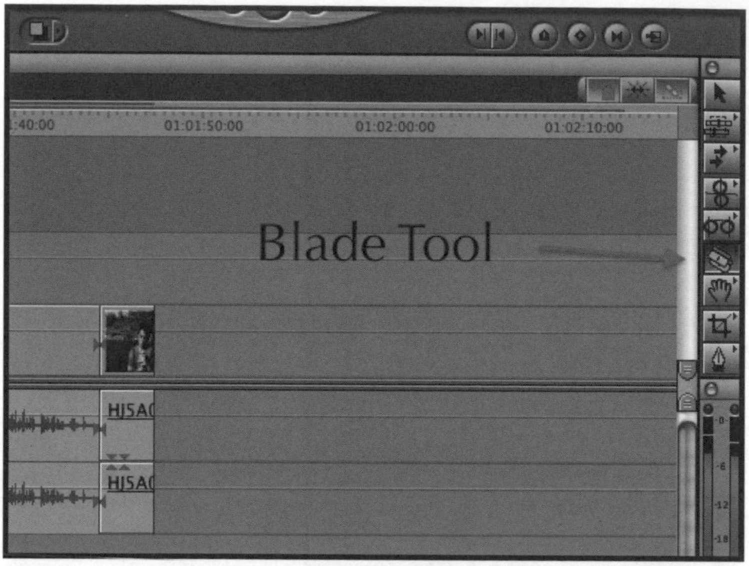

26.5 Blade tool

26.6 Render window

START

CHAPTER 27

Final Draft

By Joel Levin, Final Draft Vice President, Technical Support

Final Draft is the number-one selling software specifically designed for writing movie scripts, television episodes, stage plays and new media, combining powerful word processing with professional script formatting in one self-contained, easy-to-use package. There is no need to learn about script formatting rules—Final Draft automatically paginates and formats your script to industry standards as you write. Final Draft can take you smoothly from idea to outline to first draft to final draft to production script. Find out more at www.finaldraft.com

Writing with Final Draft

When the program is opened for the first time, you'll be looking at a blinking cursor at the top of a blank, industry-standard screenplay document. Since it's not necessary or even recommended to begin a screenplay with a fade in, you can simply start with the first scene heading.

In this example, the first scene takes place in an interior, so type the letter I. The SmartType window will come up with all the choices that match the letter I. In this case we want interior, so accept that choice with the Tab key.

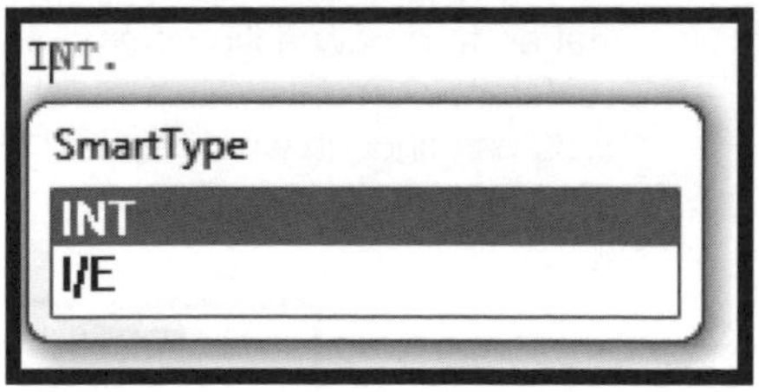

This will enter what you need and move the cursor to the next section of the scene heading, the location. Type "kitchen" (without quotes) and then hit the tab key.

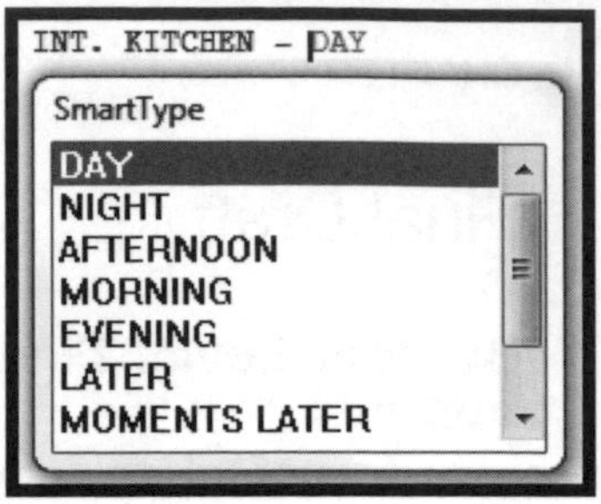

Next, choose the time of day by either clicking with the mouse, typing the first letter of what you want, or using the arrow keys on the keyboard. When the scene heading is done, press Enter to move to the next element, action. It's clear when you're in an action element because the program displays it at the top of the screen on Windows and at the bottom left on Mac.

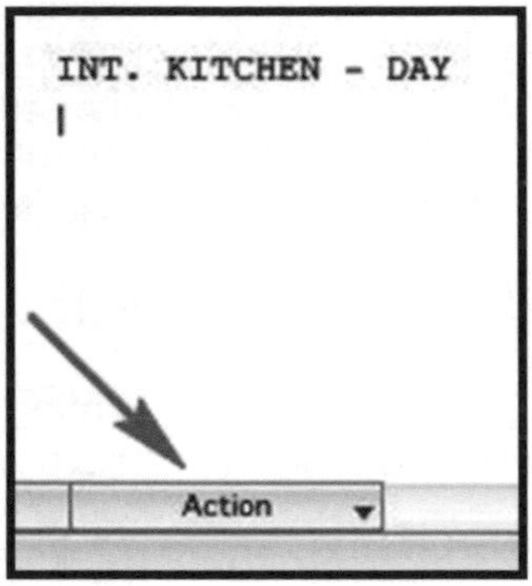

Type the action: "a woman enters and sits down at the table." (without quotes). The first letter of the sentence is capitalized automatically. You can set up the program to not capitalize the first letter of a sentence through the Options menu on Windows and the Preferences menu on Mac.

Press Enter again to move to the next element. By default, you'll be taken to a new action element. Since action elements can be followed by different elements, such as another action element or character element, you can choose what the next element is going to be from a drop-down list. To get the list, press Enter.

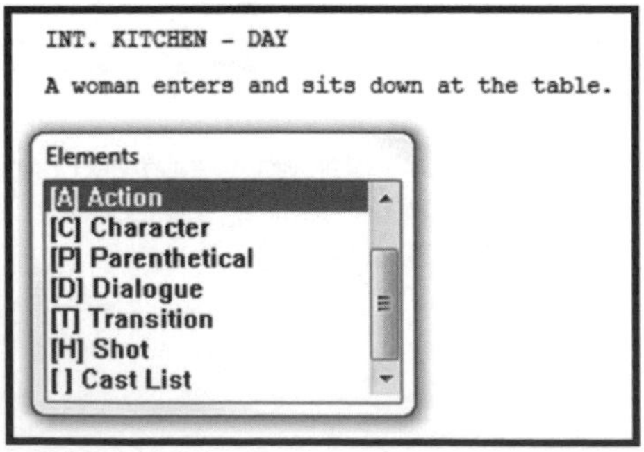

Final Draft will always let you know what the Tab and Enter key will do, depending on where the blinking cursor is. In the screenshot below, it's indicating that if the Tab key is pressed, a new character element will be inserted and if the Enter key is pressed, an action element will come up.

It's time for the character to speak, so either simply press Tab to get to a new character element or press Enter and then C to insert a blank character element. Type the name "sue" (without quotes), then press Enter to set up a blank dialogue element. Type "Hi, I'm Sue." (without quotes).

To cue the reader and eventually the actor that the next line is meant to be yelled, a parenthetical element can be used. A check of the status bar shows that Enter will insert a new dialogue element, the first logical choice after a character name, and Tab will insert the second logical choice, a parenthetical.

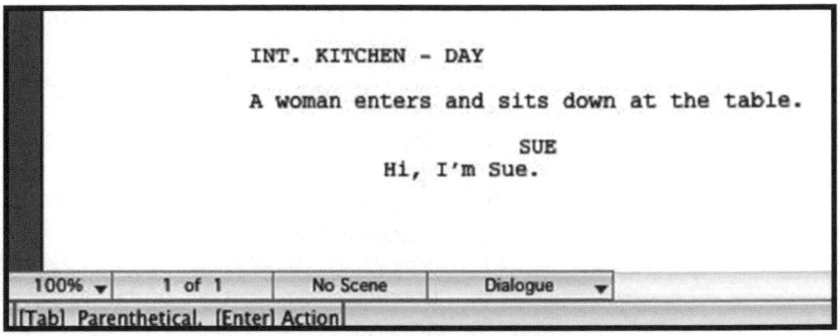

Hit Tab and you can now type in the word "yelling" (without quotes), then press Enter and type the line, "i'm mad as hell and I'm not gonna take it anymore!" (without quotes). Press Enter to continue to the next element.

Another way to insert a new blank element is to use keyboard shortcuts. On Windows, hold down the Control key to display a set of number-coded elements. Control + 1 will put in a new scene heading, control 1 2 will insert an action element, and so on. On a Mac, you would press the Command or Apple key.

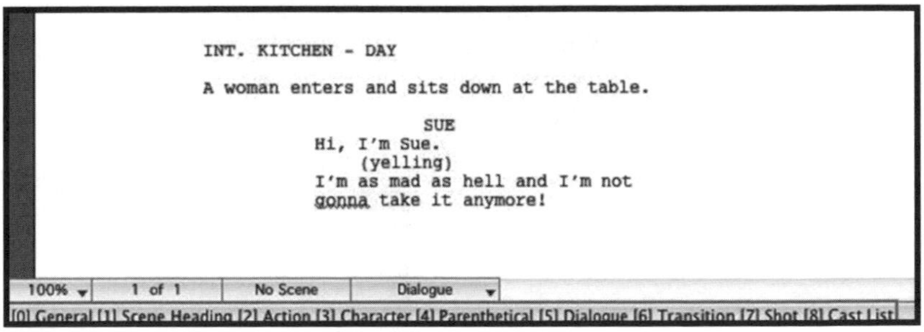

It's time to move to the next scene. Press Enter to get the elements menu and choose scene heading. This shot is an exterior, so hit the letter E. Accept "exterior" with the tab key and type the location, kay's house. From this point forward, when you type the letter k, the location field of a scene heading, KAY'S HOUSE can, along with KITCHEN, be inserted with just one keystroke.

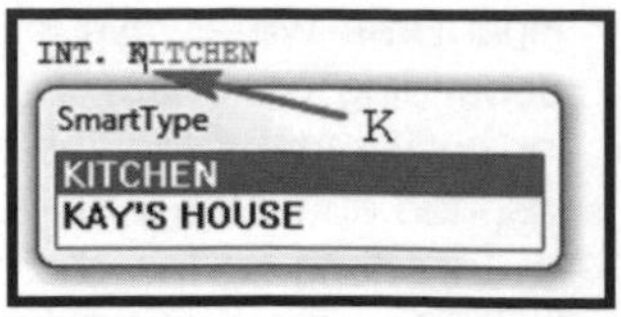

Final Draft remembers your character names in exactly the same way.

After typing “kay’s house”:

1. <Tab>
2. Choose night.
3. <Enter>

Now you’re ready to type this scene’s action:

1. “sue walks up to the door and knocks.”
2. <Enter>
3. <Tab>
4. “sue”
5. <Enter>
6. “is anyone home?”
7. <Enter>. You’ll be taken to an action element.
8. “bob sticks his head out of the window.”
9. <Enter>
10. <Tab>
11. “bob”
12. <Enter>
13. “hi sue.”
14. <Enter>

Now Sue and Bob are going to have a conversation. In order to skip some keystrokes, you can change a setting in the program that will make it a little easier to write back-and-forth dialogue.

Go to Format > Elements and tell Final Draft that the Enter key should now transition to a new character name after dialogue instead of action. Choose Dialogue from the list on the left and choose Character from the Enter dropdown menu.

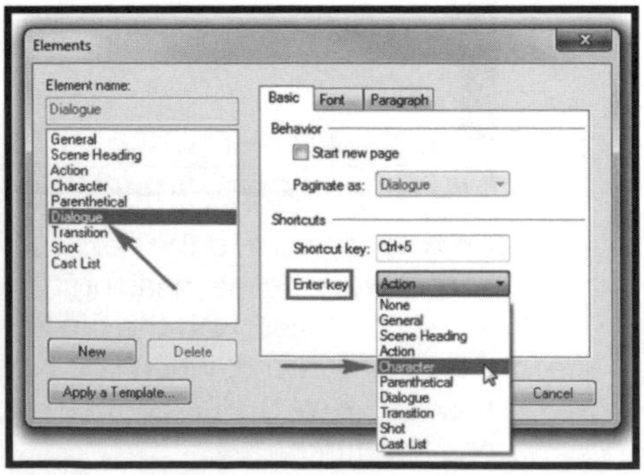

Now when Enter is pressed after a dialogue element, the program now brings up Sue.

1. Enter(to accept the name)
2. "hi bob."
3. <Enter> (to move to the next character name)
4. <Enter> (to accept BOB, the SmartType suggestion)
5. "what's new, sue?"

Now you're ready to write your snappy, clever dialogue with the absolute minimum number of keystrokes. As you write your characters and locations, they're stored for you to use again and again, so you'll reach a point where you're pretty much typing nothing but action and dialogue.

Opening Files Written in Other Programs

Final Draft can import plain and rich text that have been created in other programs. It cannot directly open (for example) Word or PDF files, but if the data can be converted to either a .TXT or .RTF file, Final Draft can import it in and render it in the default screenplay template.

1. Open the script in the program in which it was created;
2. Go to File > Save As or File > Export, or wherever the program's file export command is;
3. Choose the Desktop as the save-to location and from the Save as Type or Format dropdown menu at the bottom of the window, choose Plain Text, Text Only or ASCII Text file (they're all the same). Save the file;
4. Close this program;
5. In Final Draft, go to File > Open;
6. Navigate this dialogue box to look on the Desktop. (On Windows only, change the Files of Type to read Text Documents);
7. Double-click the text copy of your script;
8. You'll be asked to choose to format it as a Script or Text. Choose Script;
9. Final Draft will import the text and render it as a feature screenplay;
10. Go to File > Save and save the script with any file name modifications you might want, such as today's date or the word "master" (without quotes);

IMPORTANT: Although onscreen text looks identical on many different kinds of programs, it's not. Text you read on a web page is rendered differently from text you see in a graphics program, which is different from MS Word, which is different from Final Draft. Copying and pasting text from a source other than Final Draft will bring with it foreign formatting code and Final Draft will not be able to handle it. It might work fine in the short term, but eventually a .fdx file which contains both Final Draft text and (for example) HTML from a web page will become corrupted. Instead, paste it into a word processor and save it out of the word processor as a text or RTF file, then import that text or RTF into Final Draft, as above.

Saving Files for Other Programs
If you need to send a script to another word processor, save it as a Rich Text File (.RTF). When a Final Draft-generated RTF is opened in a standard word processor, it will NOT be paginated accurately but it will look like a screenplay (e.g. all-caps Scene Headings, all-caps Character Name towards the center of the page, sentence-case dialogue below that, etc.). This file will also be editable.

Other File Formats

- HTML—Openable by any web browser. Final Draft gives you the option of saving the HTML file in sections or as one long page.
- FCF—Used by Final Draft AV and in the event that you have to save the file for Final Draft v.4 or older.

File > Export

The File > Export command is used for exporting material to other production programs.

- Movie Magic/EP Scheduling (.sex)
- Avid Script-based editing (.txt)
- ScriptNote Export (.xml)
- PDF

There are two ways to do this. If you want to save the entire script as a PDF, go to File > Save As PDF. A standard Save As dialogue box will come up and allow you to save the PDF wherever you want. There will be a check-box to include or exclude the title page.

If you need only certain pages or scenes or a particular revision set saved as a PDF, go to File > Print (or Control + P on Windows, Command + P on Mac). At the bottom of the Print sheet are options for the export. Check the appropriate radio buttons and checkboxes and when you're ready to export, choose Print to PDF (Windows). Even though the button says print, this will allow you to save the PDF. A regular Save As dialogue box will come up and allow you to save the PDF wherever you want.

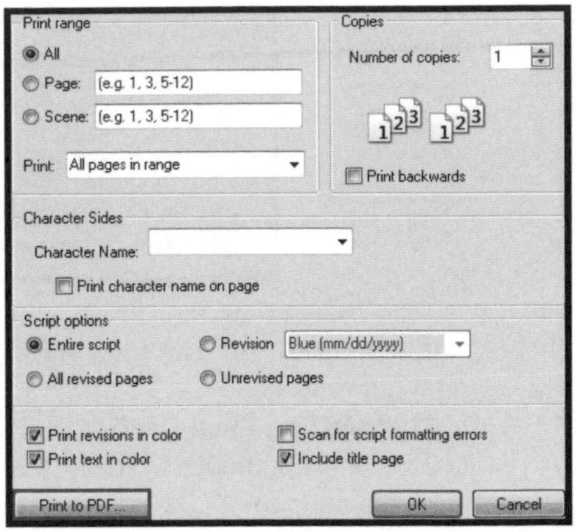

On Mac, go to File > Print >PDF > Save As PDF.

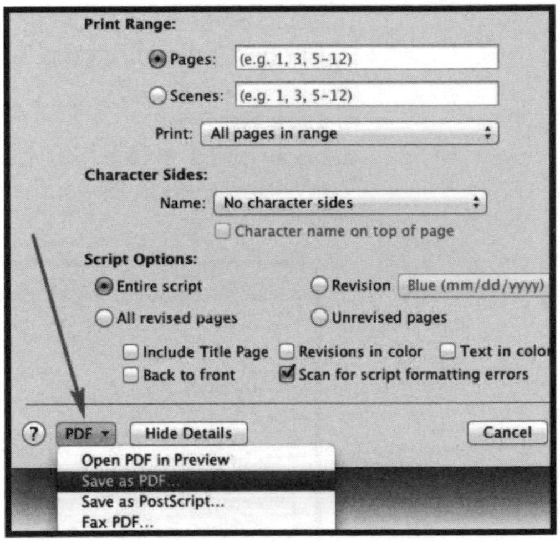

A dialogue box will come up. Choose the file name and save-to location and click Save.

If the next window appears, choose Use PDF:

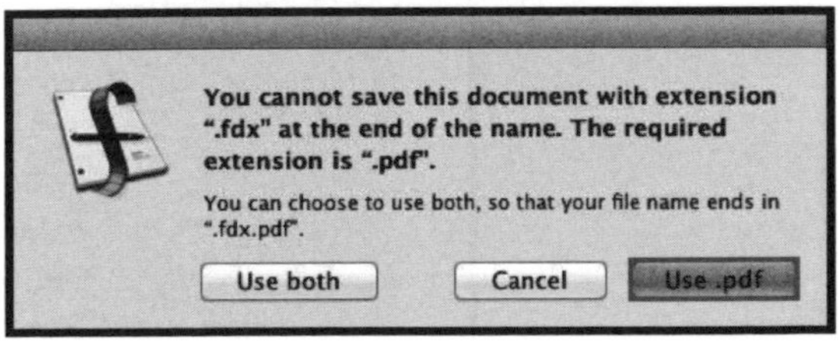

At the next window, click Print Now to create the PDF. If you want to have the Format Assistant scan your script for errors before the PDF is made, choose Scan Now.

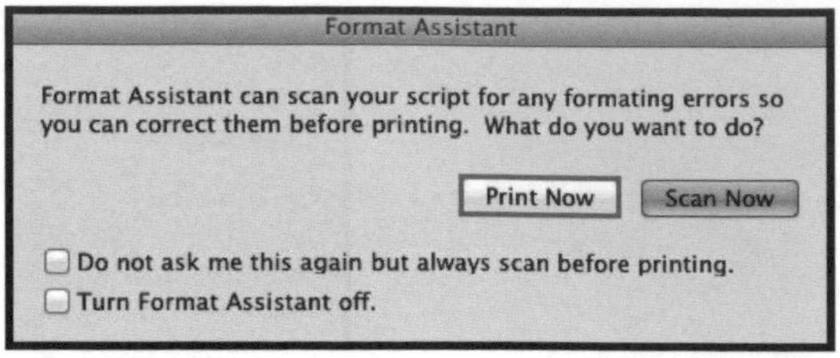

IMPORTANT: Be sure to give the PDF the correct file name.

Customizing Final Draft
Format > Elements is really the brain of the Final Draft program. In the Elements control panel, you can globally change any attribute of any element at any time. For example, if you want all of your action to be in italics:

1. Go to Format > Elements;
2. Choose Action from the list on the left;
3. Click the Font tab;
4. Click Set Font;
5. Click Italics in the Style Attributes box (Mac) or Font Style box (Windows) and OK your way back to the script.

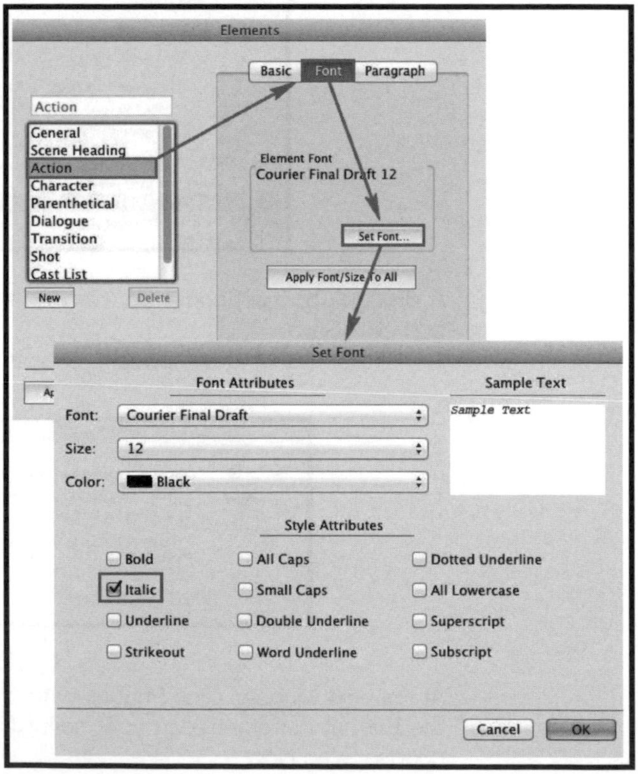

This will render all action in italics:

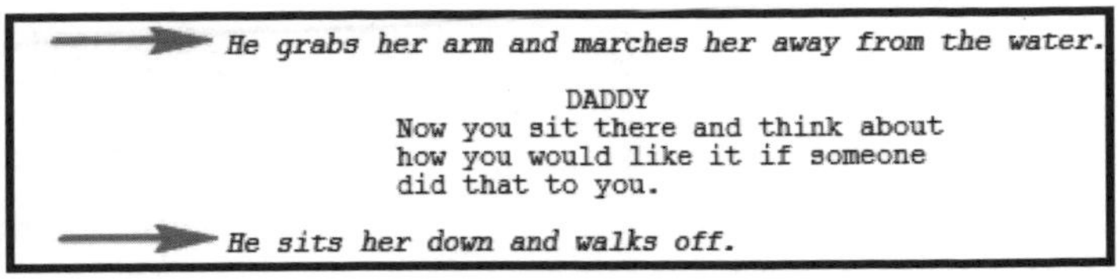
He grabs her arm and marches her away from the water.

DADDY
Now you sit there and think about
how you would like it if someone
did that to you.

He sits her down and walks off.

You can change an element's font style—i.e. Scene Headings underlined, Shots bold, etc.—or an element's font color—i.e. all Dialogue blue—from this control panel as well. It's also here that you can change an element's look, behavior, shortcut key and margins.

You can also create your own custom elements. Go to Format > Elements and choose New. In the Element Name box, overtype the text that's there with the name of your new element. In this example, it's "SFX."

1. Set the new element's behavior, font and formatting with the controls on the Basic, Font and Paragraph tabs. In this case we want the font all uppercase and italicized ...

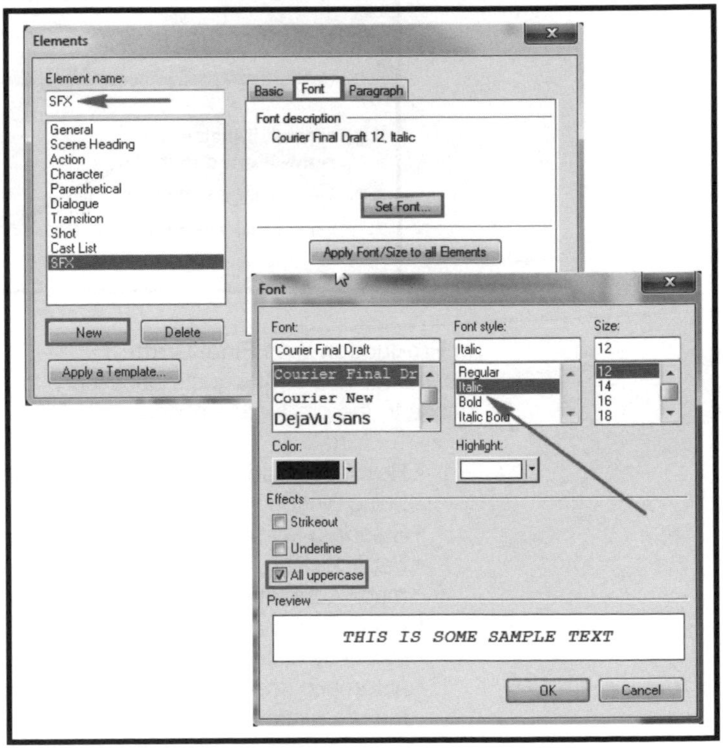

2. and the text to be aligned to the right.

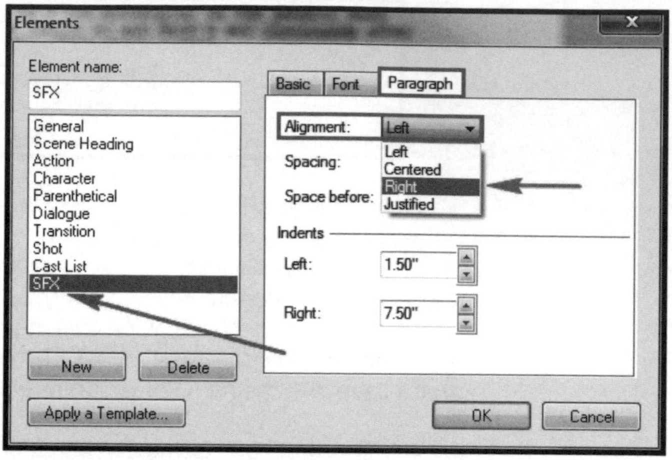

3. Click OK when you're done.

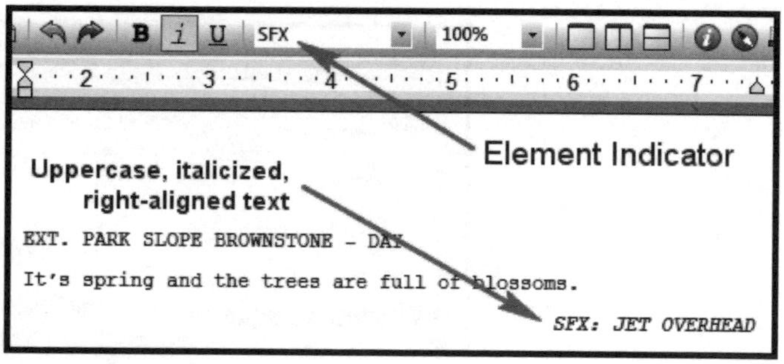

In Production with Final Draft

Final Draft has all the tools necessary to move a script from the writing phase to the production phase:

- Revision mode, which visually sets off new text from older text as it's being written;
- Standard revision set colors, which can be used as-is or customized;
- Page locking, which preserves original pagination no matter how much content is added or removed from the script;
- Filtered output, which allows the script coordinator to easily and efficiently distribute new pages to cast and crew;
- Automatic scene numbering (and A and B numbering), which helps the production crew follow new scenes as they're added;
- Omit Scene function, which accounts for deleted scenes in a locked script;
- Tagger, a standalone application that tags a script's characters, props, wardrobe, set dressing and all other production components in preparation for use in standard production scheduling and budgeting programs.

Final Draft Reports

Final Draft can generate a number of separate, editable reports that can be saved as .FDX, plain text, rich text, or PDF. The reports are found under Tools > Reports.

Reports are NOT interactive—they are snapshots of the script at a particular point in time. Editing a report will not change the script and editing the script will not change an existing report. If you make changes to the script, the reports you've already made will become obsolete. You will need to create new reports.

Available Reports:

- Scene Report: gives information about each scene: scene heading, page number, length in 8ths, cast;
- Location Report: gives information about which scenes play in which locations and the page numbers;
- Character Report: gives stats about how many times the selected character speaks and with whom they speak the most. Also contains all of their dialogue in each scene;
- Cast Report: reports on every character with information on each one's total number of dialogues, speaking scenes and total scenes;
- Script Report: allows you to select which elements are to be included in the document. An example would be to show only scene headings and action. If you choose every element, you're simply replicating the whole script;
- ScriptNote Report: displays the contents of all ScriptNotes and the pages in which they're embedded;
- Statistics Report: word count, paragraph count, number of each element (i.e. 100 scene headings, 200 action elements, etc.). Has character interactions (i.e. Character X speaks N times (M%) for a total of NN words (MM%). Interacts most with Character Y and appears in the following scenes.

Tagger

Tagger is a separate application included and installed with Final Draft that enables you to break down a Final Draft script into its various elements (components) and then export the results into popular movie scheduling and breakdown programs including:

- EP Schedule—from Entertainment Partners
- Movie Magic Scheduling—from Entertainment Partners
- Gorilla Scheduling—from Jungle Software
- CompanyMOVEShowPlanner—from Novko

Tagger should be thought of as an interface between a Final Draft script and production breakdown and scheduling programs.

You can write a script in Final Draft v.8, open the same file in Tagger, tag your props, wardrobe, vehicles, etc., and then open that file in Final Draft again for more revisions. Tagger will scan the script for revisions and if the new content has items that have been tagged in the older content, Tagger will automatically tag these items as well.

To tag a script:

1. Select the text to be tagged;
2. Click the selected text with the right mouse button (Ctrl-Click for Mac). The Add Element dialog appears;
3. Change the category by clicking it. In this case, the category we want is Props;
4. Click OK (or double-click the category name). The Confirm dialog appears;
5. Click Yes.

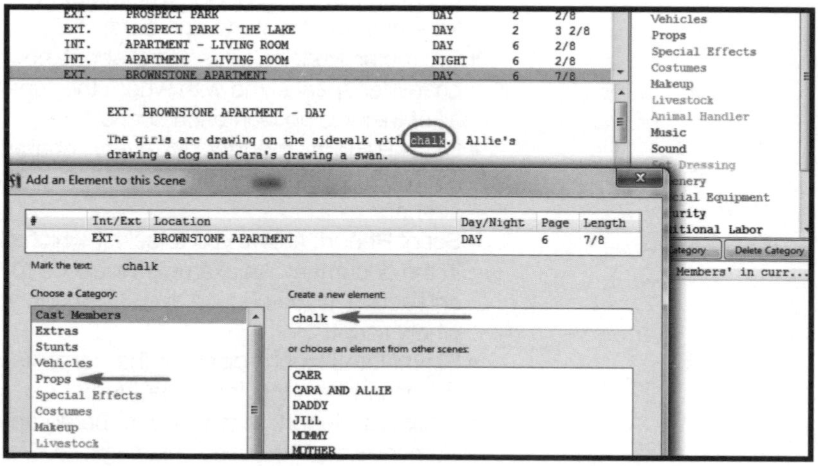

The tagged text now appears in whatever color the chosen category is set to. A plus sign (+) appears next to the Props category, indicating that an element in this scene has been tagged as a Prop.

To export a file to most scheduling/budgeting programs, go to File > Export to Schedule.

Final Draft Mobile

Final Draft offers a screenwriting tool for the iPad, designed to be a companion piece to the full desktop program. In addition to its use as an app with which you can write features, shorts, TV episodes, and stage plays, it is intended for use on films sets. It gives the production office the ability to distribute new pages to cast and crew electronically, even from the set. The writer can adjust a scene while sitting next to the camera and send out the new pages; the prop master gets them instantly.

The Final Draft Writer for iPad retains the pagination of the full desktop application, so a script at exactly 50 and 3/8ths pages in Final Draft will be exactly 50 and 3/8ths pages in the Writer app. This ability makes the Final Draft Writer for iPad the only professional-grade screenwriting program for the iPad.

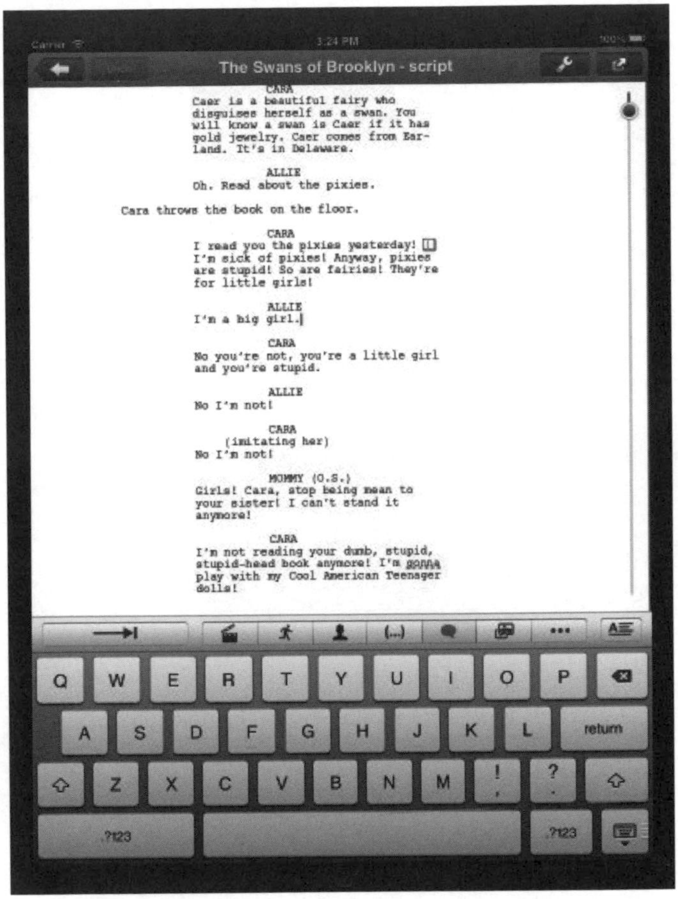

Features:

- Professionally formatted TV, Film, and Stageplay templates to help get you started;
- *SmartType* remembers your Character Names, Scene Headings, and more;
- Quickly change elements with Tab and Enter quick-navigation;
- Add, categorize, and edit *ScriptNotes;*
- Character Highlighting allows you to keep track of your characters for table reads or character development;
- Shows Active or Collated Revisions with Colored Pages;
- Includes production features like Scene Numbering and Locked Pages;
- Quickly switch from one revision set to another;

STOP

All images courtesy of Final Draft, Inc.

START

CHAPTER 28

Movie Magic Budgeting and Scheduling

By Dr Laurence Sargent

Whether raising finance, planning different scenarios or coping with the unexpected, the success or failure of a production depends on an accurate Budget and Schedule. Movie Magic Budgeting and Scheduling from Entertainment Partners enable fast and accurate estimation of the cost of shooting, an easy breakdown of the script, and the management of virtually any production schedule. Together, they help deliver the best on screen results within the finances available.

Free Trial

Registered users can trial Movie Magic Budgeting and Scheduling by downloading and installing a fully functional, time limited, trial version from the Entertainment Partners website, https://store.entertainmentpartners.com/demoregistration.

Further Information

A very useful source of further information is Entertainment Partners' YouTube channel, BroadcastEP. A range of videos are available covering many aspects of Budgeting and Scheduling with Movie Magic. To watch them visit: http://www.youtube.com/broadcastep.

Movie Magic Scheduling

Movie Magic Scheduling is a powerful software solution that takes the pain out of translating a screenplay into an actionable plan for shooting a film. It delivers a detailed and versatile production schedule that includes a sequence for shooting, a record of working days for each actor, a Breakdown Sheet for each scene listing all elements required, a Calendar, Shooting Schedules, and Day Out of Days reports that can be printed and distributed.

Navigating the Schedule

Movie Magic Scheduling offers intuitive navigation with a combination of easy-to-use toolbars and menus.[1] Menus provide access to all major modules of the program, each with its own functional controls available via a toolbar. Keyboard shortcut keys are also available throughout the application used in combination with the Control (CTRL) key in Windows® or the Command (CMD) key on a Mac®.

Getting Started

To get started create a **New Schedule from Template** by using the keyboard shortcut **CTRL + N** or **CMD + N**. Alternatively select **New Schedule from Template** from the top **File Menu.** Production Information will be required throughout the Schedule and can be entered by selecting **Production Information** from the **Design** menu.

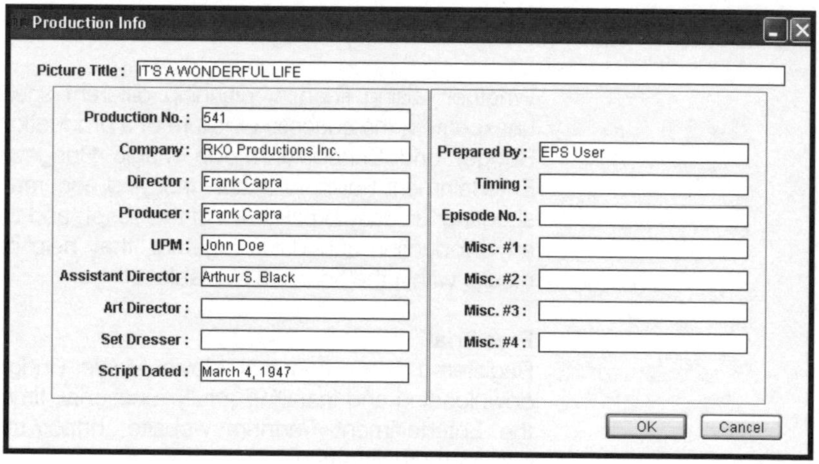

Script Import

Having finished the script and marked it up the information is now ready to be entered into Movie Magic Scheduling. To make this easier certain Elements can be imported directly from script-writing software. For example, you can import a native .FDX file created in Final Draft 8 by selecting **Import** from the **File menu**. Cast, Scene and Set information will import, along with other Elements, populating scenes on the Breakdown Sheet.

TIP: The first page will remain blank after import as it is the default Breakdown Sheet. This can be deleted by clicking the **Delete Sheet** button on the Breakdown Sheet Toolbar or by clicking on Delete Sheet from the top Actions Menu.

Breakdown Sheet

A breakdown is an analysis of everything contained within the script for Budgeting and Scheduling purposes. The Breakdown Sheet in Movie Magic Scheduling is used to enter Elements like the traditional, paper-based Breakdown Sheet. The Breakdown Sheet can be added tumor modified, as information becomes available. A printable version is available that closely resembles the traditional Breakdown Sheet.

TIP: A good breakdown should contain things that are not on the written page as well as those that are obvious to the reader.

To go to the Breakdown Sheet go to **Breakdown** and select **Breakdown Sheet** or use the keyboard shortcut **CTRL + Y or CMD + Y**. The Breakdown Sheet is divided in several parts; Scene Information, Categories, Elements and Storyboard Images.

Scene Information

Shown on the top half of the Breakdown Sheet are fields including the Scene Number, Int/Ext, Set, Day/Night, Synopsis, and Location. Each Breakdown Sheet (usually) corresponds to a single scene. For scheduling purposes, eighths of a page are used to measure the scene. An eighth of a page should not be confused with the timing in minutes and seconds.
TIP: Typically, when formatted correctly, one page of script should equate to approximately one minute of screen time, but this will depend on the content of the scene.

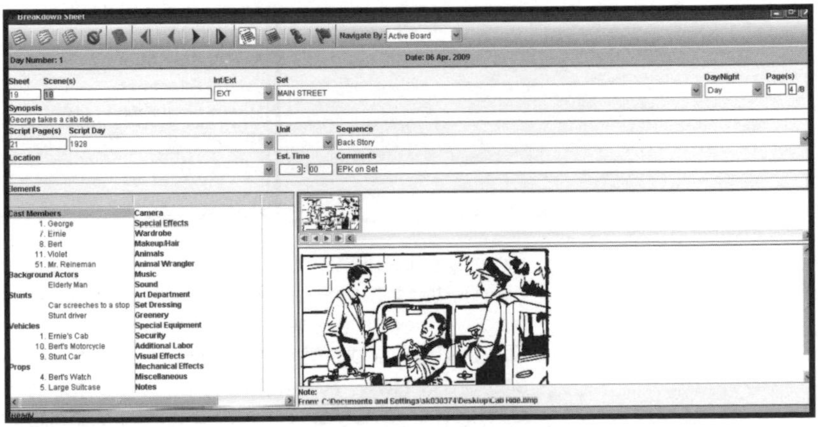

Categories and Elements

The bottom half of the Breakdown Sheet contains Elements divided into Categories, such as Cast Members, Props, and Scenery. The **Category Manager** lists all the categories that have been created in the Schedule. The Category Manager is available from the top **Design Menu**.

Elements are highlighted in the script using a color-coding system and can be inserted into any of the categories shown on the Breakdown Screen. To quickly enter an element from the breakdown sheet, click on the **Element Quick Entry** icon, choose the category, typing in the name of the element and press **New**. Alternatively, when the focus is on the Categories press **CTRL 1 +** or **CMD + I** and a cursor will appear. Start typing and the list filter will update automatically. Highlight the element using the up and down arrows and press **Enter** to confirm.

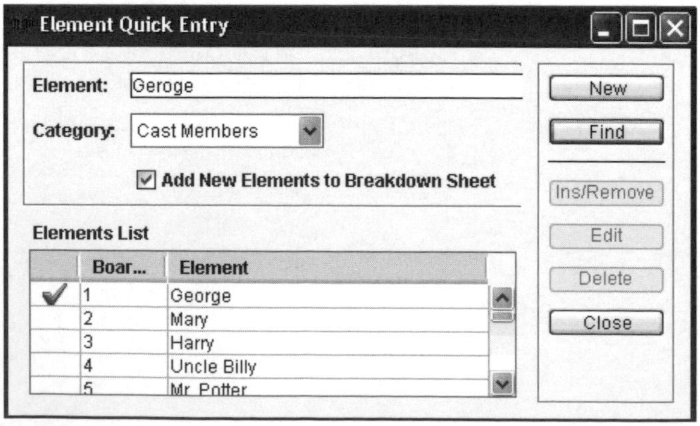

The Element Manager offers a convenient method to view, edit, and manage the Elements. To access the Element Manager go to **Breakdown** and select **Element Manager**. Each Element is listed with its Board ID, Name, and Number of Occurrences in the schedule. Elements can be numbered, re-numbered, or ordered. Elements can also be linked. For instance, if a cast member always appears on screen with a dog and a book, they can be linked to ensure they are always scheduled together. When the cast member (Anchor Element) is inserted next time, the dog and the book (Linked Elements) are automatically inserted.

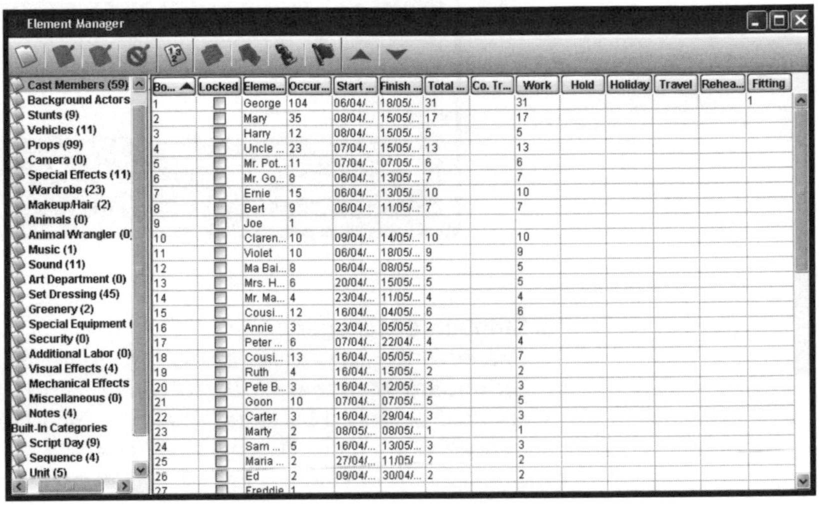

Storyboard Images

Storyboards and other Images can be added to the Breakdown Sheet to help create a visual image of the Scene. **Double-clicking** on the blank area of the **Image Pane** on the Breakdown Sheet will launch the Image Manager. To add an image click on the **Add Image** button on the top left of the screen, browse to the image on your computer and click **Open**.

Stripboard

The Stripboard provides an overview of the Schedule and a summary of Scenes and activities for any given day. The Movie Magic Scheduling Stripboard has a similar look and feel to a traditional Stripboard. Each strip corresponds to one Breakdown Sheet and can be dragged and dropped with the cursor. To view the strip board click on the **Board** button on the Main Toolbar, select **Stripboard** from the top **Schedule Menu** or use the shortcut **CTRL + U** or **CMD + U**.

TIP: Strip colors can be changed by using the **Strip Colors** option in the **Design** Menu.

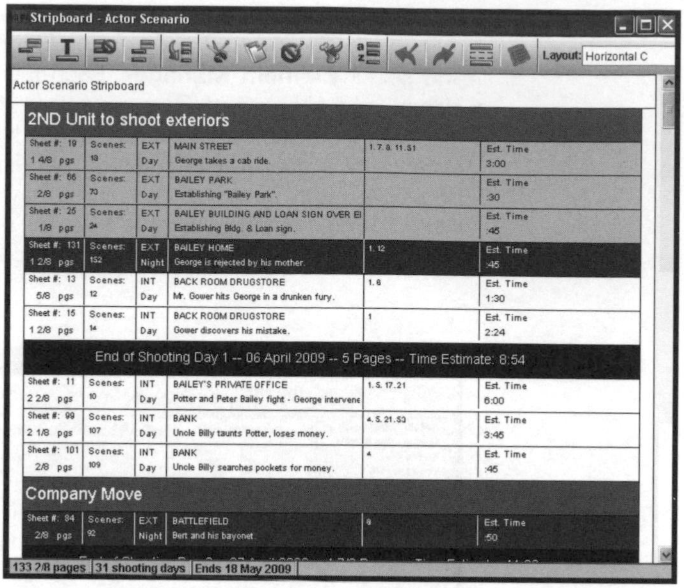

Stripboard Manager

To access the Stripboard Manager go to the **Schedule Menu** and select **Stripboard Manager**. A default Stripboard is available in the Schedule, and can be edited by selecting and clicking the **Edit Stripboard** button to change the name or associated calendar. Multiple Stripboards can be created to allow planning for different shooting scenarios.

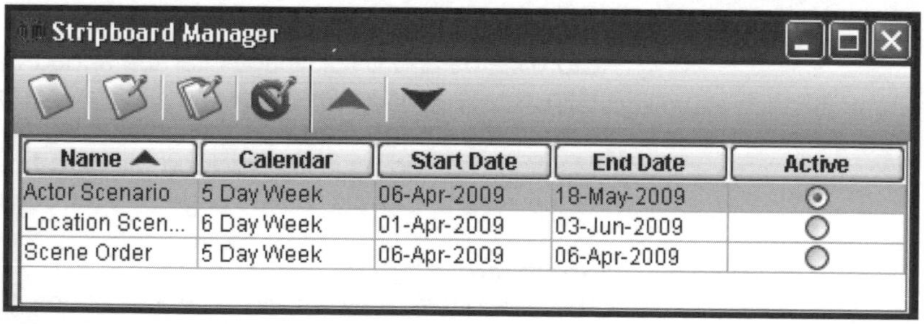

Boneyard

Unscheduled strips can be found in the Boneyard. The Boneyard is opened in a separate window by clicking on the **Show Boneyard** button at the top of the Stripboard window or using the shortcut **CTRL + SHIFT + U** or **CMD + SHIFT + U**. This makes it easy to drag-and-drop Strips between the Boneyard and the Stripboard. Each Stripboard has its own Boneyard.

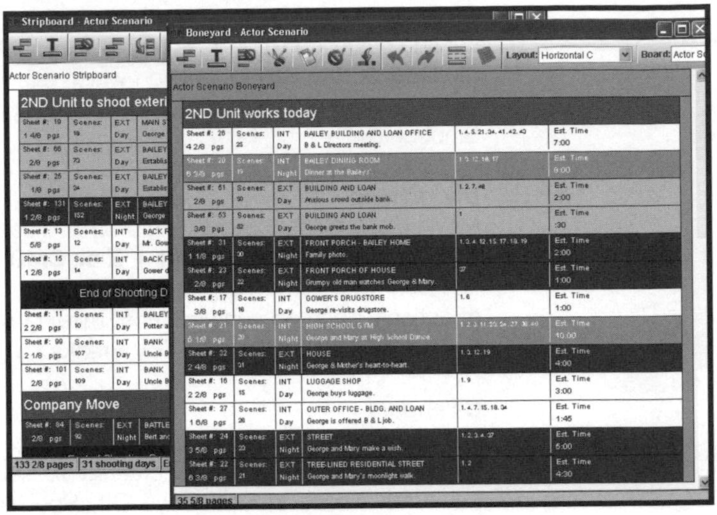

Scheduling a Day Break

Day Breaks highlight the end of a production day, making the stripboard easier to read. They are also essential as, without them, some reports cannot be generated. They can be added automatically using the **Auto Day Breaks** feature which will ensure that a specified maximum number of pages per day is not exceeded. They can also be added manually using the Insert Day Break option or the keyboard shortcut **CTRL +, or CMD + SHIFT +**.

Scheduling a Banner

Banners can be used to add narrative anywhere in the schedule by clicking on the **Insert Banner** button or by using the shortcut **CTRL + B or CMD + B**. They can be added at the beginning of the day to show additional information or used to highlight travel or rehearsal days.

Sorting and Ordering Strips

By clicking on the **Sort** button at the top of the Stripboard window or by using the keyboard shortcut **CTRL + T or CMD + T**S trips can be sorted by a range of fields including Set, Location, Unit, or Day/Night.

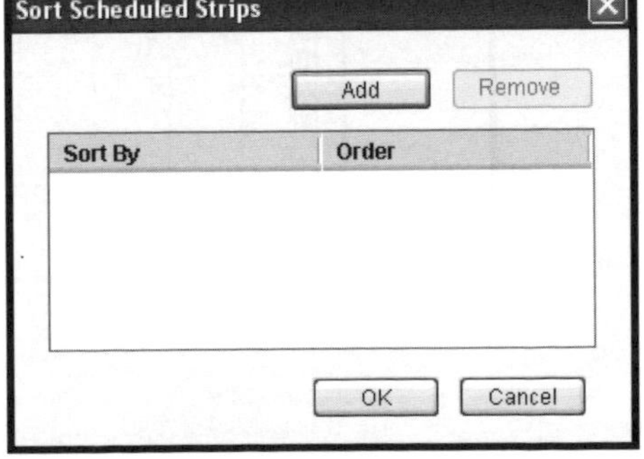

Strips can also be ordered and re-ordered by dragging-and-dropping, using cut and paste (**CTRL + X, CTRL + V or CMD + X, CMD + V**) or by using the **Reordering Strips** function which allows strips to be placed in a new order by typing the Sheet Numbers in the order they are to appear on the Stripboard.

Undo/Redo

Movie Magic Scheduling allows unlimited use of Undo (**CTRL + Z or CMD + Z**) and Redo (**CTRL + Shift + Z or CMD + Shift + Z**) in the Stripboard and Boneyard up until the last **Save** action. This will undo or redo a number of actions, such as cutting strips, moving strips, sorting strips, modifying text on a Banner, or moving Day Breaks.

Calendars

The **Calendar Manager** is available from the **Schedule Menu** and is where Calendars can be created to set the date parameters of the Schedule. These include Days Off, Special Days (such as Holiday and Travel), and Production Dates (such as the Start and End of Production). Multiple Calendars can be created and individually applied to specific Stripboards for different scenarios.

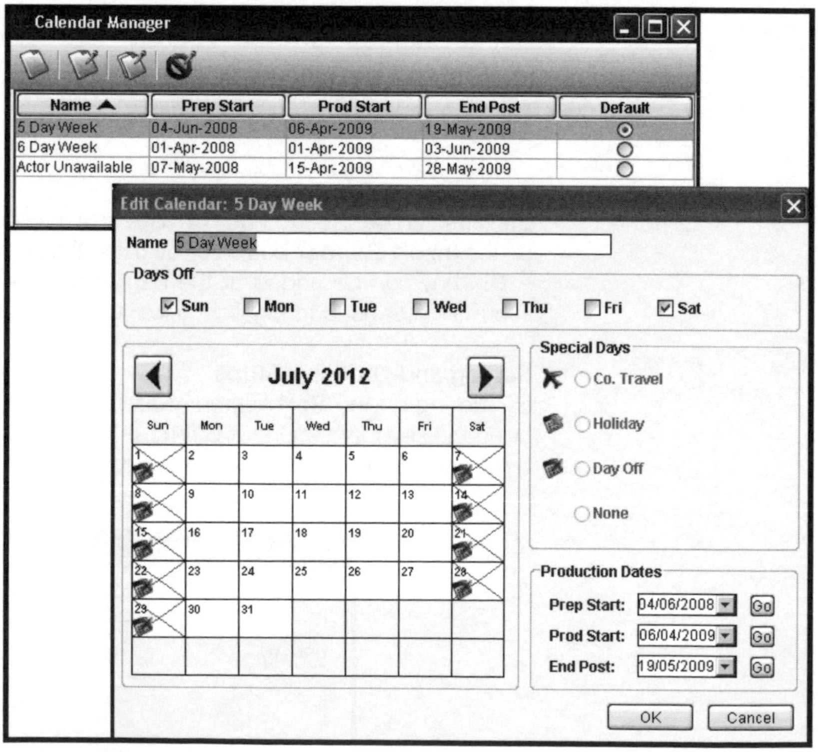

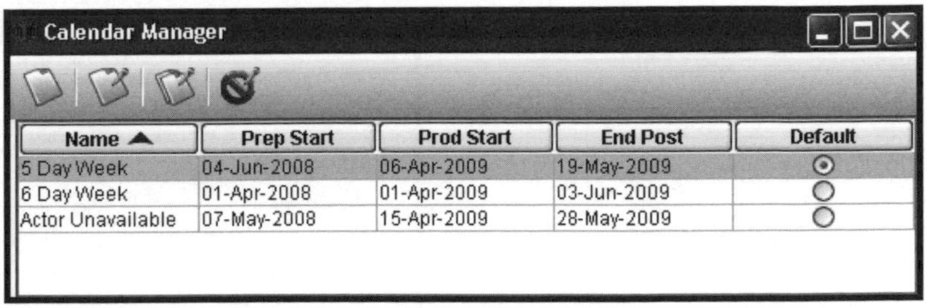

Red Flags

Warnings can be added to avoid Scheduling conflicts. To enter a Red Flag click the **Red Flag** button on the Breakdown Sheet, shortcut **CTRL + K or CMD + K**, and select the Element(s) that the Red Flag should be attached to. Next, select the date(s) that the Red Flag should cover. Finally, select a Red Flag Category. Additional categories can be added by clicking the **Red Flag Manager** button in the bottom left-hand corner of the window or from the **Schedule Menu**.

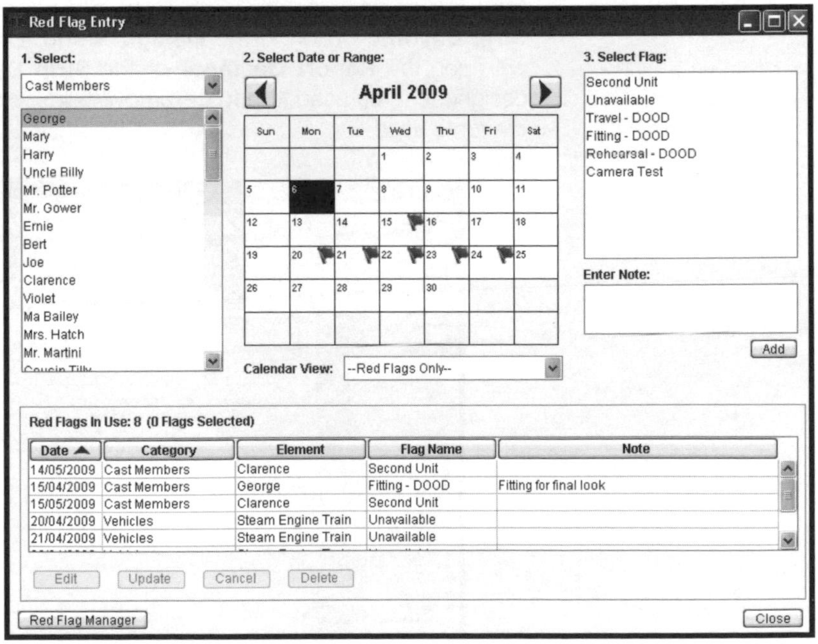

Reports

Reports can be generated from any stage of the scheduling process by selecting **Print / View** from the **File Menu**, or clicking on the Print button in the top toolbar. A number of Report formats are provided, making it quick and easy to get started. All reports are grouped by Strips, Reports, Images, and Day out of Days with optional settings available for each.

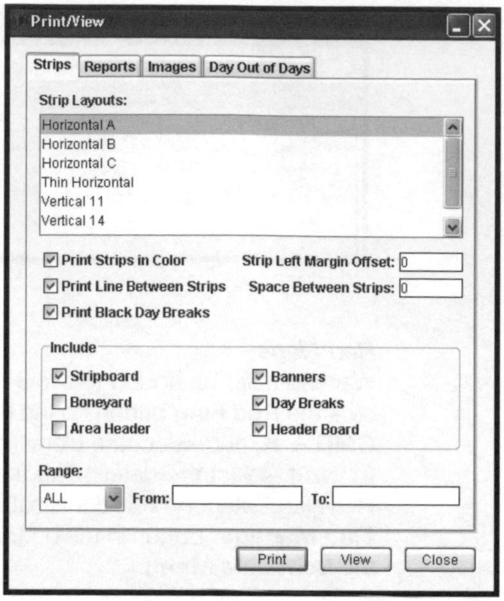

New layouts can also be designed by clicking on the **Report Layouts** or **Strip Layouts** option in the **Design Menu**. Double clicking on a layout will open the **Report Designer** or the **Strip Designer** respectively. The designer can be used to add or remove fields, change the layout or modify the fonts used.

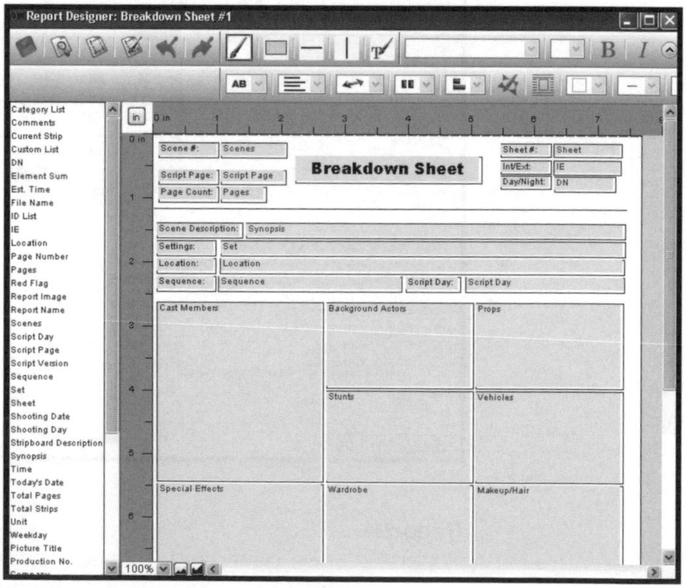

Reports can be resized when printing or viewing by selecting **Print / View** from the **File Menu**, choosing a report and clicking **View**. In the upper right—hand corner of the window there is a slide bar and drop down menu to scale either the **Contents** or the **Page**.

Movie Magic Budgeting

Movie Magic Budgeting is an innovative budgeting and cost-estimation tool used by production professionals all around the world. It allows simple or complex film and television production budgets to be created with ease and accuracy.

There are four major steps to budgeting in Movie Magic Budgeting. First, a broad category of accounts is created in the Topsheet. Second, accounts are added to the Accounts Level. Next, the Budget Preferences and tables are defined (i.e. Units, Globals, Groups, Fringes, Locations, Sets, Currencies). Finally, amounts can be entered into the Details Level, applying the Fringes, Globals, Groups, and other properties as necessary with reference to 4th Level worksheets if required.

TIP: Even with a broken down schedule the script should always be read carefully before budgeting as, for example, a "village in flames" can be created using different VFX and SFX techniques.

Navigating the Budget

Movie Magic Budgeting offers intuitive navigation with a combination of easy-to-use toolbars, tabs, and menus. The **Movie Magic Budgeting Toolbar** offers access to all major features of the program and it also allows easy navigation between budget levels. Budget levels can be navigated using the **Navigation Ball**, clicking on the corresponding Toolbar icon or by entering an Account number and clicking on the **Go** button. Keyboard shortcut keys are also available throughout the application used in combination with the Control (CTRL) key in Windows® or the Command (CMD) key on a Mac®.

Getting Started

To create a blank Budget, select **Create Blank Budget** from the **File Menu.** To create a new Budget from a template, select **New Budget** from the **File Menu** or use the shortcut **CTRL + N** or **CMD + N**. A range of budget templates are provided. Multiple Budgets can be opened and viewed in separate windows within the application.

TIP: To track Budget and Revision select **Budget Info ...** from the **File Menu**.

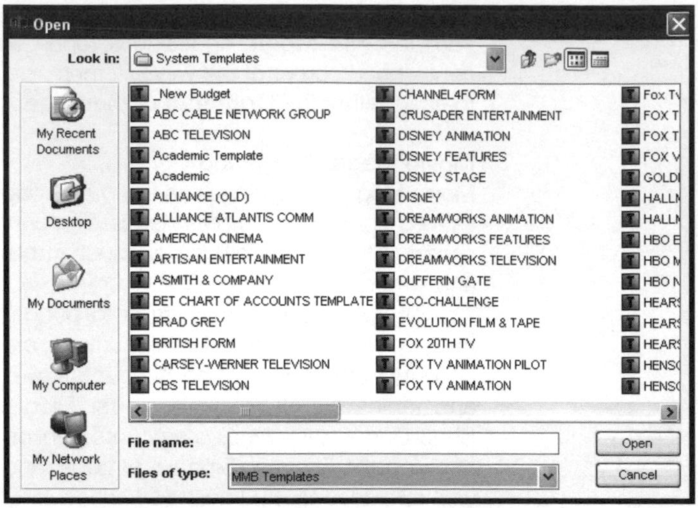

Topsheet

The Budget Topsheet provides a summary of the Budget. To navigate to the Topsheet click on the button labeled **T** in the Toolbar, select **Topsheet** from the **Go to Menu** or use the **Navigation Ball Up Arrow**. Category names (or major Account names) of a Budget, such as Art Direction, Set Construction, and Production Staff as well as their Account Numbers are entered in the Topsheet. New Categories can be added by selecting **Insert Row** from the **Edit Menu** or by using the keyboard shortcut **CTRL + I** or **CMD + I**. With the exception of Contractual Charges and Applied Credits, monetary amounts are not entered on the Topsheet, they are entered in the Details Level.

Right-clicking (**CTRL + click** on the Mac®) on the green bar on the Topsheet allows Original & Variance Columns to be shown or hidden, Fringe Total Columns to be shown or hidden and Original Column Totals to be updated in order to track changes to the budget. Above the Topsheet, Session and Change Totals are also shown along with the Budget Total.

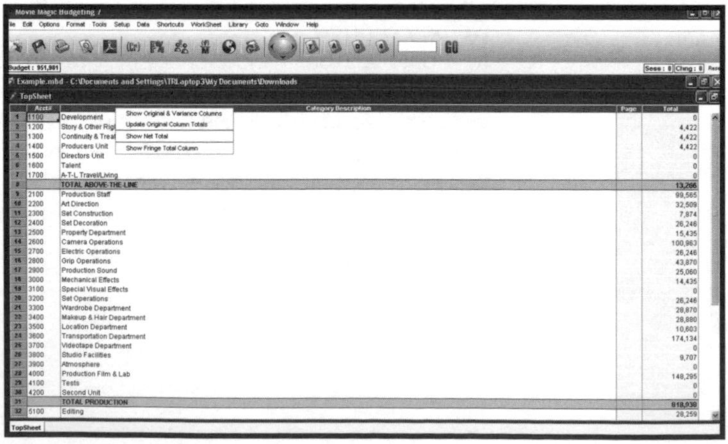

Production Totals

Production Totals can be added to the Topsheet by selecting the Category row above where the Production Total row is to be inserted. Go to **Edit** and select **Insert Production Total**. A Level Break, titled "*Untitled Production Total*," will be displayed above the selected row.

Contractual Charges

Contractual Charges are entered as a flat rate or a percentage by selecting **Insert Contractual Charge** from the **Edit Menu**. Examples include Contingency, Bond Fees, and Insurance Charges. Specific Budget amounts can be excluded from the calculation by value or by Group. For example copyright fees do not typically need insurance or bonding. Contractual Charges are usually placed on the after, the last Level Break and before the Budget Grand Total. They can be assigned an Account Number.

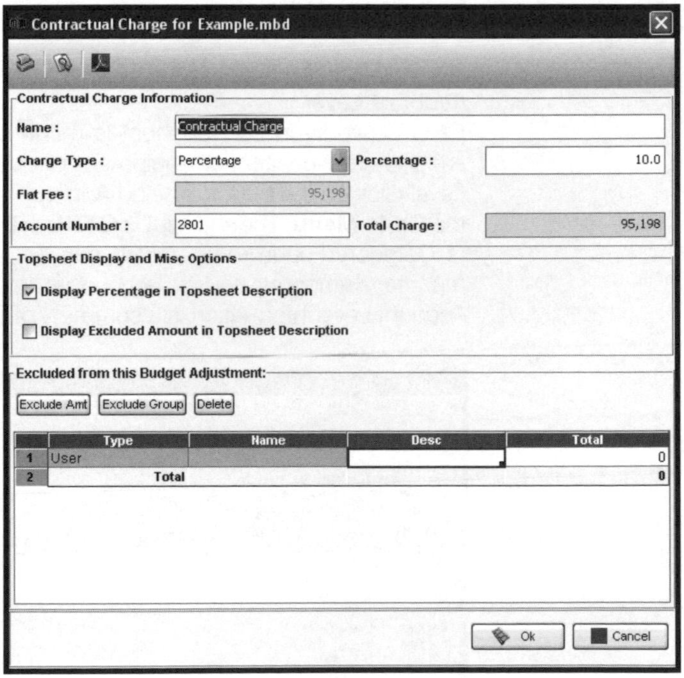

Applied Credits

The Applied Credit tool helps track production incentives applied against a Budget. Go to **Edit** and select **Insert Applied Credit** to add an Applied Credit below the Grand Total. A Net Total will appear to reflect the Budget total after the credits. Depending on shooting location, different credits may apply to different lines of detail. Using Groups to specify these items allows complex credits to be applied.

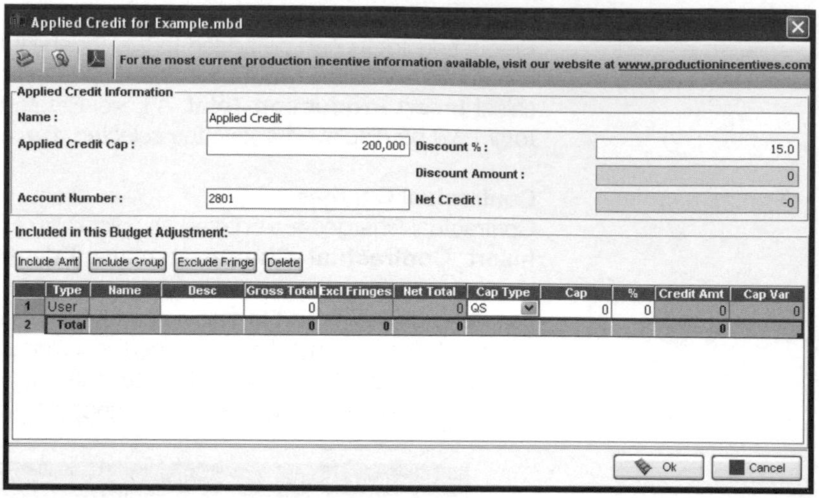

Account Level

Each Category in the Topsheet is made up of Accounts, for example, a specific crew position or equipment package. To navigate to the Account Level click on the button labeled **A** in the Toolbar or select **Accounts** from the **Go to Menu**. The shortcut is **CTRL + E** or **CMD + E** with the exception of Category Fringe rows, which can be setup in **Budget Preferences**, monetary amounts and other budget information are not entered here. Account Level information is a summary of data entered at the Details Level.

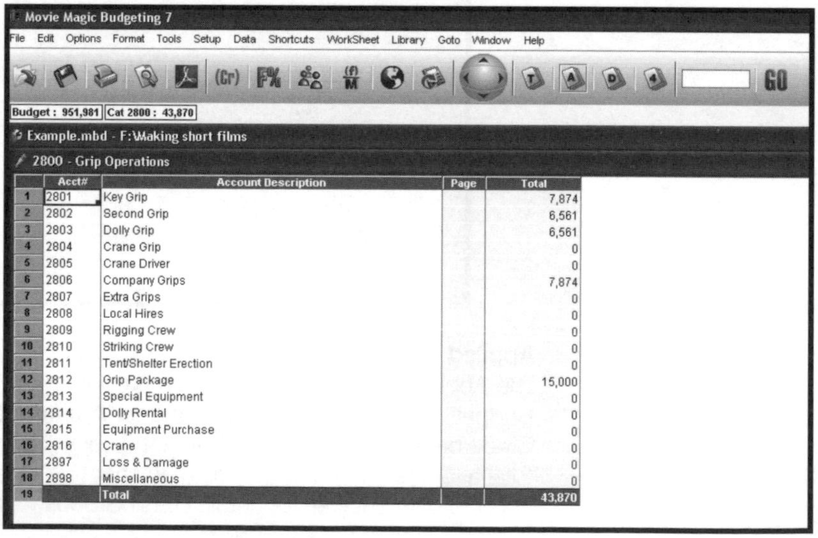

Budget Setup

The following options are available from the **Setup Menu**, allowing the behavior, structure, and presentation of the Budget to be controlled. To avoid having to repeat the setup process, a Budget Template can be saved by selecting **Make Template** from the **File Menu**. New Budgets can then be created using the Template.

Budget Preferences

Budget Preferences can be set by selecting **Budget Preferences** from the **Setup Menu**. Options are grouped into six sections: General Properties, Fringe, Detail Level, Currency, Totals, Account Format, and Optional Columns.

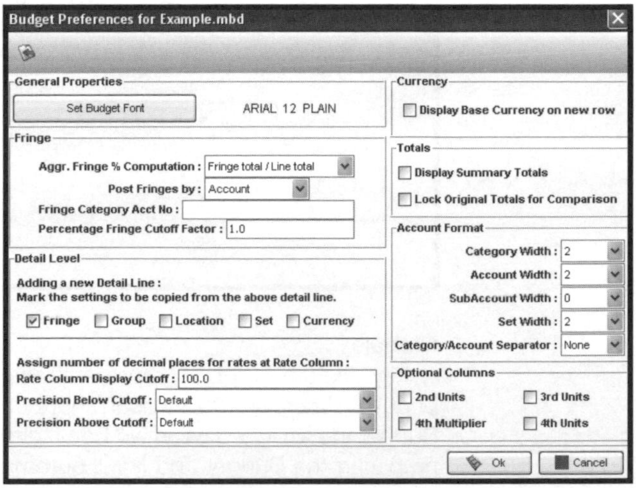

Captions

Captions are budget labels, such as **Category Description**, **Total**, **Groups**, or **Set**. Movie Magic Budgeting allows these captions to be replaced with alternative text which can be especially helpful if budgeting in another language.

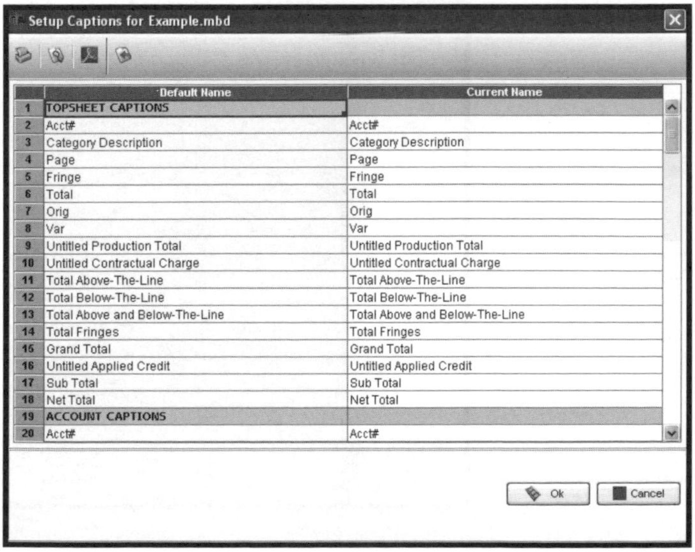

Currencies

The default currency is the US Dollar, but any currency can be used to calculate the Budget. Add the currencies to be used in budgeting into the Currency table. They can be applied in the Dedicated Currency Column at the Details Level of a budget. To setup Currencies the keyboard shortcut is **CTRL + 6** or **CMD + 6**.

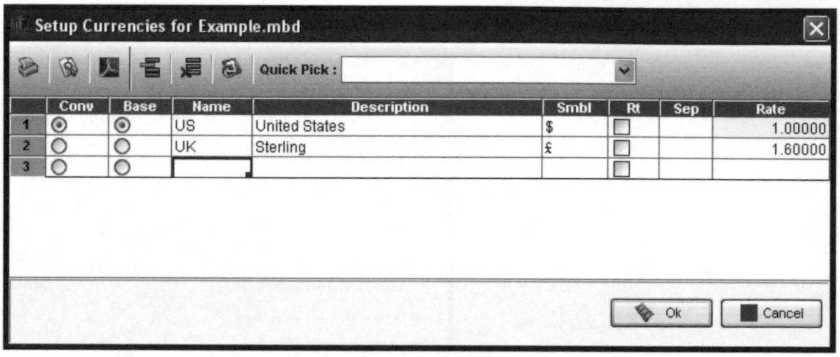

	Conv	Base	Name	Description	Smbl	Rt	Sep	Rate
1	⦿	⦿	US	United States	$	☐		1.00000
2	○	○	UK	Sterling	£	☐		1.60000
3	○	○				☐		

Globals

A key feature, Globals represent assigned values used throughout a budget. Wherever the Global shortcut letter or code is entered into a Budget the assigned value will be displayed. Change the Global value while preparing the Budget and it will automatically update throughout. Globals are assigned to Global Groups for quick reference. To setup Globals the keyboard shortcut is **CTRL + G** or **CMD + G**.

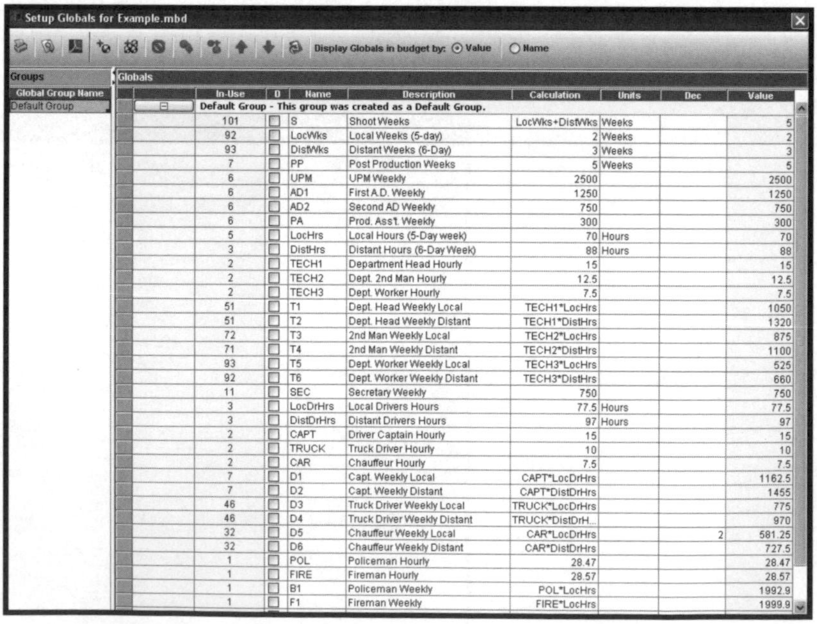

In-Use	D	Name	Description	Calculation	Units	Dec	Value
Default Group - This group was created as a Default Group.							
101	☐	S	Shoot Weeks	LocWks+DistWks	Weeks		5
92	☐	LocWks	Local Weeks (5-day)	2	Weeks		2
93	☐	DistWks	Distant Weeks (6-Day)	3	Weeks		3
7	☐	PP	Post Production Weeks	5	Weeks		5
6	☐	UPM	UPM Weekly	2500			2500
6	☐	AD1	First A.D. Weekly	1250			1250
6	☐	AD2	Second AD Weekly	750			750
6	☐	PA	Prod. Ass't. Weekly	300			300
5	☐	LocHrs	Local Hours (5-Day week)	70	Hours		70
3	☐	DistHrs	Distant Hours (6-Day Week)	88	Hours		88
2	☐	TECH1	Department Head Hourly	15			15
2	☐	TECH2	Dept. 2nd Man Hourly	12.5			12.5
2	☐	TECH3	Dept. Worker Hourly	7.5			7.5
51	☐	T1	Dept. Head Weekly Local	TECH1*LocHrs			1050
51	☐	T2	Dept. Head Weekly Distant	TECH1*DistHrs			1320
72	☐	T3	2nd Man Weekly Local	TECH2*LocHrs			875
71	☐	T4	2nd Man Weekly Distant	TECH2*DistHrs			1100
93	☐	T5	Dept. Worker Weekly Local	TECH3*LocHrs			525
92	☐	T6	Dept. Worker Weekly Distant	TECH3*DistHrs			660
11	☐	SEC	Secretary Weekly	750			750
3	☐	LocDrHrs	Local Drivers Hours	77.5	Hours		77.5
3	☐	DistDrHrs	Distant Drivers Hours	97	Hours		97
2	☐	CAPT	Driver Captain Hourly	15			15
2	☐	TRUCK	Truck Driver Hourly	10			10
2	☐	CAR	Chauffeur Hourly	7.5			7.5
7	☐	D1	Capt. Weekly Local	CAPT*LocDrHrs			1162.5
7	☐	D2	Capt. Weekly Distant	CAPT*DistDrHrs			1455
46	☐	D3	Truck Driver Weekly Local	TRUCK*LocDrHrs			775
46	☐	D4	Truck Driver Weekly Distant	TRUCK*DistDrH...			970
32	☐	D5	Chauffeur Weekly Local	CAR*LocDrHrs		2	581.25
32	☐	D6	Chauffeur Weekly Distant	CAR*DistDrHrs			727.5
1	☐	POL	Policeman Hourly	28.47			28.47
1	☐	FIRE	Fireman Hourly	28.57			28.57
1	☐	B1	Policeman Weekly	POL*LocHrs			1992.9
1	☐	F1	Fireman Weekly	FIRE*LocHrs			1999.9

Fringes

Fringes are additional charges for a contracted price of a budgeted item. Typical Fringes include payroll taxes, such as FICA, FUI, SUI, and Workers' Compensation in the United States or Social Security contributions, such as National Insurance, in the United Kingdom. As with Globals, if changes need to be made to a Fringe, edit the Fringe table and changes will automatically occur throughout. To setup Fringes the keyboard shortcut is **CTRL + 3** or **CMD + 3**.

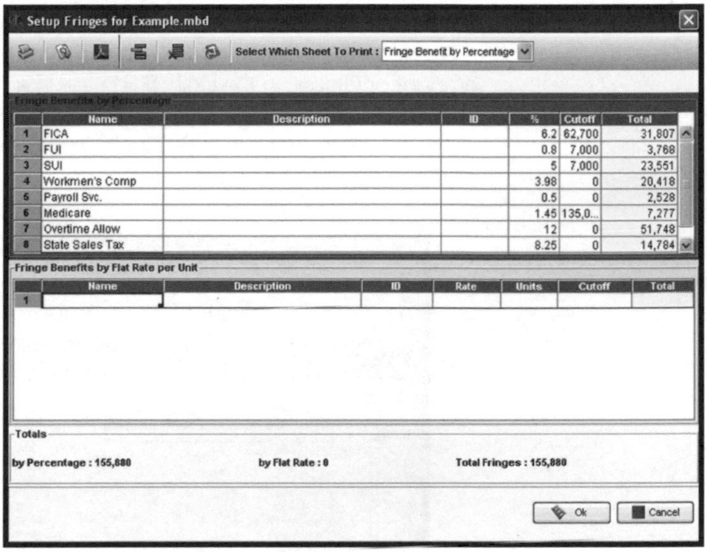

Groups

Grouping lines of Detail allows for including or excluding them collectively from a Budget, without actually deleting anything. This is useful for budget comparisons in *"what-if"* scenarios. A number of settings exist that control the Budget calculation of non-grouped detail lines, whether or not to show Fringe amounts in Group Totals and how to handle Group status conflicts where an item of detail is included in two groups and only one is included. To add or update an existing Group use the keyboard shortcut **CTRL + 4** or **CMD + 4**.

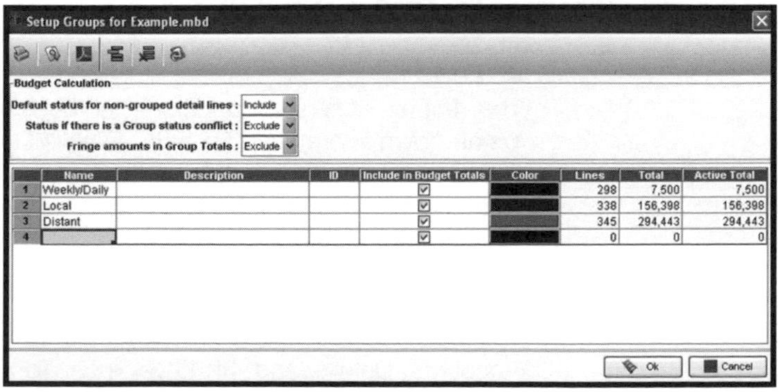

Locations & Sets

Locations and Sets can be added to the Budget in order to help analyze costs in more detail. To setup Locations use the keyboard shortcut **CTRL + 5** or **CMD + 5**, for Sets use **CTRL + 8** or **CMD + 8**.

Details Level

The Details Level is where monetary values are entered. To navigate to the Details Level click on the button labeled **D** in the Toolbar or select **Details** from the **Go to Menu**. The keyboard shortcut is **CTRL 1 K** or **CMD 1 K**. To enter data Tab to or click between fields. In a blank Description field type in a Name or Description of the expense. In the Amount field, type a number amount or Global. In the Units field type in a Unit or Unit shortcut. (If a Global is used, this is unnecessary.) In the next field, X (quantity),enter the quantity of the line item (default is 1). Finally in the Rates field enter the Detail Rate, or use a Global once again.

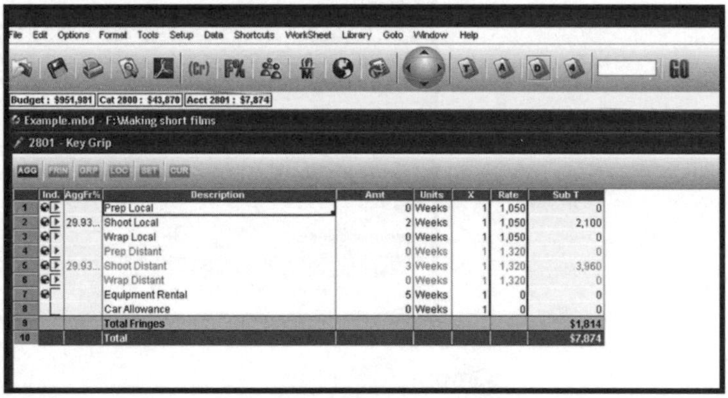

Import from Movie Magic Scheduling

Information exported from Movie Magic Scheduling, such as lists of characters and number of action vehicles, can be imported into lines of Detail in the Budget using the Library Manager. First select a row at the Details Level, then select **Show Library Manager** from the **Library Menu** and click on Insert Data.

TIP: To copy and paste into the same level, i.e. from Topsheet to Topsheet, of the same, or a second Budget use the shortcuts **CTRL + C and CTRL + V** or **CMD + C and CMD + V**.

4th Level

The 4th Level offers an additional spreadsheet-style application to further break down information from the Details Level. The 4th Level data can be linked to corresponding data on the Details Level. The linkable data ensures that changes made to 4th Level data will be updated wherever they occur throughout the budget.

Budget Notes

The Note Tool allows short messages to be attached to individual Topsheet, Accounts, Details, and 4th Level lines. To attach a Note select a line and go to the **Data Menu**, select **Note**. Alternatively **right-click** (Mac: **CMD 1 click**) on highlighted row and select **Note**. The Note window will open. Type the Note directly into the window. Select the **Include in Print Report** box to include the current Note when printing a budget report. Any budget lines with attached Notes are indicated with a red pin icon to the right of each line. *TIP*: To add a new line to a Note, type Alt-Enter.

Sub-Budgets

The Create Sub Budget feature is a quick and easy method to see a new Budget version without affecting an original Budget. Go to **File** and select **Create Sub Budget . . .** By filtering, it is possible to choose what is included in a Sub Budget. For example, a Budget may be viewed by isolating a specific Currency or Location cost without altering the original Budget.

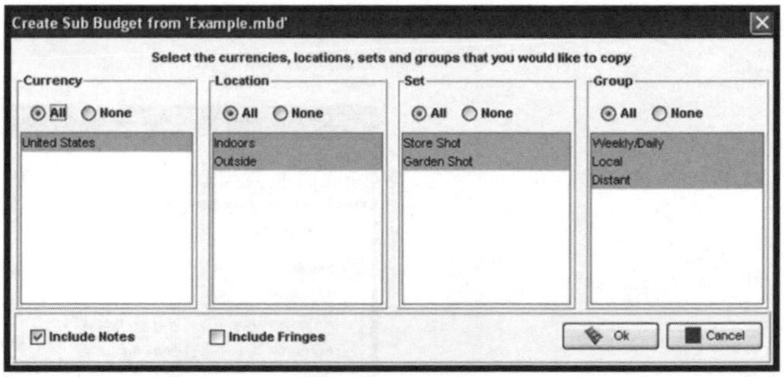

Budget Comparison

To compare several different Budgets at once go to **File** and select **Budget Comparison**. The Create Budget Comparison Report window will open. Select a number of Budgets to compare and click on the **Add** button. Select the type of report with which the Budget Comparison is to be generated; Variance, Average, or Both. Next, select how the Budget Comparison report is to be viewed: All Accounts, Topsheet, or by specified Account. Finally, click **OK** to generate the report.
TIP: Budgets can also be compared against Vista Accounting Cost Reports (*.vis) at the Accounts Level.

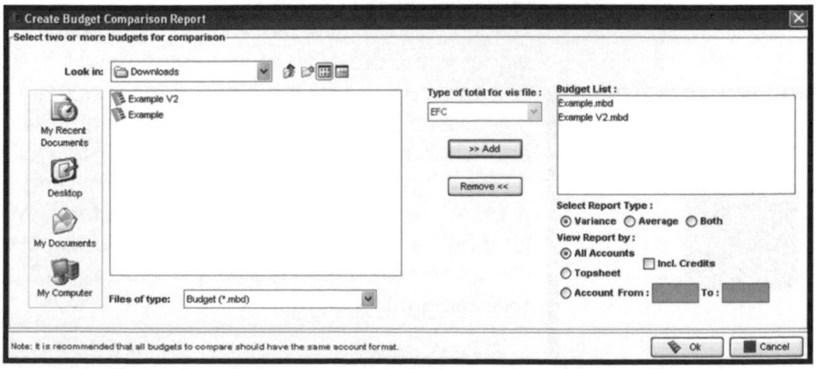

Reports

Movie Magic Budgeting provides a range of specific reports, from the Topsheet and tables to the columns in the Details Level. Once the Budget has been entered, the layout and settings for the Budget Report can be set by going to **File** and selecting **Print Setup**.

The **Print Selection** tab allows information shown on the report to be defined, including Budget Levels, Setup tables and Budget Information. The Account Range can also be specified. The **Print Settings** tab allows additional columns from the Details Level to be shown and other formatting to be set. To update the Budget Header or Footer, click the **Edit Header/Footer** button and select the text to edit by choosing either **Topsheet Only** or **Report**.

To print, click on the Print icon. Alternatively reports can be previewed or saved as a .PDF file to share electronically.

TIP: If printing by Account Range, the Print Account option will revert to the All default setting once the Print Setup window is closed and reopened again.

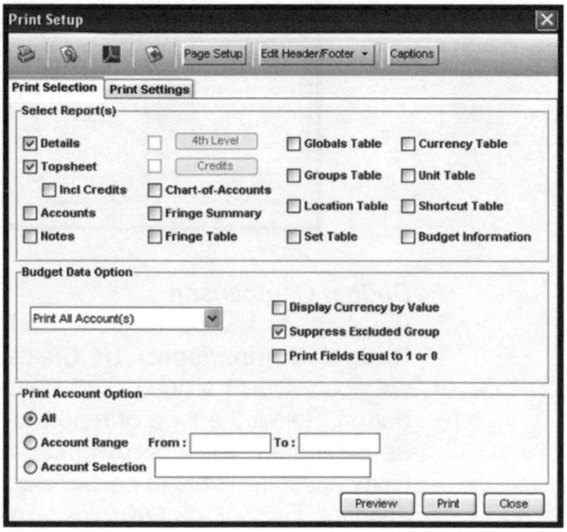

About the author

Laurence Sargent is a Director of Sargent-Disc, the European distributor of Movie Magic Budgeting and Movie Magic Scheduling. Founded in 1986, Sargent-Disc is affiliated with Entertainment Partners and is the market leader in the provision of integrated payroll and residuals, accounting and software services for the entertainment industry in the UK.

Based at Pinewood Studios, Sargent-Disc offers Movie Magic training and support throughout Europe. Clients include the major Hollywood studios, broadcasters, independent film and television producers, and a broad range of clients within the entertainment industry. Sargent-Disc supports a range of organizations including Women in Film and TV, The Production Guild, and is also an official BAFTA partner.

www.sargent-disc.com

STOP

PART

VIII

TITLE

The film buff

START

CHAPTER 29

Careers

So, you want to be in the movies?

Making a short film could be the first step. A short that gets noticed may fund the next short, festival awards, a feature, fame, and a first-class ticket to Hollywood. That is the goal of many who set out on this path but, like baby turtles scurrying out to sea, the odds are tough, only one in a thousand returns to their place of birth to breed as fully grown turtles. You have to be determined, conscientious, you have to go the extra mile; you need bundles of talent; you have to know movies like a GP knows how to treat his patients, classics as well as new trends and innovations; film language, film news. And like the surviving turtles, you need to be lucky.

The media, filmmaking in particular, is the most popular and sought after career path in the world today. Students dream of being film directors and news readers. But these jobs are at the tip of an iceberg consisting of all the other crafts in the many behind-the-scenes departments. If you do want a career in film, you have to be realistic about what it is you personally can do. Do you have the mind-set, flair and creative energy to be a director? Or are you methodical, good with numbers, and organization? More a producer? Would you be happy spending several hours a day fretting over the turning points, conflicts, reversals and beats of a 10-minute screenplay? That's the writer's job—and many successful screenwriters dream of being directors. Are you more comfortable with the kit than the cast? Because there are fulfilling careers to be had in the camera department, the editing suites and sound studios, in set design, costume, and make-up.

Many producers begin their careers as the lowly runner and, on a short film, the runner gets to know exactly what is done in each department and how those departments interact. On a well-planned film, nothing is left to chance. The dress the leading lady wears will be chosen by the wardrobe mistress in consultation with the art director's sketches for the sets and will need to be costed by the line-producer and approved by the director—while, incidentally, the director is busy drawing storyboards (with an artist or with his own pen), creating a shot list with the DP and discussing locations with the location manager, if he's lucky enough to have one.

Where do you fit in this intricate puzzle?

By getting involved in filmmaking at any level and learning as much as you can about the different career paths, you are more likely to find where your talent lies and where you should focus your energy and training in order to reach your goal. What distinguishes film crews from professionals in most other occupations is their total commitment to the cause. Making a film, even a short film, is like a battle, an addiction, a race—against time, the weather, the bank balance. People don't take a day off because they might have a cold coming, or someone's scheduled to repair the roof. They take flu remedies and let the roof leak. Like the good doctor, film is a vocation, a calling—and if you hear the call you are called for life.

Flip forward to Chapter 31: A Brief History of Short Films, to see that none of the film pioneers had formal training. The Lumière Brothers, William Kennedy-Laurie Dickson, and Georges Méliès developed their own equipment, devised stories suitable for the new medium and improved their skill base by making films. Life in the digital era is much easier. Most universities and colleges across the world offer film and media courses with knowledgeable tutors and loads of gear to play with. It seems like a soft option, watching movies and discussing the merits of different directors. But the soft option, conversely, requires greater tenacity, commitment and involvement in the process.

If a group of friends or students are making a film and you get the chance to take part, then do so, do anything. The next generation of filmmakers will be those who work as runners whenever the opportunity arises, the people who offer to carry the gear, stand in the rain holding light stands, help clean up a location and return home, flip a DVD in the laptop and study the last short they worked on.

Some 50,000 people in the UK are regularly employed in film and television production. In the United States the number is about ten times that figure and, across the world, those numbers will grow. Runners graduate to being third-assistant directors, assistant editors, focus pullers, clapper loaders. With the constantly changing technology, directors, DPs, even producers and writers need to be multi-skilled in order to be able to communicate fully with the other departments. The process is accumulative. The more you know, the more you can do, the more you have to offer—and the more you extend your network of contacts. If you are certain that film is your calling but are unsure of your career options, there is a list of job profiles at uknetguide: www.uknetguide.co.uk.

INTERNSHIPS

Internships are a good way to get your foot in the door, but there are unscrupulous companies that take on students and young filmmakers to do work that has nothing to do with film production—filing, answering phones, sorting newspaper clippings, delivering packages, collecting coffee.

People will take on these jobs at no pay because they hope it will look good on their CV and lead to paid employment. Perhaps it will. But do be aware of exactly what you are expected to do as an intern and what you may learn. If you do take on a job and there is a possibility to get out on location with the crew, work doubly hard until you get the chance.

As always, the web is a good place to search for relevant internships: www.InternMatch.com lists hundreds of openings by state, and says: "Internships in film help you secure connections within the industry that could be used for networking later on in your career. Any directors or producers you work with who are impressed by your talent will either recommend you, or be willing to work with you again. You may even get the chance to work with your favorite director or see one of your favorite actors at work! Though your best bets will be in Los Angeles or New York, opportunities can be found in any state."

Most media companies offer a variety of internships, so it's worth checking their sites. More general places to start include: www.internships.com and www.summerinternships.com.

PAUSE

THE TRUE FILMMAKERS' GUIDE

What true filmmakers have in common can be summed up in four words: Passion. Focus. Commitment. Resiliency.

Talent, perhaps, too. But you'll never really know if you have talent without the other four. Despite the common view that talent is either in you or not, I've seen the work of a lot of filmmakers mature in ways I never would have imagined through their passion, focus, commitment, and resiliency.

True filmmakers are obsessively creative people who constantly find ways to feed their creativity, even if it has nothing to do with filmmaking. All make their films without regard for their commercial potential, nor their own career aspirations, nor how the film will, in any other way, "pay off"—even though many of those thoughts take center stage when their films are complete and in major festivals.

True filmmakers make their film by hook or by crook, some having all the money and resources practically handed to them while others take years and use every trick in the book to push their film to completion.

Having a life as a filmmaker is not dependent on having a career as a filmmaker. Few will have a career as a filmmaker, but nearly all of us can build a life as a filmmaker. And if a career is your goal, it will not come to you unless you have committed to a life as a filmmaker. That is, if you are not passionate, focused, committed, and resilient.

Jacques Thelemaque, Withoutabox—www.withoutabox.com

ON THE GRAPEVINE

Students graduating from film and media courses will be made aware of their options by tutors and contemporaries—the grapevine is alive and well in the film industry. For those people with an inclination to pick up a camera and go out and shoot guerrilla style, a wide variety of courses and workshops can be found in just about every major city—hit the Internet, go to the library, telephone the film officer on the local council. Courses may be one-day events; writing a horror movie; directing actors; film festival survival; or night classes spread over several weeks where you may learn the basics in shooting, directing, and editing a short film. At the very least, what these courses do is allow new filmmakers to be in a film environment and get their hands on the equipment.

As of 2012, the BFI (www.bfi.org.uk) directory lists over 6,000 media and multimedia courses in the UK, including film, television, video, radio, and web authoring courses. In the United States there are too many to count, and certainly too many to list here. In the next chapter we have included four interviews about film school, but to get started here is a list of the crème de la crème:

TOP FIVE FILM SCHOOLS AROUND THE WORLD

29.1 *Blue Velvet* (1986)

▶▶ P.382

1. American Film Institute (USA)

AFI's Center for Advanced Film and Television Studies offers a two-year program for students to specialize in areas that include directing, producing, and writing. Most students already have some industry experience, the average age being 27. One perk is the freedom to create a thesis film in the final year, with access to SAG members for their casts and $13,500 in financing.
TUITION: $38,416 for first year; $37,112 for second year (plus $8,033 for thesis).
DEGREES: MFA certificate.
NOTABLE ALUMNI: Terrence Malick (*The Tree of Life*), David Lynch (*Blue Velvet*), Darren Aronofsky (*Black Swan*).

29.2 *Avatar*

▶▶ P.382

2. University of Southern California (USA)

The richest film school in the world, with former student George Lucas donating $175 million alone, and more than 10,000 other alumni who donate millions towards great facilities. The Peter Stark Producing Program, under *The Graduate* producer Larry Turman, is the best place for aspiring producers and execs to truly understand the culture of filmmaking.
TUITION: $42,000 (plus room and board).
DEGREES: Critical studies, B.A., M.A., MFA and Ph.D. programs in everything from film and TV to animation and digital arts.
NOTABLE ALUMNI: George Lucas (*Star Wars*), Ron Howard (*A Beautiful Mind*), Jon Landau (*Avatar*).

29.3 *House of Flying Daggers* (2004)

▶▶ P.382

3. Beijing Film Academy (China)

China's elite school for film direction, production, and writing accepts just 500 students annually from 100,000 applications and is closely linked with the Beijing Film Studio. Directors Zhang Yimou and Chen Kaige learnt the ropes at this prestigious academy—the people responsible for creating some of the most distinct new wave of filmmaking of this generation.
TUITION: Program fees range from $1,240 to $1,550 for local students; international students pay $6,665 to $7,905 per year for film programs.
DEGREES: B.A., M.A. and Ph.D. programs in everything from performance and direction to cinematography and animation.
NOTABLE ALUMNI: Zhang Yimou (*House of Flying Daggers*), Chen Kaige (*Farewell My Concubine*), Tian Zhuangzhuang (*The Blue Kite*).

29.4 *No Country for Old Men* (2007)

P.382

4. New York University Tisch School of the Arts (USA)

New York has a different flavor to Hollywood, but provided a route to the top for artists including Martin Scorsese, Oliver Stone and *Breaking Bad* creator Vince Gilligan. Nowhere else could a class of just 12 students listen to James Franco teach how to turn a poem into a movie. Graduates also compete for a $200,000 prize to create a debut feature film. There is also a campus in Singapore.

TUITION: $45,674.

DEGREES: B.A., BFA, MFA, MPS, M.A. and Ph.D. degrees in moving-image archiving and preservation, performance studies and cinema studies.

NOTABLE ALUMNI: Todd Phillips (*The Hangover*), Joel Coen (*No Country for Old Men*), Charlie Kaufman (*Being John Malkovich*).

29.5 *The Godfather* (1972)

P.382

5. University of California Los Angeles (USA)

UCLA's School of Theater, Film and Television has a different vibe to its richer rival USC, with a multicultural campus, but still ranks among the best in California. Prestigious graduates including Francis Ford Coppola and Alexander Payne prove it has what it takes to foster genius, under the supervision of teachers including producer Peter Guber.

TUITION: B.A.: $12,842 (California resident), $35,720 (non-resident).

DEGREES: B.A., M.A., MFA and Ph.D.

NOTABLE ALUMNI: Francis Ford Coppola (*The Godfather*), Tim Robbins (*Dead Man Walking*), Alexander Payne (*Sideways*).[1]

STOP

29.1 A still from AFI Graduate David Lynch's *Blue Velvet* (1986)

29.2 *Avatar* is the highest-grossing movie of all time, co-produced by USC graduate Jon Landau

29.3 Beijing Film Academy's Zhang Yimou used strong colors in *House of Flying Daggers* (2004)

29.4 Tisch School graduate Joel Coen's *No Country for Old Men* (2007) won the Oscar for Best Picture

29.5 UCLA's Francis Ford Coppola created a masterpiece with *The Godfather* (1972)

START

CHAPTER 30

Film School

If you are still reading, you must be set to make a go of it. You WILL be a filmmaker.

Now, what is the best way to get into such a tough industry?

The obvious answer is to attend a film school. That has been the route of many big names in the industry. But, then, on the other hand, Sir Ridley Scott, James Cameron, and Steven Spielberg have all had epic careers and 18 Oscar nominations between them without formal teaching.

Whether film school is right for you depends on your personality, financial resources, and life situation. While it does give you training, like-minded people to work with, and access to equipment, this doesn't automatically turn you into a filmmaker. As James Cameron said, "I think the most important thing if you're an aspiring film-maker is to get rid of the 'aspiring' ... You shoot it, you put your name on it, you're a filmmaker. Everything after that, you're just negotiating your budget."

This chapter includes four different viewpoints: convincing arguments in favor of film school from USC Senior Lecturer Pablo Frasconi; the current experiences of film student Tony Dinsey; some fresh ideas from Edward Housden, whose graduating film premiered at Cannes, and motivating words from Stuart Holt, who has created over 200 short films without going to film school. All interviews were conducted in 2012.

PABLO FRASCONI – SENIOR LECTURER USC, SCHOOL OF CINEMATIC ARTS

www.pablofrasconi.net

30.1 Pablo Frasconi

1. Why would you recommend film school to a college graduate?

Film school allows for the creation of an instant community of individuals with a shared passion for, and commitment to, cinema. This community might be formed in other ways outside of school over time, but it would not be as efficiently created as it is at USC's School of Cinematic Arts. For an emerging filmmaker, film school allows for a focus on production values and personal expression, two areas that otherwise might take a decade or more to acquire comparable experiences outside. Film school does wonders for students in terms of learning time management, organization, collaborative skills, and the ethics of production.

2. Do most students, in your experience, fully understand what they are getting themselves into?
They usually do not predict the breadth that studying film requires and allows, nor the needed commitment, nor the joy of actually finding their passions as part of a team.

3. Does the community-side of film school play an important role in a graduate's future film career?
Because we are in Los Angeles, students frequently enter the workforce as "buddies" and help each other get their feet in doors. Collaborators in SCA frequently become collaborators in the industry.

4. How are courses structured at USC and how much does it cost?
I am most familiar with the Grad production program. I co-ordinate the first year and helped to design it. Most students get their MFA in 3—4 years. (See price structures in box below.)

5. Do you think that attending a film school helps entry into the business?
It helps, absolutely. I have seen it happen hundreds of times in many ways.

6. Do you have any advice for applying for a film course? Are there any obvious mistakes that come up every year? Is there anything aspiring filmmakers should be doing before they apply?
The best thing to do is to tell SCA how you are different from the masses that apply. What will you bring to the media? What is your unique perspective? What kind of films do you want to make? Do you have an ear and eye for story?

7. "Networking" is the buzzword in many filmmaking guides. How can students achieve this? Does attending film school help?
Oh yes! At USC, we have an office of "Student-Industry Relations" which supports getting students' films into festivals, helps them to obtain internships, and guides and advises them in the right direction throughout their stay.

8. What kinds of films do USC students like to watch and draw their influences from?
You name it. We have hundreds of students. I teach an elective, "Creating Poetic Cinema" each year which fills up in days, and our multi-cam TV courses are very popular too. Students' tastes range to everything in between and beyond . . .

9. How has the study and creation of films changed over the past five years?
I think the field went through a period of unprecedented digital developments in the last 5—10 years with steep learning and adjustment curves,

expanding horizons, and some disarray. But recently, technology has diminished as an idea of growth—it has leveled off—costs are lowered, technological changes are fewer ... at film school we can now focus on developing new, unique voices. A good story is a good story no matter what technology is out there. Graduating students are making personal films, aspiring for niche markets, and their films are reaching larger audiences sooner. Film students are learning how to promote their own films—and themselves—in classes where they learn to pitch, network, and create production packages. Overall, they emerge with greater savvy about the world and the marketplace.

10. Do the majority of the students make a career in film after graduation?

Yes. As long as we agree to define film as all of the cinematic arts. I had a graduate who went to work making films for PETA, another interned with an installation artist, another was asked to direct a feature, another is a regular "YouTube Star," making a living from advertisers, as he creates one adventure-episode per week. Income is turning up in areas that never existed five years ago.

11. Any advice for a new filmmaker?

Be inventive, committed, have passion, and collaborate.

12. What film guides or books would you recommend to film students?

Voice & Vision by Mick Hurbis-Cherrier

p U.S. Film Schools (according to education-portal.com)

PAUSE

USC COURSES

Production I (507), which includes 8 weeks of "Fundamentals of Directing," (which includes casting, rehearsing, shooting, directing, and editing a pre-existing scene); 8 weeks of HD Cinematography; 8 weeks of creating their own projects (one non-dialogue, a second with dialogue and a small crew); and short workshops in editing (AVID), producing, and sound recording and design. Concurrently they take "Creating the Short Film" in the writing program, and "Concepts of Cinematic Production."

Production II (508), in which trios create three dialogue pieces in 16 weeks, rotating through the roles: Student A: Writer/Director/Sound Designer; Student B: Cinematographer; Student C: Producer/Picture Editor. There are 5 faculty: Producing, Directing, Cinematography, Editing, and Sound, and 4 student assistants for each of 4 sections of 15 students. Each film is 6 minutes max, shot in HD, edited in AVID, sound designed and mixed in ProTools. Concurrently, students take writing, and "Concepts of Post-Production."

Production III, in which 3 crews of 8–12 students create 15–20 minute HD projects in 16 weeks. The scripts (or documentary projects) are selected by faculty, and students focus on one role during the semester. We have a narrative section (546), and a documentary section (547), with 5 faculty and student assistants in each.

Production IV: Advanced Projects. Students are paired up with a faculty mentor who supervises projects that the students design as their final "calling card" film.

Budgets are covered by the students (except for using our facilities) and range from $5,000–$50,000. Many are selected for international festivals and lead students to professional work and contacts.

USC—The University of Southern California in Los Angeles, was founded in 1929 as the United States' first film school. Today, it houses departments devoted to production for film and television, criticism, animation, screenwriting, producing, and interactive media.

Costs for an MFA in Production can be found at http://www.usc.edu

30.2 Tony Dinsey

TONY DINSEY—CURRENTLY STUDYING IN FILM SCHOOL AT BASINGSTOKE COLLEGE OF TECHNOLOGY (BCOT) DOING A NATIONAL DIPLOMA IN INTERACTIVE MEDIA.

1. Why did you decide to go to film school?
I was bored with the humdrum of normal working life and wanted to achieve more and be more creative.

2. What were your expectations, and is it living up to them?
My expectations were to learn from the ground up as I only had a very basic knowledge of things to start off with, and I learnt a great deal.

3. What directors inspire you?
Peter Jackson, David Lynch, Martin Scorsese, Quentin Tarantino, Takeshi Kitano and David Fincher.

4. Do you feel attending film school was the right decision for you?
Yes definitely. I have gained a vast amount of knowledge, networked and made good contacts, achieved a lot of good work, and been very happy for the last three years.

5. What have you learnt/achieved that you probably would have been unable to do if you had not attended film school?
I have learnt how to pre-prepare for projects and this really is a vital piece of a filmmaking process, i.e. storyboards and planning camera shots and angles. I have also learnt various software packages that really help with filmmaking.

6. What does your course cover?
Film making, planning, web design, photography, advertising, animation, and many other aspects.

7. Do you feel that it is good value for money?
I was government funded so it was very good value for money.

8. Do you feel you are making useful contacts for when you finish?
Indeed. I tried to network as much as possible and using other social media such as LinkedIn and Twitter I feel I have made quite a few good contacts.

9. Are you optimistic for the future?
Yes, I'm starting uni shortly and really looking forward to it.

10. Have you made a short film?
I have made a few. My favorite is called *Sick Of It* and can be found on YouTube. I worked with a great guy on it and it was very well planned—unlike previous projects.

30.3 Edward Housden

EDWARD HOUSDEN—FILM SCHOOL GRADUATE

www.edwardhousden.com

1. Why did you decide to go to film school?
Going to film school seemed like the natural progression of things for me. As a kid in Australia, I guess I didn't really have huge understanding of the film industry and was a little naive as to how to go about getting into it. So going to film school was the way to go for me. Also being in an environment where you are surrounded by film, watching films, making films, talking about films with like-minded people seemed like a good way to spend three years.

2. Did you learn/achieve anything that you probably would have been unable to do if you had not attended film school?
I think so. For me, being there everyday, watching films you might not have watched, and having people critique your ideas, being encouraged to write differently, shoot differently, etc., pushed me to experiment and do things I might not have done before. I think it ultimately made me a better filmmaker.

3. Do you feel that it is good value for money?
I think so. In Australia, the government pays tuition fees essentially as a loan that one pays back once earning over a certain threshold. It's not overly expensive, and we got access to gear, we shot a lot of 16mm, which is great. I worry that shooting on actual celluloid will get phased out in the future at film school, that would be a huge shame.

4. Did you make any useful contacts that helped you when you graduated?
Yes, I made a lot of contacts by people seeing *Muscles* which definitely has helped me since leaving film school.

5. What directors inspire you, and why?
I'm a chump for '70s New Hollywood directors. Watching *Apocalypse Now*

makes me just wanna get some film stock and go and loose my shit in the jungle . . .!

6. Your graduating film *Muscles* premiered in the Official Selection at Cannes. How did this make you feel?
It was pretty amazing, it's not something I expected at all. I had pretty much no festival experience prior to *Muscles*, so to come out of film school and into the biggest festival in the world was quite overwhelming. I was behind the wheel of a truck when I received a phone call from France and was given the news. I was pretty ecstatic, and a little concerned I might have a crash. I was also very paranoid that it was a big practical joke.

7. Did the festival live up to your expectations, and did you learn anything by attending?
I really didn't know what to expect, but it was an amazing experience. I guess it gave me a better understanding of how festivals work. It's good to learn how to maneuver that situation and I got some great things out of it, and great contacts. It's good to just enjoy it too. Though I think it's important to try not to get too overwhelmed by all of that and remain focused on making the best films you can make.

8. You have also worked as a sound recordist and best boy. Does understanding all aspects of a film crew help make you a better producer/director?
That is another advantage of going to film school and working on your classmates' films, you get to experience most crew roles, which really helps in terms of understanding the workings of a film set.

9. What are you currently working on?
At the moment, I'm directing commercials and music videos, as well as writing a new film project.

30.4 Still from *Muscles* (2010)

10. What advice do you have for someone considering going to film school?
In my experience, I would recommend it. I met great people and had the chance to make a lot of films, being able to experiment, shoot on film, be challenged. While the bureaucracy in film school can seem completely ridiculous and unnecessary at times, find a way to work it, the bureaucracy continues outside. Be a renegade, but a charming one.

30.5 Stuart Holt

STUART HOLT—LEARNING FILM ON THE CHALK FACE

www.themostinterestingperson.com

1. What is the *Most Interesting* Person project and how did you come up with the concept?
Most Interesting Person started as a conversation on a road trip with my good friend, philosopher, ex-university tutor, PhD, DJ, Producer, Suade Bergemann. Suade is an incredibly interesting fellow to go on a road trip

with. He has a heightened state of logic which he applies lavishly to his day-to-day thinking. It occurred to me that Suade ought to find most people boring, or at least tending to talk rubbish. But at the same time, the person Suade finds most interesting would be someone, as a photographer, I would love to meet, and to photograph. And so I asked him, "Suade, who is the most interesting person you know?" And he told me about his uncle, Sir Roger Graef. Then one day I met Roger and figured his most interesting person would be someone exceptional also and so asked him the same question. He told me about his colleague, the undercover journalist Angie Mason, whom I had the good fortune to meet too and ask the same question. This is the point at which I picked up the camera, and how it all started. That was eight years ago, and the first of what I call a "trail". A trail is a group constructed through this linear format of one person interviewing the next, who interviews the next, and so on. I have initiated trails around the world, exploring how we each define what "interesting" means differently, and how our cultural network effects these definitions in different places and environments. To date, we have produced trails in London, Berlin, LA, São Paulo, Sheffield, and Amsterdam and have filmed approximately 200 people through the format.

2. What has it achieved, and how much further would you like to take the project?
The fact that it lives, despite some really difficult moments, emotionally, financially, technically, and otherwise is something of an achievement. But its greatest achievement is that it is fundamentally democratic and philanthropic in nature. There is no centralized producer directing the course of action. It can be taken in any direction by whoever happens to participate and is therefore not only somewhat subversive, which I like, but an eye-opener, and a reflection of the contradiction, perspective, disparity, coincidence, and mystery at the heart of humanity.

3. What first attracted you to filmmaking?
I was not attracted to filmmaking in the beginning. I am a photographer, and *Most Interesting Person* began life as a photographic project. However stills could not communicate the stories being told and so I turned to filmmaking because this medium allows for more complex storytelling.

4. How did you go about making your first short film?
I really didn't have a clue what I was doing from a filmmaking point of view. The terminology and the culture was intimidatingly alien . . . To make matters worse, it was extremely nerve wracking because the first film included an interview with Sir Roger Graef, one of the world's great documentary filmmakers and the head of the highly influential production company, Films of Record. Despite his supportive nature I felt like a total fraud, in fact I was a total fraud. However, I enjoy people. I am interested in them, whether I'm interviewing them, collaborating with them, photographing them, filming them—and would say, eight years on, that this remains the most important thing in achieving intriguing results. Also I was lucky to be able to call on the expertise of friends Joel Mishcon, from Chrome Productions, Neil Gordon, and Arnold Beutenmuller.

5. How did you teach yourself the technical aspects of filmmaking?
Fortunately the photographic principles of framing, exposure, perspective, color harmony, and so on, translated easily into film for me. I had already worked as a self-taught photographer running a small studio in London working with various publishing houses photographing all sorts of people; models, athletes, musicians, and products in all sorts of different environments where at times I would need to manipulate the available lighting to suit the look I was after. I was already familiar with off-camera lighting as I am interested in the Strobist movement; photographers using cheap DIY strobes to create portable yet professionally lit results. This real-life experience gave me a good grounding, and in some ways perhaps an advantage because I was able to focus on the subject, rather than the technology.

6. Do you think you would have benefited from attending film school?
Yes, certainly I would have benefited. There remain gaping, and probably quite basic gaps in my filmmaking knowledge which would have been covered in film school. In particular I think of the skill of constructing a narrative arc in the edit. This is more akin to writing music than taking a photograph and contains often beautiful layers of intrigue. I'm sure this would have proved compelling learning in an academic context.

7. Are there any merits of not attending film school?
Yes, there is a flip side in that I do not fetishize the technology or the filmmaking process per se. I learn about the stuff I need, when I need it and this has made the creative process much more organic, and fun.

8. Do you have any aspirations for making a feature film?
I'm in the early developmental stages of a 90-minute feature. I'll say no more, but watch this space!

9. What advice do you have for someone who hasn't gone to film school but is thinking about making their first short film?
We are flooded with information and resources online. Technology is advanced and cheap, communication is easy. This is both good and bad. Good because there is virtually nothing that can't be achieved creatively on a relatively small budget. Bad because you will never be able to learn everything that is out there, so it is easy to get lost in possibility, never pinning anything down. My advice would be to start by engaging yourself creatively, forget about what other people are doing, forget about what you should be doing, or haven't done, forget about the technical stuff. Take pride in your own thinking. In short, start, and start now. Everything else will happen as a matter of course.

STOP

START

CHAPTER 31

A Brief History of Short Films

AN INVENTION WITHOUT A FUTURE

It was a cold December night three days after Christmas in 1895 when guests filed curiously into the dimly lit basement at the Grand Café on the Boulevard des Capucines in Paris. It was the age of marvels, of new inventions, and what the people had come that night to see was a magic show performed by Auguste and Louis Lumière.[1]

The Lumière Brothers had set up a box of tricks called Le Cinematographe and, after a brief introduction, the lights were extinguished and the audience sat with breath held, waiting in the darkness. The machine in its wooden case with brass fittings was cranked to life and, what those people saw projected on the wall was a low-angle close-up of a train looming down the tracks in a swirling cloud of steam. There was no sound but, so realistic was this magic trick, as the train drew closer, the people threw themselves under the tables and chairs screaming with fear.

The lights were lit again. The members of the audience quickly regained their composure, such are the effects of magic, and watched the rest of the show. The Lumière Brothers screened ten short films lasting twenty minutes, and those people that December night in 1895 were without their knowing, witnesses to a moment in history. The cinema had begun.

31.1 Lumière Brothers

▶▶ P.402

31.2 The Lumières' breakthrough projection

▶▶ P.402

Auguste and Louis Lumière had been on the trail of the moving image for most of their adult lives. They had attended a technical school in Lyon and had grown up surrounded by the paraphernalia in their father's photographic studio. During the last years of the nineteenth century, photographers and inventors across Europe and the United States had been trying to film and reproduce motion, but it was Le Cinematographe, a hand-held, relatively lightweight device functioning as a camera, projector and printer all in one, that was the first to screen what can accurately be called short films to an audience.

The Lumière Brothers had taken their camera out into the street and shot what they called *actualities*—scenes of everyday life, the steaming train being the best known. Being techies, they didn't immediately grasp the potential for creating entertainment. Louis Lumière famously said: "The cinema is an invention without a future," a remark that was to transform from irony to paradox through the years of his pioneering work as a filmmaker. Even before aircraft were seen in the skies, the Lumière Brothers had captured the first aerial shots and, in the coming years, they would go on to shoot almost 1,500 short films, and created the first short-film catalogue.

Louis Lumière lived long enough to regret his slip of the tongue. Far from having no future, the movies had an instant appeal to the public imagination. Fine art and literature habitually serve an educated elite. The theater requires actors on stage being paid day in day out. But a cinema program can be shown eight or ten times a day and, with such economies, every factory worker and housemaid at the turn of the twentieth century could afford a ticket. Finally, we had an art form/entertainment/business, call it what you will, that had mass appeal and, moreover, could reach the entire world. James Cameron's *Avatar* took almost $3 billion at the box office and has been seen by hundreds of millions of people.

There is, as is often said, something magical about the movies, something that appeals to our primitive nature. As we sit in the darkened auditorium waiting for the show to begin we are taking part in the same cultural ritual as our ancestors when they squatted around the camp fire staring at the flames and listening to the elders. Through time and across cultures, man has been recounting legends that endorse and celebrate our humanity, our innate belief in equanimity, our sensitivity to the needs of others, what George Orwell called "common human decency." You find the parable of the Good Samaritan in Luke 10.25—37, but with variances on the theme, every religion and society tells the same story.

IN SEARCH OF THE MOVING IMAGE

Man has always been intrigued by the moving image and has watched since the dawn of time the sun and moon describe reflections on the landscape. We are captivated by the way birds and animals appear in shadows on the wall when we shape our fingers before the light. We are mesmerized by visual trickery, optical illusions, the mirage, the mystery of Camera Obscura.

The first credible moving pictures were projected by a magic lantern. A simple version can be created by drawing a silhouette on a sheet of paper that is then rolled into a tube. The tube is cut strategically with flaps and placed on a circular base that revolves on a pivot. The heat from a lighted candle drives the tube in circles and the figure, a galloping horse, for example, will appear to be racing along as its shadow crosses the walls. In the seventeenth century, Athanasius Kircher[2], the Italian inventor credited with coining the term magic lantern, created a lens through which images from transparencies could be projected on a screen using a candle as the source of light, an early design for the slide projector. Examples of seventeenth century magic lanterns can be found in museums, although their use goes back much further. In Victorian times in Britain, the magic lantern became a sophisticated piece of apparatus used to aid lectures, as well as for entertainment in lantern theaters.

A flick book, a progression of drawings, each slightly different, will give the appearance of movement by flicking quickly through the pages. This illusion of motion was described as "the persistence of vision" and was first studied by the British physician Peter Roget in the 1820s, although the public didn't get its first taste, or rather glimpse, of the movies until 1832 with the invention of the Fantascope. The machine was the work of the Belgian Joseph Plateau, whose device simulated the same motion as a flick book. A string of separate pictures showing the moment by moment changes of an activity, juggling balls or a dancing bear, were sketched around the edge of a slotted disk. When the disk was rotated before a mirror the viewer was treated to the perception of the balls moving through the air, the bear stamping its feet in a dance.

Plateau's Fantascope was quickly superseded by the Daedalum in 1834 created in Britain by William Horner. What he had done was place strips of photographs or drawings in sequence in a rotating drum. Through regularly spaced slots, as the drum was set spinning, the viewer could see a moving image. The device was improved and renamed the Zoetrope in 1867 by the American William Lincoln.[3]

The quest to capture the moving image was growing intense. Back in France, Charles Emile Reynaud took the Zoetrope a stage further in 1877 with what he called the Praxinoscope, a drum interspersed with mirrors, rather than slots, and the first machine with the capacity to project a series of images onto a screen. Several years before the Lumière Brothers rolled up at the Grand Café with Le Cinematographe, Reynaud had shown a 15-minute "movie" at the Theater Optique in Paris.

Two years after Reynaud's success, another invention with a fanciful name came from British photographer Eadweard Muybridge[4], whose Zoopraxiscope created a more persuasive illusion of motion by projecting images in rapid succession onto a screen from photographs printed on a rotating glass disc. He called his machine a motion-picture projector.

Muybridge's photographs were widely published at the time and had been used cut into strips like film by his rival Charles Reynaud for his Praxinoscope. Muybridge found a wealthy patron in the United States after demonstrating his photographic "loco-motion" studies; for example, at the race track in Sacramento, California, he set up a row of a dozen cameras to record the movement of a galloping horse, the sequence showing that all four of the horse's feet were at certain moments off the ground at the same time.

SHOOTING FILM

Up until this time, innovators had merely been able to create the illusion of motion. We return again to France for the illusion to become reality. The Parisian physiologist Etienne-Jules Marey[5] in the 1880s was studying animals in motion and developed what he called a "photographic gun," a camera that could in rapid succession take 12 photographs per second and record these multiple images of movement on the same camera plate. He called the development chronophotography, although the more evocative photo-gun caught on and the term "shooting film" almost certainly derives from Marey's developments.

Rather than Auguste and Louis Lumière, it is Etienne-Jules Marey who is normally described as the "inventor of cinema," and for good reason. After recording his multiple exposures on glass plates, the revolutionary step that took us closer to the modern movie camera was to expose his photographs on strips of sensitized paper that passed mechanically through a camera of his own design. Further experimentation was conducted by Marey's fellow countryman Louis Aime Augustin Le Prince, who developed rolls of sensitized paper covered with photographic emulsion for a camera that he devised and patented. A fragment from his 1888 film *Traffic Crossing Leeds Bridge* is available on YouTube.

Le Prince said at the time that he filmed Leeds Bridge because it provided action. A valuable movie lesson had been learned.

While Le Prince was filming in Leeds, George Eastman in the United States that same year was preparing to launch his celebrated black box Kodak with celluloid film on a roll. His camera was for photographing stills, but movie innovators took special note a year later when Eastman put perforations in the celluloid.

Thomas Alva Edison's[6] electric light bulb first flickered to life in 1879 and now provided the stable, continuous source of light essential for shooting movies. It was at Edison's laboratories in West Orange, New Jersey that, over the coming years, some of the most important developments in film technology took place thanks to the appearance of William Kennedy-Laurie Dickson. A French-born Scot related to the House of the Royal Stuarts, Dickson's mother, Elizabeth, was a talented musician immortalized in the ballad *Annie Laurie*, and his father, James Waite Dickson, was an artist and astronomer who drew a line back through his family tree to the painter William Hogarth. With these weighty antecedents, Bill Dickson had packed his trunks and set sail as a young man for New York with the intention of making a name for himself.

At Edison's laboratories, Dickson outlined his theories for co-ordinating film with sound, and was given a job. His experiments were largely unsuccessful, but as he became familiar with movie cameras, he devised in 1890 what he called the Kinetograph, a motor-driven machine with a synchronized shutter and sprocket system that advanced film across the lens under the controlled speed of an electric motor. Like Eastman's Kodak, the addition of sprocket holes was designed to keep the celluloid rigid and allow the film to be paused momentarily before the shutter to create a photographic frame.

That was the design, but the 19mm film turned out to be neither stable nor constant. Dickson calculated that it would require film practically twice that width in order to maintain stability and, in the long run, progress the technology. It set off one of the great debates in movie history. Edison, his co-designer and funder, was at first reluctant to go to the expense of building a new machine, but Dickson finally won the day and received his patent for 35mm double-sided sprocket film on the 7th of January 1894, the standard that remains to this day.

Having developed the Kinetograph, Dickson began to experiment with his Kinetoscope, a projector based on William Lincoln's Zoetrope technology. The device he constructed was a cabinet as tall as a man standing on its end like a grandfather clock, and which allowed a single viewer to watch a continuous loop of film on a small screen. A decade before motor cars were rolling down the conveyor-belt at the Ford factory in Detroit, Edison had recognized that only mass production would make the inventions coming out of his workshops commercially viable. If people were paying to see vaudeville, he concluded, they would pay to watch movies. After convincing Dickson, they added a coin-operated mechanism to the Kinetoscope, then took their vision to Andrew and George Holland,[7] Canadian businessmen who had dabbled in publishing, shipping, typewriters and, most importantly, the Edison Phonograph.

The Holland Brothers bought five machines and opened in April 1894 the first Kinetoscope Parlour in the heart of the theater district in New York's Broadway. Some 500 people came to pay their 25 cents to watch films such as *Blacksmith Working* and *Highland Dancing*. Within a month, the brothers opened a second parlor at the Masonic Temple in Chicago with a further ten machines and some exciting new titles, *Trapeze, Barber Shop*, *Cock Fight* and *Wrestling*. The "peep-show" craze caught on immediately and spread like a prairie fire with new parlors opening in major cities across the United States. By setting up a delivery system, the framework for cinema distribution was taking shape.

As with the birth of stills photography, as soon as filmmakers had the expertise to screen the moving image, the bawdy crowd were shooting soft core pornography. In the belle epoch when a woman's ankle set a man's pulse racing, *What The Butler Saw* must have broken box office records.

The Kinetograph became known in Britain as a "What The Butler Saw" machine and the contraptions filled arcades at seaside resorts showing a minute's worth of a woman undressing or a woman posing as an artist's model. Where the British enjoyed the saucy nature of the peep-show, in France films of a more refined eroticism were already being shot in 1896 by Eugène Pirou and Albert Kirchner under their company name Léar. The oldest surviving film was titled *Le Coucher de la Marie* and shows Louise Willy performing a striptease. Kirchner is also remembered as the first cineste to produce a film about the life of Christ, *Le Passion du Christ*.

With the growing demand for peep-show product, in 1893 the first film production studio was constructed in the grounds of Edison's New Jersey laboratories. Edison and Dickson filmed vaudeville and magic shows, boxing matches, Broadway plays and acts from Buffalo Bill's Wild West Show. Most of the clips were short, about one minute, but the private, voyeuristic nature of the Kinetograph was mesmerizing and people remained glued to the screens even when the activities they were watching were mundane and repetitive.

Dickson parted company from Edison in 1895. He formed the American Mutoscope Company[8] and began developing his hand-cranked peep-show machine at a time when the boom was about ready to bust. That same year, while Dickson and Edison were undergoing their acrimonious parting of the ways, Auguste and Louis Lumière were constructing Le Cinematographe, their portable, all-in-one camera and projector, and with it stole a march on the Americans by screening the first films to an audience. The Lumière Brothers used Dickson's 35mm film and shot at a speed of 16 frames per second, which remained the standard until the talkies 20 years later, when 24 frames per second became the norm.

The word cinema derives from *Cinematographe*. The age of the Kinetoscope was at an end.

A TRIP TO THE MOON

The first cinema built for the sole purpose of screening films opened in Paris in 1897. The first in the United States was the 200-seat Electric Theater launched by Thomas L. Talley in Los Angeles five years behind the French, although a steady supply of 10—12 minute one-reelers were being exhibited as part of vaudeville shows, at fairgrounds, carnivals, and in church halls. Films in the dying days of the Gay Nineties on both sides of the Atlantic were in the main *actualities*, documentary-like scenes from everyday life, although the first comedies were being shot and were instantly popular.

The breakthrough to what we think of as movies today was made largely by the French pioneer Georges Méliès.[9] Where the Lumière Brothers had been content to record a train pulling into the station and workers flooding from the factory gates, their compatriot was a stage magician versed in the art of bringing rabbits from a hat and silk scarves from the palm of his hand. Méliès realized that it was the manipulation of film that made it interesting and, with his theatrical ability to deceive the eye by skillful intercutting, he can safely be described as the Father of Film Editors.

Méliès—as producer, writer, director, and actor—experimented with the medium by making more than 100 shorts before completing in 1902 *Le Voyage Dans la Lune* (*A Trip to the Moon*) a 14-minute one-reeler considered the first true movie. With a rocket voyaging into space, circling planets and alien life forms that wouldn't look out of place in a George Lucas film, Méliès had planted the magic seeds that would grow into the palms that edge the boulevards of Cannes and Hollywood and turned moving pictures into the great art form of the twentieth century.

31.3 *A Trip to the Moon* (1902)

▶▶ P.**402**

When the former Kinetoscope operator Edwin Porter[10] was given the job on Edison's New Jersey lot of directing a narrative documentary called *The Life of An American Fireman* in 1903, he made a study of Méliès's work and came to realize that it was the Frenchman's astute editing that made his films compelling. In his six-minute short, rather than merely filming firemen at work, Porter had them re-stage various activities, he used close-ups to show emotion and, whether in homage or imitation of Georges Méliès, took the viewer into the heart of the drama by cross-cutting between the interior and exterior of a burning house.

What Porter brought back to the lot was so original, at least in the United States, it took Thomas Edison months re-watching *The Life of An American Fireman* before he fully appreciated what the director had achieved; as many of the most inventive *auteurs* and artists discover, anything too novel, too ahead of its times, will be met by confusion, even anger. Hollywood moguls aren't looking for the unique and innovative, they want to see a fresh spin on the previous year's blockbuster.

Edison, though, was a shrewd entrepreneur, as well as a filmmaker, and later that same year, 1903, put Porter back in the director's chair to shoot a fictionalized account of a true story. Just as young American directors in the sixties analyzed the work of the iconoclastic *Nouvelle Vague* (New Wave) aesthetics of François Truffaut, Claude Chabrol, Jean-Luc Godard, Éric Rohmer and Jacques Rivette, Edwin Porter steeped himself in

31.4 Poster of the *The Great Train Robbery* (1903)

▶▶ P.402

the work of filmmakers working across Europe before beginning to film his milestone movie *The Great Train Robbery*.

The 10-minute short was taken from a popular stage play loosely based on the real life heist by Butch Cassidy's Hole in the Wall gang in 1900. Butch (George Leroy Parker) and the boys halted a Union Pacific Railroad train in a sparsely populated stretch of wilderness outside Table Rock, Wyoming. They threw the fireman off the moving train, they forced the conductor to uncouple the passenger cars and dynamited the safe in the mail wagon before escaping with $5,000 in cash.

Porter dressed locations in New Jersey to look like the Wild West and, in what was the first true Western, created the stock elements of the genre: the robbery, the shoot-out, the chase on horseback, the gathering of the posse. Using both the newspaper transcripts and the structure from the stage play, Porter in 14 scenes created a vibrant narrative but, what made *The Great Train Robbery* so important, was Porter's extension of film language. First, it was one of the first films not to be shot in chronological order. Porter showed parallel-action between simultaneous events—inter-cutting, for example, between the bandits and the telegraph operator—and moved between scenes without using fades or dissolves. Another first, was having shown the fireman as he is about to be thrown off the train, Porter cuts back to see the figure (a dummy) rolling into the dust. One last Porter innovation was an added scene that could be placed either at the beginning or the end of the film (depending on the exhibitor) showing a bandit shooting his six-gun dead eye at the audience.

Edison was aware that he had a hot property on his hands. In the film catalogue out in January 1904 *The Great Train Robbery* got the following billing:

This sensational and highly tragic subject will certainly make a decided 'hit' whenever shown. In every respect we consider it absolutely the superior of any moving picture ever made. It has been posed and acted in faithful duplication of the genuine 'Hold Ups' made famous by various outlaw bands in the far West, and only recently the East has been shocked by several crimes of the frontier order, which fact will increase the popular interest in this great Headline Attraction.

A STAR IS BORN

Edwin Porter achieved a great deal with his 10-minute film: he established the Western as an American genre, he co-wrote (with Scott Marble) and directed the first film to make a significant financial return, he showed the unlimited scope for fiction, and proved that, far from being just another vaudeville act, film had the potential to grow into an industry.

31.5 Edwin Porters Wardrobe Van (1908)

▶▶ P.402

Another "first" for Porter was launching the career of Gilbert M. Anderson,[11] a key figure in movie history belatedly honored with a life-achievement Oscar in 1957. Anderson, a travelling salesman and failed stage actor, got his movie break in Porter's intriguingly titled *Messenger Boy Mistake* in 1902. The following year, in *The Great Train Robbery*, Anderson was cast in three roles, as a bandit, a shot passenger, and a "tenderfoot dancer"—the guy who hops about with bullets from the baddie's six-guns spitting about his feet, another cowboy cliché introduced by Porter.

After *The Great Train Robbery*, Anderson continued acting in short films and finally hit the big time playing Bronco Billy in *The Bandit Makes Good*. Over the course of the next several years, he appeared in almost 400 Bronco Billy one-reelers and became one of the first recognizable stars. While still acting and directing, Anderson teamed up with George K. Spoor to form the Essanay company, the name taken from the first letters of their surnames. They opened studios in California and produced a series of films featuring Ben Turpin, the New Orleans-born vaudeville and circus performer with trademark cross-eyes and an act so similar to that of the well-spoken young Englishman Charlie Chaplin, it remains debatable as to who gave birth to the Little Tramp.

Charlie Chaplin left the Keystone Studio in 1908 and at Essanay was given the freedom to develop his amiable if hapless hobo across a slate of ambitious movies where character development and plot were beginning to prevail over mere slapstick to capture the hearts—and loyalty—of the audience. Chaplin and his contemporaries created a language as central to filmmaking as the rules for drama set down by the Greeks. Filming techniques developed in the silent era evolved at a frantic pace, as did the supremacy of the omnipotent studios. In Europe, the First World War brought progress to a standstill, but in the United States the industry flourished with the growth of Hollywood. When Charlie Chaplin left Essanay in 1916, he was one of the biggest stars of all time and American movies were reaching audiences across the world.

It had taken just ten years from the release of Porter's *The Great Train Robbery* for film's capacity to influence the public to be understood and co-opted by forces more potent than the moguls. President Woodrow Wilson was re-elected as the "peace candidate" in 1916 and forged a nation of immigrants into an homogenous whole through a propaganda machine fueled by war newsreels and Hollywood movies with titles such as *The Kaiser: The Beast of Berlin*, and *Wolves of Kultur*. *To Hell With The Kaiser* was so popular that Massachusetts riot police had to be summoned to deal with an angry mob denied admission at a full house.

In 1917, America went to war.[12]

A night at the cinema had long been a passion. Now it had become a patriotic duty. Movies were affectionately known as *flickers;* the term "short film" didn't exist. All films were short films. With the coming of the two-reeler, the prototype feature, the short continued to play a fundamental role at the studios as a training ground for writers, directors, cameramen, and the flood of wannabe actors and actresses arriving in Hollywood looking for their shot at the big time. As star-led features began to dominate theater programs, short films were sold to cinema chains as part of a "block booking," the package including the feature, a cartoon, a newsreel, and a serial that ended with a cliff-hanger that ensured the audience would be filling the auditorium the following week.

It could be said that the American Dream was born in the cinema. People worked hard for modest wages, often in conditions where strike breakers and criminal involvement in big business was the norm. For the price of a ticket you could live the dream, at least for a couple of hours.

The movies were an escape and what people wanted from their films was glamour, adventure, a glimpse at other worlds and, at the same time, confirmation of their own values. What the studios typically provided was just that, morality tales that reinforced a Puritan ethic, clearly-defined leads, sub-plots that added wisdom or humor, usually played by popular character actors, and, for the most part, a fairy tale ending that sent the people home with a spring in their step and the energy to get up and go back to their jobs next day.

A night at the *flicks* was an occasion. It was special. Perfect for first dates. For families. People relaxed. They smoked cigarettes. They wore their best clothes and uniformed doormen dripping in gold braid greeted their arrival as they hurried up the polished steps for this weekly ritual. Theaters were plush with imposing entrances like temples, thick cushioned carpets, comfortable seats and the alluring whiff of popcorn and hotdogs. Before the advent of sound in the 1920s, in the pit below the screen there would be a piano or an organ, and in some cities with competing theaters, a full orchestra would file in just as the lights went down. Music that enhanced the mood and action on screen was crucial—in general that remains the case—and complete scores normally arrived with the big cans of film stock.

The talkies quickly eclipsed silent movies as well as the careers of some of the most famous silent movie stars; many had come from Europe and a lack of good American English didn't sound right to the native ear. The American gift for risk taking, for forging ahead, even through war and depression, resulted in the combined film product from across the world representing only a fraction of the films being produced in America. The cinema wasn't an American invention, but they had made it their own.

THE NEW WAVE

Before the term "short film" gained wide currency, shorts in the US were known as the "short subject" and included cartoons, travelogues, news clips, and comedies featuring stars such as Buster Keaton, Laurel and Hardy, the Three Stooges and the ever popular Charlie Chaplin. After the 1930s, fewer shorts were made for theatrical release; these were generally produced by picture companies that either owned their own theater chains, like Loews Theaters, or obliged theaters to take their shorts by selling them in the same package as their big-name features. When the practice of "block booking" was judged illegal by the US Supreme Court, the theater chains were required to sell off their movie studios and this commonsense division between production and exhibition remains in place.

31.6 Chaplin and the Kid

▶▶ P.**403**

Back at the turn of the century, Georges Méliès had experimented with color by hand-painting film negatives, but audiences seemed indifferent to color and its introduction was a slow process that only gathered speed when producers saw the need to compete with television, a principally black and white medium right up until the 1960s. Shorts continued to be made as an educational tool, the corporate video/DVD continues the practice, but with the rise of the double feature, the commercial short film was virtually dead, and the cartoon short was on its way to the same celluloid grave.

While new writers and directors in Hollywood now cut their teeth making B pictures, in Europe among independent filmmakers the short continued to be a showcase for experimental films and new talent. France had produced more than its share of film pioneers and, as the light in the art world is said to move from one part of the globe to another, the short-film light was switched on in Paris with the emergence of *la Nouvelle Vague,* the New Wave,[13] the term coined to describe a loosely-knit assortment of young filmmakers who in the 1950s rejected classical movie structure to develop new narrative forms and a radical visual style.

31.7 *À Propos de Nice* (1937)

▶▶ P.403

As students at film school today are likely to be trawling through the subtleties of Todd Solondz (*Happiness*), Paul Haggis (*Crash*) and the Korean masters Park Chan-wook (*Oldboy*) and Takashi Miike (*Audition*), the French New Wave were inspired by Jean Renoir, Jean Vigo, Orson Welles, and Alfred Hitchcock, directors with a style written like a signature into their work. They deconstructed every reel of film that passed through Paris, and outlined their theories in—among other publications—*Cahiers du cinéma,* the influential film magazine co-founded by André Bazin, the legendary critic considered the most prominent film-writer since the end of World War Two.

Cahiers du cinéma continues its tradition in excellent movie criticism and can be read online in English. Free.

www.cahiersducinema.com

Enouraged by Bazin, *Cahiers du cinéma* writer François Truffaut directed in 1955 his first film, the 8-minute short *Un Visite*. Jacques Rivette was behind the camera and, the following year, Rivette made his début short, *Le Coup du Berger*, written by Claude Chabrol with a cast that included fellow film critics Truffaut, Jean-Luc Godard, Chabrol, and Rivette himself. It was this group of filmmakers, with Éric Rohmer, who set out to redefine film as art and created the mood that would lead us to independent cinema.

31.8 Francois Truffaut

▶▶ P.403

New Wave films were sensual, melancholic, capturing the *zeitgeist* and reflecting the turbulent social and political changes that characterized the 1950s and 1960s. The Paris Riots in May 1968 could have been scripted by writers of the New Wave. Through critiques and editorials, they conceived the principle that the director, like the author of a book, was the *auteur* of the film and introduced the credit *A Film By*—a format adopted by directors everywhere. More significantly, *Nouvelle Vague* filmmakers challenged the commercial Hollywood notion of movies as being *just* entertainment—or business, or propaganda—and perceived film as an art form. As *the* art form.

Although these writer/directors inevitably moved on to make features, they had provided new dignity and a sense of place to the short film. In a short there is an opportunity to reshuffle the cards of film language and take on themes commercial producers avoid on both commercial grounds and the fear of the new. There is a certain comfort in the dull warmth of Plato's cave, our backs to the sun watching shadows on the wall. Show us a glimpse of life beyond the walls of our own narrow world, and the mind will not immediately compute what it is seeing. Thomas Edison had faced this moment of doubt the first time he viewed *The Life of An American Fireman*. Anything strikingly original is likely to be rejected by the status quo, yet it is the brave artist prepared to swim against the tide who in the long run often finds the greatest success; or at least critical success.

The growth of impressionistic, poetic, surreal, transgressional, boundary breaking, avant-garde films gave rise to the festival circuit, as well as the introduction of independent arthouse cinema where audiences could expect to see films that were difficult, complex, controversial, or just plain foreign. The hegemony of the American studios with their undemanding diet of thrillers, actioners, romcoms, war, Westerns, and gangster films had been broken and, in the wake of the French New Wave, young American auteurs such as Martin Scorsese, Francis Ford Coppola, Spike Lee, Jim Jarmusch, Robert Rodriguez, and Quentin Tarantino rose up in a rolling tsunami that washed away preconceived conventions and introduced a new American aesthetic. Big-budget actioners still storm the box office but indie films made by indie filmmakers have carved out a sizeable niche in the market.

YOUTUBE

According to a report by the Pew Research Centre, ten years ago 14 percent of Americans got their news from the Internet.[14] Today, that figure is 41 percent. Streaming short films over the web—drama, animation, documentaries, video diaries, hidden-camera comedies and mishaps—has grown prodigiously since the coming of net broadcasters such as YouTube.

Before Robert Rodriguez made his classic low budget *El Mariachi*, he shot the 8-minute *Bedhead*. The first title on Martin Scorsese's filmography is the short film *Vesuvius VI*. William Kennedy-Laurie Dickson and Thomas Edison 100 years ago were making one-minute films for the Kinetograph machine. Today people are shooting and sharing one-minute films on their smartphones. The Lumière Brothers 100 years ago screened a train steaming down the tracks. Today Internet broadcasters are screening the same kind of *actualities* on the net. Major television channels are finding more slots for short films, the number of short-film-dedicated festivals is on the increase, and the oldest of film genres is alive and kicking.

STOP

31.1 The Lumière Brothers

31.2 The Lumière's breakthrough projection of a train steaming into the station

31.3 *A trip to the Moon* (1902) – inspiring George Lucas

31.4 Poster from Edwin Porter's 1903 masterpiece *The Great Train Robbery*

31.5 Edwin Porter's mobile wardrobe – about 1908

31.6 A scene from *Chaplin and the Kid*

31.7 *À Propos de Nice* – promenade on the boulevard

31.8 Francois Truffaut

PART

IX

TITLE

Useful info

START

CHAPTER 32

Example Production and Release Forms

Everyone that appears in your film must sign a release form—giving consent for you to use their performances/appearances. We've included example contracts for paid actors, paid extras, and a copyright waiver for unpaid collaborations. These and other contracts/release forms can be found at Shooting People—www.shootingpeople.org/resources. Be sure to read their disclaimer, and note that these contracts are intended only as a guide. All productions are different, and ideally a lawyer will check all contracts. The publishers and authors cannot accept any responsibility if you ignore this advice. The release forms are followed by a blank Top Sheet for budgeting. The same form, as well as hundreds of other downloadablecontracts and forms can be found at Filmmaker IQ—www.filmmakeriq.com.

Finally production sheets from the short film Greta May are replicated, including a call sheet, two days of a shooting schedule and a shot list.

ACTORS AGREEMENT

[Headed paper or Name and address of film company or producer].
Date:
RE: [NAME OF THE FILM] (working title of "the film")
[NAME, ADDRESS OF ACTOR]
The above named actor agrees to take part in "the film".

1. Start Date:

2. Period of Engagement: to
(These dates may vary from time to time).

3. Rate of pay: £ per hour/day/month

4. Agreed Expenses:

5. Conditions: Producer agrees to obtain standard cast insurance for the Artist.

6. The Artist knows of no reason why he cannot freely enter this agreement.

7. The Artist gives all consents required under the Copyright Designs and Patents Act 1988 or any re-enactment consolidation or amendment thereof in order that the Producer may make full use of the Artist's services and any other moral rights to which the Artist may be entitled under any existing or future legislation.

8. The Artist agrees that the Artist shall:

8.1 perform and record the Artist's part to the best of the Artist's skill and ability

8.2 attend for fittings rehearsals and the taking of still photographs

8.3 dress, make up and wear the Artist's hair (subject to prior consultation with the Artist) as directed by the Director

8.4 comply with all reasonable and notified directions given by the Producer or the Director

8.5 keep the Producer informed of the Artist's whereabouts and telephone number at all material times

8.6 not pledge the credit of the Producer nor incur or purport to incur any liability on its behalf or in its name.

9. All rights in any way attaching to the Film and all photographs and sound recordings shall belong absolutely to the Producer throughout all periods to the extent permitted by the law. The Artist waives the right to receive any further remuneration in relation to the exploitation of the rights.

10. The Producer shall be entitled by written notice to the Artist given at any time to suspend the engagement of the Artist if:

10.1 the film is prevented suspended interrupted or postponed by reasons not within the control of the Producer

10.2 the voice of the Artist shall become unsatisfactory

10.3 the Artist shall by reason of any illness or physical or mental incapacity or disability be unable to perform his duties

10.4 the Artist's full services shall fail material obligations under this Agreement.

11. Any suspension shall be effective from the date of the event giving rise to such suspension and shall continue for the duration of such event.

11.1 the Producer shall during the period of suspension cease to be liable to make payments to the Artist save such installments of remuneration which have become due.

12. The Producer shall be entitled to terminate the engagement of the Artist hereunder by delivery of written notice of such termination to the Artist at any time if:

12.1 any of the circumstances under Clause 10 continue for at least 28 (twenty-eight) days consecutively or in the aggregate,

12.2 the circumstances under Clause 10.1 continue for at least 2 (two) consecutive days or 3 (three) days in the aggregate, or

12.3 any of the circumstances in Clauses 10.2–10.4 occur, subject to the Producer giving prior written notice of such default to the Artist and the Artist not curing such default within 2 (two) days of receipt of such notice.

12.4 any suspension under the provisions of Clause 12.1 shall continue for six weeks or more then the Artist shall be entitled to terminate this engagement by seven days' written notice.

13. In the event of termination of the engagement or death of the Artist

13.1 any claim which the Producer may have shall not be affected or prejudiced

13.2 the Producer's title to and ownership of all copyrights and all other rights in or in connection with the services rendered shall be or remain vested in the Producer

13.3 payment of the installments of remuneration due and payable to the Artist shall operate as payment in full and final discharge and settlement of all claims.

14. All consents granted hereunder to the Producer are irrevocable.

15. Credit will be given only if the Artist appears recognizably in the Film as released if this Agreement has not been terminated for the default of the Artist.

16. The Artist shall keep as confidential the provisions of and any information which may come to the Artist's attention in connection with this agreement.

17. This agreement is governed by and construed in accordance with the laws of England and subject to the exclusive jurisdiction of the Courts of England

Signed ……………………………………… Dated ……………………
[Artist]
Signed ……………………………………… Dated ……………………
[Producer]

EXTRA RELEASE FORM

[Headed paper or Name and address of film company or producer].

[Name and address of extra]

I (the undersigned) do hereby confirm that I have agreed to be filmed and photographed as an extra (non-speaking role) in connection with the film [Title] (working title) on the [date].

I hereby grant to you, your successors, assigns and licensees, to use as you desire in any manner or in any media currently existing or which may be developed in the future, all video, still and motion pictures that you may take of me.

I understand that I shall receive [no fee/ a fee of £x] for my appearance in and participation in the film.

I am over 18 years of age

Signed ....
Print..
Print Name

COPYRIGHT WAIVER FORM

[Headed paper or Name and address of film company or producer].

Date:

[NAME OF THE FILM] (working title)
[ROLE OF CONTRIBUTOR ON FILM]

I agree to collaborate on this short film and to assign to [NAME OF THE ASSIGNEE], with full title guarantee, the following:

i) all of my rights, title, interest and property in [NAME OF THE FILM] (the "Intellectual Property Rights");

ii) the full and exclusive benefit of all the Intellectual Property Rights including all forms of protection and all rights, privileges and advantages appertaining thereto;

iii) the right to recover and to bring proceedings to recover damages and/or to obtain other remedies in respect of infringement of the Intellectual Property Rights whether committed before or after the date of this Agreement.

AND to hold the same unto [NAME OF THE ASSIGNEE] absolutely.

Further, I hereby agree to waive all moral rights in the Intellectual Property Rights.

The nature of the project and my role in it has been explained to me and I have agreed to collaborate on this project for [NO FEE/ FEE OF £X].

I understand that this film (or part of it) may be distributed by the producer in any medium in any part of the world.

I shall, at the request of [NAME OF THE ASSIGNEE], sign all instruments, applications or other documents and to do all such acts as shall be reasonably required by [NAME OF THE ASSIGNEE] to enable [NAME OF THE ASSIGNEE] or its nominee to enjoy the full and exclusive benefit of the Intellectual Property Rights and to fully and effectively vest the same in [NAME OF THE ASSIGNEE] including, where necessary, the registration of [NAME OF THE ASSIGNEE]'s title in the Intellectual Property Rights in the appropriate intellectual property office at which the Intellectual Property Rights are (or at the nomination of the [NAME OF THE ASSIGNEE] shall be) registered.

Signed ....
Print.......................................

EXAMPLE BUDGET TOP SHEET

Sheet # 1
Page # 1

Production: ______ Budget Draft Date: ______
Length: ______ Shooting Dates: ______
Location: ______

Account #	Category	Specifics	Cost	w/Tax	Budget	Actual Cost
001	Script & Rights					
002	Producer					
003	Director					
004	Cast					
		ABOVE THE LINE TOTAL:			$0	$0
005	Travel					
006	Hotel & Lodging					
007	Food					
008	Camera	Kit, Crew, Expendables				
009	Lighting	Kit, Crew, Expendables				
010	Sound	Kit, Crew, Accessories				
011	Locations	Fees & Permits				
012	Art Dept	Props, Wardrobe etc.				
013	Office Expenses	Paper supplies, fax, internet etc.				
014	Petty Cash					
015	Film or Tape Stock					
016	Lab	Developing, dailies, etc.				
017	Insurance					
018	Editing					
019	Shipping					
020	Still Photos	Photographer, film, developing, etc.				
021	Contingency	10% of production costs			$0	$0
		PRODUCTION TOTAL:			$0	$0
022	Final Post Online	Conform, Color Correction, etc.				
023	Final Post Mix	Sound mixing session				
024	Marketing	Festival fees, screeners, postage				
		POST PRODUCTION TOTAL:			$0	$0

GRAND TOTAL ESTIMATE: $0
GRAND TOTAL BUDGET: $0
ACTUAL GRAND TOTAL: $0

GRETA MAY CALL SHEET

"GRETA MAY"

Metro 7 Ltd
Gastigny House, Lever Street, London, EC1V 3SU
Tel. 020 7689 XXXXEmail: GretaMay@Metro7.com

CALL SHEET NO.1

RISK ASSESSMENTS AVAILABLE FROM PRODUCTION

Executive Producer:
Date : Thursday 28 October 2004
MAUREEN MURRAY (mobile: 07860 xxxxxx)
Producer:
Unit Call : 07:00 On Loc.
SACHA VAN SPALL (mobile: 07984 xxxxxx)

Writer/Director: **Sunrise: 07.44**
Hrs
CLIFFORD THURLOW (mobile: 07748 xxxxxx)
Sunset: 17.43
Hrs

Location:
BATTERSEA ARTS CENTRE
Lavender Hill
London SW1V 2DY
Contact: Anna Martin: Tel: 020 7326 8234. Mobile: 07905 xxxxxx.
Email: AnnaM@BAC.org.uk
& Edel Ryan (Front of House Co-ordinator) Mobile: 07947 xxxxxx

SC.	Set / Description	D/N	PGS.	CAST
1	INT-THEATER FOYER (DAY 1) Richard recognises Greta and gives her his telephone number.	EVE	1 3/8	GRETA RICHARD
2pt	INT – STAGE (FLASHBACK) Fleeting image of Greta in ultra sexy outfit. She looks terrified.	N	1/8	GRETA
5pt	INT – STAGE (FLASHBACK) Fleeting image of Greta in ultra sexy outfit. She sees Oliver behind her.	N	1/8	GRETA OLIVER

7	INT – STAGE (FLASHBACK) Greta & Oliver act out their brutal scene. The director is dissatisfied.	N	5/8	GRETA OLIVER (DIRECTOR O/S)
12 & 12A	INT – STAGE (FLASHBACK) The director decides to use the French girl. Oliver tacitly agrees. Greta is left stunned. We see Richard.	N	1	GRETA RICHARD OLIVER DIRECTOR

	ARTIST	CHARACTER	P/UP	M/UP	W/D	L/UP	**ON-SET**
1	JESS MURPHY	GRETA MAY	O/T	07.00	0745	------	0800
2	PHILIP DESMEULES	RICHARD BATES	O/T	07.45	07.30	------	0800
3	THOMAS SNOWDON	OLIVER MORRELL	O/T	11.15	11.30	------	1145
5	DAVID STERNE	DIRECTOR	10.00	11.30	1200	-------	1215

Weather: Sunny. Max Temp 16 degrees C

Total Pages 3 2/8

REQUIREMENTS.

TRAVEL: **10.00 p/u Mr Sterne from home & transport to Location. On wrap deliver Mr Sterne home.**

ART DEPT/PROPS : **As per script to include :**
Sc. 1: flyers for "You're Not Alone", Richard's newspaper (& rpts), Richard's pen.
Sc. 2pt, 5pt, 7, 12 & 12A: sofa with throw, rug, lampstand & shade, director's clipboard, script & pen & reading light.

CAMERA: **As per Jean-Philippe Gossart (mob. 07906 xxxxxx)**

SOUND: **As per Daniel Rosen (mob. 07712 xxxxxx)**

HAIR/M-UP: **As per Jenny Spelling (mob. 07900 xxxxxx) to inc.**
Greta's m/u change from Sc. 1 to Flashback scenes.

COSTUME: **As per Maja Meschede (mob. 07810 xxxxxx) to inc.**
Greta's sexy red underwear, Oliver's belt. Modesty dressing gown for Miss Murphy.

RUSHES : **Picture/Sound Rushes to be given to Renee Willis at the end of the day.**

ELECTRICAL: **As per Pete Carrier (mob. 07748 xxxxxx).**

CATERING: **07.00: Juice & hand-held continental buffet on arrival. Production to set up buffet table in corner of Foyer.**
10.00—10.30: Mid-morning break in BAC Café.
13.00—14.00: Lunch in BAC Café.

HEALTH & SAFETY: **Local Hospital:**
The Bolingbroke Hospital, Clapham Junction, London SW11
Tel: 020 7223 7411.

PRODUCTION NOTES: **ON WRAP CREW WILL TRAVEL TO MAIN LOCATION (77 NEW KINGS ROAD, LONDON SW6) AND SET UP FOR SC. 15.**
SCHEDULED AS FIRST SCENE OF THE FOLLOWING DAY.

ADVANCED SCHEDULE

Friday 29 October 2004

SC.	Set / Description	D/N	PGS.	CAST
15	INT – RICHARD'S HOUSE (DAY 2) Greta asks Richard for breakfast in bed with the papers – but there's no hurry.	D	1	GRETA RICHARD
2	INT – GRETA'S FLAT – KITCHEN (DAY 1) Rachel tells depressed Greta to get over Oliver. Cake is not the answer.	N	2	GRETA RACHEL
3	INT – GRETA'S FLAT – KITCHEN (DAY 1) Greta phones Richard.	N	4/8	GRETA
5	INT – GRETA'S FLAT – GRETA'S BEDROOM (DAY 1) Greta tries on different outfits.	N	1/8	GRETA

Total Pages 3 5/8 **Maureen Murray—Exec. Producer)**

GRETA MAY

SHOOTING SCHEDULE
Prepared by Maureen Murray

Thursday 28 October 2004

Location: Battersea Arts Centre

Sc. 1	INT – THEATER FOYER – EVENING (DAY 1) Richard recognises Greta and gives her his telephone number
Sc. 2pt	INT – STAGE – NIGHT (FLASHBACK) Fleeting image of Greta in ultra sexy outfit. She looks terrified.
Sc. 5pt	INT – STAGE – NIGHT (FLASHBACK) Fleeting image of Greta in sexy outfit. She sees Oliver behind her.
Sc. 7	INT – STAGE – NIGHT (FLASHBACK) Greta & Oliver act out their brutal scene. The director is dissatisfied.
Sc. 12	INT – STAGE – NIGHT (FLASHBACK) The director decides to use the French girl, Oliver tacitly agrees. Greta is left stunned. We see Richard.

Unit Move: 77 New Kings Road & set up for Sc. 15

Friday 29 October 2004

Location: 77 New Kings Road

Sc. 15	INT – RICHARD'S HOUSE – BEDROOM – MORNING (DAY 2) Greta asks Richard for breakfast in bed with the papers – but there's no hurry.
Sc. 2	INT – GRETA'S FLAT – KITCHEN – NIGHT (DAY 1) Rachel tells depressed Greta to get over Oliver. Cake is not the answer.

Sc. 3 INT – GRETA'S FLAT – KITCHEN – NIGHT (DAY 1)
Greta phones Richard.

Sc. 5pt INT – GRETA'S FLAT – GRETA'S BEDROOM – NIGHT (DAY 1)
Greta tries on James Dean outfit etc.

GRETA MAY SHOT LIST (as at 26/10/04)
DAY 1 THURSDAY 28TH OCTOBER

Loc: Battersea Arts Centre Foyer
Sc.1 INT—THEATER FOYER—EVENING (DAY 1)
Richard recognises Greta and gives her his telephone number.

1) Dolly Position 1:
WS to 2 shot following Greta, from start of scene (*Greta May descends* to *Greta moves past Richard* on page 2).
59 secs.

2) Dolly Position 1:
C/U Greta looking at flyer.

3) Dolly Position 2:
Tracking 2 shot (from *Richard scribbles number* to end of Scene 1.)
25 secs.

4) Sticks:
Richard's p.o.v. of Greta leaving.

Loc: Battersea Arts Centre Studio 2
Sc.2pt INT—STAGE—NIGHT (FLASHBACK)
Fleeting image of Greta in ultra sexy outfit. She looks terrified.

5) Sticks:
WS, no shadow. Time limit 3 secs.

Sc. 5pt INT—STAGE—NIGHT (FLASHBACK)
Fleeting image of Greta in sexy outfit. She sees Oliver behind her.

6) Sticks:
Full or mid length shot. 3 secs.

Sc.7 INT—STAGE—NIGHT (FLASHBACK)
Greta & Oliver act out their brutal scene. The director is dissatisfied.

7) Dolly Position 1:
MS from director's point of view, ending on CU of Greta's face (neck-up),
Greta smiles (to match immediate subsequent cab shot of Greta smiles). 23 secs.

Sc.12 & 12A INT—STAGE—NIGHT (FLASHBACK)

The Director decides to use French girl. Oliver agrees, Greta left stunned, Richard revealed.

8) Dolly Position 1:
Long lens, from director's pov, jib up to reveal LH side of director and foot tapping, continue into 12A until *"Oliver, a word please...."* 25 secs.

11. Dolly Position 2:
Greta's pov—MS 2 shot Oliver and director. 18 secs.

12. Sticks:
Richard's pov—CU of Greta (dark, then lighting change). 5 secs.

13. Sticks:
Richard's pov—full length of Greta, in the spotlight. 3 secs.

14. Sticks:
CU on Richard—revealed as lighting guy. (5 secs)

STOP

START

CHAPTER 33

Useful Links

Innovative sites with new concepts that can aid every aspect of filmmaking appear at a dizzying speed. Many are hard to categorize as they cover numerous aspects of the filmmaking process. We have included and described numerous sites throughout these pages, so have not included them here. Below is a far-from comprehensive list of some new sites that have promise and some of the established old-timers.

Backstory—www.backstory.net
Currently available on the iPad with a web version coming soon, short films are played in their entirety as well as interviews with the filmmakers.

Creative COW—www.creativecow.net
Vast amounts of information on all aspects of filmmaking, with a free e-zine.

DV Creators—www.dvcreators.net
One of the best digital video training companies around, their mission is "To help you improve the quality of your digital video projects and workflow." A good place to buy products, with a forum and DV Knowledgebase.

Filmlinker—www.filmlinker.com
The sites tagline states: "Linking filmmakers to helpful resources", and with almost 4,000 links to other film sites over 11 categories, it certainly does what it says on the tin.

Final Cut King—www.finalcutking.com
Film student Zach King provides a large amount of free videos, and others that can be bought, for learning programs including Final Cut Pro, Color, Motion, and more.

Go Into The Story—www.gointothestory.com
Screenwriting professor Scott Myers, of the University of North Carolina, posts daily blogs about the screenwriting process. He labels the site as "a professional and creative approach to writing screenplays."

Kays—www.kays.co.uk
A directory of contact details for over 50,000 companies and freelance technicians working in the European film and TV industry, searchable by country, category, name, and credits.

KFTV—www.kftv.com
Formerly known as Kemps, a huge database of film, television, and commercial production services companies in 149 countries worldwide, with everything from aerial photography to video equipment.

The Writers Store—www.writersstore.com
Features exhaustive lists of books, DVDs, software, courses, and contents all about screenwriting. It should be the first stop for any aspiring script writer.

Filmmaker.com—www.filmmaker.com
A resource for filmmakers on a budget with a regular blog with everything from helpful tips to software updates. There's also a useful section called D.U.M.P.S.: Directing Unsuccessful Motion Picture Shorts which lists common pitfalls of first time filmmakers.

Filmmaker Magazine—www.filmmakermagazine.com
Alongside the traditional printed volume, Filmmaker is packed full of interviews, information on financing and distribution, festival reports, technical updates, and much more. With a readership of over 60,000 it must be doing something right.

Filmmaker IQ—www.filmmakeriq.com
Labeled as the website "for filmmakers created by filmmakers," it's a good place to network, share knowledge, and get inspired, as well as featuring articles on everything from screenwriting to distribution and regular news updates.

Filmmaking.net—www.filmmaking.net
A huge site running through everything from festivals to film schools, latest books and software with a lively message area.

Making Short Films—www.making-short-films.com
The website connected to Making Short Film edition 3. If you've enjoyed the book, you'll love the site.

Movieola—www.movieola.ca
Movieola lays claim to being the first digital TV channel devoted exclusively to short films—*a feature film experience in a fraction of the time* is this Canadian broadcaster's motto.

Ripple Training—www.rippletraining.com
A number of professionals have created comprehensive video tutorials for Apple's Final Cut Studio for purchase—with a few freebies thrown in. Training is offered in both DVD-ROM and iTunes/iPad editions.

Ron Dexter—www.rondexter.com
A huge database of tips and articles on cinematography, covering everything from crane terms and technologies to camcorder hints to book reviews.

Student Filmmakers—www.studentfilmmakers.com
A huge site packed with everything from lists of contests to events, networking opportunities to workshops to magazines to film schools. And it's not just aimed at students.

The Knowledge—www.theknowledgeonline.com
Over 20,000 UK and international production suppliers are listed, it's free to use and you don't need to register. For suppliers, over 25,000 unique users visit every month.

PAUSE

A trio of sites that should be on every moviemakers list of favorites is the British Film Institute (BFI), the American Film Institute (AFI), and the Australian Film Institute (AFI)—the latter two sharing the same initials. These three organizations offer a variety of services particularly useful to those starting out in the industry.

British Film Institute—**www.bfi.org.uk**
Established in 1933, the BFI has the largest film archive in the world, a vast collection of film stills and posters, and leads the field in film restoration and preservation, as well as financing new talent.

MEMO FROM THE BFI

The BFI offers the following advice:

- Get online—from production information to sales, distribution and exhibition, marketing and publicity, the Internet is an invaluable resource for filmmakers.
- Have at least one very strong production still. This will be used endlessly.
- Have all clearances (especially music clearance) in place before approaching buyers.
- Make sure you allow enough time to get the film print right before your first exhibition opportunity.
- See as many films as you can, both contemporary and from the history of world cinema. Check out shorts on the internet.
- Information is power! Find out all you can about the industry by reading the weekly trade press (*Screen International, Variety,* etc.).
- Working at any level in the industry will gain you valuable experience. Unpaid/expenses only work experience placements are a way in.

American Film Institute—www.afi.com

The AFI, formed in 1967, is the pre-eminent national organization in the United States dedicated to advancing and preserving film, television and other forms of the moving image, and "promotes innovation and excellence through teaching, presenting, preserving and redefining the art form." With New Media Ventures (NMV), AFI has developed digital filmmaking coursework, student monitoring and teacher training programs in the AFI Screen Education Centre and for online film studies. The Institute sits on an eight acre site in the hills overlooking Hollywood and is guided by four primary missions:

1. Training the next generation of filmmakers.
2. Presenting the moving image in its many forms to a national and international public.
3. Preserving America's great movie heritage.
4. Redefining the moving image in the new digital era.

Australian Film Institute—www.afi.org.au
Founded in 1958, the AFI is Australia's foremost screen culture organization and is responsible for producing Australia's annual AFI Awards, the country's premier film and television awards. As a producer of the industry's night of nights, the AFI plays a central role in the way in which the Australian film industry is known and understood, both locally and internationally, and is crucial to the definition, business and culture of the Australian film, television and other moving image industries.

STOP

START

CHAPTER 34

Film Festivals

PICK OF THE FESTIVALS

North America

Chicago Intl Film Festival (October)
30 East Adams, Suite 800
Chicago, Illinois 60603
Tel: 312 683-0121
info@chicagofilmfestival.com
www.chicagofilmfestival.com

Cinequest: The San José Film Festival (Feb–March)
P.O. Box 720040
San Jose CA 95172-0040
Tel: 408 295-3378
contact@cinequest.org
www.cinequest.org

Florida Film Festival (June)
1300 South Orlando Ave
Maitland, FL 32751
Tel: 407 629-1088
Email through website
www.floridafilmfestival.com

Slamdance Film Festival (January)
5634 Melrose Ave.
Los Angeles, California 90038
Tel: 323 466-1786
submissions@slamdance.com
www.slamdance.com

Sundance (January)
5900 Wilshire Blvd. Suite 800
Los Angeles, CA 90036
Tel: 310-360-1981
Institute@sundance.org
www.sundance.org

SXSW Film Festival (March)
1000 East 40th Street
Austin, Texas 78751
Tel: 512 467-7979
film@sxsw.com
www.sxsw.com

Telluride Film Festival (July)
800 Jones Street
Berkeley, CA94710
Tel: 510 665-9494
Mail@telluridefilmfestival.org
www.telluridefilmfestival.org

Toronto Intl Film Festival (September)
Reitman Square, 350 King Street West
Toronto, Ontario, M5V 3X5
Tel: 416 599-8433 (x.3285)
submissions@tiff.net
www.tiff.net

Europe

Berlin Film Festival (February)
Potsdamer Stra 5
Berlin D-10785
Tel: +49 30 259–200
info@berlinale.de
www.berlinale.de

Cannes Film Festival (May)
3, rue Amélie
75007 Paris – France
Tel: +33 (0) 1 53 59 61 00
Email through website
www.festival-cannes.fr

London Film Festival (November)
National Film Theater
South Bank, Waterloo
London SE1 8XT
Tel: +44 20 7957 8957.
indaccred@bfi.org.uk
www.bfi.org.uk

Venice Film Festival (Aug–Sept)
Palazzo del Cinema, Lungomare Marconi
30126 Lido di Venezia
Tel: +39 041 2726501
cinema@labiennale.org
www.labiennale.org

Australia

Brisbane International Film Festival (November)
Level 3, 167 Queen Street
Brisbane Qld 4000
Tel: +61 7 3224 4114
biff@biff.com.au
www.biff.com.au

Flickerfest Short Film Festival (January)
Bondi Beach
Sydney Australia, PO Box 7416
Tel: 02 9365 6888
coordinator@flickerfest.com.au
www.flickerfest.com.au

Melbourne International Film Festival (July–August)
GPO Box 4982,
Melbourne, 3001
Tel: +613 9662 3722
miff@miff.com.au
www.miff.com.au

Sydney Film Festival (June)
PO Box 96
Strawberry Hills, NSW 2012
Tel: +61 2 9690 5333
info@sff.org.au
www.sff.org.au

OSCARS SHORT FILMS AWARDS FESTIVALS LIST
To be able to be considered for an Academy Award, a short film must first have won an award at one of these festivals:

AFI Fest (California, USA)
www.afi.com

Academia De Las Artes Y Ciencias Cinematograficas De España (Spain)
www.academiadecine.com

Académie Des Arts Et Techniques Du Cinéma [César] (France)
www.lescesarsducinema.com

Academy Of Canadian Cinema & Television [Genie] (Canada)
www.academy.ca

Academy Of Motion Picture Arts And Sciences [Student Academy Awards] (California, USA)
www.oscars.org

Anima Mundi (Brazil)
www.animamundi.com.br

Ann Arbor Film Festival (Michigan, USA)
www.aafilmfest.org

Annecy Festival Int'l Du Cinema D'animation (France)
www.annecy.org

Aspen Shortsfest (Colorado, USA)
www.aspenfilm.org

Athens Int'l Film Festival (Ohio, USA)
www.athensfest.org

Atlanta Film Festival (Georgia, USA)
www.atlantafilmfestival.com

Austin Film Festival (Texas, USA)
www.berlinale.de

Bermuda International Film Festival (Bermuda)
www.biff.bm

Bilbao Int'l Festival Of Documentary & Short Films (Spain)
www.zinebi.com

British Academy Of Film And Television Arts [Bafta] Awards(England)
www.bafta.org

Canadian Film Centre's Worldwide Short Film Festival (Canada)
www.worldwideshortfilmfest.com

Cannes Festival Int'l Du Film (France)
www.festival-cannes.fr

Cartagena Int'l Film Festival (Colombia)
www.festicinecartagena.org

Chicago Int'l Children's Film Festival (Illinois, USA)
www.cicff.org

Chicago Int'l Film Festival (Illinois, USA)
www.chicagofilmfestival.org

Cinanima Int'l Animation Film Festival (Portugal)
www.cinanima.pt

Cinequest Film Festival (California, USA)
www.cinequest.org

Clermont-Ferrand International Short Film Festival (France)
www.clermont-filmfest.com

Cleveland International Film Festival (Ohio, USA)
www.clevelandfilm.org

David Di Donatello Award [Accademia Del Cinema Italiano] (Italy)
www.daviddidonatello.it

Encounters International Film Festival (U.K.)
www.encounters-festival.org.uk

Festival De Cine De Huesca (Spain)
www.huesca-filmfestival.com

Flickerfest International Short Films Festival (Australia)
www.flickerfest.com.au

Florida Film Festival (Florida, USA)
www.floridafilmfestival.com

Foyle Film Festival (Ireland)
www.foylefilmfestival.org

Galway Film Fleadh
www.galwayfilmfleadh.com

Gijon Int'l Film Festival For Young People (Spain)
www.gijonfilmfestival.com

Guanajuato International Film Festival, Expresion En Corto (Mexico)
www.guanajuatofilmfestival.com

The Hamptons International Film Festival (New York, USA)
www.hamptonsfilmfest.org

Heartland Film Festival
www.trulymovingpictures.org/heartland-film-festival

Hiroshima Int'l Animation Festival (Japan)
www.urban.ne.jp/home/hiroanim

Krakow Film Festival (Poland)
www.kff.com.pl

Leeds International Film Festival
www.leedsfilm.com

Locarno Int'l Film Festival (Switzerland)
www.pardo.ch

Los Angeles Film Festival (California, USA)
www.lafilmfest.com

Los Angeles Int'l. Short Film Festival (California, USA)
www.lashortsfest.com

Los Angeles Latino International Film Festival (California, USA)
www.latinofilm.org

Melbourne Int'l Film Festival (Australia)
www.melbournefilmfestival.com.au

Montreal Festival Du Nouveau Cinema (Canada)
www.nouveaucinema.ca

Montreal World Film Festival (Canada)
www.ffm-montreal.org

Morelia International Film Festival (Mexico)
www.moreliafilmfest.com

Nashville Film Festival (Tennessee, USA)
www.nashvillefilmfestival.org

New York International Children's Film Festival
www.gkids.com

Nordisk Panorama – 5 Cities Film Festival (Five Nordic Countries)
www.nordiskpanorama.com

Oberhausen Int'l Short Film Festival (Germany)
www.kurzfilmtage.de

Ottawa Int'l Animation Festival (Canada)
www.awn.com/ottawa

Palm Springs Int'l Festival Of Short Films (California, USA)
www.psfilmfest.org

Raindance Film Festival
www.raindance.co.uk

Rhode Island International Film Festival (Rhode Island, USA)
www.film-festival.org

Rio De Janeiro International Short Film Festival (Brazil)
www.curtacinema.com.br

St. Louis Int'l Film Festival (Missouri, USA)
www.cinemastlouis.org

San Francisco Int'l Film Festival (California, USA)
www.sffs.org

Santa Barbara Int'l Film Festival (California, USA)
www.sbfilmfestival.org

Seattle International Film Festival (Washington, USA)
www.seattlefilm.com

Shortshorts Film Festival (California, USA)
www.shortshorts.org

Siggraph (USA)
www.siggraph.org

Slamdance Film Festival (Utah, USA)
www.slamdance.com

South By Southwest (Texas, USA)
www.sxsw.com

Stuttgart Int'l Animation Festival (Germany)
www.itfs.de

Sundance Film Festival (Utah, USA)
www.festival.sundance.org

Sydney Film Festival (Australia)
www.sydneyfilmfestival.org

Tampere Int'l Short Film Festival (Finland)
www.tamperefilmfestival.fi

Tribeca Film Festival (New York, USA)
www.tribecafilm.com

Uppsala Int'l Short Film Festival (Sweden)
www.shortfilmfestival.com

Urbanworld Film Festival
www.urbanworld.com

USA Film Festival – National Short Film & Video Competition (Texas, USA)
www.USAfilmfestival.com

Venice Int'l Film Festival (Italy)
www.labiennale.org

Warsaw Film Festival
www.wff.pl/en

Zagreb World Festival Of Animated Films (Croatia)
www.animafest.hr

STOP

START

CHAPTER 35

Glossary Of Film Terms

A

Above The Line Costs
The creative elements as detailed at the top of the budget sheet. Includes story rights and screenplay, producer and executive producer, director, principal cast and all associated costs.

ADR: Automated Dialogue Replacement, looping
Re-recorded dialogue to replace unfit recordings. Normally done back at a studio with the actors lip-synching.

AMPAS: Academy of Motion Picture Arts and Sciences
American professional honorary organization composed of more than 6,000 motion picture craftsmen and women.

Ambient Sound
Background sound in addition to dialogue picked up by the mike

Anamorphic lens
A projection lens used to produce Widescreen images at the cinema.

Ancillary Rights
Rights to the commercial potential of a project aside from direct exploitation of the film. Includes, computer games rights, television spin-off, prequel, sequel, and remake, book publishing rights, merchandising rights, soundtrack album rights, and the music publishing rights to the score.

Answer Print
The composition print that emerges from the laboratory after the combination of the graded picture with sound, soundtrack, and optical effects.

Aperture
Camera opening controlling the amount of light that touches the film; its size can be varied to vary the amount of light.

Aspect ratio
The width-to-height ratio of a movie frame and screen. Standard aspect ratio is 1.33 to 1; CinemaScope uses 2.35 to 1.

Audience positioning
The relationship between the audience and the media product. How the media tries to determine the response of an audience to its products.

Auteur
A film-maker, usually a writer/director, with a recognizable, strong personal style.

B

Backlighting
Lighting placed behind a subject to create a silhouette.

BAFTA: British Academy of Film and Television Arts
British professional honorary organization.

BBFC: British Board of Film Classification
The organization that issues certificates to films and videos, stating whether they are suitable for children or young people to watch.

Below The Line Costs
Section of budget that includes technical, insurance, production, general expenses, editing, and post production costs.

Best boy
The chief assistant to the gaffer on a set.

Bollywood
Nickname of the Indian film industry (a fusion of “Bombay” and “Hollywood”).

Boom
A movable arm that holds a microphone over actors’ heads during filming.

Buzz track, Presence, Atmos
Recorded atmospheric sound. The sound of silence. Also used as a backdrop for ADR.

C

Call Sheet
Schedule of each day's filming normally created by the Line Producer.

CGI: Computer Generated Imagery
Used for creating everything from full on *Lord of the Rings* battle scenes to cleaning up minor details such as an errant watch on Napoleon's wrist.

Chain of Title
The route by which the producer's right to use copyright material may be traced from the author to the producer through a "chain" of assignments and transfers.

Chroma key
A device that allows an image to be filmed in front of a background that has been produced elsewhere.

Cineaste
A film or movie enthusiast.

Cinerama
A Widescreen process using three projectors to produce an image on a curved screen.

CinemaScope
The trademark used for an anamorphic wide-screen process.

Cinéma vérité
A style of film-making that stresses unbiased realism and often contains unedited sequences.

Clapperboard
A board on which details of each Take are written in chalk, and which is "clapped" in order to synchronize sound and vision.

Cliff-Hanger
Device used principally in early film serials and latterly on television whereby the action ends at the highest point of the drama ensuring the audience tunes in for the next episode.

Collection Agent
A mutually agreed company appointed to collect the proceeds from a film and distribute to the financiers and other contractually agreed benefactors.

Completion Guarantee
An agreement under which a guaranteeing company guarantees to financiers that the film will be completed and delivered by a given date.

Contingency
An amount added to the budget of a film to cover unforeseen circumstances, usually 10% of the budgeted costs.

Continuity
Ensuring that each shot in a film or TV programme has details that match.

Co-production Treaty
An arrangement between two or more countries allowing film-makers to access tax incentives in each country.

Coverage
The shots, including close-ups and reverse angles which a director takes in addition to the master shot.

Crane Shot
A shot from above, using a device of the same name.

Crash Zoom
Rapid zoom in on a subject; also **zoom-in** and **zoom-out**, to move closer and move further away.

Cross Collateralization
Used by distributors and sales agents to apply costs from one territory or exploitation right to all other income revenues from all other territories and exploitations.

Cut
1. The instruction to stop the camera and the action in front of the camera.
2. The process of editing a film or shortening a scene.

Cutaway
A brief shot that interrupts the continuity of the main action of a film, often used to depict related matter or indicate concurrent action.

D

DAT: Digital Audio Tape
Tape used to store Digital recordings of a high quality.

Day for Night
A shot filmed during the day, which appears on the screen as a night scene. (Title of a 1973 movie by François Truffaut.)

Deep focus
A cinematic technique whereby objects are kept in focus in both foreground and background.

Deferment
Payment from revenues derived from the exploitation of the film, after the deduction of distribution fees and expenses and, usually, after financiers have recovered all of the sums. Most short films are made with deferments.

Degeneration or Drop Out
The lowering of quality as images and sound are transferred from tape to tape.

Diagetic sound
Sound that belongs naturally with what can be seen in the picture.

Diffusion
The reduction of the harshness or intensity of light achieved by using a screen, glass filter, or smoke.

Director of Photography (DP)
The movie photographer responsible for camera technique and lighting during production. Also called cinematographer.

Director's Cut
Director's version of a film, which usually includes scenes cut from the original.

Dissolve
The gradual transformation of one scene to the next by overlapping a fade-out with a fade-in.

Distributor
Company responsible for the distribution and placement of a film in cinemas and other agreed media.

Dolby
A technique in sound recording that helps cut out background noise and distortion.

Dolly shot
A moving shot that uses a wheeled camera platform known as a dolly.

Domestic rights
The rights to distribute a film in North America or other originating country where specified.

Down Time
The late hours and off-peak times at an editing suite where you may be able to cut your film on a budget.

E

E&O: Errors and Omissions insurance
Insurance against claims arising out of infringements of copyright, defamation and unauthorized use of names, trade names, trademarks or characters.

Establishing shot
The first shot of a scene showing a wide shot of the location in which the action takes place.

Edit Controller
Machine linking a player, or video camera, to a recorder in order to assemble and edit shots; they come in various sizes with a range of extras.

Editor
The person usually responsible for the final structure of a film.

Equity
British equivalent of the US SAG (Screen Actors Guild)

External Microphone
Mike that plugs into the camera.

F

Fade-in
A gradual transition from complete black to full exposure.

Fade-out
A gradual transition from full exposure to complete black.

Field of Vision
The area your camera *sees* and will record.

Film gauge
The size or width of film, e.g. 35 mm or 16 mm.

Final cut
The last version of an edited film prior to release.

Flickers
Early nickname for the movies stemming from the flickering effect they had.

Foreign rights
Opposite of domestic rights, the rights to distribute a film outside America.

Four Walling
The renting of a cinema by a producer for a period allowing for the retention of all box office returns.

Frame Accurate Editing
Editing system that allows editors to stop and start cuts exactly where they want.

Frame/FPS frames per second
An individual unit of movie film. The American standard film speed is 24 frames per second; there are 16 frames per foot of 35mm film.

Freeze-frame
A still picture during a movie, made by running a series of identical frames.

G

Gaffer
The main electrician and supervisor of lighting on set.

Gaffer Tape
A strong and versatile multi-purpose cloth tape used for everything from marking floor positions to fixing equipment.

Gag
A furry object for reducing the amount of wind sound that the mike picks up.

Gap Financing
Lending arrangement whereby a bank will lend the difference between production finance raised and the minimum expected from sales by a reputable sales agent.

Gate
The part of a camera or projector in front of the lens, through which the film passes.

Gel
Colored transparent sheets that are placed in front of lights to change the color and ambience, or over windows to maintain a white balance in the picture.

General release
The exhibition of a film that is shown in cinemas across a country.

Grip
Crew member who adjusts scenery, flags lights, and often operates the camera cranes and dollies.

Gross participation
An arrangement whereby a participant in a film, usually a major artist, takes a share in the gross, rather than net receipts.

H

Holdback
A period during which a particular form of exploitation is not allowed. An example would be a six-month holdback on video rentals to allow sufficient time for a theatrical release.

Hook
It is the special "selling" point that gets the buyers interested in your script and keeps the audience in their seats when the film is made. Every tale must have one.

I

In-camera editing
A technique used when shooting on video. Requires shooting in sequence and re-recording over unwanted scenes.

J

Jump cut
A cut made in the middle of a continuous shot rather than between shots, creating discontinuity in time and drawing attention to the film itself instead of its content.

K

Key grip
The head grip who supervises the grip crew and receives orders from the gaffer.

Key light
The primary light in a scene.

Klieg light
A powerful carbon-arc lamp producing an intense light that is commonly used in film-making.

L

Laveliers
Small omnidirectional microphones usually attached to an actor's chest.

Loan out agreement
An agreement where the services of an individual are made available through a production company, usually owned or controlled by that individual.

Low-angle shot
Shot with the camera placed low (which makes people look bigger and stronger) as opposed to **high-angle shot** (which makes you look small and insignificant. An **aerial-shot** is a bird's eye view of the scene.

M

M & E track
A mixed music and effects track, which is free from dialogue. Used for foreign language versions.

Master shot
A continuous take that covers the entire set or all of the action in a scene.

Matching
It's all about the money. This is a funding process where funds are granted to equal those that are already in the pot.

Matte shot
A partially opaque shot in the frame area. The shot can be printed with another frame, hiding unwanted content and permitting the addition of another scene on a reverse matte.

Minimum guarantee
The minimum sum a distributor guarantees will be payable to a producer as a result of the distributor's distribution of the film.

Mise-en-scène
From French meaning "Arranging the scène." The physical setting of the action and environment. It defines the mood, color, style, and feeling of the world. It includes the style of art, camera movement, and lighting; architecture, terrain, atmosphere, and color palettes.

Mix
To put together sound or images program, or the sounds on a record.

Montage
The putting together of visual images to form a sequence.

N

Negative
An image that has been shot onto film from which a Print or Positive is taken.

Negative pick-up
A distribution agreement where the advance is payable only on delivery of the finished film to the distributor.

Net profits
The revenues from the exploitation of the film after distribution fees and expenses, deferments, repayment of any loans and investments raised to finance production.

Non-diagetic sound
Sound that does not come from anything that can be seen in the picture—i.e. the musical score or a voiceover (VO).

Non-linear Editing
Editing style where shots can be edited in a way that does not conform to, or affect, the scheduled story order.

NTSC: National Television Standards Committee
A broadcast and video format using a fixed vertical resolution of 525 horizontal lines. NTSC countries are: USA, Antigua, Bahamas, Barbados, Belize, Bermuda, Bolivia, Burma, Canada, Chile, Colombia, Costa Rica, Cuba, Dominican Republic, Ecuador, El Salvador, Greenland, Guam, Guatemala, Guyana, Honduras, Jamaica, Japan, South Korea, Mexico, Netherlands Antilles, Nicaragua, Panama, Peru, Philippines, Puerto Rico, St. Vincent & the Grenadines, St. Kitts, Saipan, Samoa, Surinam, Taiwan, Tobago, Trinidad, Venezuela, Virgin Islands.

O

Optical
A visual device such as a fade, dissolve, or wipe, also includes superimposing and other special effects.

Option agreement
The right to exploit, during a specific period of time, for a specific sum, a book, screenplay, short story, or contributors services for the making of a film.

Out-take
A shot or scene that is shot but not used in the final print of the film.

Overages
Distribution revenues payable to the producer after the advance or minimum guarantee has been recouped.

Overexposure
When too much light gets through the aperture during filming, often caused by the sun's sudden appearance through clouds. The makes faces and shiny surfaces glossy. It is more commonly called **flare** or **bleach**. You may wish to overexpose film for dream sequences and flashbacks.
See underexposure below.

P

P & A commitments/spend
A contractual obligation imposed on a distributor to spend specified minimum sums on prints and advertising to support the initial theatrical release of a film.

PACT
Producers Alliance for Cinema and Television, the UK trade association for film and television producers.

PAL: Phase Alternating Line
Broadcast and video standard which is used mainly in Western Europe, Australia and some areas of Africa and the Middle East and provides a clearer image than NTSC. This standard is based on 625 horizontal scan lines and 50 frames per second.

Pan
A horizontal movement of the camera from a fixed point.

Paper Edit
Written guide to the planned chronology of the film footage, soundtrack and other effects; also called the **edit script**.

Pay or play
A commitment to pay a director or performer made before production commences, regardless of whether the production actually goes ahead.

Pitch
Verbal summary of a film delivered to busy executives; the *elevator pitch* gives the filmmaker two minutes to tell his story and get backing.

Points
Shares of the net profits of a film, measured in percentage points.

POV: Point of View
A shot that depicts the outlook or position of a character.

Post-production
The final stage in the production of a film or a television program, typically involving editing and the addition of soundtracks. Also called post.

Pre-production
The planning stage of a film or television program involving budgeting, scheduling, casting, design, and location selection.

Pre-screen
To see a movie before it is released for the public.

Press Kit
Essential marketing document containing film-makers' contact details, film synopsis, behind the scenes production details, key profiles and photos, credits of key players, press clippings. Other handy tools: flyers, posters, stickers, and business cards.

Producer
The person responsible for initiating, organizing, and financing a venture.

Product placement
A form of sponsorship in which advertisers pay the producers of films to have characters use their products.

R

Reaction Shot
Just what it says. It's usually a cutaway shot to show someone's reaction, the bigger the close-up the greater the reaction.

Recce
Short for reconnaissance, this is an essential part of pre-production where the director and key personnel go and look at locations prior to filming.

Recoupment order
The order in which investors and financiers are repaid their loans and investments.

Redhead
Standard type of lighting equipment.

Reverse Shot
Filming from opposite angles. In this way, a moving object can appear to change directions.

Rush
The print of the camera footage from one day's shooting. Also called the *daily*.

S

SAG: Screen Actors Guild
American equivalent of British Actors Equity.

Sales agent
An agent appointed by the producer to act as agent for the sale of a film.

Set
This is the place where it all happens, where the actors act, the technicians set up their gear, the DP rolls that camera and the director yells (through a megaphone if need be) ACTION. This is an interior space decorated by the set designer, as opposed to an exterior location.

SCART
A 21-pin plug connector for audio and video between VCRs, camcorders and televisions.

Scene
A succession of shots that conveys a unified element of a movie's story.

Screenplay
The script for a film.

Sequence
A succession of scenes that comprises a dramatic unit of the film.

SFX
Special effects or devices used to create particular visual illusions.

Shooting script
The final version of a script with the scenes arranged in the sequence in which the film is to be shot.

Shot
The basic building block of film narrative – the single unedited piece of film.

Short Subject
Before they were called short films, the term was short subject and studios in the US sold their short subject as part of a block booking package that included the feature, a cartoon, news clips, a comedy, and occasionally a travelogue.

Slate
The digital board that is held in front of the camera and identifies shot number, director, cameraperson, studio and title. The data was originally written with chalk on a piece of slate. This footage is used in the laboratory and editing room to identify the shot.

Soft focus
The device of shooting the subject a little out of focus to create a specific effect, usually to do with nostalgia, an attractive female star, or dreams.

Sound stage
A soundproof room or studio used in movie production.

Source material
The original work on which the screenplay for a film is based.

SteadiCam
A hydraulically balanced apparatus that harnesses a camera to an operator's body providing smooth tracking shots without using a track.

Stop date
The last date on which a performer or director can be obliged to work. Allows an agent to schedule projects for a client.

Storyboard
The sketches depicting plot, action, and characters in the sequential scenes of a film, television show, or advertisement.

Strobing
A system of digital editing employed to make video look more like film.

Sub-genre
A genre within a genre.

Sync
When sound and images are linked properly together in time.

T

Take
The filming of a shot in a particular camera set-up. The director usually films several takes before approving the shot.

Take-over
Completion guarantors and some financiers require the right to take over the production of a film if the producer becomes insolvent, commits a material breach of its obligations to the completion guarantor or the financier encounters serious production problems.

Television rights
The collective expression for different forms of television, i.e. free and pay television, terrestrial, cable, and satellite television.

Third Party Material
Such things as music, film clips, or text used but not owned by the filmmaker.

Tilt
A vertical camera movement from a fixed position.

Time Code
The numerical sequence shown in a camera view finder, or tape player to help locate shots.

Time lapse
A technique of filming single frames of action at delayed intervals and replaying them at normal speed, to speed up dramatically an action or event.

Tracking shot
A shot that moves in one plane by moving the camera dolly along fixed tracks.

Trailer
A short filmed preview or advertisement for a movie.

Treatment
A detailed synopsis of a movie's story, with action and character rendered in prose form. An essential weapon.

Turnaround
Occurs when an agreed period in which to put a project into production expires. The producer is entitled to buy the project back from the financier, usually for all or a proportion of the sums advanced by the financier.

Two Shot
Just as it sounds: a shot with two people dominating the frame.

U

Underexposure
The opposite of overexposure, underexposure occurs when the sun suddenly vanishes into clouds or not having the aperture open enough. Underexposure is useful to create the effect of night and twilight.

V

Video assist
Video assist (or video tap) takes some of the image and sends it to a video monitor that allows the crew/director to check footage immediately.

Voiceover
The voice of an unseen narrator or of an onscreen character not seen speaking in a movie.

W

Whip Pan
Favorite of the MTV directors, like a pan only quicker, in fact so quick the shot comes out streaked or blurred.

Wildtrack
A recording of background or atmospheric noise that can be used at the editing stage. *See also* **Buzztrack**

Z

Zoom in/Zoom out
Zooming in makes the object in the frame steadily larger or smaller, depending on the direction of the zoom.

PART

X

TITLE

Top 10s

START

Top 10 Short Films You Must See

1. **Ballet Méchanique** (1924): Dadaist film by Fernand Léger and Dudley Murphy, with cinematography by Man Ray, showing abstract shapes moving hypnotcally to the music of George Antheil.

2. **Un Chien Andalou** (1929): Luis Buñuel and Salvador Dalí collaborated on this surreal masterpiece where a woman's eyeball is sliced with a razor, priests and dead donkeys are strapped to a piano and live ants pour from the palm of a woman's hand.

3. **À Propos de Nice** (1930): Jean Vigo's legendary travelogue takes us along the Riviera revealing the rich and poor living their separate lives together.
4. **The Mascot** (1934): Wladyslaw Starewicz's macabre *bal masque* features Satan and a multitude of gruesome creatures made from household items. Sometimes titled *The Devil's Ball*.

5. **Duck and Cover** (1951): Uncredited, wickedly parodied civil defence training film showing children how to protect themselves from nuclear attack by diving under school desks.
6. **The Red Balloon** (1956): Albert Lamorrise's award-winning film is a childhood story about innocence found and lost, and lessons learned.
7. **La Jetée** (1962): Chris Marker's puzzling study of time, memory, and imagination, a premise that inspired Terry Gilliam's *12 Monkeys*.
8. **The Hold Up** (1972): Abel Ferrara's short film about three men who plan to hold up a gas station after being laid off work shows the early promise of *Driller Killer* and *Bad Lieutenant*.
9. **Tale of Tales** (1979): This awe-inspiring film by the Russian Yuriy Norshteyn was selected by an international jury as the best animated film of all time at the 1984 Los Angeles Olympiad of Animation.

10. **Little Terrorist** (2004): Ashvin Kumar's Oscar-nominated film tells the story of Jamal, a 10-year-old Muslim cricketer who by accident crosses the landmine-strewn border between Pakistan and India. Returned in safety by a Hindu Brahmin, the film brilliantly captures the absurdity of divisions and borders everywhere.

START

Top 10 Directors According to TopTenReviews[1]

		Director	No of Films	Career Span	Top 4 Movies
1	 **Steven Splieberg**	Steven Spielberg	32	1950s – 1 1960s – 3 1970s – 3 1980s – 7 1990s – 7 2000s – 9 2010s – 2	*Raiders of the Lost Ark (1981)* *E.T. the Extra-Terrestrial (1982)* *Jaws (1975)* *Saving Private Ryan (1998)*
2	 **Alfred Hitchcock**	Alfred Hitchcock	58	1920s – 11 1930s – 15 1940s – 14 1950s – 11 1960s – 5 1970s – 2	*Rear Window (1954)* *Psycho (1960)* *Vertigo (1958)* *Shadow of a Doubt (1943)*
3	 **Woody Allen**	Woody Allen	40	1960s – 1 1970s – 7 1980s – 9 1990s – 10 2000s – 13	*Annie Hall (1977)* *Manhattan (1979)* *Hannah and Her Sisters (1986)* *Radio Days (1987)*

4	 **Martin Scorsese**	Martin Scorsese	32	1950s – 1 1960s – 1 1970s – 8 1980s – 5 1990s – 8 2000s – 8 2010s – 1	*Goodfellas (1990)* *Taxi Driver (1976)* *Raging Bull (1980)* *Departed, The (2006)*
5	 **Stanley Kubrick**	Stanley Kubrick	14	1950s – 6 1960s – 4 1970s – 1 1980s – 2 1990s – 1	*Dr. Strangelove or: How I Learned to Stop Worrying and Love the Bomb (1964)* *2001: A Space Odyssey (1968)* *Paths of Glory (1958)* *Spartacus (1960)*
6	 **Quentin Tarantino**	Quentin Tarantino	7	1990s – 3 2000s – 4	*Pulp Fiction (1994)* *Reservoir Dogs (1992)* *Kill Bill: Vol. 1 (2003)* *Django Unchained (2012)*
7	 **Peter Jackson**	Peter Jackson	11	1970s – 1 1980s – 2 1990s – 3 2000s – 4 2010s – 1	*Lord of the Rings: The Fellowship of the Ring, (2001)* *Lord of the Rings: The Return of the King, The (2003)* *Lord of the Rings: The Two Towers, The (2002)* *King Kong (2005)*
8	 **Joel Cohen**	Joel Coen	15	1980s – 2 1990s – 5 2000s – 7 2010s – 1	*No Country for Old Men (2007)* *Serious Man, A (2009)* *Fargo (1996)* *Barton Fink (1991)*

9	 **Clint Eastwood**	Clint Eastwood	34	1970s – 7 1980s – 7 1990s – 8 2000s – 10 2010s – 2	*Million Dollar Baby (2004)* *Unforgiven (1992)* *Letters From Iwo Jima (2006)* *Mystic River (2003)*
10	 **Francis Ford Coppola**	Francis Ford Coppola	17	1960s – 2 1970s – 5 1980s – 4 1990s – 4 2000s – 2	*Godfather, The (1972)* *Godfather: Part II, The (1974)* *Conversation, The (1974)* *Apocalypse Now (1979)*

START

Top 10 Podcasts

1. American Film Institute (www.AFI.com)
Exclusive filmmaker discussions and audience Q&A sessions as podcasts.

2. The Documentary Blog Podcast (www.thedocumentaryblog.com)
Documentary news and interviews—created by and for documentary fans and filmmakers.

3. Indy Mogul (www.indymogul.com)
A network dedicated to film fanatics and aspiring auteurs alike. Shows are focused on DIY filmmaking, cheap special effects, movie reviews, and conversations with high-profile filmmakers.

4. Moviola (www.moviola.com)
A weekly in-depth conversation with digital filmmakers covering topics related to pre-production, production, and post. Subjects include everything from workflows, HD, 3D, Stereography, Final Cut, Avid, and Compositing.

5. New Mediacracy (www.newmediacracy.com)
An audio podcast about the world of web video and new media featuring industry producers, directors, writers, and other content creators.

6. Filmspotting (www.filmspotting.net)
Weekly film podcast/WBEZ radio show from Chicago featuring in-depth reviews, top 5 lists and interviews. Hosted by Adam Kempenaar and Josh Larsen.

7. The Q&A with Jeff Goldsmith (www.theqandapodcast.com)
Jeff Goldsmith interviews screenwriters and filmmakers alike about their creative process. Also be sure to check his Creative Screenwriting podcast, and new website www.backstory.net, which screens short films and interviews with the filmmakers.

8. The Cutting Room (www.aotg.com)
Part of The Art of the Guillotine's podcast section, every week sees new interviews with editors from around the world about their technique and approach to film editing.

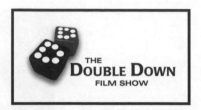

9. DoubleDownFilmShow (www.blogtalkradio.com)
An hour long experience of "real talk" about what it takes to get your project from script to screen. Pete Chatmon and Anthony Artis deliver all of the production, technology, business, and motivational support that filmmakers need to achieve their filmmaking dreams.

10. Screenwriter's Corner (www.screenwriterscorner.com)
Screenwriting Guru Syd Field guides listeners through the tips and techniques of writing screenplays.

START

Top 10 Filmmaking Blogs

Blogs are rated by 20 different factors including monthly visitors, pages per visit, RSS membership, incoming links, Compete Alexa and Technorati ranking, and social sites popularity. Thanks to BlogRank—www.invesp.com/blog-rank

1. The Art of the Title Sequence—www.artofthetitle.com
2. indieWIRE Recent—www.indiewire.com
3. Indy Mogul—DIY filmmaking—www.indymogul.com
4. Motionographer—www.motionographer.com
5. Directors Notes—www.directorsnotes.com
6. Film Directing Tips—www.filmdirectingtips.com
7. Filmmaker.com—www.filmmaker.com
8. Cinematical—http://news.moviefone.com
9. Filmmaking Central—www.filmmakingcentral.com
10. Screenwriting from Iowa—www.screenwritingfromiowa.wordpress.com

START

Top 10 iPhone Apps

1. The Biz by The Content Beast, LLC. (Cost: $0.99)
www.actorsandcrew.com

The latest Entertainment Industry content and information: constantly updated. Everything from jobs and auditions, to tips for breaking into the business, advice on marketing, labor relations issues in Hollywood ... and much more.

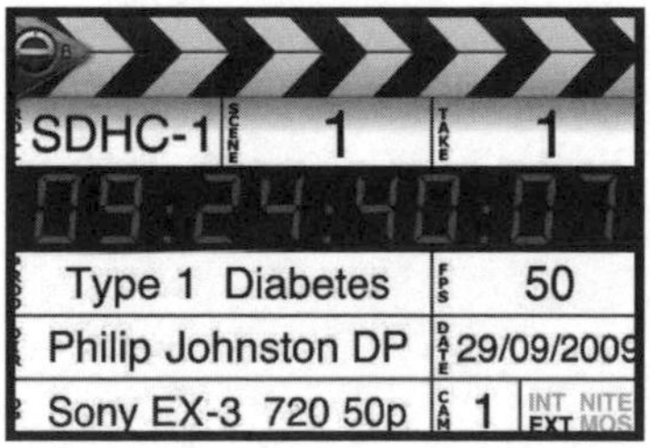

2. Movie Slate by PureBlend Software. (Cost: $4.99)
www.movie-slate.com

A professional film and video production tool to log footage and take notes as you shoot—saving time later when capturing/editing, and creating reports. As well as logging notes as you shoot and exporting in multi-formats, MovieSlate is a clapperboard—great for syncing picture with sound, and photographing shot/production info when starting and ending takes.

3. Storyboard Composer by Cinemekinc. (Cost: $14.99)
www.cinemek.com/storyboard

A mobile storyboard and pre-visualization composer designed for Directors, Directors of Photography, Producers, Writers, Animators, Art Directors, film students, and anyone who wants to be able to visualize their story. Traditional storyboarding markups such as dolly, track, zoom, and pan can be added, and a duration for each storyboard panel can be set and played back to get real time feedback on pacing and framing.

4. Screenplay by Black Mana Studios. (Cost: $2.99)
www.blackmana.com

A fully-functional mobile screenwriting application, allowing professionals and hobbyists to write complete movie and television screenplays directly on the iPhone. It can also be synced with Final Draft (v8 and above).

5. FiRe 2 by Audiofile Engineering. (Cost: $5.99)
www.audiofile-engineering.com/fire

The first iPhone recorder to display an accurate audio waveform in real time, it has advanced to support markers, Broadcast WAVE metadata, and the instant downloading of files in multiple file formats. It also offers SoundCloud integration, advanced editing, Dropbox integration, and more.

6. Gel Swatch Library By Wybron ($9.99)
www.wybron.com
Lighting production personnel can browse, search, and compare over 1,000 gel color filters made by manufacturers including Apollo, GAM, Lee, and Rosco. Among other uses, gels can be searched for by name or number, similar colors can be compared, and every color can be examined with a detailed Spectral Energy Distribution graphs by turning the iPhone sideways.

7. pCAM Film+Digital Calculator by David Eubank ($29.99)
www.davideubank.com
A Cinematography and Still Photography calculator that works out the Depth of Field—Hyperfocal—Image Circle—Splits/Aperture Finder—Field of View (Picture Sizes)—Field of View Preview (with images to size shots)—Angle of View—Focal Length (lens) Matching—Triangulate—Exposure—Running Time to Length—Shooting to Screen Time, and a whole load of other things only serious DPs and photographers even understand.

8. Set Lighting by Enlightened Shenanigans ($9.99)
www.esthegripapp.com
The application is an instructional and educational tool which is a reference for lighting equipment. The application includes equipment, and specs from manufacturers including Arri, Mole Richardson, Kino Flo, Dedo, CMC, K5600 Lighting, Kobold, Briese, Airstar.

9. Exposure Assistant by Kigra Software ($0.99)
www.kigrasoft.com

A handy photographer's utility that helps calculate correct exposure settings for those times when the in-camera exposure options are not flexible enough. It helps when determining long exposure shutter speeds, as many modern cameras will not calculate shutter speeds greater than 30 seconds and is especially useful for time-lapse and long-duration exposures.

10. Helios Sun Position Calculator by Chemical Wedding ($29.99)
www.chemicalwedding.tv

Graphically representing the position of the sun from dusk to dawn, on any given day, in any given place, this calculator is a great tool for working in natural light. Six modes include the HelioMeter, which represents the direction of the sun on a compass dial, indicating elevation and shadow length. Virtual Sun View, which shows the sun's path overlaid onto the camera image and Map View, showing the direction of the sun overlaid onto a map of the location.

START

Acknowledgements for the Third Edition

The aim of this book is to place the short film in its historic context and trace the journey through the process from writing to screening shorts.

In this revised and expanded edition we have added new chapters on scheduling and budgeting, marketing, and distribution; practical information on cameras, lights and sound; detailed software guides to Final Cut Pro, Movie Magic Budgeting and Scheduling and Final Draft; example contracts and production forms as well as five "top tens." There is also the 2012 Oscar-nominated short screenplay *Time Freak*, and an interview with its producer Gigi Causey. Eighteen other interviews with movers and shakers in the film industry have also been added, from USC Lecturer Pablo Frasconi, starting filmmakers on their journey, through to one of the leaders in new world distribution Peter Broderick, with all major film careers covered in between.

Along with everyone who contributed and helped with the first two editions of this book, we are grateful to Adam Greves for writing the Camera Tips, as well as reading and making valuable comments on the manuscript. Emily Heaton for her illustrations and Jenna Ramsden, Maya Fiala, Christopher Reddy and Jacek Bielarz for letting us use their photographs. Thanks to Jeremy Stamas, Zach King, Laurence Sargent and Joel Levin for contributing instructional chapters on the latest hardware and software, as well as the respective teams at Camcorder Info, Apple, Entertainment Partners, and Final Draft for the support along the way.

Thanks also to Jesse Douma at The Writer's Store, Tom Hutchings for his sound knowledge, Maureen Murray for her scheduling help, Steve Annalls, Interfit for the use of their product shots, and Betty Sheehan at Taylor & Francis. Everyone who has been interviewed for the third edition has provided thoughtful and inspirational answers. Special credit to Roland Heap and Victoria Poland for providing additional "top tips" and to Peter Broderick for his thoughtful advice and proofing of the Hybrid Distribution chapter. Finally, but most importantly, to Katie Gallof at Bloomsbury for making it happen and her support along the way.

START

Bibliography

Alpert, Hollis (1986)—*Fellini, A Life* (Atheneum Publishing)

Ashcroft, James (2006)—*Making A Killing* (Virgin Books)

Baxter, John (1997)—*Stanley Kubrick, A Biography* (Harper Collins)

Berger, John (1972)—*Ways of seeing*, (Penguin)

Biskind, Peter (1983)—*Seeing is Believing* (Bloomsbury Publishing)

Callow, Simon (1995)—*Orson Welles The Road to Xanadu* (Jonathan Cape)

Cameron, Julia (1995)—*The Artist's Way* (Pan Books)

Campbell, Joseph (1993)—*The Hero with a Thousand Faces* (Fontana Press)

Cook, Pam (1999)—*The Cinema Book* (BFI Publishing)

Crofts, Andrew (2002)—*The Freelance Writer's Handbook* (Piatkus Publishing)

Eisenstein, Serge (1970)—*The Film Sense* (Faber and Faber)

Field, Syd (1998)—*The Screenwriter's Problem Solver* (Dell Publishing)

—(1984)—*The Screenwriter's Workbook* (Dell Publishing)

Fonda, Afdera (1987)—*Never Before Noon* (Weidenfeld & Nicolson)

Freeman, D. J. (1995)—*The Language of Film Finance* (Pact)

Frensham, Raymond G. (1996)—*Teach Yourself Screenwriting* (Teach Yourself Books)

Gates, Tudor (1995)—*How to Get into the Film and TV Business* (Alma House)

—(2002)—*Scenario, The Craft of Screenwriting* (Wallflower Press)

Gibbs, John (2002)—*Mise-en-Scène, Film Style and Interpretation* (Wallflower Press)

Giles, Jane (2001)—*A Filmmakers' Guide to Distribution and Exhibition* (Film Council)

Goldman, William (1997)—*Adventures in the Screen Trade* (Abacus)

—(2000)—*Which Lie Did I Tell? More Adventures in the Screen Trade* (Bloomsbury)

Gore, Chris (2001)—*The Ultimate Film Festival Survival Guide* (Lone Eagle Publishing)

Hammond, Paul (1997)—*L'Âge d'Or* (BFI Publishing)

Hancock, Caroline and Wistreich, Nic (2003)—*Get Your Film Funded*, *UK Film Finance Guide* (Shooting People Press)

Hill, John and Church Gibson, Pamela (1997)—*The Oxford Guide to Film Studies* (Oxford University Press)

Houghton, Buck (1991)—*What a Producer Does, The Art of Moviemaking* (Silman James Press)

Jones, Chris and Genevieve Jolliffe (2000)—*The Guerrilla Film Makers Handbook* (Continuum)

Katz, Steve (1991)—*Film Directing Shot by Shot: Visualizing from Concept to Screen* (Michael Wiese Productions)

Minghella, Anthony (Ed. by Timothy Bricknell) (2005)—*Minghella on Minghella* (Faber and Faber)

Parker, Philip (1998)—*The Art & Science of Screenwriting* (Intellect Books)

Reiss, Jon (2012)—*Think Outside the Box Office* (Hybrid Cinema)

Stoller, Bryan Michael (2008)—*Filmmaking for Dummies, 2nd Edition* (Wiley)

Thompson, Kristin and Bordwell, David (2002)—*Film History: An Introduction* (McGraw-Hill)

Thurlow, Clifford (2000)—*Sex, Surrealism, Dalí and Me* (Razor Books)

Tobias, Ronald B. (1993)—*Twenty Master Plots and How To Build Them* (Piatkus Publishing)

Vogler, Christopher (1998)—*The Writer's Journey* (Michael Wiese Productions)

Wakelin, Michael (1997)—*J. Arthur Rank* (Lion Hudson)

Weston, Judith (1999)—*Directing Actors: Creating Memorable Performances for Film and Television* (Michael Wise).

—(2003)—*The Film Director's Intuition: Script Analysis and Rehearsal Techniques* (Michael Wiese Productions)

Wexman Wright, Virginia (2005)—*A History of Film 6th Edition* (Allyn & Bacon)

White, Carol (1982)—*Carol Comes Home*, *An Autobiography* (New English Library)

Wiegand, Chris (2005)—*French New Wave* (Pocket Essentials)

Worle Alec (2005)—*Empires of the Imagination: A Critical Survey of Fantasy Cinema from Georges Méliès to the "Lord of the Rings."* (McFarland)

START

Images List

- Below is a list of all images, screenshots, and logos.
- Copyright listed where necessary, if not listed the permission has come directly from the owner (including logos and interview pictures).

1 Lights, Camera, Action © Emily Heaton

1.1 Sidney Poitier and Rod Steiger reaching boiling point in the racially charged *In the Heat of the Night* (1967). © BFI
1.2 Ready for the long ride: Geena Davis and Susan Sarandon in *Thelma and Louise* (1991). Photo Roland Neveu. © BFI
1.3 Ashvin Kumar directing *The Little Terrorist* (2004)
1.4 Oscar nominee Ashvin Kumar
1.5 *Babel* (2006) film poster. © BFI
1.6 Screenshot of www.bmyers.com.

2.1 George Clooney and fellow travelers take on commie hunter Senator Joseph McCarthy in *Good Night and Good Luck* (2005) © BFI
2.2 *"Are you looking at me?"* Robert de Niro in *Taxi Driver* (1976) © BFI
2.3 *Belle de Jour* (1967)

3.1 Christina Ricci, ready for anything in *The Opposite of Sex* (1998) © BFI
3.2 Jack Nicholson and Faye Dunaway in Roman Polanski's noir thriller *Chinatown* (1974) © BFI
3.3 John Travolta and Samuel L. Jackson shooting up LA in *Pulp Fiction* (1994) © BFI
3.4 Billy Bob Thornton in *The Man Who Wasn't There* (2001) © BFI
3.5 Rooney Mara in *The Girl with the Dragon Tattoo* (2011) © BFI
3.6 *La Dolce Vita* (1960)—Marcello Mastroianni and Anita Ekberg in a rainy street © BFI
3.7 *La Dolce Vita*—Marcello Mastroianni and Anouk Aimée in party mood © BFI

3.8 Carol White and Ray Brooks in a scene from Ken Loach's moving account of homelessness in *Cathy Come Home* (1966) © BFI
3.9 Protesters in Nigel Cole's *Made in Dagenham* (2010) © BFI

4.1 Grand Hunt in movie *Ran* (1985) © Kurosawa Productions
4.2 Screenshot of StoryBoard Quick © PowerProduction Software, www.powerproduction.com
4.3 Screenshot of StoryBoard Quick © PowerProduction Software, www.powerproduction.com

5.1 A still from Robert Rodriguez's low budget *El Mariachi* (1992) © BFI
5.2 *Senna* (2010) is about the legendary Brazilian Formula One racer © BFI
5.3 Nim Chimpsky starring in James Marsh's *Project Nim* (2011) © BFI
5.4 Pete Postlethwaite as The Archivist in *The Age of Stupid* (2009) © Spanner Films
5.5 Villagers follow filmmaker Franny. © Spanner Films
5.6 indiegogo
5.7 Buzzbnk
5.8 Kickstarter

6.1 Victoria Poland
6.2 The Makeup Artist Handbook © Focal Press (Taylor & Francis Group, LLC)
6.3 Make-Up, Hair and Costume for Film and Television © Focal Press (Taylor & Francis Group, LLC)

7.1 Erica Arvold
7.2 Pere Costa © Maya Fiala

8.1 *Perfume* (2006) film poster © BFI
8.2 Mick Ratman
8.3 Greg Babcock

9.1 Canon HF G10. The HF G10 straddles the line between consumer and professional.
9.2 Salt flats in Uyuni, Bolivia pictured, adhering to the Rule of Thirds © Emily Heaton
9.3 Panasonic HC-X900M. Panasonic's past three flagship models have offered excellent bang for their buck.
9.4a The aperture can be changed to adjust the amount of light entering the camera. © Emily Heaton
9.4b Aperture © Nayukim http://creativecommons.org/licenses/by/2.0/
9.5 Canon 60D. The 60D performed nearly as well as the Canon 7D in our video tests.
9.6 A shallow depth of field blurs out the background © Christopher Reddy
9.7 Sony NEX-VG20. The NEX-VG20 works with any Sony E-mount lens.

30.1 Pablo Frasconi
30.2 Tony Dinsey
30.3 Edward Housden
30.4 Still from *Muscles* (2010)
30.5 Stuart Holt

31.1 The Lumière Brothers
31.2 The Lumières' breakthrough projection of a train steaming into the station
31.3 *A Trip to the Moon* (1902)—inspiring George Lucas
31.4 Poster from Edwin Porter's 1903 masterpiece *The Great Train Robbery*
31.5 Edwin Porter's mobile wardrobe—about 1908
31.6 A scene from *Chaplin and the Kid*
31.7 *À Propos de Nice* (1937)—Promenade on the boulevard
31.8 François Truffaut

PART X – TOP 10S

Top 10 podcasts and apps. All logos courtesy of companies

Top 10 Directors:

1. Steven Spielberg © 🅭—(share Alike) 2011 Gerald Geronimo
2. Alfred Hitchcock PD-PRE1964; PD-US-NOT RENEWED.
3. Woody Allen, © 🅭—(Attribution 3.0 Unported) 2009 David Shankbone) http://creativecommons.org/licenses/by/3.0/deed.en
4. Martin Scorsese © GNU FDL 2007 David Shankbone Copyright (2012) Max Thurlow. Permission is granted to copy, distribute and/or modify this document under the terms of the GNU Free Documentation License, Version 1.3 or any later version published by the Free Software Foundation; with no Invariant Sections, no Front-Cover Texts, and no Back-Cover Texts. A copy of the license is included in the section entitled "GNU Free Documentation License."
5. Stanley Kubrick Public domain image
6. Quentin Tarantino © 🅭—(Attribution 3.0 Unported) 2009 Siebbi
7. Peter Jackson © 🅭—2009 Natasha Baucas
8. Joel Cohen © 🅭—(share Alike) 2001 Rita Molnár
9. Clint Eastwood © 🅭—(share Alike) 2010 gdcgraphics
10. Francis Ford Coppola © 🅭—(BY-SA-2.0) 2011 Gerald Geronimo

START

Notes

INTRODUCTION

1 Paul Hammond's excellent study *L'Âge d'Or is* published by the BFI. All books and articles quoted in the text are listed in the Bibliography.

CHAPTER 1: THE WRITER

1 Throughout the text, I use masculine nouns and pronouns to refer to both sexes; while this avoids clumsy tags like cameraman/woman or soundperson, it should also be made clear that there are now just as many female producers in the industry as males, as indeed there are many female directors, editors, etc.
2 Joseph Campbell, *The Hero With A Thousand Faces* (Fontana Press 1993)
3 Callie Khouri, *Thelma and Louise*
4 Truman Capote
5 From AMPAS (Academy of Motion Picture Arts and Sciences) http://web.archive.org/web/20080302160301/http://www.oscars.org/nicholl/format.html
6 Thanks to ListVerse.com
7 Jean Cocteau

CHAPTER 2: THE PRODUCER

1 John Walker
2 Franz Kafka
3 Samuel Beckett
4 Michael Wakelin, *J. Arthur Rank* (Lion Hudson 1997)
5 The quotations in this chapter from Dawn Sharpless and Elliot Grove are from interviews with the author.
6 *Minghella on Minghella*, Edited by Timothy Bricknell (Faber and Faber 2005)

CHAPTER 3: THE DIRECTOR

1 John Gibbs, *Mise-en-Scène, Film Style and Interpretation* (Wallflower Press, 2002)
2 Gary Oldman
3 Burt Lancaster, in a live interview at the National Film Theater, 1988
4 Steve Biddulph
5 Paul Wells, *The Horror Genre* (Wallflower Press, 2001)
6 John Berger, *Ways of Seeing*, (Penguin 1972)

7 Federico Fellini
8 Andrew Sarris
9 Hollis Alpert, *Fellini, A Life* (Atheneum Publishing, 1986)
10 The quotations in this chapter from Cedric Behrel, Alexis Bicât and Terence Doyle are from interviews with the author.
11 *Minghella on Minghella*, Edited by Timothy Bricknell (Faber and Faber, 2005)

CHAPTER 7: CASTING

1 Judith Weston, *Directing Actors: Creating Memorable Performances for Film and Television* (Michael Wise 1999). There is a chapter devoted to the casting process.

CHAPTER 10: LIGHTS

1 Thanks to www.lowel.com

CHAPTER 11: SOUND

1 Neal Baldwin, *Edison: Inventing the Century* (Hyperion 1995)
2 David Cook, *A History of Narrative Film* (W.W. Norton 2004)
3 Michael Chion (frwd Walter Murch), *Audio-Vision: Sound on Screen* (Columbia University Press 1994)

CHAPTER 12: THE EDITOR

1 Simon Callow, *Orson Welles, The Road to Xanadu* (Jonathan Cape, 1995)
2 Ibid.
3 Ibid.
4 Paul Hammond, *L'Âge d'Or* (BFI Publishing, 1997)
5 Cecil B. de Mille
6 Frank Capra
7 Hedda Hopper
8 The quotations from Martin Scorcese and Harvey Weinstein are from an interview by Alex Williams, the Guardian, 3 January 2003.
9 The quotations in this chapter from Sam Small are from an interview with the author.

CHAPTER 13: MUSIC

1 http://www.afi.com/100years/scores.aspx

CHAPTER 16: HYBRID DISTRIBUTION

1 From a Sundance press release: http://www.sundance.org/press-center/release/sundance-institute-artist-services-expands-self-distribution-opportunities

CHAPTER 22: NOISE CONTROL

1 The quotations in this chapter from Terence Doyle and Danielle Anneman are from interviews with the authors.

CHAPTER 23: G.M.

1 Martin Pickles, script notes.
2 The quotations in this chapter from Martin Pickles are from an interview with the author.

CHAPTER 24: ROOM ELEVEN

1 The quotations in this chapter from Maureen Murray, Philip Robertson, Roger Tooley, Clive Brill and Maedhbh McMahon are from interviews with the authors.

2 Garrett Brown, in John Baxter, *Stanley Kubrick, A Biography* (Harper Collins, 1997).

3 Ibid.

CHAPTER 25: GRETA MAY—THE ADAPTATION

1 *Zoetrope: All-Story* runs online workshops and short story competitions www.all-story.com

2 The quotations in this chapter from Jean-Philippe Gossart and Alexander Atwater are from an interview with the author.

3 Soho Images is a full service Film Laboratory and Digital Post Production Facility located all under one roof in the heart of Soho's Post Production community.

CHAPTER 28: MOVIE MAGIC BUDGETING AND SCHEDULING

1 "Screen shot created using Movie Magic Scheduling software owned by DISC Intellectual Properties, LLC dba Entertainment Partners. For more information, http://www.entertainmentpartners.com/products and_services/products/mm_scheduling/"
"Screen shot created using Movie Magic Budgeting software owned by DISC Intellectual Properties, LLC dba Entertainment Partners. For more information, http://www.entertainmentpartners.com/products_and_services/products/mm_budgeting/s upport/"

CHAPTER 29: CAREERS

1 Sourced from The Hollywood Reporter www.hollywoodreporter.com

CHAPTER 31: A BRIEF HISTORY OF SHORT FILMS

1 Steve Parker, *The Lumière Brothers and Cinema* (Belitha Press, 1995)

2 Tim Dirks, <www.filmsite.org>

3 The Bill Dougles Centre for the History of Cinema and Popular Culture <www.centres.ex.as.uk>

4 Gordon Hendricks, *Edweard Muybridge* (Dover Publications 2001)

5 Marta Braun and Etienne-Jules Marey, *Picturing Time: Work of Etienne-Jules Marey* (University of Chicago Press, 1994)

6 Neal Baldwin, *Edison: Inventing the Century* (Hyperion 1995)

7 Charles Tepperman, www.canadianfilm.com

8 <www.biographycompany.com>

9 Alec Worley, *Empires of the Imagination: A Critical Survey of Fantasy Cinema from Georges Méliès to the Lord of the Rings* (McFarland 2005)

10 Luke McKernan, <www.victorian-cinema.net>

11 Sandra Brennan, *All Movie Guide* (2006)

12 Aaron Delwiche, <www.firstworldwar.com>

13 Chris Wiegand, *French New Wave* (Pocket Essentials 2005)

14 http://www.people-press.org/2011/01/04/internet-gains-on-television-as-publics-main-news-source

PART X: TOP 10s

1 http://movies.toptenreviews.com/directors/list_all_time_director.htm

START

Index